THE
TITFORD FAMILY
1547 ~ 1947

Photo: Steve Bavister

JOHN TITFORD M.A., M.ès.L., L.H.G., J.P., was born in London in 1945 and educated at Haberdashers' Aske's School, Elstree, and St John's College, Cambridge, where he took a degree in English. He taught and studied in Paris for a year and completed a Master's degree at the Sorbonne before taking a Certificate in Education at the University of Newcastle upon Tyne. In 1972 he was awarded a Graduate Fellowship by the Rotary International Foundation to spend a year following a film studies programme at San Francisco State University, California, where he gained First Prize in the American Society for Cinema Studies' Annual Scholarly Writing Competition for an article on German Expressionist Cinema.

He has since been a school teacher in Grammar, Public, Secondary Modern and Comprehensive schools, and is currently Senior Lecturer and Staff Development Officer at South-East Derbyshire College.

He is the co-author and publisher of a number of books on Derbyshire dialect, and has produced an L.P. record called 'Ey Up Mi Duck' with Richard Scollins. He has written a number of articles for historical and genealogical journals, is a regular book reviewer for *Family Tree*, and is the co-author with Geoff Gration and John Reilly of *Communication and Media Studies: An Introductory Coursebook*, published by MacMillan in 1989.

He has a keen interest in folk music, playing the guitar, melodeon and concertina, and was Founder Chairman of the Ilkeston (Derbyshire) Civic Society. He is a member of the Ilkeston Round Table 41 Club, and a Justice of the Peace for the Derbyshire Commission of the Peace.

He began researching family history in 1978 and gained first Prize in a competition organised by the Institute of Heraldic and Genealogical Studies for his family-history study, 'Come Wind, Come Weather' in 1984. He was awarded the Licentiateship of the Institute in 1985, became a member of its council in 1986, and is a member of the Society of Genealogists and the Wiltshire and Somerset and Dorset Family History Societies.

THE
TITFORD FAMILY
1547~1947

Come Wind, Come Weather

John Titford

with contributions by
Anthony Richard Titford
Donald George Titford
Russell John Titford

Best wishes !

John Titford

Phillimore

1989

Published by
PHILLIMORE & CO., LTD
Shopwyke Hall, Chichester, Sussex

ISBN 0 85033 681 3

Printed and bound in Great Britain by
RICHARD CLAY LTD.
Bungay, Suffolk

To
my parents
my uncles and aunts
my millions of cousins
and
all my ancestors
(known and unknown)
with love and respect

The author would be very pleased to hear from anyone who can shed any light on the history of the Titford family in any of its branches, and would be glad to provide information from his files to help family members compile their own pedigrees. Please address any correspondence to John Titford, care of the publisher.

Contents

Note

It should perhaps be pointed out that this book was originally entered in the Institute of Heraldic and Genealogical Studies' competition under the title 'Come Wind, Come Weather'. The present title, *The Titford Family, 1547-1947*, with the sub-title 'Come Wind, Come Weather' has been considered more suitable for general publication.

The chapter arrangement runs as follows: after the first four, which may be thought of as 'The common heritage', chapters five to 25 follow a particular line of descent, taking each adult male within a family in order of age, the eldest first.

List of Pedigrees

List of Illustrations

Acknowledgements
The author is grateful to the following for permission to reproduce illustrations: The Public
Record Office, 2, 3, 10, 24, 38, 47; Wiltshire Record Office, 4, 5, 7, 11; The Syndics of
Cambridge University Library, 6; The Marquess of Bath, Longleat House, Warminster,
Wiltshire, 13, 20; Somerset Record Office, Taunton, 15, 18, 22, 27, 28; Kent Archives Office,
16; Mr. Tony Titford, West Horsley, Surrey, 17, 30, 34; Bristol Baptist College, 19; Mr.
David Wills, 21; Greater London Record Office, 31, 37; The Worshipful Company of
Weavers, 32; His Grace the Archbishop of Canterbury and the Trustees of Lambeth Palace
Library, 36.

Foreword

by His Grace the Duke of Norfolk, K.G., G.C.V.O., C.B., C.B.E., M.C., D.L.,
Patron of The Institute of Heraldic and Genealogical Studies

The oldest part of the buildings of The Institute of Heraldic and Genealogical Studies in Canterbury is the hall house dating from 1283. To celebrate the coming of age of its journal *Family History* the Institute challenged family historians to put up their efforts for judgement. The ruse was the 700-year-old building and there were £700 in prizes, enough to encourage well over a hundred entries to the competition. 'Come Wind, Come Weather' is a tremendous effort by John Titford and an excellent example of how to compile a family history. Clearly, the Institute's educational policies have paid dividends and all concerned should be praised for seeing the first prize through to publication.

Norfolk.

Preface

by Cecil Humphery-Smith, F.S.A., Principal of The Institute of Heraldic and Genealogical Studies

It is thirty years ago since my essay 'Introducing Family History' was published by duplication on an Elam flat screen. Expanded over the years, that, and a growing movement inside and outside the many classes that I have taught since the early 1950s, has greatly assisted the spread of the concept of family history. After some years of detailed preparation and much floundering, the Institute was eventually established in Canterbury by a document dated the 6th February 1961. A few years later it acquired a solid constitution as a registered educational trust. It has since been incorporated with extensive powers to teach and research in the field of the history and structure of family life.

At the beginning of this decade the trustees of The Institute of Heraldic and Genealogical Studies saw that they would have a double cause for celebration in 1983. They agreed to mark the 700th anniversary of the building of the oldest part of their premises with a competition to find the best family histories that had been written and which would discover if the beliefs and values of the Institute which have been communicated over the years through classes and our journal, *Family History*, have fallen on fertile ground. Amateurs and professionals alike were encouraged to enter and a £500 first prize and four other prizes were offered.

More than 130 entries were received for the competition and the judges, Dr. Robert Lloyd Roberts and Dr. Teddy Church, both medical practitioners and exceedingly keen genealogists, eventually reduced this number to twelve. The writers were each presented with a certificate of commendation and a pewter goblet inscribed with the Institute's coat of arms. The five best entries were also entertained at Luncheon at the *Savoy Hotel* on Thursday, the 26th July 1985 and the Institute's president, Major-General the Viscount Monckton of Brenchley, presented the prizes as follows:

1st   John Titford: 'Come Wind, Come Weather'
2nd   Francis Warneford and Elisabeth McDougall: 'An English Family through Eight
        Centuries: The Warnefords'
3rd   Meriel Lucas: 'The Reynells and Their England, 1150- 1900'
4th   Neville Wood: 'The Woods: A Gloucestershire Family'
5th   Peter Marsden: 'The Marsden Family of Paythorne and Nelson, 1666-1981'

It is the Institute's earnest wish that these family histories, or at least extracts from them, might be published as examples. Some of the competitors have ventured to publish their own, and I have prepared a volume of abstracts for publication which may appear shortly. For the time being, 'Come Wind, Come Weather', is presented here.

The judges had great difficulty in deciding between the first prize winners, but they said of 'Come Wind, Come Weather' that it was 'lovely' and a 'masterpiece' as a study of all the male members of one branch of a family seen within the context of the political, social and economic developments of pre- and post-industrial England.

The old Hall House built in the July of 1283 has had additions in the 16th, 19th and 20th centuries, and 1986 commemorated the Silver Jubilee of the foundation of this Institute which occupies these buildings and where family history is taught and studied. I hope that the publication now, soon after these events, of the prize-winning entry from the competition may encourage family historians throughout the world to make their own studies in the same depth and to commit themselves to print for posterity. Once more, let me congratulate John Titford and commend him for his hard labours and fruitful production.

Cecil R. Humphery-Smith.

Acknowledgements

I have gathered a posy of other men's flowers, and nothing but the thread that binds them is my own
Montaigne

It is more than conventional humility that prompts any author of a work on family history to acknowledge the invaluable help provided by friends and relations, genealogical professionals and genealogical amateurs. Without the generous and unstinting help and encouragement of such people, no such work could ever see the light of day.

One of the joys of researching one's own family is the way in which new relations are discovered and become firm friends. Three such distant cousins of the present author have a very special part to play here, all having made invaluable contributions to the ever-evolving story as it has unfolded, as well as having offered their advice, encouragement and friendship.

Tony Titford of Surrey has been the pioneer Titford researcher, wrestling alone with the intricacies of the family's history long before anyone else joined him in his efforts. All subsequent research, then, owes a special debt of gratitude to him for his careful and wide-ranging work over the years. His special interest has been the life and career of William Jowett Titford, author of the *Hortus Botanicus Americanus*, and his monograph on the subject was published in 1977.

Donald Titford of Bath is the author of the first three chapters of this book (Richard the Servant, Thomas the Shoemaker and Thomas the Alehousekeeper) – a signal contribution, consolidated by various illustrations throughout the book and other material on various family branches which awaits a further volume to do it justice. A substantial chapter on Charles Titford, innholder of London (1614-1675), is already on the stocks, as is the story of the Titfords of Wylye, Wiltshire, and London, and a detailed study of the Titfords of Warminster, Wiltshire. The subtitle of the present work – *Come Wind, Come Weather*, from the famous hymn by John Bunyan – was first suggested by Donald Titford.

Russell Titford of Upminster has been a tireless and meticulous researcher, whose findings have provided material for very many pages of text and illustrations. Matters nautical have had his keenest attention (he is, after all, a descendant of Robert Titford, Master Mariner . . .) and his researches in a number of London record repositories have been invaluable. Over the years he has made the Guildhall Library his second home, and he and the author shared the hopes and frustrations of many months of thought and research which culminated in the discovery of the marriage entry for their mutual ancestor, 'Ben the Outrider', tucked away in the register of All Hallows, Barking, next to the Tower of London.

To all three of these cousins and to their families this history owes an incalculable debt.

Other members of the extended Titford family have searched their memories and their archives to help illuminate the story and put flesh on the bones. The author's parents, Sidney and Beth Titford, and his Aunt Doris have been priceless stores of information in this respect, and very little could have been achieved without them.

Other Titfords – both friends and relations – who merit affectionate thanks for all their many kindnesses include Arthur and Muriel Titford and their family and Joyce Titford and her family; 'Auntie Florrie' Titford of Clacton-on-Sea; and Reg, Pamela and Graham Titford, descendants of the Titfords of Wylye.

Other acknowledgements will of necessity be selective, with the sincerest of apologies to those who may inadvertently have been omitted.

Special and specific researches have been undertaken by Matthew Copus of Tunbridge Wells in Kent, Paula Lewis of Ilminster, Somerset, and Sir John Willoughby of Codford St Peter, Wilts. In thanking them, we should also make reference to the many record repositories in London and elsewhere which have been invaluable mines of information; in particular, mention should be made of K. H. Rogers, Esq., County and Diocesan Archivist, and his staff at the Wiltshire Record Office in Trowbridge; D. M. M. Shorrocks, Esq., County Archivist, and his staff at the Somerset Record Office in Taunton; the librarian and staff of the Guildhall Library, and the staff at the library of the Society of Genealogists in London. Our thanks must also be extended to Miss Jane Fowles, onetime archivist at Longleat House, and R. H. Mellish, Esq., agent to the Wilton Estate, for allowing us the opportunity of examining some of the records relating to the estates of the Marquess of Bath and the Earl of Pembroke. Rev. C. Sidney Hall showed a similar kindness in making available a number of documents now in the keeping of Bristol Baptist College, and allowing the author to spend two days there extracting details from them.

No list of acknowledgements would be complete without some mention of Frome, Somerset; lucky indeed is the researcher whose path takes him to this town – books by Peter Belham, Michael McGarvie and Derek Gill give him the wealth of detail he would wish for, while the activities of the Frome Society for Local Study can frequently save him hours of fruitless searching. The help afforded the author by the indefatigable Hilda Massey, Church and Museum Archivist, has been of untold value, while the assistance offered by Derek Gill and Michael McGarvie has been deeply appreciated; if errors still remain in the text, they are of the author's making – no-one could have asked for better or more freely-given advice. Further thanks are owed to Mr. and Mrs. Butler of Dommetts Lane, Frome, for making available all the records relating to Sheppards Barton Baptist Chapel.

Our further gratitude must be extended to Mr. and Mrs. Donald Mounter of Curry Rivel, Somerset; to Mr. Ray Burrows of Street, Somerset; to the Branch Library of the Church of Jesus Christ of Latterday Saints in Loughborough; to the editors of the journals of the Wiltshire and Somerset and Dorset Family History Societies; to the compilers of a number of Marriage Indexes, especially Mrs. Barbara Carter of Wiltshire; and to a number of friendly incumbents who have allowed access to be had to their parish records.

Finally, we must express our gratitude to Richard Scollins for his help and encouragement – and especially for his conjectural illustration of 'Ben the Outrider'; also to Alan Tew, whose enthusiasm for his own family history awoke a latent interest in the present author some eleven years ago; and last, but by no means least, our deepest thanks go to Gwen Jones and Angela Osborn for their sterling efforts in typing the original manuscript – and to Heather Bridge for her generous help just at a time when help was needed most.

Mr. Trevor Hodgkison of Belper carried out the necessary artwork for the family trees and the map showing Titford migration from Bratton.

Preamble

What we call the beginning is often the end
And to make an end is to make a beginning.
The end is where we start from

T. S. Eliot

It is always the wrong time to put your ideas into print. Just around the corner, it seems, lies the day when your story will be definitive for all time, complete, accurate and exactly as you always wanted it to be. Alas, how many major and minor historical works have been lost to us because their compilers took such a view and never committed themselves to paper at all!

All history is conjecture; whoever tells us that he has written the definitive historical account of anything at all is deluding himself and us. What we need is knowledge, not completion, truth and not neatness – or rather, the truth *so far*. James Joyce had originally called the novel which eventually became *Finnegan's Wake* nothing more than *Work in Progress* – and that is what the present account of the Titford family attempts to be. Research will go on – and in that sense Eliot's phrase: 'The end is where we start from' is very relevant in its paradoxical way. All we have done is taken a snapshot mid-way, held things up temporarily to consolidate the state of knowledge so far – but history and historical research is a process, not a fixed entity. It is our ardent wish that the day after this present work is finished, something will turn up which will add to its findings, point out its errors, or at least modify some of the hypotheses we have proposed. 'To publish and be damned' would seem to have less to do with any risk of being sued for libel than with the decision to commit oneself to print with the strong possibility that a piece of writing might contain inaccuracies. A book with *errata* is better than no book at all.

The best any piece of historical writing can do is to be honest about when and where it is introducing uncertainties, and this we have tried to do, both in the narrative itself and on the family trees with their broken lines and question marks. We would hope, as time goes on, that some of these areas of doubt will be resolved – but at least we know where they lie. This story is intended to take an overall view of the history of one branch of a family in the male line from 1547 to 1947, though the precise line of descent, the further we move back through the centuries, will involve degrees of conjecture. That is only to be expected, after all; and even the most apparently gilt-edged of male-line pedigrees must take on trust the belief that every son is really the blood-descendant of his supposed father. Few men, as Strindberg once proposed with cruel devilment in his play *The Father*, can be sure in the final analysis that their children are really their own: mothers are quite unequivocally mothers; fathers must take their fatherhood on faith.

Any family history research will have its swings and its roundabouts – there will be good luck we feel we hardly deserve, followed by bad luck which makes us feel the world is against us. At times there has seemed to be what we have referred to, only half-jokingly, as a 'Little Titford in the sky'; he it is, it seems, who decides what we shall uncover and what we shall not. The part of our story set in Frome, for example, has had to be compiled with no family wills (the one which did exist was destroyed at Exeter during the war); no gravestones; no manor court rolls, and a host of missing baptisms and marriages. Yet where such records are missing, forced willy-nilly to look elsewhere, we have managed to find diaries, property indentures, an 18th-century census, Baptist Chapel minute books and the like. And in the search for such material the existence in Frome of a dedicated and scholarly group of local historians has been invaluable. Much of any credit which may be due is theirs, not ours.

Some ancestors have tried to hide themselves away in dark corners, hoping, perhaps, that we would never find them? The marriage of Benjamin Titford the 'Outrider' (1786-1816) was tucked away in the registers of one of the very few churches in the City of London whose records have not been deposited in the Guildhall Library. The event could have taken place in any parish between Somerset and London – or not taken place at all. In the event, it was only by following Benjamin's wife's family, the Hasteds, who were moving steadily southwards every ten years or so within the City, that we finally homed in on All Hallows by the Tower and found the entry we sought. Similarly, his eldest son Robert, a captain of a merchant ship, turned out to be a master of evasion: his seaman's ticket is registered under the name of 'Tilford', Lloyd's register lists him as 'Fitford', and he died leaving no death certificate. Only a search through the documents pertaining to his ship, the *Orynthia*, uncovered the details of his untimely demise – in Honduras, in Central America, in 1839.

A rare surname is, indeed, a great advantage in our case; or rather, it would have been, had not scores of Titfords been called 'William'; there have been times when 'Hephzibah Smith' or 'Alefounder Brown' would have been easier to trace!

If scarcity of documentary evidence is a problem in the early years of a family's history, then an excess of material, an *embarras de richesse*, takes over as we approach the present day. Before, we knew too little – now we know too much, and conjecture of a different kind sets in. When opinions vary even in the present about people and places, it should be no surprise to find that memory is both fallible and variable from one person to the next. Was Aunt Jenny a kind, considerate person, or a bit of a harridan? We may well get different answers from a series of people, each answering in total honesty. So-called historical accuracy is as enigmatic a concept when we are studying the present as it is when we are studying the past; not just history, but day-to-day reality itself, we may say, can only be perceived as through a glass, darkly. With all this in mind, the reader will notice a change in tone and approach as the story of the Titfords progresses; the early chapters try to present and to weigh up such documentary evidence as exists, though they can only get as close to individuals in the family as available information will allow. As we approach the present day, however, and encounter people who are still alive or still remembered, we have tried to be more homely in our tone – there is, after all, little point in speaking about the living as if they were long-since dead, just raw material for historical analysis. And to finish with, we have decided to let Sidney Horace Titford speak for himself; every other character is seen from the outside – but here we have recorded an individuals's own perception of his life – in itself only one possible perception, of course, but one that gives his story a different perspective from all the others. His account brings our story, not to a close, but to a temporary resting-point. To make an end is to make a beginning . . .

Introduction

TETFORDS, TEFORDS, TIFFORDS AND TITFORDS:
LINCOLNSHIRE, BEDFORDSHIRE AND WILTSHIRE

When you have eliminated the impossible, whatever remains, however improbable, must be the truth.

Sir Arthur Conan Doyle: *The Sign of Four*

The canonization of Oedipus as the patron saint of family historians is long overdue; his quest for self-knowledge through an unravelling of the mysteries of his origins is essentially the same as that undertaken in a more modest way and with less harrowing consequences by thousands of 20th-century family history researchers. Genealogy is, of course, a subject of enormous fascination whichever family we might be investigating; yet there can be something especially moving and almost eerie about tracing our own direct ancestry, warts and all.

The present study consists of an account of four hundred years in the history of one branch of a family in the male line of descent; it attempts, in a sense, to be a kind of family counterpart to what Rowland Parker has done for a single village in *The Common Stream*. Parker's settlement of Foxton in Cambridgeshire is fascinating precisely because it has been so unexceptional through the years; the Titford family which will be our central interest here is a Foxton of families – extraordinary in being so very ordinary, a series of no-ones-in-particular whose story can therefore, in its way, be seen as that of the common man of England in miniature.

Strictly speaking, of course, any family history like this one is in effect the history not of one, but of a series of families, each descended from the one before it. And no such series of histories, we may say, can be typical or truly representative in any meaningful statistical way – no self-respecting demographer, for example, would be content with such a small sample upon which to base more general conclusions. Nevertheless, so many books and articles on social history covering the last four hundred years do appear to be telling the story of the Titfords, almost as if the family unwittingly followed the norm and went along with national or regional trends. The reason why that should appear to be so is a very simple one: namely, that families, like individuals, do have only a limited range of choices open to them as to how they will live their lives – and the poorer the family, the fewer the choices. There have been Titford entrepreneurs and fortune-seekers aplenty over the years, those who appeared to transcend the financial and geographical constraints which might have bound them; but much of the time our story is of the family as victim. To others the luxury of moulding history; the characters in our tale seem so often to have been moulded by it; restricted, like so many of their fellow-countrymen, by the laws of the manor courts, the Church and parliament, by the apprenticeship and settlement Acts, and above all by the economic facts of everyday life, they managed to live comfortably at best, but were too often caught in the vicious circle of poverty whenever things took a turn for the worse. And as they bobbed up and down on the sea of economic circumstance they do appear, after all, to be typical of a thousand other such humble families. If we seek a barometer of the times through which they lived, they very often provide us with one.

All of this is neither a hopeless nor a pessimistic view; what it does mean is that the dignity which these people's lives had, together with whatever influence they may have managed to wield over their own destinies, existed within fairly narrow confines, like a detailed painting on a small canvas. Jane Austen, we may say by way of comparison, was no less a novelist than Tolstoy simply because her characters lived out their lives in rural backwaters, while his might cross an entire continent. The local and family historian, as David Dymond has said, '. . . has no greater reward than to be able to show that the lives of ordinary people had meaning and dignity'.[1]

Where should our story start? 'To begin at the beginning . . .' would be an ideal, if hackneyed, introduction if this were a work of fiction – but we are dealing with the world of facts, albeit facts eked out with a sprinkling of necessary conjecture. We usually know where our own family's history ends – it ends with ourselves, at least for the time being; but where does it begin? The challenge is a daunting one – to research a history from the present back into the past, and then to write it up forwards in time, as a chronological narrative. We are, in a sense, assembling a jigsaw puzzle; the picture looks simple enough once it has been put together, but there are times when certain pieces just will not seem to fit – do they come from a different jigsaw altogether? What make the task so intriguing, in the last analysis, is that it satisfies the basic human desire to impose order on chaos – providing always that we never let our desire for neatness and completeness override our honesty and sense of historical integrity. Any piece of family history research will be valuable to the extent to which it admits areas of doubt and conjecture which others may be able to elucidate at a later date.

Our delvings into the very early years of Titford history will be little more than an exercise in conjecture, a look at a range of possibilities. We can begin by disposing of what is almost certainly a red herring. Deep in the Black Country, near the town of Oldbury, lies the Titford Valley; neither green nor fertile, it is in effect a shallow depression on the flanks of the Rowley Hills, its contours now obscured by high-rise flats, railway embankments and an elevated section of the M5 motorway. On the floor of the valley lies the Titford Canal, a humble and apparently superfluous branch of the Birmingham Canal Navigation, opened in 1837 after an enabling act of 17th June, 1835:

> . . . a canal from and out of the Birmingham Canal, at or near a Piece of enclosed Land lying between Two Bridges of the said Canal, Called Anchor Bridge and Stoney Lane Bridge . . . and extending along a Line of Feeder belonging to the said Company, and from thence in one Direction to a Piece of Land called Minley's Piece, in the Occupation of William Jarvis Hodgetts, and in another Direction to a piece of enclosed land near Titford Bridge, in the Occupation of Sarah Brinton.[2]

Nor is the canal itself the only evidence of the 'Titford' name in the area – there is also the Titford Valley itself, Titford Bridge, Titford Pools, Titford Pumping Station – and even Titford Road.

The area of Titford itself pre-dates canals or pumping stations: the court rolls of Halesowen make reference to 'Tottefordfeld' in the Oldbury/Langley region in 1299, while a deed of 1521 mentions 'Tetford Brugge'.[3] And, indeed, members of the Titford family could in theory have come from this part of what is now the industrial belt of the West Midlands – but, with the exception of a certain Ambrose Titford who moved from Warminster in Wiltshire to make his home in Birmingham in the late 18th century, no documentary evidence exists of any Titford family connexion with the area whatever.[4] This line of research, like the Titford Canal itself, is probably no more than an intriguing impasse.

A more fruitful possibility in the search for early origins would seem to be offered by the inclusion in Burke's *General Armory of England, Scotland, Ireland and Wales* (1884) of a reference to a Titford family coat-of-arms: 'Gu. Three lions heads erased or', and a crest: 'A demi lion ramp or'. Fairbairn's *Crests of the families of Great Britain* corroborates the details of this crest – and also the fact that scores of families would lay claim to it, alongside the Titfords.

Correspondence with the Lancaster Herald at the College of Arms in London, however, has only confirmed what might have been guessed in advance: that is, that the 'Titford' arms were not officially registered for any family, though are attributed by Burke to both Titford and Strode. Papworth's *Ordinary of Arms* ascribes the 'Titford' coat to the families of Teford and Rion, while the same coat with lions 'argent' is that of Sir William Teford and also of Titford. So far so good, except that the identity of Sir William Teford has yet to be established – as has that of Sir John Tefford, who is credited with the 'argent' version of the arms in the manuscript armory known as *EDN Alphabet*.[5]

Finally, Thomas Robson in *The British Herald* (1830) gives the same coat, with no mention of tinctures, which he ascribes to 'Titford', with the lions 'argent' coat being attached to the family of Teford.

News of the Titford crest is no more heartening: it is officially registered in the name of Strode . . .[6]

Through all this detail one clear fact seems to emerge – that the Titfords never had any official claim either to arms or to a crest; we may follow this with a further hypothesis – namely, that some enterprising Titford decided of his own volition to lay claim to a modified version of a 'Teford' family coat of arms, with no official by-your-leave.

1. The Titford arms and crest as used by Isaac Titford (1760-1834) of Cranbrook in Kent and Jamaica. He has added a crescent as a mark of cadency denoting a second son.

Who may this purloiner of arms have been? Of all possible Titford rogues, perhaps the most likely candidate would be Isaac (1760-1834), military surgeon, slave-owner and planter, a descendant of William Titford of Frome, Somerset, and Cranbrook, Kent. Isaac had an eye to the main chance in most things; if he invented armorial bearings for himself, he began a fashion which has long persisted in many family branches – to this day there are Titfords who know of, or have used, the hallowed family arms.

There is no substitute, of course, for tracing a family's history back through parish registers and other primary sources, and this has been done; all present-day Titfords would appear to be descended from a line stretching back to the village of Bratton in Wiltshire, where Richard Tuttford and Alice Smith were married in 1547. Yet the Bratton Titfords seem to have been new arrivals in Wiltshire at that period – precisely at the time when parish registers can be of no further use to us in tracing a pedigree. At this point we must turn elsewhere for clues – and specifically to C. W. Bardsley's *Dictionary of English and Welsh Surnames* and Harrison's *Surnames of the United Kingdom*. Both these authorities agree on the origin of the name Titford: 'Local, "of Tetford", a parish in Co. Lincoln, six miles from Horncastle'.[7]

Two possibilities exist: either Bardsley and Harrison are in error, associating a Wiltshire family with Lincolnshire, or – and much more likely – the Titfords were in Lincolnshire before moving to Bratton.

This immediately opens up a new avenue of research: what we do find in Lincolnshire, as early as the 12th century, are many members of a family or families known variously as Tiford, Teford or Tetford. Not only that, but references to such names are becoming rarer by the early years of the 16th century – just as the Bratton Titfords begin to appear in Wiltshire. If a family called 'Tiford' or 'Tetford' did move from Lincolnshire to Wiltshire at this period, then the general destablizing effects of such a migration together with dialect variations between the two counties could well have resulted in a change to 'Tutford' in Bratton, finally settling at 'Titford'. Vowel-sounds are notoriously variable both in terms of spelling and pronunciation, so 'Tetford' could readily become 'Titford'. Not only that, but as very few speakers indeed would articulate the second 't' in 'Titford' with its full plosive force, but use a glottal stop instead, then the phonetic difference between 'Tiford' and 'Titford' is a fairly subtle one – subtle enough, certainly, for the one name to slip almost imperceptibly into the other.

A present-day map of Lincolnshire will include the village of Tetford, north-west of Horncastle; what it will not show us is the now-extinct settlement of Tetforthe or Thetford further south in the county, once in the wapentake of Ness, near Stamford.[8] Croyland Abbey had owned much of the land in this area, and there are references in 1529 and 1539 to the vicarage of Tetforthe and the chapel of Baston. The Lincolnshire Hearth Tax returns for Baston in Ness wapentake include 'John Gromitt for Tetford', though all that remains of the village today is the farmstead of Thetford.[9]

Anyone called 'Tetford' or 'de Tetford' or any variation of these, then, could in theory originate from the Tetford near Horncastle or from its now-disappeared more southerly namesake. As early as the 14th century there is documentary evidence of a Philip de Tetford of Aslackby, 10 miles to the north of Baston; much later another family group was to be settled nearby in the parish of Spalding: Jenet Tetforth left a will there in the 1530s, and there are references early in the 17th century to Thomas Tetforth of nearby Weston (a will of 1616), Simon Thedford, a glover of Spalding (a will of 1617) and William Tetforth of Cowbit (a will of 1626). Even as late as 1711 we find there is a baptismal entry for Mathew, son of Mathew Tedforth, at Gosberton, five miles north of Spalding. This looks on the surface like one family group spanning a number of generations – possibly named after the vanished Tetford near Baston?

Some miles to the west, in Grantham, we have the opportunity of seeing the surname change and settle before our very eyes in the parish registers. In 1563 a certain Robert Titferth was baptised; over the next sixty years that surname becomes Titferne, Tettffear, Titfeare – and finally, with a marriage of 10 February 1621, the registers include an Alice Titford. The name had finally settled down to its modern form in exactly the same year, by a strange coincidence, that the Bratton registers in Wiltshire first use 'Titford' instead of 'Tutford'. It seems almost as if the move towards 'Titford' was somehow inexorable, as people in various parts of the country eventually adopted this form in preference to all others.

Other references to the surname 'Tetford' and its variants in Lincolnshire come from a good deal further to the north – many centred on the present-day village of Tetford itself, which is situated among the wooded uplands of the Wolds. In the Domesday Book it was called 'Tedforde' – etymologically identical with the name 'Thetford', and meaning 'The people's ford' or 'Chief ford'.[10] This is a very Anglo-Saxon name, to be sure, for a village which is surrounded by countless others with names ending in the Old Norse suffix '-by'. But then maybe we shouldn't discount the possibility that the original Tetfords were Vikings?

The extant Tetford parish registers only begin in 1709, but the family references we seek antedate those registers by many centuries: just over a hundred years after the Norman Conquest there is evidence of a William, son of Alured de Tiford, holding land in Enderby in the year 1195.[11] Bag Enderby is two miles south of Tetford, while Mavis Enderby lies further south still, towards Old Bolingbroke; whichever settlement is being referred to here, William de Tiford appears to have been living, or at least owning land, outside the village which had given him his name. That name itself very probably reflected the fact that he was a landowner, rather than being one given to him almost by way of a nickname once he had moved away from his home base. Few enough people bore surnames at all in the 12th century; this particular one, relating to a comparatively small settlement, would survive in one form or another over the years, though it is by no means certain that every person who bore the name Tiford, Tetford or Titford subsequently was a direct descendant of this original William and his father Alured (or Alfred).

Within seven years of this original Tiford reference, the Lincolnshire Assize Rolls for 1202 for Hill Wapentake, which includes the village of Tetford, make mention of Hugo de Teford and his son Gaufrido, alongside Gilbert de Tefford and his son Robert. Another Gilbert de Teford, alias Theford, is mentioned in a 1256-7 Feet of Fines, together with free tenements which he had of Richard Trussebud in Barkwith, Kingthorpe and Wragby – all to the west of Horncastle. The family or families were spreading out geographically, then, but still within ten miles or so of Tetford itself.

In 1298 Philip de Tetford and William de Tetford, son of Agnes, were jurors for Hill Wapentake, whilst during the next century some individuals were moving slightly further afield: in 1373-5 Nicholas de Tetford was in Raithby and Roger de Tetford was in Lissington, while John de Tetford had even strayed as far as Caistor, a good twenty miles to the north. Slightly closer at hand, nearer the coast, were those 'de Tetfords' who owed their allegiance to the manor court of Ingoldmells. At a 'Court of Ingoldmeles held at Burgh on Wednesday next before the Feast of St Peter in Cathedra, 13 Edw. II' (i.e., 20 February, 1319-20), there was Philip de Tetford featured alongside great landowners like Nicholas de Cantilupe, 'attached by the pledge of Richard Bonde to do fealty to the lord, and he has not come, therefore the said Richard is in mercy, and nevertheless let the said Philip be distrained for fealty, etc.'.[12]

Nine years later it was the turn of Philip's wife to be mentioned, in 1328/9: 'It is ordered, as often, to distrain all the tenants of the lands of Waytecroft to show how they hold, etc., and for default to suit of court, except Joan who was the wife of Philip de Teford'. The surname, we may note in passing, is characteristically unstable – Philip 'de Tetford' of 1319-20 becoming Philip 'de Teford' a few years later.

The last reference worthy of note in the Ingoldmells court roll appears in the records of the court held on the Saturday before Palm Sunday, 1349-50: 'It is ordered, as often, to distrain William de Teford for fealty'. The exact limits of the manor of Ingoldmells at this period are unknown – but with the court proceedings taking place at what is now Burgh-le-Marsh, it clearly stretched significantly inland. About seven miles west of Burgh itself lies East Keal, high on a winding road on the southern slopes of the Wolds; it is here we come across our next reference to the Tetford family, by way of a man who may well be a descendant of that William of the Ingoldmells court who was distrained for fealty in 1349-50.

A Chancery case of the late 15th century concerns William Boleyn, gentleman (son of William Boleyn), John Langholme and William Tetford of Keel, 'feoffees to uses'. Land belonging to the late William Boleyn, senior, is mentioned in Stockford, Enderby, Lusby, West Keal and Hareby – all situated five to ten miles south of Tetford.[13] No longer are we speaking of 'de Tetfords', then: here for the first time is a straight and unadorned example of a William *Tetford* – the ancestor, perhaps, of more than a few 'William Titfords' of later centuries?

William Tetford had somehow lost possession of his own former lands in East Keal by the year 1527; the will of Thomas Bruster made on 12 October of that year with 'my lord Thomas the abbott of Revesby' as the supervisor, defines in detail the properties he wishes to leave to his two sons – both of whom, confusingly, are called 'John Bruster'. One legacy consists of 'ij rygges off londe lying in the same felde next betwyx the landes off the prioresse and convent of Stykeswolde off the weste parte, and off the landes off the Lord off Willughby toward the north', with another being 'a lyttyll crofte lying in Esterkele, off layt Hugh Eland off Sturton, lying next betwyx the landes of John Gregby off the south parte, and toward the est upon the hy way, and upon the landes sumtyme *William Tedforth* off the weste parte . . .'.[14]

These Lands, then, were 'sumtyme' William Tedforth, but his no longer; perhaps he had died, or moved elsewhere? Indeed, the family as a whole was beginning to abandon the Lincolnshire Wolds; a later William Tedford and his wife Ann who took a son for baptism at Old Bolingbroke in 1617 – just to the west of East Keal – do look like the last of their line still remaining in the area.

Where had the family gone to? Some, no doubt, had died without male issue; some may have moved to the southern part of the county around Spalding and Grantham – that is a possible explanation for the presence of 'Tetfords' there which would be an alternative to our earlier hypothesis about individuals being named after the Tetford near Baston. Other than that, it does very much look as if various branches of the family migrated further afield in a generally southerly direction, modifying their name in the process. Circumstantial evidence would support the proposition that those who called themselves 'Tifford' moved to Huntingdonshire, while the 'Titfords' settle in Bedfordshire and Wiltshire.

The name 'Tifford', with its variants 'Tifferd', 'Teffert', 'Tyffyrt' and the rest, does have a habit of popping up unexpectedly in a number of different places. It was used in Lincolnshire itself, as we know; then there was a Robert Tyfford of Hengham ad Castrum in Essex, who left a will in 1491; there are Tiffords in Devon and Cornwall, in Gloucestershire and Dorset.[15] The most well-documented family line bearing this surname, however, is first in evidence owning land in St Ives in Huntingdonshire in the 1590s – possibly emigrants, then, from Lincolnshire? Thomas Tifferd and An Beton were married in St Ives in 1593, and began a family line which would include a series of further Thomases in each generation – the first a prosperous butcher and alderman of Cambridge, the next a Cambridge-educated clergyman, and then his son, a Citizen and Upholder living in the City of London.

Land, wealth and status are all inter-related in this particular Tifford story. Their land in St Ives gave them a firm base from which to operate; freehold houses and acreage in Cambridge built upon that base; a man with property could readily become an alderman, and an alderman, we may suppose, could easily acquire more property; status would be consolidated by having a graduate clergyman in the family, and the clergyman's son would have the wherewithal to become a Freeman of the City of London. And most significant of all, perhaps, is the fact that Thomas Tifford of London would still have some of the original family land in St Ives to include in his will of 1689; country landowners and their descendants might become successful craftsmen or businessmen in the big city, but many of them were far too wise to let the agricultural foundation of their wealth slip away.

The Tiffords seem to have had all the wealth that many of their supposed cousins the Titfords lacked; the Wiltshire Titfords were very definitely poorer relations, but another family group which settled in Bedfordshire – and may well have moved there from Lincolnshire – did at least contain a few landowning yeomen.

The Bedfordshire Titfords deserve a mention, if only in passing; they were once very prolific, and they do appear in local records from at least as early as the late 16th century. How long had this Titford branch been in that county? We can only say with certainty that members of the family feature in four parishes almost from the beginning of the earliest extant parish registers: from 1575 in Cardington, 1576 in Wootton-by-Bedford, 1602 in Willington, and from 1591 in Blunham.

Cardington has the earliest Titford reference – a marriage entry of 1575 for Thomas Titford and Agnes Davie, which gives us our first-ever spelling of the family name in exactly its modern form; we have assumed, with some degree of conjecture, that this marriage was that of Thomas of Bratton in Wiltshire, a shoemaker, who may have been visiting his Bedfordshire cousins before taking his new wife back to his own little village on the northern edge of Salisbury Plain.

At least one Titford owned land in Cardington – William, a yeoman of Cotton End, whose decision to leave most of his property to his little illegitimate daughter and her husband in his will of 1604 led eventually to an acrid squabble in Chancery – the case of Foster vs. Titford of 1617.[16]

The Titford presence in Cardington was eventually brought to an end as a result of William the Yeoman's will; some young males from there chose to slip across the border into Hertfordshire to find themselves wives, as did their cousins from Wootton-by-Bedford. The Wootton branch were to use rather distinctive Christian names for their male offspring – Peter, Michael and Augustine appear in one generation – but through other naming patterns which favoured boys' names like Christopher, Robert and Roger, we are able to make an informed guess that the Wootton Titfords eventually settled in Surrey during the 1620s – first at Merrow, then West Clandon, and finally in East Horsley. Here the family fondness for litigation manifested itself all over again: the provision made for his relations by Christopher Titford of West Clandon, also a Citizen of Madras in the East Indies, failed to satisfy all the legatees; this time the parties fell to blows in the Archbishop of Canterbury's Court of Arches in 1693, with the case of Parsons vs. Fox, alias Richmond.[17]

The Bedfordshire Titfords were by no means paupers, after all; those who were settled in the other two parishes we have already mentioned – Blunham and Willington – also managed to achieve a very respectable degree of financial solidity as the years went by. When a certain Alice Titford, widow of Richard, decreed in her will of 1637 that her little cottage in Ravensden be sold and that the proceeds, together with various items of household furniture, be divided between her five sons and her 10 grandchildren, she was giving her boys only a modestly solid foundation in life. One son, Michael, would become a labourer, dying in the October of 1665 – a victim of the plague, we may suppose; but his elder brother Richard would eventually put his mother's legacy and his own best endeavours to very good effect. His will was proved at the prestigious Prerogative Court of Canterbury in 1659, leaving his only son Isaac a fairly healthy inheritance which he in turn was to build upon. Isaac, like his father, was a woodward, and a literate one at that, who would sign his own name on the will which he made in 1679/80. In the event he needed to be able to read and write: his employer, Sir Edward Gostwick, Baronet, a scion of one of the county's more eminent families, was both deaf and dumb.

Isaac's job was at once a simple but yet a daunting one: he had responsibility for

Sheerhatch Wood, a sizeable forested area to the south-east of Willington, still in existence today. As 'Isaacke Titford of Willington, Beds., Woodward' he found himself summoned as a witness at a Chancery case concerning Sheerhatch during the Commonwealth, in 1654; having given his opinion that a theoretical felling of the trees therein would bring in about £45 or £46 per acre, he was no doubt thanked for his trouble and was free to get back to work once more.[18]

Isaac prospered; whether through his own hard work, his master's munificence or his ability to make an illegal penny or two behind the deaf and dumb Sir Edward's back, he succeeded in acquiring quite substantial tracts of freehold land in Blunham, Northill, Moggerhanger and elsewhere. Isaac had been the only son of his father, and had just one male child of his own, Richard, to leave his land to. By the time of Richard's death in 1699, that land was still intact; but eschewing the temptation to bequeath it all *en bloc* to his eldest son, Richard had the fairness of mind instead to divide everything between his four boys – William, Isaac, Richard and Walter, all minors under their mother's guardianship following their father's death.

To divide land might be fair, but it put an end to two generations of yeomen, Isaac and Richard. Richard's eldest son, William, became an innholder and moved to Biggleswade where he died in 1713, followed twenty years later by his only son, Isaac. The period 1707-1716 would see the deaths of all four of the sons of Richard the Yeoman; not one of them even reached his thirtieth birthday – all were carried off in their twenties, the three bachelors being described at the time of their deaths as sons of Sarah Titford, widow. A generation of males had been decimated within nine years.

The youngest son, Walter, had been away from home for a number of years before returning to Willington and a premature death. Having attended a private school in Roxton, a few miles to the north-east of Willington, he was admitted as a sizar at Peterhouse, the oldest of the colleges of Cambridge University, in 1711. A sizar would pay reduced fees, and could be expected to perform menial tasks around the college. Walter and two of his Roxton school friends, John Rewse and Robert Jones, were placed under the care and tutelage of Mr. Stukes. Walter himself was then aged 15; having passed the necessary examination to complete the admissions procedure, he became a Poor Scholar in the November of 1711, a Pensioner in January of 1712/3, and a Woodward Scholar in June of that year.[19]

The young undergraduate should not have been as poor as he appears to have been at Peterhouse – except that, during his minority, his mother was holding his legacy of a messuage or tenement in Potton in trust for him. He only just lived long enough to inherit that property on his twenty-first birthday, and never did graduate from the University; in 1714, at the age of twenty-two, Cambridge education or no Cambridge education, he was buried in Willington, 'son of Widow Titford'.

The Titfords of Bedfordshire had spread out and about from their original late 16th-century parishes – to Sandy, Northill, Ravensden, Ampthill, Biggleswade and elsewhere in Bedfordshire, to Great Hormead and St Albans in Hertfordshire, across the border into Cambridgeshire to be married in Gamlingay or Fen Ditton, and even down to faraway Surrey. That geographical mobility was matched by the diversity of their standing in the social structure, whereby one man, a labourer, could have an elder brother who was a woodward and would father a landowning yeoman.

Most remarkable and strange of all, however, is the fact that, wherever they moved to or however many children they had, the Bedfordshire Titfords eventually died out altogether in the male line of descent. With the burial of Isaac Titford, son of William the Innholder in 1732, all such lines come to an end, and every known Titford alive in the 1980s is a descendant, not of Richard the Woodward or Isaac the Yeoman, William the Innholder or Christopher of the East Indies, but of the Titford family of Bratton in Wiltshire.

The time has come then, to introduce the Bratton story. How and when did the Lincolnshire Tetfords travel down to Wiltshire and become Titfords – if that is, indeed, what they did? The Lincolnshire narrative has had, of necessity, to be a long-distance view of the family in the broadest sense, an attempt at outlining who lived where and when, with few enough exact relationships known to us. The Wolds story of the area around Tetford itself took us as far as William Tedforth, no longer in possession of his lands in East Keal by 1527. Had he or his descendants left for Wiltshire?

Rowland Parker in *The Common Stream* says that scores of new families flooded into the village of Foxton, Cambs., between 1548 and 1603.[20] The same could be said of Bratton in Wiltshire. Some landowning or commercially-wealthy families like the Whitakers and Ballards were well established in the village by the middle of the 16th century, and stayed there. But around 1550 or so a number of new surnames first appear – often the very names which would then vanish again in the early 17th century, such as Bannocke, Boucher, Appleyard, Godpathe, Noble – and Titford itself. All of this was by no means untypical: in Nottinghamshire, for example, only between ten and twenty per cent of the surnames featured in the 1544 tax assessment would still be found in the same town or village in 1641.[21]

We would do well, then, not to underestimate the extent to which many labouring people and others in England were geographically mobile in the 16th and 17th centuries. The influx of new names into Bratton around 1550, for example, might be accounted for quite simply by the arrival of a different Lord of the Manor, who possibly installed his own men on his newly-acquired land. The main Bratton lordship had been held by Thomas Seymour, uncle to Edward VI; he had been granted lands in both Bratton and Edington in 1539, following the Dissolution of the Monasteries, and these remained in his possession until his execution for high treason ten years later. In 1550 the Earldom of Wiltshire was revived and conferred on William Paulet of Basing, Hants., and Nunney, Somerset; he was granted the lands in Bratton in that year, just at the time when so many new families first appear in the village.[22]

But the Titfords had been in Bratton since at least as early as 1547, in which year Richard Tuttford married Alice Smyth – in other words, before the time of the change in lordship. Perhaps they were tenants of a different lord, one with both Lincolnshire and Wiltshire connexions – like the Earls of Rutland, for example, one of whom, the sixth Earl, had landed interests in Corsley, near Bratton, which are mentioned in a Chancery case of 1631.[23]

Alternatively, the Titfords may have chosen to leave for Wiltshire during the aftermath of the Pilgrimage of Grace and the Lincolnshire Uprising, which was quelled by Henry VIII in 1536. The Titfords of Bratton, one of whom married an erstwhile priest in 1549, while others were presented for non-attendance at church in the early years of the 17th century, might well be the descendants of a man or men of nonconformist tendencies who had found living in strongly-Catholic Lincolnshire a bit too much to bear, and had chosen to move to another sheep-rearing county, off along the Fosse Way to seek a better life in the south-west.

The story of Bratton itself will be told very shortly; this introductory chapter should end by outlining one final hypothesis which attempts to forge that link which we seek between the Tetfords of Linconshire and the Titfords of Wiltshire.

The 1527 will of Thomas Bruster of East Keal, we may remember, mentions 'landes off the Lord off Willughby'. The Willoughby family had originally come from Willoughby in Lincolnshire itself, but the prudent marriage made by Sir William de Willougby, Kt., (d. 1306) to Alice, heiress of Baron Bek of Eresby, brought Eresby House into the family. The

TITFORD:

HENRY = Marian Lyne
m. 7·1·1557/8.
Westbury, Wilts.

THOMAS = ? Agnes Davie
b. 1558. Bratton.   m 16·10·1575,
d. 1624. Bratton.   Cardington, Beds.
SHOEMAKER

WILLIAM = Mary Smyth
m. 24·4·1625.
d. 1678/9   Frome, Somerset
Frome.

WILLIAM = Margaret
b. 1635, Frome
d. 1717. Frome
WIREDRAWER

WILLIAM = Joan
b. 1681/2 Frome
d. 1746. Cranbrook.
Kent.
CARD MAKER

CHARLES = Frances Ballard
b. 1717,   m. 22·4·1747.
Hawkhurst   Cranbrook, Kent.
d. 1784,
Cranbrook
CARDMAKER

WILLIAM = Susannah Vandome
b. 1752,   m. 29·11·1774,
Cranbrook,   Christ Church,
d. 1824,   Spitalfields, London.
Walworth, Surrey
SILK WEAVER

RICHARD = Elizabeth Walters
b. 1780, London m. 18·10·1809.
d. 1841, London St. Botolph Bishopsgate,
SILK   London.
MANUFACTURER.

ROBERT = Eliza Stafford
b. 1809 London   (née.........)
d. 1839 Honduras m. 22·8·1831,
MASTER MARINER St. Leonard's Shoreditch

WILLIAM = Jane Wilkinson
b. 1810, London m. 1838,
d. 1882, London Cannon Street Register
SCALE   Office, London.
MANUFACTURER.

ROBERT EDWARD = Sarah Ann Farrow
b. 1834. London   m. 26·4·1857.
d. 1923. London   St Mary's,
TRAVELLER   Bermondsey.

EDGAR = Louisa Constance
b. 1844, London Jones.
d. 1930, London m. 1877.
SCALE   Islington, London.
MANUFACTURER.

ROBERT HENRY = Alice Maud Davis
b. 1860, London m. 1885,
d. 1928, London Hackney
TOBACCONIST, PUBLICAN

HERBERT EDGAR = Bertha Warren
b. 1879. London.   (née Reeves)
d. 1967. London.   m. 14·10·1908,
SCALE   St Mary the Virgin,
MANUFACTURER. Monken Hadley, Herts.

ROBERT JOHN = Daisy Alice Ellis
b. 1886. London   m. 10·5·1922.
d 1967. London   Hackney.
BUILDER & DECORATOR

ANTHONY RICHARD = Jeannette
b. 1917. London.   Leslie Hallam.
m. 23·5·1945
CIVIL ENGINEER.   Bangalore, S. India.

RUSSELL JOHN = Janet Patricia Bellingham
b 1930 London   m. 24·10·1959.
St Saviour's, Walthamstow.
STOCKBROKER

Relationship between John Stuart Titford and: Russell John Titford (fourth cousins)
Anthony Richard Titford (seventh cousins) Donald George Titford (tenth cousins, once removed)

```
- - - - - - - - - - - - - - - - - - - - ┐        HENRY ══ ? Joan Henton
                                          │                m. 29·4·1582
                                          │                Bratton, Wilts.
                                          │
                                          WILLIAM ══ Rachel
                                          b. 1600,
                                          Sutton Veny, Wilts.
                                          SHEPHERD
                                          │
                                          WILLIAM ══ Emary
                                          b. 1622/3,
                                          Wylye, Wilts.
                                          d. 1670/1, Wylye
                                          │
THOMAS ══ Sarah Lacey                     WILLIAM ══ Anne Bath
b. 1688, Frome   m 5·2·1732/3,            b. 1654, Wylye   m. 6·10·1684,
d. 1771. Frome   Frome, Somerset.         d. 1730. Wylye   Wylye, Wilts.
CARDMAKER                                 │
                                          │
CHARLES ══ Elizabeth Carpenter            WILLIAM ══ Elizabeth Taylor
b.c. 1749   m. 9·7·1770.                   b. 1693, Wylye   m. 19·1·1720
d 1802 Frome   Frome, Somerset.           d. 1762, Wylye   Wylye, Wilts.
CHEESEMONGER                              SHEPHERD
                                          │
                                          │
BENJAMIN ══ Elizabeth Hasted              WILLIAM ══ Christian Duke
b. 1786 Frome   m. 24·1·1808              b. 1725, Wylye   m. 22·4·1751.
d. 1816 London   All Hallows by the       d. 1806, Wylye   Teffont Evias, Wilts.
OUTRIDER   Tower, London.                 SHEPHERD
                                          │
BENJAMIN ══ Elizabeth Augusta             WILLIAM ══ Elizabeth Oram
b. 1814 London   Josephine Parkes.        b. 1755, Wylye   m. 11·4·1779,
d. 1879 London   m. 22·3·1846,            d. 1837, Wylye   Fisherton Delamere, Wilts.
SILVERSMITH   Christ Church, Watney
           Street, London
WILLIAM ══ Mary Ann Keziah                JAMES ══ Mary Leach
b. 1849, London   Parkes.                 b. 1780, Wylye   m. 23·8·1802,
d. 1918, London   m. 2·3·1872.            d. 1862, London   Fisherton Anger, Wilts.
GOLD   St James, Clerkenwell,             AGRICULTURAL
ENGRAVER   London.                        LABOURER
HENRY JAMES ══ Margaret Willox Archibald. WILLIAM ══ Anne Eliza Brenchley
b. 1875 London   m. 8·9·1902              b. 1817, Wylye   m. 5·3·1838.
d. 1967 London   Arundel Square Chapel,   d. 1880, London   St Pancras, London
GOLD BEATER.   Islington, London          UNDERTAKER
SIDNEY HORACE ══ Ethel May Buckler        MAURICE ══ Eliza May Bennett
b. 1904, London   m. 26·6·1930            b. 1847, London   m. 22·6·1875,
COMPANY   St John's, Queens Drive,        d. 1908, London   St Lawrence's Aberdeen
SECRETARY   Finsbury Park, London.        UNDERTAKER   Park, Islington
                                          PERCY MAURICE ══ Emily Hannah McLaren
JOHN STUART                               b. 1876, London   m. 13·11·1912
b. 1945, London.                          d. 1968, Sunbury-   St Pancras, London
                                              on-Thames
COLLEGE LECTURER                          UNDERTAKER
                                          DONALD GEORGE
                                          b. 1925, London
                                          REAR-ADMIRAL, R.N.
```

house itself, just south of Spilsby, was only a mile to the north-east of East Keal, where it stood until a fire destroyed it in 1769.

The Willoughbys de Eresby would eventually make their chief home in Grimsthorpe Castle in the south of the county, but in the meantime a further advantageous marriage had been undertaken during the 15th century by another member of the family: John, son and heir of Sir Thomas Willoughby, Kt., found a wealthy match in Ann, one of the daughters and coheirs of Sir Edmund Cheney of Broke in Wiltshire. Their son, Sir Robert Willoughby, on the victorious side at Bosworth in 1485, would be granted a peerage by the grateful King Henry VII on 12th August, 1491, becoming the first Baron Willoughby de Broke.[24]

Broke itself, now known as 'Brook', and 'so-called from a little torrent which runs there', lies on the outskirts of Westbury, a mere three miles west of Bratton.[25] If one branch of the Willoughby family in the 15th century moved from within a mile of East Keal in Lincolnshire to within three miles of Bratton in Wiltshire, then could not they, or other Willougbys later, have taken the Tetford or Titford family with them, as tenants, servants, shepherds or the like? The first known occupation for any Titford in Bratton is that of Richard, servant to John Rawlings in 1580. Significantly or not, the Hungerford Rent Roll of 1609 lists other members of the Rawlings family who are paying rent in Brook itself: 'Margaret, wife of John Rawlins and John Rawlins son of John Rawlins. i close in Brookes Wood with a cottage built'.[26] Had the Rawlings, too, come direct to Brook from Lincolnshire?

Whether the Titfords did or did not accompany the Willoughbys remains uncertain; what is not at issue is the Titford family's presence in Bratton itself, for which there is abundant evidence; and here the four-hundred year history of the Titfords begins in earnest.

CHAPTER 1

Richard the Servant (?-1603)

Bratton, Wiltshire

DISSOLUTION AND REFORMATION

I praise God and ever shall,
It is the sheep has paid for all.

Anon.

The White Horse of Westbury, carved into the chalk of Salisbury Plain above the little village of Bratton, is reputed to be the oldest of the white horses of Wiltshire. Two miles to the east lies Edington, probable site of the battle of Ethandune, and some historians believe that the White Horse commemorates the victory there of Alfred the Great over the army of Guthrum the Dane in A.D. 878. Close to the Westbury White Horse are the remains of an Iron Age fort known as Bratton Castle whose great ditches and earthworks still command the steep descent into the Vale of Wiltshire where Alfred saved Wessex from the Danes more than a thousand years ago.

In the Domesday Survey of 1086 it is recorded that the lands around Edington had been granted to the Convent of Romsey by King Edgar in A.D. 968, but there is no mention of Bratton. Nevertheless, the little 15th-century church of St James with its Norman tower stands on Saxon foundations, and if there had been a Saxon church in Bratton before the Conquest then there surely was a Saxon village – a village which, during the Middle Ages, became the three tythings of Bratton, Melbourne and Little Stoke, strategically straddling the main road which ran from Westbury through Edington to Devizes.[1]

Bratton must have been a prosperous community at that time.[2] The Poll Tax of 1377 reports that there were '167 lay persons dwelling there beyond the age of 14 years', and they could not have lacked employment. The lush meadows of the Vale of Wiltshire provided rich pasture for their dairy herds whilst above, on the Plain, their sheep grazed the short grass amongst the ancient burial mounds. Wiltshire folk still contrast these two agricultural life-styles as being 'as different as chalk from cheese', but although Bratton enjoyed the benefits of both, it was probably the wool which provided the main source of income for the villagers.

The wool trade was not merely of local significance. The wealthy weavers and staplers of nearby Steeple Ashton might truly have claimed that 'it is the sheep has paid for all' when they praised God in the elaborate church of St Mary the Virgin, but in far-off London the Woolsack, from which the Lord Chancellor presided over the deliberations of his fellow peers, was a symbol and a recognition that the wealth, not only of Wiltshire but of all England, was carried on the backs of sheep.

Apart from tending their valuable sheep, the villagers of Bratton had other opportunities for employment in neighbouring Edington where William, Bishop of Salisbury, had erected the great monastery of the Bonhommes Order of St Augustine in the 14th century. The scale of employment provided by the monastery is suggested by William of Edington's will, which lists no fewer than 132 beneficiaries ranging in social status from Archbishop Langham and his fellow prelate, William of Wickham, to John Romsey 'my barber', Philip and Thomas 'who work in the brewhouse', and 'the boy in the bakery'. Other young servants at

1

Edington monastery are remembered by name: 'I leave to John Moul, the page who looks after my palfrey, sixty shillings; to William, the boy who leads the first cart, £5; to John, the boy who leads the second cart, £5'.[3]

The boys must have been delighted at such a handsome windfall, but their successors at the monastery were witness to less happy events. In 1450, during Jack Cade's rebellion, another Bishop of Salisbury, Bishop Ascough, was robbed of 10,000 marks by Cade's followers as he fled from his palace to take refuge in the Priory Church at Edington, from whence, whilst celebrating Mass, he was dragged from the High Altar by the mob and taken to the top of a neighbouring hill where 'his head was clave in sunder'.[4]

After that traumatic interlude, however, life in the villages under the Plain returned to its customary tranquility for a further eighty years, and the Court Rolls of the monastery's manor of Bratton record only how one villager was directed to repair his cottage, another to renew his fence, or how another was fined for allowing his pigs to stray. The names of all these villagers are preserved for posterity, even that of John Fetypase, 'who the jury say is a natural idiot', and those of the six archers and three billmen who filled the Muster Roll 'for the tithings of Bratton and Stoke in the Hundred of Westbury in the County of Wiltshire in 1538, the thirteenth year of the reign of King Henry VIII'.[5]

In their entirety the records of Bratton contain the names of hundreds of villagers who were sufficiently fortunate – or unfortunate – to achieve local prominence: villagers who leased land, paid taxes, were directed to repair their property, committed misdemeanours or suffered unnatural deaths. But elsewhere in the realm more weighty matters were being resolved: the reformation of the church following the break with Rome and the imposition of a new discipline on the clergy by licence and injunction at the command of Thomas Cromwell, acting in the name of its new Supreme Head, the King himself. And the twelfth injunction of Thomas Cromwell, issued on 5 September 1538, was designed to ensure that henceforth not only the notable and notorious, but every man and woman in the kingdom, should have his or her name recorded for posterity – or, more probably, for taxation purposes! The injunction was succinct:

> Item. That you, every parson, vicar or curate within the Dioces, shall for every churche kepe one boke or registere wherein ye shall write the day and yere of every weddyng, christenyng and buryeng made within your parish for your time and so every man succeeding you likewise, and also insert there every persons name that shalbe so weddid, christened or buried.

Although this injunction had to be repeated on several occasions over the next decades before each parish priest was persuaded to comply with Thomas Cromwell's decree of 1538, the Parish Register was born.

The following year an even more dramatic event disturbed the tranquility of village life in Bratton, an event which had been foreshadowed by the ominous arrival in Edington in 1535 of the royal Commissioners charged with assessing the wealth of the monastery for the *Valor Ecclesiasticus* as a preliminary to its dissolution. A start was made with the dissolution of the smaller monasteries throughout England in 1536, but Edington was one of the largest and wealthiest in the realm, and it was not until 31 March 1539 that Paul Bush, Rector of Edington, surrendered the monastery and all its lands to the King's Commissioners, leaving intact only the priory church of St Mary.[6]

Meanwhile the injunction of Thomas Cromwell that every parish priest should 'kepe one boke or registere' had to be obeyed, and although Bratton had no resident priest of its own and was in dispute with the Vicar of Westbury, obeyed it was.[7] Whilst the Bratton Registers date only from 1542 and the first entries are, in fact, copies made on parchment from the original paper records, they are amongst the earliest surviving Parish Registers in Wiltshire.[8] And the seventh 'weddyng' to be recorded, on 13 October 1547, was that of Richard Tuttford and Alice Smyth.

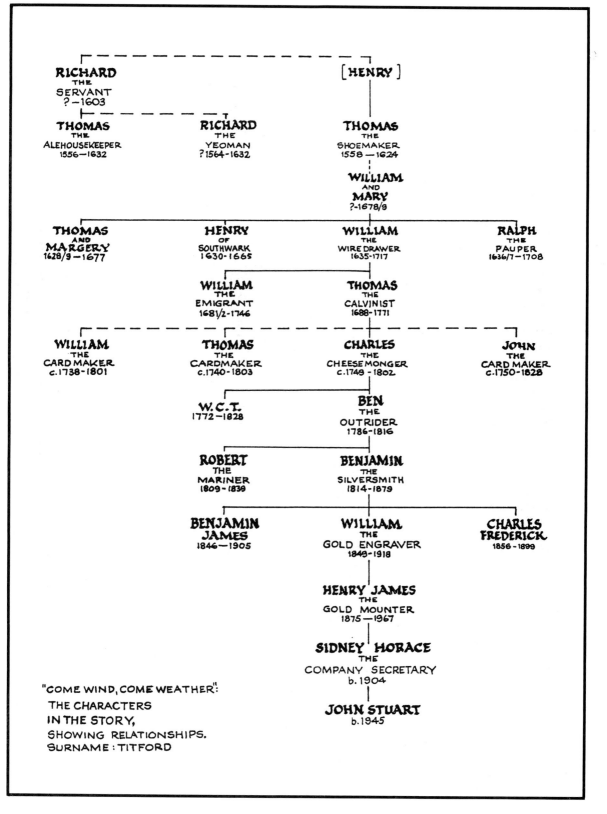

RICHARD
THE
SERVANT
?–1603

[HENRY]

THOMAS
THE
ALEHOUSEKEEPER
1556–1632

RICHARD
THE
YEOMAN
?1564–1632

THOMAS
THE
SHOEMAKER
1558–1624

WILLIAM
AND
MARY
?–1678/9

THOMAS
AND
MARGERY
1628/9–1677

HENRY
OF
SOUTHWARK
1630–1665

WILLIAM
THE
WIRE DRAWER
1635–1717

RALPH
THE
PAUPER
1636/7–1708

WILLIAM
THE
EMIGRANT
1681/2–1746

THOMAS
THE
CALVINIST
1688–1771

WILLIAM
THE
CARD MAKER
c.1738–1801

THOMAS
THE
CARDMAKER
c.1740–1803

CHARLES
THE
CHEESEMONGER
c.1749–1802

JOHN
THE
CARD MAKER
c.1750–1828

W.C.T.
1772–1828

BEN
THE
OUTRIDER
1786–1816

ROBERT
THE
MARINER
1809–1839

BENJAMIN
THE
SILVERSMITH
1814–1879

**BENJAMIN
JAMES**
1846–1905

WILLIAM
THE
GOLD ENGRAVER
1849–1918

**CHARLES
FREDERICK**
1856–1899

HENRY JAMES
THE
GOLD MOUNTER
1875–1967

SIDNEY HORACE
THE
COMPANY SECRETARY
b.1904

JOHN STUART
b.1945

"COME WIND, COME WEATHER":
THE CHARACTERS
IN THE STORY,
SHOWING RELATIONSHIPS.
SURNAME : TITFORD

2. The will of John Rawlings of Bratton, Wilts., 1580. 'I bequeathe unto Richard Tittforde my servaunte one heiffer of three yeares of age & twoe chilver sheepe.' The handwriting here is a fine example of 16th-century secretary hand. (PRO Prob 11/63.)

This entry, made in the same year as Henry VIII died and his Protestant son Edward VI came to the throne, is the first mention of a 'Titford' in any Bratton document. Throughout the next eighty years, however, the name 'Tuttford' or 'Tutford', as the scribe of the Bratton Parish Register – and he alone – insisted it should be spelt, appears many times amongst those who were 'weddid, christened or buried', and it would seem that the Titfords were prominent, at least in numbers if not in social standing, in a village of some two hundred inhabitants. One in seven of all entries in the Parish Registers between 1570 and 1590 mentions a 'Tutford'; there is evidence of at least nine family members of the same generation living in Bratton in the middle of the 16th century, and although only three of these had large families, a further five are known to have married.

There are also many omissions from the Parish Register. At some time in the past an attempt was made to clean its pages with a compound containing gall, and in consequence the first few records of baptisms are almost entirely obscured by a brown stain, whilst several entries on later pages have become illegible through age. Omissions were also caused by human frailty, and there were at least two occasions when the pastor failed to comply with the twelfth injunction of Thomas Cromwell at all! In 1558, when Queen Elizabeth came to the throne and an epidemic swept across England, there is an entry in the register: 'here also are certaine christenings lost', whilst a footnote of 1595 reads:

> Now about this time Mr Augustine Carewell, the curate of this church deceased whom one Robert Marshall succeeded and so continued curate here until the xxvth March Ano dmi 1597 in all which time so neglected to register all suche thinges which he ought to have done. Wherefore this booke is destitute of alle suche christenings, buryalls and weddings which were accomplished from the xiith day of June Ano dmi 1595 until the xxvth of March 1597.[9]

Nor would it seem that Robert Marshall's successor served his flock much better since, on 1 October 1597, the churchwardens of Bratton made a 'presentment' to the Precentor of Salisbury in which they complained that 'our vicar hath not been resident with us this hole yeare at the least, and he is noe man's chaplin to our knowledge'.[10]

Whereas these omissions probably consigned to oblivion the baptism, marriage or burial of more than one Titford, the burials of both Richard Tuttford and his wife Alice were duly recorded. Richard was buried in Bratton on 14 November 1603 – in the same year that Queen Elizabeth died – and Alice on 28 October 1611, by which time she must have been a very old lady.

The occupation of Richard Tuttford is also known, since he is mentioned as one of the beneficiaries in the will of John Rawlings of Bratton who died in 1580/1 – probably during another epidemic. The will reads in part: 'I bequeathe unto Richarde Tittforde my servaunte, one heiffer of three yeares of age & two chilver sheepe'.[11]

Nor, if he were the 'Richard Tytworthe' listed amongst those taxed by the Lay Subsidy of 1575, did 'Richard the Servant' lack substance – even compared with the value of 'Goodis' attributed to his Master, John Rawlings, on the same list:[12]

Landdis:	Wylliam Alredge	xx s.	ij s. viij d.
	Henry Wheataker	xx s.	ij s. viij d.
		Summa partis 8 s. prolatur.	
Goodis:	Jame Ballard	xj li.	x s.
	Richarde Axeford	xj li.	x s.
	Agnes Alredge	iiij li.	vj s. viij d.
	John Bowecher sen.	iij li.	v s.
	Richarde Tytworthe	iij li.	v s.
	John Alredge	iij li.	v s.
	Richarde Aplegaidge	iij li.	v s.
	Thomas Gardener	iij li.	v s.
	John Rawlyns	vij li.	xj s. viij d.
	John Bucher	vij li.	xj s. viij d.
		Summa partis 75 s. prolatur.	

It would seem that 'Richard the Servant' lived a comparatively comfortable and conventional life, but not all the Titfords of his generation in Bratton were so fortunate. Eight lines below the entry in the Parish Register which recorded his marriage to Alice Smyth appears the name of another Tutford – and this marriage entry marks an event which must have caused quite a sensation in the village: 'Thomas Seven of Edington, priest, and Katherine Tutford. 3rd June 1549'.

According to the canons of the Roman Catholic Church priests were not allowed to marry, and even with the rejection of Papal authority by Henry VIII that prohibition remained in force throughout his lifetime. It was not until the Protestant Reformation was consolidated in the reign of his son, Edward VI, that the rules of celibacy were relaxed for the clergy, but even in 1549 such a novel event as the marriage of a village girl to a priest from the erstwhile Monastery of Edington must have caused heads to shake and tongues to wag. And there would have been more gossip and speculation when, with the return to the discipline of the Roman Catholic Church decreed by Mary Tudor, the prohibition on priestly marriages was reimposed in 1553, and those priests who had taken advantage of the indulgence of Edward VI were required either to leave the priesthood or to have their marriages annulled. Which of these unwelcome alternatives was chosen by Thomas Seven and Katherine is not known, but it may be significant that the Bratton parish registers contain no mention of the baptisms of any children by their marriage, nor of the burial of either Thomas or Katherine Seven.

This priestly wedding was not the only village scandal to enliven alehouse gossip during the long winter evenings in Bratton. Immoral conduct or other offences against the wide spectrum of canon law were 'presented' by the churchwardens to the Precentor of Salisbury during his periodic routine 'visitations' to the parish, but the Dean of Salisbury himself also made occasional visits to Bratton, and for these important events the churchwardens must have prepared their 'presentments' with particular relish. On one such visit in the middle of the century a certain Bengemyn Gilbert was presented to the Dean because, despite 'having a wife of his owen', he 'doth suspitiously resort the company of M'garet Butcher and, beinge forbyden by the officers of her company, doth nev'theless resort her'. This was highly reprehensible in itself, but there was worse to come. 'And about Whitsuntyde last', the presentment continues, 'they both deptd the pishe and he not yet returned, but she returned home againe about three days past'. And then, presumably referring to events which took place before Bengemyn's mysterious disappearance, the churchwardens involve others in the scandal with a triumphant dénouement designed to send a shiver of righteous horror through the Dean's chasuble. 'The foresaid Bengemyn and M'garet resorted together dyvers tymes to the howses of Ralfe Hevill and Thomas Harres to what ende we knowe not.'[13]

The tinge of disappointment that the village nosey-parker had not provided more information is clearly evident in the phrase '. . . to what ende we knowe not', but, given that the churchwardens were men of the world, they must have had a pretty good idea of what Bengemyn and M'garet were up to – whilst the Dean, who presumably led a more sheltered life, may well have been suitably horrified by all this 'resorting'. But to the Tutfords of Bratton the involvement of Ralfe Hevill was equally disturbing, since Ralfe was, or was about to become, one of their kinsmen, marrying Agnes Tutford on 16 October 1558.[14]

Nor did the Tutfords of Bratton fail to learn the lesson implicit in this 'presentment'. Clearly, subterfuge was necessary if one wished to escape the prying eyes of the village busy-bodies, and when Henry Tutford married Marian Lyne on 7 January 1557/8, the happy couple took the unusual step of having their union solemnised in the nearby town of Westbury, rather than in Bratton. There was, as so often was the case, an epidemic that winter, and it could be that Henry and Marian went to Westbury to escape infection. But there is a less charitable explanation. It was a mere seven months after their wedding that their first child, Thomas, was born, suggesting to the ill-disposed that it was not fear of infection which had prompted them to leave Bratton for their wedding, but an understandable reluctance to face the gossip of their neighbours and the censure of the churchwardens in their native village for anticipating the joys of matrimony so shamelessly.

But as one of the pillars of the next generation of the Tutfords of Bratton, their embarrassingly forward child (who was to become 'Thomas the Shoemaker') was to make good use of the two months start in life which his parents had provided!

CHAPTER 2

Thomas the Shoemaker (1558-1624)

Bratton, Wiltshire

CHURCHWARDENS AND JURYMEN

Brave *shoemakers*, all gentle men of a gentle craft.
Thomas Dekker, 1572-1632

When a son was born to Henry Tutford and Marian Lyne only seven months after their marriage in Westbury they called him Thomas – possibly after one of his grandfathers. Young Thomas, who was baptised in Bratton on 28th August 1558, was a precocious child: not only was his mother's pregnancy a suspicious two months shorter than was normal, but it would seem that Thomas himself married when he was only just seventeen. And if he were the same 'Thomas Titford' whose wedding with Agnes Davie was recorded in the parish register of far-away Cardington in Bedfordshire on 16 October 1575, then he, like his father, chose to be married at some safe distance from Bratton.

The curate or clerk who entered this particular marriage in the Cardington Register spelt the name as 'Titford', and this is the first occasion on which this form of spelling is known to have been used. The surname was again spelt 'Titford', however, when, on 9 December 1576, the first son of Thomas and Agnes was baptised at Cardington with the forename Henry, and also on 20 May 1580 when a second son, Richard, was christened there.

Little Richard Titford, it would seem, died as an infant just before or just after the family's return to Bratton, where another boy was born and baptised on 17 November 1581 with the same Christian name as his dead baby-brother. Other children followed: Agnes in 1584, John in 1586, Matilda in 1591 and, conjecturally, William sometime between 1595 and 1597, when Robert Marshall, the curate of Bratton, 'neglected to register all suche thinges which he ought to have done'.

By profession Thomas was a shoemaker.[1] But he was also something more. Through his kinsman, William Boudget, who had married Matilde Tutford in Bratton on 19 September 1582, Thomas Tytford (as his name was spelt when he crossed the border into Somerset) held by indenture a house, garden, orchard and two parcels of land in Nunney within that county – including a close of $17\frac{1}{2}$ acres of pasture called 'Budgetts Coome' and an acre of meadow on the common.[2] The indenture provided Thomas with a lease on the land for 21 years from December 1596, but his association with William Boudget was to be of much shorter duration for, in 1597, William died – to be buried in Nunney on 27 May of that year.

Clearly Thomas was not a poor man, and although his title to the land in Nunney was by indenture rather than freehold, nevertheless, in 1604, he became one of the 24 'good and lawful men' chosen by Sir Thomas Thynne, Sheriff of Wiltshire, to sit on the Jury for the Hundred of Westbury, in which capacity he was to continue to serve until 1615 – with breaks in service totalling only three years during all this time.[3]

The Jury of the Hundred, like the superior Grand Jury, was a 'jury of presentment' rather than a 'jury of trial', and its function was to 'present' to John Kent, the Clerk of the Peace, all alleged offences against civil or criminal law which occurred in its locality. The Clerk

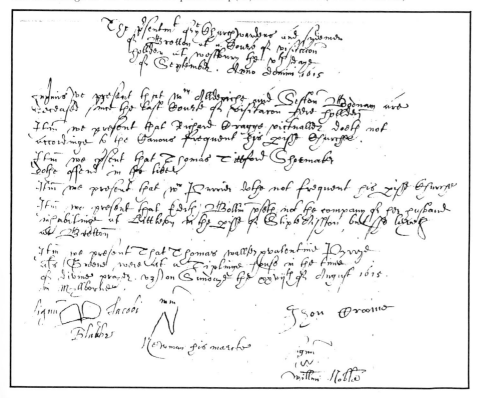

3. Nunney, Somerset: survey of 1597. Reference is made to Thomas Tytford's house and lands held by virtue of a lease dated December 1596, '. . . of the demise of Willm Budgett'. (PRO C110/36.)

4. Churchwardens' presentment, Bratton, Wilts., 1615. This is 'The presentment of ye Churchwardens and sidemen of Bratton at a Courte of visitacon holden at Westbury the vth. daye of September. Anno Domini 1615·'. The presentment includes the charge that 'Thomas Tittford Shoemaker dothe offend in the like' – i.e., 'doeth not accordingly to the Canons frequent his p(ar)ish Churche'. (WRO D25/12.)

of the Peace would then submit such 'presentments' – whether from juries of hundreds, churchwardens, constables, public-minded citizens, or mere informers – to the Grand Jury who would examine them and, if the jurors thought that there was a case to answer, they would, in their turn, 'present' the allegations to the Justices of the Peace at Quarter Sessions. It was only then that a case could go to trial before a Petty Jury of 'twelve good men and true' nominated by the Sheriff.[4] Thomas not only served on the Jury of the Hundred of Westbury, but on at least four occasions between 1604 and 1615 was a member of a petty jury at Quarter Sessions.

The presentments of Thomas and his fellow jurors of the Hundred of Westbury were generally heard at Warminster during the Trinity Quarter Sessions, and many of the original presentments still exist, endorsed at the bottom: 'Be it knowene that we the jurye aforesaid have sett our names and mark in the backside of this our presentment'. Although presentments could cover a multitude of sins, the religious zeal of the strongly-Protestant King James would seem to be reflected in many of the allegations presented at Warminster during this period – with 'not coming to church these last three months' being the most commonly-reported misdemeanour. There were occasional variations on the theme, however, as in the case of Thomas Budd of Clay Close, Dilton, 'husbandman, of the age xxx yeares and upwarde', whom Thomas Titford and his fellow jurors presented 'for livinge idly, never cominge to his parish churche for the space of half a yeare but lyeth at home fighting and brawlinge in the time of Divine service'.[5]

This presentment of 1607 marked a temporary end to Thomas Titford's service as a juror. The following year he found himself, if not actually on the wrong side of the law, then at least a little too close for comfort. And his brush with authority came from an unexpected quarter.

At the Somerset Quarter Sessions in October 1608 a certain Robert Thomas was charged with horse-stealing. Robert Thomas was a surgeon who lived in Langport and, when charged, he admitted that some two years previously he had bought a bay mare for which he was unable to pay. The mare was therefore returned to its owner, but at a later date Robert Thomas saw a similar mare on Langport Moor and, apparently overlooking the fact that it belonged to someone else, he took it to Bratton, 'which is in the parish of Westbury under the Plain', and sold it to one Ralph Aldridge. When asked what he was doing in Bratton, Robert Thomas replied that 'he had come to see his brother-in-law, Thomas Tetford, with intent also to sell the said mare'.

Robert Thomas's theft would, in all probability, have gone undetected except that he later bought a second mare from a man called Pasque Hill whom he met on the way to Glastonbury Fair but, having only made part-payment for his purchase and headed West – presumably to avoid paying the rest – he was arrested at South Molton in Devon on suspicion of theft.[6]

Robert Thomas's evidence would not seem to provide any strong defence against the charge, but both Ralph Aldridge and 'Thomas Tetford' were, in fact, living in Bratton at that time, which would appear to confirm at least part of his story. So possibly he *did* suffer a temporary lapse of memory when it came to paying his debts! Whether or not Robert Thomas was convicted of horse-stealing and duly hanged is not known, but his implication of his 'brother-in-law, Thomas Tetford' in the crime – innocent 'though his involvement may have been – might have been the cause of Thomas Titford's name being removed from the list of Jurors for the Hundred of Westbury that year. Presumably he would no longer be considered to be 'a good and lawful man' and, in the event, it was not until 1610 that he was selected for jury service again.

By 1613, however, Thomas was not only performing his duties as a member of the Jury of the Hundred of Westbury with customary zeal, but he was also on the Petty Jury at

Quarter Sessions. In the former capacity he subscribed to the presentment of one Roger Pavvier of Bratton 'that he useth not his parish church being parish to the hamlet of Bratton within the parish of Westbury orderly as he should and as other parishioners do for the space of three monthes' and in this presentment, as in later ones, Thomas affirmed his name by making his mark – a cross with a line joining the extremities of two of the lower arms.[7] Perhaps it was only coincidence, but on 28th June that same year Thomas's youngest daughter, Matilda, married William Pavvier in the little church of St James in Bratton.

The relationship between Roger Pavvier, to whose presentment Thomas had subscribed, and Thomas's son-in-law, William Pavvier, has not yet been established but, like his presumed kinsman, William was soon in trouble with the authorities. It would seem that in one unfortunate respect – that of pre-marital pregnancy – Matilda Pavvier took after her paternal grandmother, but whilst Henry Tutford and Marian Lyne had prudently married in Westbury to escape the ever-vigilant churchwardens of Bratton, William and Matilda foolishly chose to brazen it out. And they were caught! On 23 May 1614 the churchwardens of Bratton formally reported their misdemeanour to the Precentor of Salisbury – emphasising the seriousness of the offence by putting it top of the list.

Imprimus. We present William Pavvier and Muade [sic] his wife for being with child before they were married.[8]

Early pregnancies were not uncommon in Bratton that year and, although they never quite replaced 'not going to church these three months' as the most popular misdemeanour, the very next entry in the same presentment to the Precentor makes an identical charge against William Walter and his wife. But whilst absence from church might incur a fine, having a bastard was a serious charge which, if proved, could even result in excommunication.

As for the Pavviers and Walters, there is little doubt that the charges against them were well-founded. According to the Bratton parish register, Agnes, the first child of William 'Purvior', was baptised on 15 September 1613, only three months after her parents' wedding, whilst the firstborn of William Walter and Elner Burges was baptised just four months after their marriage on 27 September that same year.

The accused were 'cited' to appear before Henry Cotton, Precentor of Salisbury, on 13 October 1614 and, according to the record of their trial in the Precentor's Act Book, William and Matilda Pavvier were fined 2s. – a lenient punishment in comparison with the fine of 4s. 6d. imposed on Richard Gardener by the same court for 'common Adultery with Elizabeth, wife of John Smith, shepherd', but still not a particularly happy start to married life for the young couple. In consequence they, together with their friends and relatives, probably felt aggrieved that they should have been singled out for punishment for what, after all, was a common human failing.[9]

The following year a party of disaffected villagers seem to have decided that an appropriate communal protest against the judgement of the Precentor's Court might be to boycott church services in a 'gesture of solidarity'. They did just that – and were inevitably presented by the churchwardens of Bratton.

The churchwardens made a rich haul. Those listed in their presentment to the Precentor of Salisbury on 5 September 1615 included Thomas Walter (who was probably William Walter's elder brother), William Pavvier, and 'Thomas Tittford, Shoemaker'. Richard Cragge, victualler, who, like the others, was also accused of failing to attend church, may have been another supporter of the protest movement, and Valentine Perry – who was associated with Thomas Walter in being 'at a tiplinge house at the time of divine prayer' – was included for good measure.[10]

The customary punishment for failing to attend church was a fine of 12d., but repetition of the word 'Contumacious' in the Latin text of his personal summons to attend the court suggests that Richard Cragge in particular (who, being top of the list of accused, was probably first to face the Precentor) was not only impenitent but also impertinent. And the mark against his name on the list of those cited '*Quorum Nomina*' implies that his indiscretion earned him not just a fine, but excommunication![11] A similar punishment was imposed on William Pavvier who, having been dealt with leniently by the Precentor the previous year for fathering a child before he and Matilda were married, was clearly in need of a sharp lesson.

What punishment was inflicted on Thomas Tittford who, as father of Matilda Pavvier, might have been considered to be one of the ring-leaders of the villagers' 'gesture of solidarity'? According to the account of his trial in the Precentor's Act Book, 'Tho. Tyttford de Bratton' made no mention in his defence of any protest movement, but in answer to the charge of 'not frequenting his parish Church att time of prayers', said that

> Edington parish church is nearer . . . than his own parish church, and that he doth rather frequent thither to hear Divine Service than to his own parish church, and further sayeth that he will hereafter frequent his own parish church . . .

Although, understandably, this excuse failed to convince the Precentor of his innocence, Thomas's statement that Edington parish church was nearer to his home than that of Bratton does suggest in passing that he lived in the hamlet of Melbourne, on the north-west edge of Bratton village, from whence it was but a short walk across the fields to Edington. His statement also implies that the protest movement had evaporated in the face of the severe punishment inflicted on Richard Cragge, and that in preparing his defence Thomas Tittford had decided that discretion was the better part of valour and that the role of penitent rather than militant was more appropriate for a juryman of the Hundred of Westbury! He was duly fined 12d. for failing to attend his parish church and the fine was recorded in the Act Book alongside his name.

In the event, possibly because of his daughter's disgrace and his own clash with the church authorities, the Jury of the Hundred of Westbury now felt that they could dispense with the services of Thomas Tittford. As a juryman whose term of service dated back to 1604, Thomas had watched the progress not only of his colleagues in the jury-room but also of the regular visitors to the dock. Thomas Budd, who back in 1607 had been presented for 'living idly' and for 'lying at home fighting and brawlinge in the time of Divine Service' had been presented again to the justices at the Quarter Sessions of 1614 as 'a common spoyler of coping hedges and underwoods by cutting them' and, in 1615, as 'a common steler of rodde and hucker of quick fryth'.[12] On all of these presentments Thomas the Shoemaker had righteously made his mark as a juror, but now that he himself had been presented for failing to attend divine service, the secular authorities may well have decided that he was no longer sufficiently law-abiding to continue to serve on the jury. Whether or not this was the reason for his dismissal, the name of Thomas Tittford ceased to appear on the list of jurors for the Hundred of Westbury after 1615.

But whilst the sheriff, who chose the jurors for secular courts, may have condemned Thomas's fall from grace, the Church – surprisingly in view of Thomas's earlier flouting of the canon law – was more forgiving. In 1617, the year in which he relinquished the tenancy of his land in Nunney, Thomas the Shoemaker appears in a new guise at Bratton – that of 'sydeman' in support of the churchwardens of the parish church of St James.

Either the church authorities saw in Thomas a 'poacher turned gamekeeper', or his contrition at his presentment in 1615 had been sufficiently eloquent to earn not only the forgiveness of the Church but also its patronage. Whatever the reason for his return to favour, however, by 1617 Thomas Tittford was a sydeman at Bratton – and a person of some local importance. To be a churchwarden, or even a sydeman, during the early 17th century was no sinecure. The Tudor monarchs had extended the traditional responsibilities

5. Wiltshire Quarter Sessions, 1615. The presentment of the jury of Westbury Hundred. Thomas Titford makes his mark. (WRO Quarter Sessions, A1/110.)

of the Church's lay officials to embrace much civil administration as well as vigilance over the canon law within their parishes, and the churchwardens' duties now included supervising the collection and distribution of money for the poor, the repair of buildings and highways, and even the destruction of vermin.[13]

In carrying out these – and many other – responsibilities, they were authorised to make presentments against alleged offenders. Transgressions against civil or criminal laws were presented to the Clerk of the Peace for the county in the same way as those made by juries of the hundreds, whilst offences against the canons of the Church were presented to the bishop, dean, precentor or sub-dean as appropriate for investigation during the next 'visitation'. And now Thomas himself was a sydeman at Bratton, an ally and aide to John Croome and William Noble, those same churchwardens who had subscribed to Thomas's own presentment to the Precentor only two years before.

Although Thomas may have found his new association with the churchwardens embarrassing, he nevertheless carried out his duties as sydeman with characteristic zeal. The vicar of Westbury still claimed authority over the church at Bratton, and the presentments of the churchwardens there increasingly reflected the villagers' dissatisfaction with the vicar of Westbury's neglect of their church fabric and the incompetence of his nominated minister or curate. The churchwardens' presentment to the Precentor of Salisbury prior to the visitation of 1617 – a presentment to which Thomas was a signatory – reads in part:

> Imprimis. We present that our chauncell is much decaied in the leads to the value of xl s. or upwards in default of Mr Chambers.[14]

Prestigious though the post of sydeman may have been, it was unpaid, and having lost the income from his tenancy in Nunney after the lease expired, Thomas decided to add to the money he earned as a shoemaker by keeping an alehouse in his spare time. And so it was that, on 22 January 1620, 'Thomas Tytford' visited the Justices of the Peace in Trowbridge where Sir Henry Vynar, Knight, and William Pawlett, Esquire, sat to receive the 'recognaissances' of every innkeeper, butcher and alehousekeeper in the area. The 'recognaissances' of 1620 were legally-binding promises not to serve meat during Lent, and the conscientious Clerk of the Peace, John Kent, was entitled to charge a fee of 2s. 6d. to each innkeeper and butcher and 1s. to every alehousekeeper whose 'recognaissance' he engrossed. With this incentive John Kent carried out his task with such thoroughness that the Lenten Recognisances of 1620 are now recognised as providing an accurate and comprehensive list of all the innkeepers, butchers and alehousekeepers trading in Wiltshire at that time. Thomas paid his shilling and his name was duly engrossed:

> Thomas Tytford of Bratton, alehousekeeper, sureties John Langden, weaver, and William Rawlyns, shoemaker, both of the same.[15]

At the age of 62, then, Thomas the Shoemaker had decided to supplement his income by keeping an alehouse, and had taken as one of his sureties William Rawlyns, a fellow-shoemaker and, conjecturally, a kinsman of John Rawlings, one-time employer of Richard Tutford.

Shoemaker, juryman, sydeman, and now alehousekeeper of Bratton, 'Thomas Tytford' must have felt himself secure. But by the standards of the 17th century he was a very old man, and in the summer of 1624 he died, to be buried in the churchyard of the Church of St James in Bratton on 4 August that year, aged sixty-six. Nor did his wife, Agnes, survive him for long. She too was buried in St James' churchyard, on 20 January 1626/7, and there, in the shade of the ancient yew-trees, Thomas Tytford and his wife still lie.

CHAPTER 3

Thomas the Alehousekeeper (1556-1632)

Steeple Ashton, Wiltshire

MANOR COURT, QUARTER SESSIONS AND STAR CHAMBER

The law doth punish man or woman that steals the goose from off the common,
But lets the greater felon loose that steals the common from the goose.

Anon.

'Thomas the Alehousekeeper' was the son of 'Richard the Servant' and Alice his wife. He was baptised at Bratton on 10 April 1556, and although he may have had elder brothers or sisters who didn't survive infancy, all record of their christenings has been obliterated by the brown stain which obscures so many of the early entries in the Bratton Registers. Indeed, the burial of 'Joan, daughter of Richard Tutford', on 10 January 1550 suggests that Thomas was not the first of Richard and Alice's children; nevertheless he is the first of their sons known to have reached manhood.

And 'manhood' for young Thomas meant that he left his parents' home to live in nearby Steeple Ashton, married before his twenty-third birthday, and fell foul of the law! The record of his marriage has not yet been found, but his wife's forename was Elizabeth and their two children, Mary and Richard, were baptised at Steeple Ashton on 20 October 1579 and 28 May 1583 respectively. Thomas's brush with the law was sufficiently serious to take him before the Justices of the Peace at Devizes during the Michaelmas Quarter Sessions of 1578. The charge against him will never be known, but the verdict of the Court has survived four hundred years:

> Fines taxed by the Court of Thomas Tytford at 2s. and John Slade at 12d. and the Hundreds of Mylksham and Seene at 5s.[1]

Nor was this to be Thomas Tytford's only appearance before the Justices. On 12 October 1586, an older but apparently not a wiser man, Thomas again stood in the dock at Devizes. As on the previous occasion details of his offence have been lost, but this time Thomas pleaded 'not guilty' to the charge. It did him little good; he was convicted and fined rather more heavily than before:

> Thomas Tytford of Stipleashton, who pleads not guilty to an indictment and presentation as of record, 2s. 6d.[2]

Thomas was a husbandman, but to supplement his income and help support his little family he decided that, in addition to working on the land, he would go into business as an alehousekeeper, just as his cousin Thomas the Shoemaker of Bratton would do thirty years later. And this decision involved him in a third – somewhat happier – visit to Devizes. As well as being judges of criminal cases (Entries), the Justices of the Peace were also responsibile for considerable local administration (Orders). Their most common administrative task was the granting of 'badges' to pedlars and of licences to innkeepers, alehousekeepers and the owners of tippling houses, and it was with this category of 'Orders' that Thomas was concerned when he appeared before the justices during the Easter Quarter Sessions of 1589.[3] It was duly recorded in the Minutes of Proceedings that: 'Thomas Tytford of Stipleashton, husbandman, came and renewed his alehouse licence'.[4]

Since Thomas was then 'renewing' his licence, it is evident that he had already been keeping an alehouse before 1589 and, with only two licensed alehouses in Steeple Ashton, Thomas probably did well.[5] But in 1597 tragedy struck. A severe epidemic swept through the little town that summer, and amongst the 42 burials recorded in the parish register between May and August is that of Elizabeth, Thomas Tytford's wife.

Epidemics were commonplace in Tudor England, but for the population of a small town literally to be decimated within the space of four months suggests that the infection which visited Steeple Ashton in 1597 was exceptionally virulent. Whatever the nature of this epidemic – smallpox, influenza or the plague – there was no known remedy, although people were well aware that, to escape infection, they must avoid contact with others. Small wonder that in neighbouring Bratton the pastor deserted his flock and in Steeple Ashton, where the alehouse rivalled the church as a community centre, Thomas Tytford would have had few customers during that terrible summer. And not only did Thomas's alehouse business suffer, but the four years of bad harvests which England experienced from 1594 to 1597 must also have threatened his livelihood as a husbandman. His wife dead, his alehouse deserted, and his children exposed to infection, Thomas decided to leave Steeple Ashton and look for a healthier and happier place to live.[6]

But where to go? The road to Devizes was familiar – all too familiar – but Devizes was unwilling to accept refugees from an infected area, and Thomas was forced to move on. From Devizes the main road took him and his two children across the Vale of Pewsey, over the Marlborough Downs, and past the ancient stone circle of Avebury into Swindon. But Swindon, too, was reluctant to accept strangers fleeing from an epidemic, so Thomas and his little family wearily set out once more along the rutted road which led across the Vale of the White Horse into Berkshire. It was not until they reached the edge of the Cotswolds that they found the refuge they were seeking, and it was in the village of Shipton-under-Wychwood that Thomas also found his second wife.

The marriage of Thomas Tytford of Steeple Ashton to Margaret Ferfield at Shipton-under-Wychwood in Oxfordshire on 25 June 1598 was only one of several out-of-parish weddings recorded in the Parish Register of Steeple Ashton that year. Many other families had fled to escape the epidemic, and some never came back. But Thomas did return, and it was in Steeple Ashton that Thomas and Margaret's first child was baptised, in the Church of St Mary the Virgin on 12 October 1599, and given the name 'Alice'. Sadly the little girl died when she was barely six months old, but the following year another daughter was born and also christened 'Alice' on 1 March 1601/2.

On his return to Steeple Ashton Thomas Tytford not only had a new wife, but also a new trade. The impracticability of earning a living as an alehousekeeper – or even as a husbandman – whilst on the road to Shipton-under-Wychwood had compelled him to adopt another occupation, and Thomas became a tailor. In repairing his own ragged clothes – and those of his children – he must have learned to sew during his travels, and finding that he could sell his new-found skill to others, he continued to practise as a tailor back in Steeple Ashton, where he doubtless discovered that tailoring was more profitable – and certainly less arduous – than full-time husbandry.

Thomas Tytford was 43 years old when he returned to Steeple Ashton, but it would seem that he still possessed that touch of lawlessness which had brought him into conflict with authority during his younger days. Six months before Margaret's first child was born Thomas became involved in a local dispute – a dispute which, three years later, resulted in a complaint by the injured party to the Queen herself through Her Majesty's Privy Council sitting in the Court of Star Chamber.[7]

In this complaint it was alleged that, on Friday 16 April 1599, 'Thomas Tetforde, taylor' was one of the four ring-leaders of a mob which attacked the person and property of John

Brewer, butcher, and, if the allegations were correct, the assault had all the ingredients of a riot. Regrettably, although John Brewer gives a graphic description of his assailants being armed with 'swords, daggers, maine-pikes, staves, forrest-bylls, iron-barrs and such other unlawful weapons' when they broke into his house and shop, terrorised his father, mother, sisters and brothers with 'divers proude, disdainful and contemptuous speeches and menacing words', and 'did most barbarously and savagely cast into the street' his 'fish and flesh there and then to be sold in the said shop', he fails to suggest any motive they may have had for their violent behaviour – merely alleging that they had 'of long time undeservedly and with out just cause or offence given to them, borne secret malice and inward grudge' against him.[8]

The defendants doubtless had a different story to tell, but their answers to John Brewer's complaint have yet to be discovered. But since 'Thomas Tetforde' in particular had been away from Steeple Ashton for more than a year, the allegation that he had 'of long time' borne a grudge against John Brewer seems somewhat excessive. The riotous mob probably considered itself to be no more than a group of right-minded vigilantes, while to John Brewer, quite understandably, they represented the hooligan element of Steeple Ashton, whom he describes as '12 persons or upward of badde, lewde, wicked and desperate behaviour'. In the event it would be difficult to find a more respectable – if disparate – trio than Thomas Tetforde's fellow-conspirators.

Cicily Stileman, who allegedly masterminded the affray, was a wealthy widow and freeholder in the manor, farming 44 acres, while Walter Stileman, another ringleader, was a 'gent' and a substantial landowner.[9] The third conspirator was 'James Gamble, smith' whose father also practised as a smith in Devizes. James Gamble's first wife, Margaret, had died in 1588 but he had subsequently remarried, and his second wife, Janet, had recently presented him with his third son. What common cause could unite such an unlikely combination of seemingly-respectable citizens in taking violent action against the local butcher?

Not that John Brewer had been the local butcher for long. At the time of the 'riot' he was only 22 years old, a bachelor who had probably taken over the butchery business from Robert Robertes – a friend of the family who, together with John Brewer's father, Walter, had stood as surety for Robert Robertes' brother John when the latter applied for an alehouse licence in 1585.[10] Walter Brewer himself was a husbandman who had dabbled in the victualling trade since at least as early as 1582, in which year he had been granted a 'badge' by the Justices of the Peace to transport corn or other victuals for sale at a profit.[11] A 'badger' had to be over 30 years old, married and a householder, and whilst Walter was all of these things, his 'house' – as described in the manorial survey of 1604 – was no more than 'a small piece of ground with a cottage'.[12] John Brewer's younger brother, Richard, was also to become an alehousekeeper, but clearly the Brewers were not a wealthy family.[13] Nor could they have offered much physical resistance to the mob. Apart from John Brewer himself and his parents, (who are described as 'aged persons') those named in the 'complaint' of 1599 as having been terrorised and abused by the rioters were all children – the oldest, John's brother, Thomas, being only 15 at the time.[14]

It thus seems possible that the 'riot' was a communal protest against John Brewer's business practices, rather than a dispute over property or the expression of personal animosity against him and his relations. It may be significant that the 'riot' took place on a Friday – a meatless day – and that the particular Friday in question was that following immediately after Easter and the long abstinence of Lent, when a butcher would have been denied any custom. Had John Brewer been selling meat illegally during Lent and roused the ire of a puritanical mob? Or could his prices have been excessive, or his meat tainted? Certainly in later years John Brewer was to show no particular regard for the niceties of the law, nor was he above using abusive behaviour himself on occasions. In 1611 he was to be one of the defendants (George Webbe, the vicar of Steeple Ashton, being another) in a complaint of libel submitted to the Court of Star Chamber by Francis Wallis, an attorney, who alleged that '. . . his reputation had been maligned by certayne ill-disposed persons, his professed enemies (who) indevored to make him odious amongst his clients'.[15] And, possibly more pertinent, in the 1620s he was to face a charge at Quarter Sessions for sheep-stealing! Not that there was any question of the stolen carcases being tainted on that particular occasion, since John Brewer had kept the sheep in question alive in some caves on Claverton Down until the hue-and-cry had subsided and he could butcher them at leisure![16]

Although the outcome of John Brewer's complaint of 1599 to the Court of Star Chamber is not known, subsequent events suggest that shortly afterwards he fell upon hard times. And in his later troubles he was, once more, to be associated with Thomas Tytford – or, more accurately, with Thomas Tytford's neighbour.

On 30 January 1601/2, a certain Roger Winslowe married for a second time, his first wife, Dorothee Purnell, having died in Steeple Ashton during the epidemic of 1597, leaving Roger with two little boys to bring up. Roger then moved into an extension built on to his cottage ('The New Building'), which was near the Manor Farm behind the church, and, sometime after 1604, his original cottage ('The Old Building') was rented by Thomas Tytford. By then Thomas's children by his first marriage were old enough to work and make some contribution to the family exchequer, but their neighbour, Roger Winslowe, was less fortunate.

Not that Roger Winslowe came from a poor family. An earlier 'Roger Winslow' had, in 1539, been copyholder of 24 acres of arable land in Eastfield, Merefield, Standellfield and Windmyllfield, together with three rods of pasture in 'Whites' and 'Dixs', and in 1545 had contributed the substantial sum of 22s. to the 'Benevolence' of that year.[17] But the Winslowes had since come down in the world, and their financial problems were exacerbated as Roger and Elizabeth, his second wife, added to the number of mouths to feed in their family – young William and Roger being joined successively by John, Anne, Christoper, Matthias, Henry, Elizabeth and, in 1616, by Edward.

Few of these children reached adulthood, but with such a large and ailing brood to support Roger found it hard to make ends meet and by 1605 was forced to accept charity from the parish. Part of this charity – in cash or in kind – was distributed at the door of the church of St Mary the Virgin by the overseers of the poor on the feast-day of St Stephen, and the names of those who received it were recorded in the churchwardens' accounts. The entry for 1605 includes the following:

> Item: Roger Winslowe's child had of canvas 1 elle and a h.

and, recalling participants in the riot of 1599:

> John Bruer's wife had of canvas 2 elles and a qr.

and

> James Gamble's child had of canvas 1 elle and a qr.[18]

Roger Winslowe, John Brewer and others received parish charity on St Stephen's Day year after year until 1619, after which the names of recipients were no longer recorded. The last entry reads:

> Of Frize: To John Brewer 3 yd. 3 qrs.
>   To Roger Winslowe 2 yd. & a h.
> In monie: To Roger Winslowe's wife in her sonnes sickness 18d.

For Roger Winslowe this was the calm before the storm. The following year William Styleman, a relative of Cecily and Walter, one of the richest freeholders in the manor and also a churchwarden, sued both Roger Winslowe and his neighbour Thomas Tytford for possession of their cottages and land, and petitioned for their rehousing on the common.

It was in the manorial court that a jury of villagers (the 'homage') met the Lord of the Manor or his Steward to decide land transactions and titles in the court baron, and although reforms by the Tudor monarchs had limited their jurisdiction, manorial courts still exercised considerable authority in country districts. This was particularly apparent in Steeple Ashton, where the manor belonged to no less a person than Charles, Prince of Wales, and although it was his steward and not the Prince himself who presided at the manor court, even the steward of the manor of Steeple Ashton was a man of consequence – Sir James Ley, Chief Justice of the King's Bench and later Lord High Treasurer of England.[19]

Nor did Sir James Ley leave room for any doubt as to where true authority lay in Steeple Ashton. Whilst the Elizabethan Poor Laws had made the provision of houses for the homeless and destitute on the common or waste but one of the many responsibilities imposed on the churchwardens and overseers of the poor, Sir James was doubtless aware that abuse of this authority was not unusual and, in Steeple Ashton, ensured that matters were conducted somewhat differently.

The ruling which Sir James Ley had given at the manor court in September 1617 on the use of common land for new housing developments was both concise and unequivocal – as we might expect from the Chief Justice of the King's Bench:

> It is ordered that no person whatsoever shall hereinafter divert or sett-by any cottage or building uppon the Prince's Highnes' wastes or commons within the manor without lycense first obteyned from the Prince's Highnes or of the Prince's Councill of Revenue or else of the officers of this Courte in payne of £5 [fine]. And it is also ordered that the baylief shall hinder the setting up of any such building before the framing or setting up thereof. And just in case the same shall notwithstanding be built, then the baylief is to seise the same into the Highness' hands'.[20]

It would have taken a bold man to contest such an order and although, as a churchwarden, William Styleman was himself empowered to rehouse Thomas Titford and Roger Winslowe on the common, prudently he chose to leave the matter to the manor court.

The eviction order was first considered by the court on 30 September 1620, and whilst judgement was given in favour of William Styleman, its terms appeared to be generous to Messrs. Tytford and Winslowe:

> It is ordered that the cottage of Roger Winslowe and Thoma. Titford be removed by the next Courte into a place on the Common where the Prince's Highness steward hath upon view appoynted the same. And Thomas Titford to have his part of the land measured and his Highness' said steward is pleased to give allowance in the common of soe much ground and halfe as much more ground and like measure for Winslowe and like allowance. And Roger Winslowe is p'hibited to take away the great appletree.[21]

Unexpectedly the court then decided that not only should Roger Winslowe and Thomas Tytford move to the common, but that John Brewer should join them there – not because anyone wanted his house and land, but simply because he didn't have any! By 1620 John Brewer, one-time butcher of Steeple Ashton, was homeless himself and needed somewhere to live.[22]

> And the foresaid John Brewer is allowed to build a cottage in the common and place aforesaid with some convenient ground for a garden plott to be allowed.

Finally the court dealt with the award of the vacated land to William Styleman and the question of removal expenses for Roger Winslowe and Thomas Tytford from their semi-detached cottages behind the church:

> . . . and the said William Styleman is to have all the ground adjoining to his close where the foresaid cottage stand and the foresaid lane and the orchard of Winslowe and to take the same into his owne ground. So as the said Styleman to be at chardg towards the removing of the foresaid cottages viz; to each of them the said Winslowe and Titford xx s. apeice whereof xiii s. iiij d. to be paid and allowed by Styleman's sonne . . .[23]

The court's unusual but explicit prohibition over the removal of 'the great apple tree' must surely have been inserted because a distraught, and perhaps not-entirely sober, Roger Winslowe had been heard to threaten to do just that – and the Chief Justice of the King's Bench left nothing to chance! But if Roger Winslowe and Thomas Titford were upset by the eviction order, they had good reason to be. Ashton Common was more than a mile from the town of Steeple Ashton, and although Thomas Tytford was no longer a licensed alehousekeeper, all his friends doubtless lived in the town, and Thomas must have resented being condemned to spend his twilight years in isolation with only those two layabouts, Winslowe and Brewer, for company.[24] As for Roger Winslowe, his third son, John, had died the previous year at the age of 17, and Roger may by then have felt himself too old to convert wasteland into the allotment he would have needed to grow fruit and vegetables for his family.

But although Sir James Ley had ordered that the eviction should be completed 'by the nexte courte' he had, perhaps, forgotten that he was in Wiltshire – and in Wiltshire things always take a little longer! And, anyway, weren't there still a few details to be settled? Like the mills of God, the manor court of Steeple Ashton may have ground slowly, but no-one could deny but that it ground exceeding small, and these details were important!

And so it was that six months later, on 14 April 1621, the manor court met again under the chairmanship of Charles Danvers, Esquire, deputy to Sir James Ley, to direct that the existing properties of Roger Winslowe and Thomas Tytford be measured so that suitable provision could be made for their accommodation on the common. At the same time, to facilitate the absorbtion of the Winslowe and Titford lands into the Styleman estate, arrangements had to be made for the lane in which the two cottages stood to be closed to traffic. And finally – almost casually – it was necessary to approve an agreement between William Styleman and Henry Greenhill by which the latter rented a major part of the erstwhile Winslowe/Tytford property. Roger Winslowe and Thomas Tytford were not merely to be evicted, they were also to be the victims of a property deal between two of the biggest landowners in the district![25]

Partly in Latin, partly in English, the orders of the manorial court were inscribed in the rolls:

> It is ordered that the baylief of the mannor and Roger Martyn and William Styleman doe view the houses and buildings in question . . . and at the next Court to certyfie what is fitt to be added & set up for ij habitacions for them to the intent which estate may be granted to each of them.
> It is ordered that the lane in which the cottages of Roger Winslowe and Thomas Tytford are situated next the close of Henry Greenhill be blocked up and no-one shall pass along the same lane under pain of 3s. 4d. for each time. And that according to the order before made, copies granted of part of the lane were made, by copy, to William Styleman together with a copy of a licence to lease out 26 perches there to Henry Greenhill for a fine of 5s. and rent, and that separate copies be made for Roger Winslowe and Thomas Titford for lands to be commensurate, and that the cottages to be removed before the feast of Pentecost by the view of the homage.[26]

A new deadline had now been set for the move, but Pentecost in 1621 fell on 20 May – scarcely a month after the Court had met – and, like Sir James Ley, Charles Danvers, Esquire, still had to learn that to 'order' something to happen carried no guarantee that it would happen in fact. Or, at least, not yet! Perhaps the Court had Pentecost *1622* in mind? But on 3 May 1622 when the manor court met again, Roger Winslowe and Thomas Tytford were still living in their original cottages, and the only progress made with their eviction was a report that their land had been measured:

> Item. That the land whereon Winslowe's cottage standeth is measured and conteyneth 37 perche in the whole whereof the said Winslowe's part of the land was 26 perche and the part of Thomas Titford 11 perche. And this land being the Prince's land is bounded out from the land of Henry Greenhill by the homage of this manor by meere stones sett and pitched att the view, and the said

6. Steeple Ashton, Wilts.: manor-court proceedings, May 1622. '. . . the said Winslowes p(ar)te of the land was xxvj perche and the p(ar)te of Thomas Titford xj perche . . .' The eviction of Roger Winslowe and Thomas Titford, both to be rehoused on the common, gets underway in the Prince of Wales's manor court of Steeple Ashton. (CUL Oo.VII.8.)

Henry Greenhill desireth 30 lugg of the said land whereof 26 lugg belong to Winslowe his cottage and four lugg of ground of the said Titford's eleaven lugg belonging to his cottage.[27]

In the event it wasn't until the *next* meeting of the manor court, on 27 September 1622, that the formalities were completed and the the file closed on the eviction of Roger Winslowe and Thomas Titford. Firstly, in Latin – and at some considerable length – the transfer of their two cottages was recorded on the Court Rolls:

And to this court came Roger Winslowe and surrendered into the lord's hands a cottage, namely the east part called New Building, and a garden and a piece of land containing one virgate of land now or lately in the tenure of the same Roger. And likewise to this same court came Thomas Titford and surrendered into the lord's hand a cottage, namely the west side called le Old Building, and a certain piece of land on the west there with the appurtenances now or lately in the tenure of the aforesaid Thomas, which same cottage by order of the last court, he was to remove to the common lands called 'le Marshe'. And thereupon, to this same court, came Henry Greenhill and took of the lord the parcel of land aforesaid so surrendered viz. 25 perches by measurement as bounded out by the homage, namely 20 perches lately in the tenure of the aforesaid Roger Winslowe, 5 perches thereof being parcel of the land lately in the tenure of the aforesaid Thomas Titford and the appurtenances.

The extent and location of Henry Greenhill's newly-acquired property was then defined:

Which same premises extend in length from the field called Keevell Field to the orchard of Thomas Silverthorne and in breadth between the lands of John Whatley and others on one side and the farm of Ashton on the other side, saving always 11 perches granted to a certain William Styleman . . .

And, finally, the manor court rolls contain a description of the properties to which Roger Winslowe and Thomas Titford had been moved and the terms and conditions of their tenure. First, Roger Winslowe:

> To this court came Roger Winslowe and took of the lord a cottage, newly erected, and a garden or piece of land adjacent with the appurtenances lying near the end of the lane called 'le Marshlane' now in the tenure of the same Roger, To Have and To Hold for himself, the aforesaid Roger, and for William his son for their lifetimes and for the survivor of them, at the will of the lord according to the custom of the manor aforesaid, rendering therefore yearly 12d. And rendering and doing all other duties, works, rents, customs and services there due before and of right accustomed, and he gives to the lord as fine nothing by reason of having moved the cottage out-side the town of Steeple Ashton, and he has made fealty to the lord and thus was admitted tenant thereof.

The formula for granting Thomas Titford tenancy of his new cottage was similar:

> To this court came Thomas Titford and took of the lord a cottage of new erection and a garden or piece of land containing by measurement (blank) now in the tenure of the same Thomas, To Have and To Hold for himself, the aforementioned Thomas, and Alice his daughter for the term of their lifetimes and for the survivor of them, at the will of the lord according to the custom of the manor aforesaid, rent there yearly 12d. And rendering and doing all other duties, works, rents, customs and services there before due and of right accustomed. And he gives to the lord as fine nothing by reason of the cottage having been moved outside the town of Steeple Ashton, and he has done fealty to the lord and is admitted thereof tenant.

It had taken two years almost to the day to evict Roger Winslowe and Thomas Titford and to rehouse them on the common, and during that time Thomas Titford's daughter, Alice, had married John Foote – the wedding taking place in the parish church of St Mary the Virgin on 28 February 1620/1. As for the other protagonists in the manor court proceedings, it is perhaps ironic that, after all the trouble he had taken to acquire the little tenancies of Winslowe and Titford, Henry Greenhill was to enjoy them for only a further two years. In 1624 he sold all his estates in Steeple Ashton to John Bennett – including the manor-house, farm and demesnes which he had inherited on the death of his father, John Greenhill, in 1618. Nor was that all. Men of property were required to accept knighthood, and pay the appropriate fee to the crown; but in 1623 Henry Greenhill 'disclaimed arms', thus incurring a fine, and having repaid the sum of £4 he had borrowed from the vestry, left Steeple Ashton for good in 1625.[28]

Another leading character in the history of Thomas Titford's eviction, Sir James Ley, was created Earl of Marlborough on the accession of Charles I in 1625, but died four years later, in which same year the Princes' Highness' manor of Steeple Ashton was sold to Edward Ditchfield and others.

Perversely, the families of Winslowe and Tytford were to retain possession of their new properties rather longer than Henry Greenhill kept his. Indeed, the inclosure map for Steeple Ashton for 1813 shows a 'Samuel Winslow' and a 'John Winslowe' as occupying two cottages on the common – nearly two hundred years after Roger Winslowe first moved there! More pertinent, another survey of the manor of Steeple Ashton taken in 1637 lists Roger Winslowe himself as then living in a cottage 'erected 15 years since' and still paying 12d. a year rent – although, with only eight luggs of land attached to the cottage, it would seem that the promise of the manor court at the time of his eviction in 1622 that he would be 'allowed soe much ground and halfe as much more ground' had not been honoured.[29] The cottage to which Thomas Tytford moved is also shown in the survey, together with six luggs of land – again, much less than Thomas had been promised – but the occupier listed in the survey of 1637 is not Thomas Tytford but John Foote, Thomas's son-in-law.[30]

Five years before this survey was made, Thomas Tytford had come to the end of his own long journey through life. 'Thomas the Alehousekeeper' who, in 1597, had travelled all the way to Shipton-under-Wychwood in Oxfordshire to find a wife, made his last, solitary journey from his cottage on the common to the parish church of St Mary the Virgin in

Steeple Ashton to be buried on 21 April 1632. The bearers couldn't carry his coffin past the door of his old home behind the church, as was the custom, because the lane in which it stood had been closed since 1621, by order of the manor court.

Thomas Tytford was 76 years old when he died, and the wife he had married in Oxfordshire so long ago was buried with him the following year. He had been born when 'Bloody Mary' was Queen, had lived all through the long and eventful reign of her sister, Elizabeth, and the uncertain age of James I, and had died when James's ill-fated son Charles – sometime lord of the Prince's Highness' manor of Steeple Ashton – was on the throne of England. Two queens and two kings! And Thomas had survived nearly all of them!

CHAPTER 4

Richard the Yeoman (?1564-1632)

Corsley and Upton Scudamore, Wiltshire

DEPRESSION AND DISPERSAL

To thrive, a *yeoman* must wive . . .
                              Thomas Tusser

The common man of England, so the accepted fairy story used to go, was tied to the land; lacking either the will or the means to be mobile, he was born and died in the same village, as were his children and his children's children and his children's children's children. Yet such a view is after all, little more than an attractive fiction, lacking the saving grace of historical accuracy: 'One of the most deeply rooted and false ideas about English social history is that the majority of our population were rooted to the soil in one place until quite recent times'.[1]

Even the most cursory glance at any long run of English parish registers reveals only too clearly the fact that roots were very often not permanent roots, after all. The landowning classes might dominate the life of a small village for hundreds of years, but many a humble family would be quite likely to arrive in a place from elsewhere, stay there for a couple of generations or so, and then pull up those seemingly deep roots and set off down the road to replant them in pastures new. We may suppose that very few working families enjoyed the luxury of waking up one sunny morning and deciding to make their home elsewhere, just for a change of scenery; if we wish to make sense of patterns of immigration and emigration between settlements, we must think, more often than not, in terms of economics. Any place where times were hard, where jobs were impossible to find, would lose its younger sons and daughters; and by the same token a village or town which was prospering would attract those very same emigrants as they sought a new means of making a livelihood.

The Titford family which is the focus of our attention can furnish us with specific examples of population mobility in the late 16th and early 17th centuries. For a start, it would seem that the Bratton Titfords, so much in evidence in the village following the marriage of Richard and Alice in 1547, were fairly new arrivals there themselves at that time, along with several other such families.[2]

Not only that, but we already have evidence of individuals who were prepared to leave Bratton temporarily or permanently when they had to or when it suited them: Henry and Marian Lyne were married in Westbury; Thomas the Shoemaker very probably found his wife in Bedfordshire, and had connexions with Nunney in Somerset; Thomas the Alehousekeeper made his home in Steeple Ashton, but was married for the second time in Oxfordshire. All of this suggests a degree of geographical mobility which might have surprised us had we adopted the 'fixed-in-one-spot' theory of English social history.

Bratton boomed when the textile industry boomed; during its heyday in the 16th century it could boast at least four mills on the stream known as the Stradbrook, and life must have seemed stable enough to comparatively rich and comparatively poor alike. Yet for the Titfords this was to be a place of temporary sojourn, not a permanent home, after all; within sixty years – a mere two generations – of the first Titford marriage recorded in the village,

24

steady family emigration was underway. Those who left Bratton chose a variety of new places in which to settle – none more than a few miles away – but the flock was scattering nevertheless. Who were these people, and where did they go?

We can start by following the fortunes of the most financially-successful of them: 'Richard the Yeoman'. He enjoys the rare distinction among Wiltshire Titfords of having been a well-to-do man of the countryside; other members of the family over the years would become as prosperous as he, if not more so, but theirs would be an urban success – especially for those who moved to London. Richard's comparative wealth, by contrast, was firmly rooted in the land.

His beginnings were humble enough: the illegible Christian name for the baptism of a 'Tutford' boy in the Bratton registers for 12 May 1564 is very probably that of our Richard, the younger brother of Thomas the Alehousekeeper and – more significantly – the son of Richard the Servant with his '. . . one heiffer of three years age and two chilver sheep', courtesy of the will of John Rawlings in 1580/1. If Richard the father had consolidated this livestock holding by the time he died in Bratton in 1603, then his own legacy to Richard, junior, may have enabled the young man to begin his career as a yeoman farmer. The burial entry for the older man describes him as 'Richard Tutford, senior', probably because his son of the same name was still in the village; but he was not there for long – this was exodus time for everyone and by 1609 young Richard had taken himself off round the western edge of the plain and settled near the little scattered village of Corsley.

This was not Richard's first time of leaving Bratton: in the January of 1591/2 his steps had taken him northwards to Bradford-on-Avon, where he married the wife who would outlive him: Katheren Godsden. The Bradford-on-Avon registers provide us with three Titford marriages during this period: that of Richard himself, that of James Titford and Mary Noble in 1585/6, and that of Mary Titford and James Hearne in 1588.[3] Some Titfords, at least, then, had decided to eschew their native parish when it came to wedding time, though these Bradford marriages took place during periods when there were few if any such ceremonies being celebrated in Bratton – a result, perhaps, of pestilence of some sort, or of that disaffection with the local clergy which was never far beneath the surface?

7.   Rent Roll, Corsley, Wilts., 1609. 'Richard Titforde holdeth by Indenture bearinge date the . . . of the graunte of Sir E Hungerforde knight j small Cottage w(i)th thapp(ur)ten(a)nces for . . . xijd. rent.' (WRO 442/2.)

We should hardly describe Richard Titford as a 'yeoman' when we first meet him in Corsley in 1609. There were three freeholders in the village at the time – William Carr, Anthony Raxworthy and Robert Fytchne – and a total of seven tenants paying rent to the Hungerfords of Farleigh Castle for their properties, including Richard Titford. He was paying less such rent than anybody: while William Lambe was assessed at £6 13s. 4d. for the half-year, and William Carr at £4 5s. 5d., Richard had to content himself with 'one small cottage and appurtenances' held by indenture from 'Sir E. Hungerford' which would cost him 6d. per half-year, '. . . payeable . . . at the ffeast of Th'annunciason of our Ladie'.[4]

If Richard felt overawed by his more plutocratic neighbours, then the remedy was in his

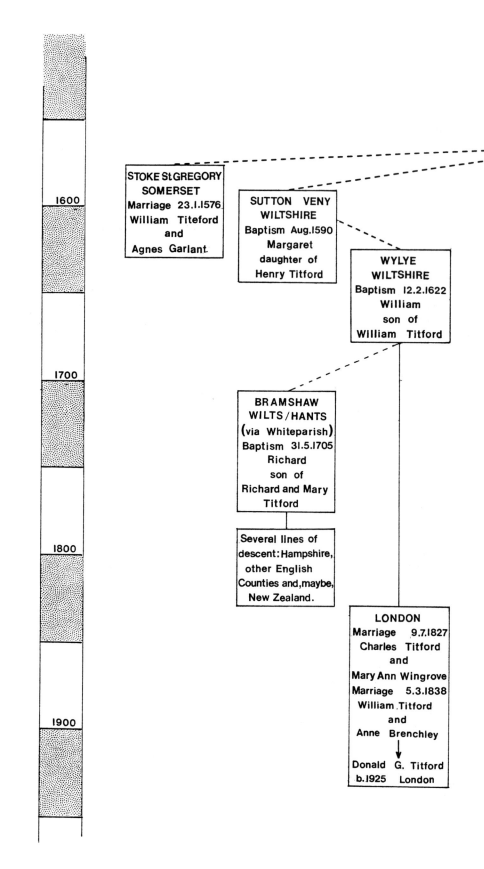

1600

1700

1800

1900

STOKE St GREGORY
SOMERSET
Marriage 23.1.1576
William Titeford
and
Agnes Garlant

SUTTON VENY
WILTSHIRE
Baptism Aug.1590
Margaret
daughter of
Henry Titford

WYLYE
WILTSHIRE
Baptism 12.2.1622
William
son of
William Titford

BRAMSHAW
WILTS / HANTS
(via Whiteparish)
Baptism 31.5.1705
Richard
son of
Richard and Mary
Titford

Several lines of
descent: Hampshire,
other English
Counties and, maybe,
New Zealand.

LONDON
Marriage 9.7.1827
Charles Titford
and
Mary Ann Wingrove
Marriage 5.3.1838
William Titford
and
Anne Brenchley
↓
Donald G. Titford
b.1925 London

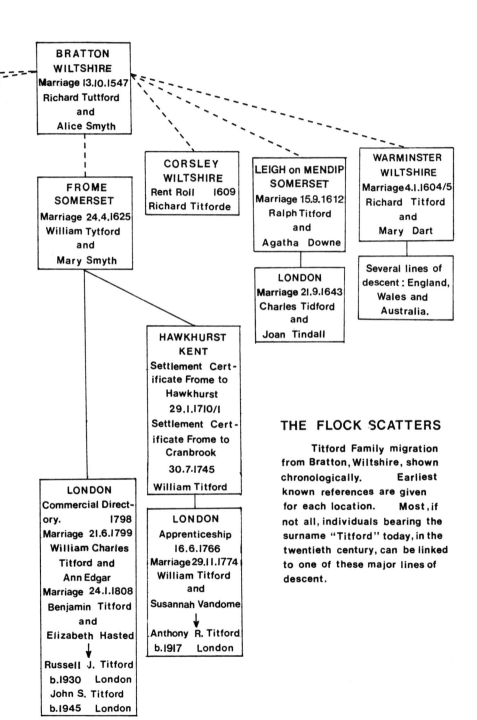

BRATTON
WILTSHIRE
Marriage 13.10.1547
Richard Tuttford
and
Alice Smyth

FROME
SOMERSET
Marriage 24.4.1625
William Tytford
and
Mary Smyth

CORSLEY
WILTSHIRE
Rent Roll   1609
Richard Titforde

LEIGH on MENDIP
SOMERSET
Marriage 15.9.1612
Ralph Titford
and
Agatha Downe

WARMINSTER
WILTSHIRE
Marriage 4.1.1604/5
Richard Titford
and
Mary Dart

LONDON
Marriage 21.9.1643
Charles Tidford
and
Joan Tindall

Several lines of
descent : England,
Wales and
Australia.

HAWKHURST
KENT
Settlement Cert-
ificate Frome to
Hawkhurst
29.1.1710/1
Settlement Cert-
ificate Frome to
Cranbrook
30.7.1745
William Titford

LONDON
Commercial Direct-
ory.   1798
Marriage 21.6.1799
William Charles
Titford and
Ann Edgar
Marriage 24.1.1808
Benjamin Titford
and
Elizabeth Hasted
↓
Russell J. Titford
b.1930 London
John S. Titford
b.1945 London

LONDON
Apprenticeship
16.6.1766
Marriage 29.11.1774
William Titford
and
Susannah Vandome
↓
Anthony R. Titford
b.1917 London

THE FLOCK SCATTERS

   Titford Family migration
from Bratton, Wiltshire, shown
chronologically.   Earliest
known references are given
for each location.   Most, if
not all, individuals bearing the
surname "Titford" today, in the
twentieth century, can be linked
to one of these major lines of
descent.

own hands: he would work and save, build up his livestock, store his grain, and expand his living accommodation. Things went well for him: by the time he died in 1632, worth a grand total of £60 3s. 6d., he could boast five 'keine', five 'horsebeats', two 'sucking colts', four yearlings, three pigs, and 15 sheep; all that, plus £10 worth of corn, together with hay, malt, bacon, cheese and 30 lb of wool. A thrifty man, indeed.

Yet farmers need land as well as beasts and crops. Richard was living at Fulmore, just north of Norridge Wood, and could easily graze some of his animals on the nearby common – all too easily, as it happens, to the point where the manor court of the Hungerfords fined him 5s. in October 1631 for allowing three of his horses and six of his cows to encroach upon the common when they had no right to be there.[5] But apart from his use (or misuse) of the common, Richard appears to have rented or leased land adjacent to his cottage: a survey of the manor of Upton Skidmore for 1804 contains details of orchards and meadow totalling two acres, two rods and 13 perches, on what by then was the Marquess of Bath's estate at Fulmore, which area was still being referred to as 'Titfords', even at that date.[6] This, surely, had been one of Richard's own fields or closes, adjoining his house in Fulmore?

Fulmore is south of the village of Upton Scudamore; to the north there lies yet further evidence of Richard the Yeoman's presence, in the shape of what is referred to today as 'Titford Farm', near Old Dilton. The 1808 Inclosure Award for Westbury makes no mention of the present farm building, but does list 'Titford Acre', 'Titford Field' and 'Tyning at Titford' in the immediate neighbourhood.[7] The brook which is now culverted outside Titford Farm once ran directly across the road, thereby creating what may have been known as the 'Titford': either that or, more likely, it was here that the redoubtable Richard Titford farmed his outlying fields as long ago as the 17th century, thereby perpetuating his name for posterity.

Richard may have given his name to a number of fields, but they were fields he held as a tenant, not his own freehold property; do such holdings and his considerable store of beasts, crops and chattels qualify him as a yeoman? That must be a matter of opinion; there are those who would claim that a yeoman – the name had originally meant simply a 'servant' – would need to earn 40s. from freehold land to deserve such a title; but there can be little doubt that the borderline between a husbandman and a yeoman was a rather hazy one in the 17th century, and that some 'yeomen' were in effect little more than subsistence farmers. Richard Titford himself was equivocal on the issue, in any case: as a witness in a Chancery suit of 1631 he described himself as a 'husbandman', while on his death-bed it occurred to him that perhaps 'yeoman' might sound more grand as he dictated his will. Not, certainly, one of those stalwart chaps with hundreds of acres who was the backbone of England, but a very comfortably-off tenant farmer with a substantial house and goods a-plenty.

In the event Richard must have felt as equivocal about his position in the local government structure as he did about his occupational status: here he was, farming at Fulmore in the parish of Upton Scudamore, but with fields across at Old Dilton, a few yards from St Mary's church – a different parish altogether. He was on the edge of Corsley – a parish which had been divided into several manors since medieval times – and found it was part of his responsibility as a tenant of the Hungerfords to attend the three-weekly court of the Hundred of Warminster as a tythingman for 'Little Corsley'.[8]

At least Richard took his role as a tythingman seriously, and left his day's work on the land to sit through the requisite court proceedings, however boring they may have been. Not all the six or seven Little Corsley men were so conscientious: one of them, at least, decided he needn't waste his time in any such pursuits, and is listed time and again under the heading of 'essoin' – that is, absent with some form of excuse. That man was Thomas Carr.

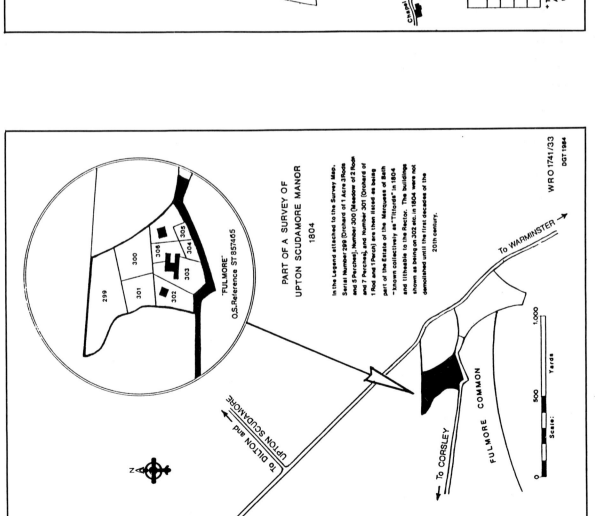

NUMBER ON MAP	NAME OF PROPRIETOR	SITUATION	QUANTITY		
			A	R	P
263	C.L. Phipps Esquire	Tyning at Tytford+	3	3	28
326	Henry Bletch, baker (Davinese)	Titford Field	5	2	24
327	Elizabeth Phipps & -?-Kemp	"	1	0	18
328	Joseph Ball	"	2	2	3

+ This allotment, annotated "X the Vicar" on Map A, is called "Titford Acre" in the associated Award Book where it is show amongst other allotments which C.L. Phipps "exchanged with the Vicar of Westbury"

9. Inclosure award for Westbury, 29 July 1808 (extracts from maps A and B). (WRO 1A/V76.)

PART OF A SURVEY OF UPTON SCUDAMORE MANOR 1804

In the Legend attached to the Survey Map, Serial Number 299 (Orchard of 1 Acre 3Rods and 5 Perches), Number 300 (Meadow of 2 Rods and 7 Perches), and Number 301 (Orchard of 1 Rod and 1 Perch) are then listed as being part of the Estate of the Marquess of Bath "known collectively as "Titfords" in 1804 and tithable to the Rector. The buildings shown as being on 302 etc. in 1804 were not demolished until the first decades of the 20th century.

8. 'Titfords' of Fulmore. (WRO 1741/33.)

Thomas Carr had other things on his mind, it is true: his family had held the farm of Little Corsley (now Cley Hill Farm) since the middle of the 16th century, but by 1631 he was in financial difficulties. In the January of that year a Chancery case was proceeding against him apace, with the Earl of Rutland and others as plaintiffs. No fewer than 36 witnesses duly arrived at Warminster to make their depositions before Sir Henry Ludlowe, Sir John Horner and Robert Drewe, Esq. Top of the list and first examined was none other than 'Richard Titfford of ffullmore in the parish of Upton Skidmore in the County of Wiltshire, husbandman, aged threescore yeares or thereabouts . . .' What could Richard possibly tell Their Worships that might interest them? Yes, he knew the plaintiff and defendant, and he knew the farm called Corsley; yes, Corsley farm was in reasonably good repair, but the oxhouse, the stable, the back house and the washing house were much in decay; yes, since the death of his father, William Carr, the said Thomas Carr had cut down a 'greate store' of trees – oak, elm and maple – oh, about four hundred of them, he would guess . . . and big trees, too . . . And he'd used about six of them to build a hay house, but had sold the rest – made about two hundred pounds or so, Richard would guess.

All this was not good news for Thomas Carr, and things grew no better for him as the witnesses took the stand one after another – a motley collection of worthies from Corsley, Upton Scudamore, Warminster and Frome. Half the men of the neighbourhood, it seemed, had taken the day off work to have their say: a whole host of husbandmen, tailors, bakers, shoemakers, a fletcher, a clerk, a carpenter, a joiner, a mason, an innholder, a weaver – and Giles Hungerford of Upton Skidmore, 'Gentelman'. All had tales to tell: one man had bought eight oak trees from the defendant, another had had nine of the same; one had purchased 740 feet of oaken board at 5s. 8d. per hundred, and another declared darkly that he had seen many trees carried . . . Few witnesses had been so unfortunate, however, as Robert Hooper: he had acted as overseer of the poor in Corsley three years previously, at which time he went to collect a debt of 8s. from Thomas Carr – owed to the 'poore of Corslie'. Carr said he had no money but told Hooper to help himself to a few trees in lieu, and 'willed him to tak what trees he would uppon Corslie ffarme for the money . . .' Always a naïve man, we may guess, Hooper agreed; choosing two trees, he felled them and carted them off to sell '. . . and could not gett more than seven shillings six pence for them, soe that he loste six pence by the bargaine . . .'.[9]

The accumulation of evidence against Carr proved all too damaging: the sheriff was ordered to remove him from Little Corsley Farm forthwith, and allow one Hopton Haynes to take possession of it. But all at once, it seemed, Carr had as many friends as he had seemed to have enemies at his trial: a 'multitude of base persons' flocked to his aid as he resisted the best efforts of Sir John Tope, the sheriff, to take over the farm. Here was the Englishman defending his home, his castle, against the incursions of an official who took his orders from an essentially foreign court of law. The rights of the individual were at risk! The sheriff's attempts to press local people from Warminster and elsewhere met with a feeble response, and when a handful of reluctant and ill-armed men did finally accompany him to the farm, their apathy and the foulness of the late-afternoon weather left him with little option but to retire and admit defeat. The populace at large, it seemed, were all for Carr and against Haynes; local men were imprisoned for their non-cooperation, but only when the gunners were called in from Bristol was Thomas Carr finally evicted.[10]

The issue, it must have seemed to the inhabitants of the area, was a simple one: their lives were lived in accordance with the customs of generations, their allegiance was to their own local community and to the manor and hundred courts; how dare an outside body, however 'legal', interfere with their affairs? They lost in the end; the long arm of centralised government and the lawcourts would ultimately reach even into their quiet and private part of the world. Rural Wiltshire in 1631 was at the watershed: the power of the manor

10. Chancery depositions, the Earl of Rutland and others vs. Thomas Carr, 1631. The first witness is 'Richard Titford of ffullmore in the p(ar)ishe of Upton Skidmore in the County of Wilts husbandman aged threescore yeares or thereabouts . . .'. (PRO C21 R28/1.)

court was already diminishing – that unit of local government which had rehoused Thomas the Alehousekeeper on the common would eventually become an impotent body, its role being taken over increasingly by vestries and by the judicial arm of national government. The Englishman's right to self-determination within his local community was fast being eroded. Those events of 1631 in Corsley must nevertheless have been exciting in the extreme for people used to a fairly tranquil life. Maybe it was all too much for Richard Titford: in the August of the following year he was dying, with little time left to make his nuncupative will – an oral statement validated by witnesses who wrote down what he had to say. Richard's was recorded 'as he spake' by William Wright and Robert Toogood, both of Upton. His wife Catherine was to inherit his 'goods chattells and household stuffs', and after her decease such goods as she then left would be given to their kindred; it would seem, failing other evidence, that the couple had no children of their own – only 'kindred' in the broadest sense.[11]

There is no surviving burial record for Richard – neither in the Bishop's Transcripts for Upton Scudamore, nor in the registers of Corsley church which, in the event, do not cover that period. Nevertheless, it was probably at Corsley that he was laid to rest; his will was proved on 2 October 1632 and two years later his widow, Katherine, decided in her generosity to present Corsley church with a wooden table listing the 'Severall Benefactors of Corsly, and the Particular Sums of Monye, giuen by them fo the vse of the Poore ofthe said Parish, for euer to Continue . . .'. There follows a list of names – four yeomen, two ministers and two vintners – who had given sums ranging from four to ten pounds for the benefit of the poor. The man who painted the wooden board duplicated the details on both its sides – one, perhaps, a dummy run? On the reverse he has entered 'Katherine Titforde' with an 'e', while on the front we read that: 'Katherine Titford widowe Gaue this table 1634'. This memorial table hangs in the church to this day. One year later a comprehensive seating plan of the church was drawn up: there is Thomas Carr, right at the front behind Sir Thomas Thynn in the south corner, and there, too, are many other familiar Corsley characters – but no Titfords; the family's association with Corsley comes to an end in 1634.

All that remains for us to do is to read with interest and fascination the slightly-damaged handwritten inventory of the 'goods, chattels . . . and householdstuffs' taken after Richard Titford's decease by a number of his worthy neighbours. From it we can make a fair guess at the layout of his house: essentially one large 'haule' after the traditional pattern, it also boasted four other rooms: 'the chamber where the testator lay', together with two chambers 'within the haule' – these probably constituting a ground-floor parlour and at least one room over it, possibly reduced in size by the stairs, and then a buttery and a 'lought over the haule' for the storage of grain. All in all, quite a substantial house of the period, enough in its own right to justify its occupier as thinking of himself as a fully-fledged 'yeoman'. Outside, just for good measure, he had a 'barton' where he kept his 'cart with the furniture'.[12]

So much, then, for one man who moved only a few miles away from Bratton and managed to prosper in the process. Not all the male Titfords of his generation fared as well as he, but they all, like him, left home in the early years of the 17th century and resettled in neighbouring towns and villages.

Another Richard Titford, cousin to the yeoman, had skirted west and then south round Salisbury Plain to settle in Warminster by 1605, soon to be followed there by John Titford, who made his home in nearby Oldfield. Their kinsman Ralph, a little more adventurous, plunged westwards into Somerset; his was a 15-mile journey ending in a steep climb, and he was well established in the little settlement of Leigh Upon Mendip a early as 1612. Here, far away as he may have felt himself to be from his home in Bratton, it was still possible to get a clear view of the Westbury White Horse which he had left behind, had he chosen to climb the church tower!

In the Haule

Item a table borde ij ... stools ...
Item ... brass panns ... brass potles ...
Item ij dozen of ... vessell ... candlesticks
Item an old cubbord ...
Item in the Chimnie ... andirons ... brandirons ...
... pann a dripping pann ...
                    Som ...

In the chamber where the testator laye

Item a bedsted ... with the furniture therof
Item ... side borde a side bed ... a little ...
Item ij paire of ...
Item all his apparell ...
                    Som ...

In the chamber within the haule

Item the bedsted bed & furniture to the same
Item a ... in the same chamber
Item bed & furniture in another chamber near the haule
Item in the buttrie ij barrells ...
    iij other ... with other old thinge
Item diverse ...
                    Som ...

In the lought over the haule

Item in mault
Item in barlie
Item in ...
Item ... of wooll
                    Som ...

Cattell corne and haye

Item ... heine
Item ... horsbeaste ...

11. Part of the inventory of all the goods, chattels and household stuff of Richard Titford, Yeoman, of Upton Scudamore, Wilts., 14 September, 1632. The goods of the deceased are noted room by room: 'In the Haule'; 'In the chamber where the testator laye'; 'In the chamber within the haule'; 'In the lought over the haule'; 'Cattell corne and haye'. There was also 'another chamber near the haule' and a buttery.

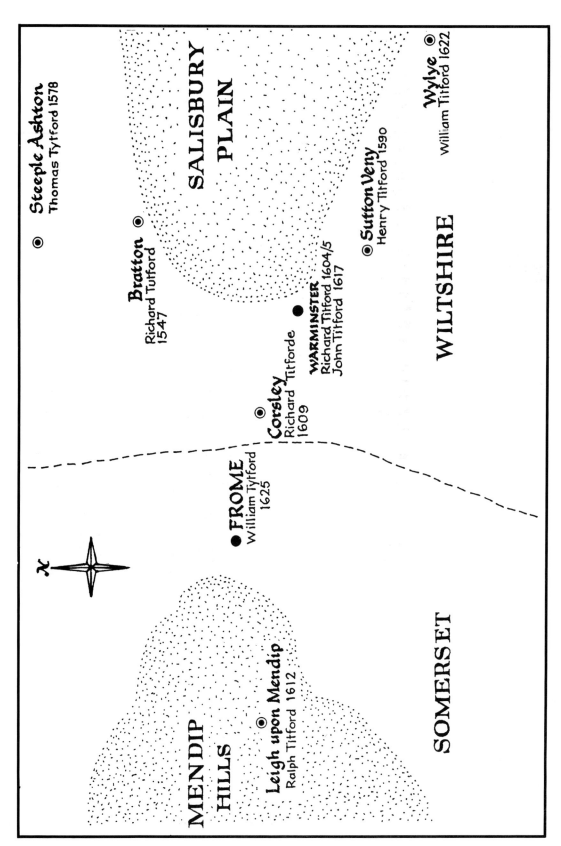

12. Titford family migration from Bratton, Wiltshire, 1578-1625, showing the earliest reference for an adult male in each location.

Within the space of five years or so, then, four young males from the same family group had left home for good; Bratton's worst economic depression was yet to come, but some here were clearly reading the early signs. Two further members of this generation, both called William Titford, remained in the village itself – but not for long. One – 'William the Shepherd' – was starting a family down in Wylye, south of the Plain, in 1622, while the other would marry in Frome in Somerset three years later. Sons were abandoning home and kindred to seek their fortunes elsewhere, leaving women folk and the older men to survive as best they could. By the 1620s that simple task of survival was not itself so easy as it had once been: many families had lost their common rights, bad harvests arrived with depressing frequency, and the plague was rampant. The resultant hardships suffered by the working people of England in the years from 1620 to 1650 have been described as the worst in the country's history.

Bratton was no place to be if you wanted to be numbered among the survivors: the undyed broadcloth trade was beginning its death throes in the village as in so many places elsewhere, with English manufacturers increasingly being driven out of business by foreign competitors – especially the Dutch. Fashion was changing so that silk and satin from abroad were all the rage; the Thirty Years War (1618-1648) did little to improve English exports, and the Privy Council was even worried that craftsmen in the wool trade, often not properly catered for by the existing poor laws, might terrorise their parishes once they found themselves out of work.

The Titfords of Bratton at this period were not numbered among such craftsmen in wool: the mature adults, we know, included a shoemaker, a husbandman and an alehousekeeper – men who, together with their sons, should have been able to make a living whatever the economic basis of village life might be. But an impoverished community spelt hard times for everyone living within it. Between 1620 and 1640 England would lose eighty thousand emigrants to the New World, all seeking a better life in one way or another; down in Wiltshire the new generation of Titfords would take shorter but no less final paths away from home, never to return.

Bratton, struggling as it was in times of general distress, was to suffer another blow to its economic stability in 1625: one branch of the prolific family of clothiers, the Whittakers, came to an abrupt end when Jeffrey Whittaker died without issue, his cloth mills thereafter vanishing altogether.

It is precisely in this year of 1625 – significantly or not – that the last of our émigrés from the village – William Titford – turns up in the Somerset town of Frome, 10 miles away.

CHAPTER 5

William and Mary (?-1678/9)

Frome, Somerset

THE CIVIL WAR AND THE COMMONWEALTH

William Titford had followed his kinsman Ralph by making the trek west; not as far as Leigh Upon Mendip, but striking out through Chapmanslade or across Dilton Marsh – neither alternative promising a particularly safe journey, we may be sure, with footpads and 'sturdy vagabonds' lying in wait. William would hardly have proved much booty for such types out for a quick penny, however: he was probably as poor as they were, and perhaps for similar reasons.

Frome was, indeed, a very obvious centre for which to aim; surrounded as it was by some fairly wild and even violent forest land, it had nevertheless long thrived as a focus of the wool industry.[1] A natural communications centre, nestling in the narrowest gap between the Mendips and the Wiltshire Downs, it acted as a market for a wide surrounding area, including villages like Lullington, Beckington, Rode and Berkley to the north, and Nunney and Wells to the south. Paradoxically, it was also rather an isolated place in its way, far from the centre of government both politically and culturally; here were fostered and bred men of independent spirit.

Although he was hardly to know it at the time, William was to begin in Frome a new period of stability for his branch of the Titford family, just as his namesake William was to do in Wylye. We have said that the family which stays in one place for three or more generations is unusual, but although William Titford's descendants were to scatter as the years went by, there would be members of the family in Frome who bore his surname for over two hundred years. The last, Sarah, died in the town in 1860.

The Frome parish registers record the marriage of William Tytford to Mary Smyth on 24 April 1625. It was not just the beginning of a new era for this family alone: the death of James I just one month before William and Mary's happy event had heralded the arrival of the hapless King Charles, whose own marriage to Henrietta Maria, the French Catholic princess, took place in that same year. The Stuart dynasty had entered what was to prove a tragic phase in its history.

But in Frome there were marriage celebrations to be enjoyed – or not enjoyed, as the case may be, since the heavy incidental expenses, not to mention the rowdy nuptial customs of the time, persuaded many a couple to marry clandestinely or at least with a minimum of publicity. It was not everyone's idea of a good time to be woken up on the wedding morning by the sound of drums and trumpets and the need to pay off the perpetrators before they would go away. Such practices, of course, were not universally adhered to, but other conventions of the time might have struck us as equally quaint or unusual: the fact that two 'bride-men' commonly appeared alongside the two bridesmaids, for example, or that symbols of the groom's trade might be strewn in his path (wood-shavings for a carpenter, grass for a farmer) alongside the more usual flowers, sweet herbs and handfuls of wheat. The Titfords may well have married in the morning between the hours of 8 and 12, as an Act of 1603 decreed, but might nevertheless have caused a few raised eyebrows by going in for a Sunday wedding as they did – that was not forbidden as such, but very much discouraged at the time.

Perhaps we would be ill-advised to linger any longer at the church door, or to focus upon the romantic side of a marriage like this; the couple would not only be cementing an emotional attachment – they were very much entering into an economic partnership.[2] It is little wonder that so few men seem to have remained unmarried in 17th-century and 18th-century England, or that we encounter childless couples so rarely: the family was the most natural and the most effective way of ensuring survival in good times as well as bad. And that family had to work for its living: the household was the main unit of production, not just of consumption; children would be expected to pull their weight just as soon as they were able, and the women shared with the men the job of keeping the economic ship afloat.

There was every opportunity for wives and daughters to engage in some form of secondary employment: the spinning-wheel – referred to by some historians as the most ubiquitous industrial tool of the period – would have been whirring away in the corner of most cottages. Six spinners could provide enough yarn for one weaver, and those weavers themselves in Frome were busy supplying not just local needs, but a growing mass market.

William Titford, in effect, had made a fateful decision in moving those few miles from Bratton to Frome – even if it were a decision made for him by circumstance. This was more than a mere trip down the road; it would be the beginning of an entirely new economic pattern of life for him and his descendants. The Titfords of Bratton had enjoyed a degree of independence: spreading their risks, as they were, by practising dual occupations, they could turn from husbandry to shoemaking or alehousekeeping in times of dearth and still survive. But that way of life was very much a thing of the past now: in Frome things were different. William had made a move in the early 17th century which many were only to make a century and a half later: he had traded the semi-independence of a subsistence economy for life in a town most of whose inhabitants were well on the way to becoming wage-dependent. It is not without significance, of course, that he probably had little choice; if a living could not be had in one place, then some alternative must be sought – as quickly as possible, and preferably as locally as possible. So Frome it was.[3]

Henceforward – and our story will bear this out – the Titfords in Frome would be like corks bobbing up and down on the sea of economic circumstnce: town dwellers like them, employees and not tied to the land, were to fare just as badly in times of scarcity as their subsistence-farmer contemporaries – when supplies were short, the market economy forced up prices. They had, in a sense, the worst of all worlds.

> Yea, I have lived to see the hour,
> In which a clothier had such power,
> That lords are glad to buy him[4]

So runs a satire of 1647. The clothiers were the lynch-pin of Frome's industrial life: their predecessors had earlier challenged the Medieval guild system in towns by setting up business in rural areas – a supply of fuller's earth and a fast-running stream would suit their purposes very well. Those, plus a pool of labour; the putting-out system would provide yarn and then cloth which the clothiers could sell in bulk for consumption at home and abroad. Such entrepreneurs, then, were financiers, traders, organisers, not producers as such – others were doing that for them.

At its worst this system of mass-production could mean that a cottage worker, isolated and powerless as he was, might even be in debt to the clothier for the very materials he was working upon. The West Country fared very badly in this respect into the 18th century, and periodic outbreaks of violence such as the weavers' riots in Frome in 1726 should perhaps not surprise us.

Where did the Titfords fit into all this? They, like the weavers, ended up selling their labour and their skills to clothier employers. William and Mary's descendants would slot into the middle range of skilled artisans, working as wiredrawers and cardmakers; and that was fine, so long as the economy was healthy. The textile trade in England during the 18th century, heavily protected as it was, would outweigh that of nearly all other industries put together, with the manufacture of woollen cloth constituting by far the greatest element in that trade. So long as a constant stream of packhorses or carts set out from Frome with supplies of cloth for Blackwell Hall in London, there would be few complaints; but when, towards the end of the 18th century, the conservative ways of the clothiers sounded the death-knell of the town's prosperity, destitution followed.

What all this meant, in effect, was that the range of choices open to an average family was severely limited; body and soul must be kept together, work must be found, and there was no option but to ebb and flow with the economic tide. Not only that, but men like William Titford and their families in the mid-17th century were trapped in other ways, too. The Statute of Artificers of 1563 had made various provisions which would limit any man's freedom of choice whether he liked it or not. Anyone wishing to follow a trade would have to bind himself as an apprentice for seven years; having chosen that trade, then, he would be almost powerless to change it. If he then engaged in gainful employment once the seven years were up, his wages would be fixed on an annual basis by the local magistrates, as would his hours of work – little incentive, then, to work harder than absolutely necessary or to show much enterprise.[5] The free man, in short, was finding his life hemmed around with the kind of restrictions which in some ways bound him as surely as he had been bound in the days of feudal tenure.

Things would not get better as the 17th century progressed: the Settlement Laws of the 1660s onwards were to tie a working man as firmly to his place of abode as the earlier act had tied him to a trade and a wage, so that:

> It is often more difficult for a poor man to pass the artificial boundary of a parish than an arm of the sea or a ridge of high mountains.[6]

The Titfords, then, would be trapped in many ways by laws not of their own making. The very skills they developed – specific to the wool trade – would not, in any case, allow them to be as mobile as, say, a wheelwright, a saddler or a tailor. Disincentives to any kind of emigration from Frome lay all around; yet emigrate they did, eventually, for all that.

Let us return to William Titford at the church door; we now know, as he can hardly have done without a crystal ball, the deep significance of his short journey away from Bratton to a new life in Frome. We may be sure that he found something more than a wife in the town – he must have found employment of some sort, since no parish looked kindly upon importing jobless paupers from surrounding towns and villages.

The abandonment of Bratton by her younger sons in the early 17th century almost certainly points to the fact that life must have been a shade easier elsewhere than in the poor, beleaguered village on the Stradbrook – but not all that much easier. Frome was no *Shangri La* for immigrants; in 1622 the inhabitants had petitioned Quarter Sessions, desperately seeking relief for the poor who were 'much impoverished by reason of the decay of clothing'.[7] By 1631 the town was still beset by poverty, and Frome hundred was said to consist of 6,506 inhabitants (five of these, by then, Titfords!), most of whom were clothiers, weavers and spinners. The only crumb of comfort for the totally destitute in all of this was the modest provision of 12 places at the Leversedge-family almshouses in town; a modest palliative, to be sure, but better than nothing.

And as if there were not enough problems arising from agrarian discontent and a flagging woollen industry, the year in which William Titford married saw the arrival in Frome of a family called Phillips from London, desperately trying to escape the effects of an outbreak of plague in the city.[8] They were shut up in a remote house once they reached town, for fear of the pestilence spreading. There they were all to die; threats to survival, it must have seemed, were lurking everywhere.

Yet amidst it all William and Mary quietly set about bringing up a family – life must go on. At least one bride in every three in the 17th century was pregnant on the day she was married – indeed, it is surprising how few childless couples one encounters in this period, almost as if mutual fertility were put to the test before marriage, just to be sure of offspring. In the event, Mary appears not to have been a pregnant bride; their first child, Martha, was baptised at St John's church on 12 March 1625/6, almost a year after the wedding. No fewer than 10 more were to follow, including four males, whose fortunes we will follow in due course – not just because they were males as such, but because through them we can follow the surname through succeeding generations.

William himself was not the only adult Titford in Frome during the 1620s and '30s.[9] In 1627 we find the baptism of a child called Barbara – one of the very few Barbara Titfords who has ever lived, in fact! – and her father was Richard Titford. Poor little Barbara was not to be a survivor in a family of survivors: she was buried in 1629, just a few days short of her second birthday, and the 'Accompt of John Hillard and Richard Harbottle, Churchwardens' for 1630 indicates retrospectively the receipt of the traditional sum of 1s. by way of payment for the 'Great Bell' to be rung at the funeral of 'Titford's child'.[10] Richard Titford is never heard of again in Frome; his exact identity remains a mystery, though he is probably that same Richard who had settled in Warminster, putting in a guest appearance in Frome with a new wife (his first, Mary, having died in 1624).

Meanwhile, during the period between the births of William's first two children, Thomas Titford the Shoemaker's widow, Agnes, had died in Bratton. The usual vagaries over spelling resulted in a parish register entry for 'Agnes Tyfford', while the Bishop's Transcripts talk of 'Agnes Tutforde, vidua'. The family was not to be subjected to many more such mishearings, misreadings or misspellings; 10 years later, on 17 February 1636/7, the burial of Christopher Titford saw the final extinction of the Titfords of Bratton. Henceforward the scattered flock was on its own.

We may imagine that conversations in church, in alehouses and on street corners in Frome while William Titford and Mary were adding to and bringing up their brood would have centred not just on the price of bread and the struggle to feed and clothe oneself and one's family, but on rumours and more reliable news filtering westwards from the capital: the King was in deep trouble. Charles and his parliament had been engaged in a power struggle from the start, and in 1629, taking refuge in his anachronistic belief in Divine Right, he vowed to do without them; there was to be a hiatus of 11 years before parliament reconvened, and by then the seeds of civil war were well and truly planted.

News in a Somerset town – even one at the centre of a vital, if lagging industry – would arrive slowly, by dribs and drabs, with varying degrees of credibility. The role of the ballad-seller and singer was crucial; his wares may not always have been accurate purveyors of news, but in a time of general illiteracy and before the advent of a national or local press, ballads would open up subjects of national importance for general discussion.

In the hey-day of the woollen industry it may well have been the sheep who paid for all; a well-known ballad circulating in 1630 told a different story, one which no doubt touched a chord in many a Frome heart:

> Me thought I was i'th'countrey,
> Where poore men take great paines,
> And labour hard continually,
> Onely for rich men's gaines:
> Like th' Israelites in Egypt,
> The poore are kept in thrall;
> The task-masters are playing kept,
> But poore men pay for all.[11]

In effect, poverty in the countryside and King Charles's problems were not unrelated. Among the causes of the Civil War, according to G. M. Trevelyan, was the '. . . gradual but constant rise of prices, largely due to the flow of silver from the Spanish-American mines into Europe.'[12] Such a situation made it impossible for Charles I to live on his own revenues; there was discontent in the country as a result of this very rise in prices, and parliament was unwilling to make up what the King regarded as the deficiency in his budget. Few Frome people, poor as most of them were and generally Puritan in outlook, can have had much sympathy with His Majesty.

The 1640s dawned; the worst decade of an already desperate period was about to begin, exacerbated by a series of disastrous harvests.

When the Civil War began in 1642, it must have seemed like the eruption of a sore that had long been festering; Somerset generally was Royalist much of the time, with the signal exception of the towns – Bath, Bridgwater, Minehead, Taunton and Frome itself – where many workers and traders in the woollen industry, already browbeaten by hard times, also strongly resented Archbishop Laud's attacks on the Elizabethan Church Settlement with its degree of protection for the individual conscience. Frome church bells would ring out to announce many a Cromwellian victory – but never a Royalist one.

Frome people can never have had the war far from their minds but, in common with much of North Somerset, the town managed to remain comparatively unscathed by the armies. Cousin Ralph Titford in Leigh Upon Mendip, only two years away from his death, was not so lucky; 1643 had seen a signficiant night-time skirmish there, and it would be little wonder if such dangerous times had not given some impetus to Ralph's ambitious son, Charles, to leave his home village and seek his fortune in London. There he prospered beyond his wildest dreams.

And so the Civil War hostilities raged; King Charles himself passed close by Frome in 1644, and nearby Nunney Castle was taken in August of the following year. But the end was in sight: finally and symbolically the whole tragic affair was ended with the execution of the King in 1649.

To say that Frome escaped the full impact of the war years is, of course, only to say that it was not used as a battlefield as such. But it would have had its widows and its maimed soldiers, probably its broken friendships, and certainly the job of cleaning out the church in 1643 after Royalist soldiers had taken lodging there. To add to the misery, the high price of corn and a constant threat of famine and plague beset the years of war, and even those who had some sympathy with the King as a human being could hardly have escaped sighing in relief that maybe his passing would herald the arrival of better times.

William Titford and his family had not lived through the war without some domestic losses; a son, John, only three years old, was buried in 1643, and before May of 1648 the churchwardens' 'Recaits for the Bell' included the usual fee of 1s. for the burial of 'Mari Titford'. Very shortly after the birth of her last daughter, William's wife had died. Whether the privations of the war itself had caused or hastened her death, we cannot be sure; but William would have had good cause for the rest of his life to look back at the struggle between king and parliament as a time of tragedy and irreparable loss. Luckily for him, then, the next decade was to see better times; Cromwell didn't have it all his own way – there was Charles II to be driven out on the one hand, and the Levellers' insurrection to be crushed in May of 1649 on the other. But by 1650, with England now a Commonwealth, the dreadful decade was over and the hard times which had lasted for about thirty years were just beginning to abate; in 1649 things were still so bad in London that the poor had been given free corn and coal, but a more prosperous era was on the horizon, one which would bring a brief taste of financial good fortune to the Titfords of Frome, before they were plunged into poverty during the closing years of the 18th century.

The establishment of a Commonwealth under Cromwell was not, of course, all good news; in Frome itself even erstwhile supporters of Parliament rioted against the new taxes imposed in 1649, and on a lesser but significant note, family historians have long blamed the Protector and his followers for the havoc caused to baptismal, marriage and burial records during the Interregnum.

In the circumstances, we are lucky that some Titford entries in registers do exist for this period: such as the occasion on which one of the Warminster Titfords, Thomas, was married to a Frome girl, Joan Newport, on 2 July 1655 by

> The Worshipfull Edward Michell, Esqr., one of the Justices of the Peace of the County of Wiltes, according to the Act latlie made for marriages births and burials & the Registering thereof.

Hardly an occasion, this, for the once-traditional light-hearted dancing and drinking of former years . . .

By this time William of Frome already had one grandchild, Ann, daughter of his son Thomas; she was duly baptised at St John's, as was another daughter, Joan, in 1661/2. Between these two, however, the register entries for their sisters Lewes (or Lucy) and Mary 'Tetford' are given as births only, according to the Commonwealth stipulations; the prayer book had been outlawed, and to comply with the new regulations the Commonwealth 'Directory' would have to be used for any ceremony celebrating the arrival of a new infant.

So we are now considering the fame and fortune – or lack of these – of a new generation of Frome Titfords. William, left a widower during the Civil War as we have seen, could now take some comfort, at least, from seeing his own children, and now their children, well settled in his adopted town. Our story will now concern itself with William's four sons; Thomas, Henry, William and Ralph. They were no doubt very different characters, and their lives were to take very diverse paths. One thing unites them – and a rather unfortunate thing, too, from the family historian's point of view – that there are no surviving records of their marriages. We know the Christian names of their wives, and we may assume, if we wish to, that they were all legally married just at that period when the Civil Wars and the 'Cromwellian Gap' were causing havoc with parish records. Either that, or they may have made their vows before witnesses by way of a common-law marriage – a practice frowned upon as irregular, but accepted as legal by Church and State in the days before Hardwicke's Marriage Act of 1753. Our only consolation when records go missing is that it is marginally less serious to lose a marriage or two than it is to lose baptisms; unregistered births will, alas, prove to be a Titford speciality when we reach the middle years of the 18th century . . .[13]

CHAPTER 6

Thomas and Margery (1628/9-1677)

Frome, Somerset

THE HEARTH TAX YEARS

So what of the four sons of William Titford?

It was not to fall to the eldest, Thomas, to pass on the family name to future generations: he and his wife Margery or Margaret had a succession of daughters – at least six – but no sons. These were particularly unhealthy times: two of Thomas's daughters, Hester and Ann, were buried in Frome within a week of each other in the November of 1657 – victims, we can make a fair guess, of one of the epidemics which were to sweep the country during that and the next two years, thought of in retrospect as a kind of 'warning plague' or ominous torchbearer for the catastrophic outbreak of 1665. Thomas and Margery survived these two little girls by exactly 20 years: Thomas, predeceasing his own father William, was laid to rest two months after his wife, in the September of 1677.

During the few years before his death, Thomas and others in the family had had some rather unwelcome visitors. Officials were making a tour of the town, trying to establish how many fireplaces there were in each person's house: there was to be a 'Hearth Tax'. The idea had been adopted by the 'Cavalier Parliament' in 1662 to provide Charles II with more revenue, and its conditions were that every householder who was '. . . rated or rateable to church and poor' should pay two shillings annually for every fireplace or stove in his or her house.

> Such direct taxation, involving as it did intrusion into the home (intrusion which might reveal all sorts of unlicensed and otherwise illegal activity) was heartily disliked and thoroughly resisted.[1]

The tax was levied twice a year between 1662 and 1689, but there were many who were exempt through poverty, refrained from paying or took other evasive measures; Frome folk must have been heartened by the fact that there was actual rioting in nearby Bristol as the population rose in protest against this blow to their pockets and their privacy. As in so many cases, however, what is bad news to people at the time is good news to family historians; it is thanks to the Hearth Tax returns for 1674 that we are able both to corroborate the presence of Titfords in Frome, and also to establish that, unless returns were falsified, all Titfords there were too poor to be charged.

Titfords in many places and at various times have been too poor to do or to pay this, that, and the other. They certainly have been beset by poverty, though one cannot help feeling from time to time that many a Titford was a little bit too canny to pay the parish or the state that which he would rather spend on himself . . .

There is quite a sizeable list of Frome townsfolk who were exempt from payment of Hearth Tax. The rubric runs:

> Wee the Minister of the Parish . . . doe hereby Certifie unto his Majesties Justices of the Peace for the said County That we doe believe That the respective Houses wherein the persons hereunder named doe Inhabit are not of greater value than twenty shillings *per annum* upon the full Improved rent, And that neither the Person so inhabiting, nor any other using the same Messuages hath, useth, or Occupieth any Lands or Tenements of their own or others of the yearly value of Twenty shillings *per annum* Nor hath any Lands, Tenements, Goods or Chattels of the value of Ten pounds in their

own Possession or in the Possession of any other in trust for them. And that the said houses have not above two Chimneys, Firehearthes and Stoves in them respectively.

Indeed, there was no shame in being exempt from this punitive tax: a quarter of the nation evaded payment on grounds of pauperism, and nearly a fifth of the population was in receipt of alms. So the vicar of Frome, two churchwardens and two overseers who signed the list of those exempt and presented it to the appropriate justices got little enough out of the Titford family. There they all are: William senior, sons Thomas and William – all with one hearth – and son Ralph with two.[2] Daughter Mary also appears on the list – but one name is missing: that of Henry Titford, William's second son. Henry, in fact, had been dead for almost 10 years by 1674, but there is more to his story than that, and the time has come to trace his fortunes.

CHAPTER 7

Henry of Southwark (1630-1665)

Frome, Somerset, and Southwark, London

VICTIM OF THE PLAGUE

'Tis plaguey news that the plague has come to *Southwark!*
Sir Ralph Verney. Early 1665

We have seen from the outset that the English working man, often owning little except his labour, was by no means as tied down to the parish of his birth as we might suppose. Nor should we assume that all journeys to a new settlement were short ones: to a tradesman or a craftsman – and that is what the Titfords of Frome were now becoming – a far-off town or city was fair game. The journey might be arduous, and certainly exciting if a little dangerous, but once there, wages would perhaps be better, customers and employers more generous.

Almost no branch of the Tiford family from the common stock of Bratton is without its adventurous entrepreneur – and their journeys in search of fame and fortune almost invariably led them to the capital itself. London was, after all, the place where the wealth circulated; it was also afflicted with a higher death-rate than the average. So you paid your money and took your choice.

The first Titford with Bratton antecedents to make the journey eastwards was Charles, son of Ralph of Leigh Upon Mendip. An amazingly energetic individual, innholder, property owner, confidence trickster and sharp businessman, the apotheosis of the unscrupulous self-made man, he proved for himself the truth of the rumour that the streets of London were paved with gold. He never looked back.

Encouraged, perhaps, by what they had heard of Charles's success, or just inquisitive by nature, at least two of his cousins made the same journey as he had made. One, it seems likely from the evidence, was Thomas of Wylye, son of William the Shepherd, who made his home near Charles in the parish of St Martin-in-the-Fields; the other, settling independently in Southwark, was Henry Titford of Frome, second son of William and Mary.

There was little enough to prevent Henry striking out on his own; the increasingly restrictive Settlement Acts of the late 17th century still lay in the future, he had a family contact in the capital and, we may suppose, a sense of adventure in his heart. Cousin Charles had left Leigh upon Mendip during the Civil War; Henry made his move during the Commonwealth period, and we find him taking his baby son to be entered in the registers of St Saviour's in Southwark on 10 June 1655. He was then just 25, married to a lady called Alice; and like his brothers William and Ralph he named his eldest boy after the child's paternal grandfather: William.

Southwark in the 17th century nestled quietly against the southern bank of the Thames, an urban spot in an agricultural landscape. To the west lay Lambeth Marshes; St George's Fields began at the end of Blackman Street, which itself was rural enough to sport a windmill, and there was a small area of development eastwards towards the church of St Mary Magdalen. Apart from that, open fields stretched as far as the eye could see. Little wonder, then, that the parish registers of St Saviour's – very well kept and more than usually informative – include entries for husbandmen from the surrounding countryside, as well as the more predictable fishermen, shoemakers, cardmakers, pinmakers and tailors.

Henry Titford was a wiredrawer; a skilled job, it was one which he might have learned in Frome along with brother William, also a 'wyerdrawer', or possibly a trade he had been apprenticed to in London. Whichever might have been the case, it suggests either that father William of Frome was sufficiently well-breeched to arrange apprenticeships for his sons, or that he was himself a wiredrawer and taught them the skills they would need. And fathers, we may be sure, very often made severe masters to their apprentice sons.

The job of the wiredrawer is integral to the processes used in the wool trade; in essence, wool is carded or combed so that the fibres are enlarged lengthways, it is then spun, woven and the resulting cloth is finished – dyed, bleached, or printed. The first stage in all of this necessitates good quality cards; card-making had been of signal importance in Frome from the 16th century, and was to be the trade that generations of male Titfords were to follow. A 'card' consisted of a wooden or leather base (made by a 'cardboard maker'), into which either teasels or wire teeth were set; the cardmaker might fix the wire to the board, or oversee the manufacture of the whole artefact, while the wiredrawer made the necessary fine, crooked teeth.

The process of carding was to be celebrated in verse by Dr. Samuel Bowden in 1738, in which year the Frome Society of Cardmakers was founded:

> . . . each pore receives a tire,
> In shining weapons clad, of stapled wire.
> As glittering cohorts, marshalled in array,
> In even files their shining arms display:
> While polished blades through every vista glide
> And in a thousand ranks the leafs divide[1]

Here was Henry Titford in London, then, practising a skill in itself vital to the wool industry of the South-West, and one which he had been able to carry with him to the metropolis. Certain craftsmen, it seems, had the wherewithal to be mobile.

Henry was to have five more children by Alice, all girls, of whom three at least died in infancy. His wife was taken from him in 1664, buried on 22 May and he lost little time in marrying again. This new bride was Margaret Dix; after the appropriate banns, they pledged themselves to each other at St Saviour's on 14 January 1664/5.

Things might have looked fairly rosy, in theory – here was the chance for a new start, a companion to replace Alice and a new mother for the children. Alas, events took a grimmer turn. Five months after their marriage an outbreak of bubonic plague spread through the dry, dusty air of the City and set about its dreadful business both there and in Southwark. Helpless and frightened, unaware that it was the fleas from rats, biting them in their beds, which spread the pestilence, the population tried the only medications they knew: olive oil, dragon water, onion, pepper, garlic, vinegar, sage, elder, bramble leaves – anything at all in desperation. Those out in the streets tried carrying nosegays, while sufferers and their families were quarantined – the healthy and the sick together – inside their homes with a red cross daubed on the door.

Plague in itself was nothing new, and the sound of the death cart with its warning bell could have been heard rattling over the cobbles many a time as London was often afflicted. What made the outbreak of 1665 so notorious, however, was its virulence: it claimed the lives of over 56,000 people in the City alone – and in August of that year it added Henry Titford to its list of victims. On the day he was buried at St Saviour's, 26 August, 25 other poor souls were also laid to rest in the same place. Henry the Wiredrawer had made his choice, picked London for his adopted home; for some it proved an Eldorado – for Henry, a graveyard.[2]

Just over a year after his death, on 2 September 1666, another tragedy was to afflict drought and plague-stricken London: the Great Fire. Little wonder, then, what with these catastrophes and the ominous appearance of two comets in 1664 and 1665, that there were many who believed and preached at this time that the end of the world was at hand.

But there we must leave London and turn once more to Somerset, picking up the story of the other sons of William Titford and Mary by turning our attention to William, junior, and Ralph. We can return to Frome at the close of the Civil War and the establishment of the Commonwealth, in 1649. William Titford junior was then 14 years old, possibly about to begin his apprenticeship, and Ralph almost two years younger, having been baptised on 15 January 1636/7.

These were still stormy times, of course; Cromwell's Navigation Acts had not exactly proved internationally popular, quite understandably, and England was to be at war, on and off, with Holland for a number of years. The churchwardens at St John's in Frome finally got around to removing the 'Kinge's Arms' from the church in 1651, though to many believers the parish church was increasingly becoming a less-than-natural place at which to worship the Almighty, and an inexorable move towards Nonconformity, however clandestine, was about to begin in the town.

Cromwell's death in 1658, to be followed by his son Richard's brief protectorship until May 1659, rocked the Commonwealth boat to the point where Charles II could return with a degree of safety; the Interregnum was over – the Restoration had begun. It was the acts passed by Charles's new 'Cavalier Parliament' in the first years of its rule which were to drive the final wedge between Anglicans and Nonconformists. By taking draconian measures against Dissenters – the so-called 'Clarendon Code' legislation – the country's new rulers opened up a number of divides, some of which had only half-existed before. At a single stroke the 1662 Act of Uniformity alienated two thousand clergy throughout the land – 62 of these in Somerset alone – who promptly left their livings. To comply with the new act, all clergymen had to be properly ordained, accept the Thirty-nine Articles, and agree to use the Book of Common Prayer; among those who found this the last straw and was forced to leave the Established Church was John Humfry of St John's, Frome. As he was replaced by Dr. Joseph Glanvill, Humfry became the leader of a Dissenting meeting at Rook Lane; the die was cast, and as further legislation aimed at Dissenters' freedom of worship followed – the Conventicle Act in 1664, and the Five-Mile Act in 1665 – Frome was well on its way to becoming what was often later described as a hot-bed of Dissent. Right at the heart of that Dissent, and worshipping as Baptists from the early 18th century if not before, was the Titford family: they were neither famous nor highly influential in the Dissenting movement, but it was to mould and control their lives in unmistakable ways.

CHAPTER 8

William the Wiredrawer (1635-1717)

Frome, Somerset

REBELLION, REVOLUTION, PROTESTATION AND PROSPERITY

O, what a brave state of the Church it would be for all ecclesiasticall causes to come before Weavers and *Wiredrawers . . .*

Lyly (?) 1589

We have seen already how the Frome Titfords were too poor to pay Hearth Tax in 1674, and also that you did not need to be particularly destitute to evade it, in any case. We have other indications, luckily, of the Titford's financial standing in Frome, from as early as 1668; in that year fairly substantial lists of ratepayers in the town were instituted by the churchwardens, who found themselves responsible for maintaining the fabric of St John's and with giving alms to the poor. Their first really comprehensive list of people paying rates, dated 3 September 1668, includes William Titford – William, senior, presumably – charged at 9d. for the property he occupied in the general area of 'Frome Cheep Street'.[1] So William may have been poor, but he was not that poor, after all; he was paying 4d. in rates during the Hearth Tax period of the early 1670s, continuing unchanged through 1677, when the wardens needed money for 'repair of the parish church and for Hospitall & mahimed souldier mony', until his death in 1678.[2]

William's neighbours in Cheap Street consisted of families into which the Titfords would eventually marry: the Lacys, the Bedfords, the Franklins, the Carpenters. We may not know exactly to what extent marriages were arranged during the 17th and 18th centuries, but Frome families certainly seemed to have intermarried to a considerable extent – and once the Baptist chapels were well established in the town, it would be a brave or foolhardy man indeed who would dare seek a wife outside the magic circle of believers.

By the time William senior died – he was buried at St John's on 23 January 1678/9 – both his sons William and Ralph had brought him further grandchildren. William junior and his wife Margaret had produced Elizabeth, William and Margaret, these last two dying as infants. More than half a dozen further children were to follow, but only two surviving males: William, named after his paternal grandfather, and Thomas. All investigations lead us to the conclusion that it is from these two men, and from them alone, that all present-day Titfords with a Frome ancestry are descended.

We must cease calling William, son of William and Mary (*née* Smyth), 'William Junior'; the mantle now falls on him, though the churchwardens refer in their rate books for Cheap Street to 'Will Titford' once he takes over payments until eventually he becomes a fully-fledged 'William' in his own right, even in their eyes. To us he will be 'William the Wiredrawer'.

By 1681 there were over 130 ratepayers listed for 'Cheep Street', and William was still paying the 4d. rate his father had paid before him. Of course, he was lucky in a sense, and fortune had favoured him against all the odds. With his two elder brothers having only daughters or dying early, the lion's share of any tenancies, goods or chattels there may have been when his father died would very probably have come to him – and, as we shall see, he built on such a foundation in the true spirit of the parable of the talents.

The churchwardens' rates are now (from 1679) complemented by those levied by the overseers of the poor, and it is thanks to their meticulous detail from this date onwards that we know as much about the Titfords of Frome as we do.[3] In 1683 the overseers were paying out for shirts, linen and shoes for bastards and widows, as well as helping paupers pay their rent. The churchwardens, meanwhile, needed financial assistance for the 'setting up of the Kinges Armes' in St John's, and William Titford paid 4d. in rates towards their expenses. If he had even then the rumblings of Dissent in his heart, we may suppose he paid that year with a sorry grace: Nonconformists had reason enough to despise Charles II and his parliament, and the prospects of contributing towards His Majesty's coat of arms in the parish church must have stuck in a few throats. Not only that, but absenteeism from church was itself becoming increasingly common both in Frome and in the other clothing towns and villages of Somerset, as further disillusionment with established religion set in.

We now turn to the Monmouth Rebellion of 1685, which was to leave probably as great a scar on the people of the county of Somerset as the Civil War itself; the whole catastrophe might never have happened, some observers believed, if there had been greater freedom of worship under Charles II. Charles had begun his reign by promising that all forms of religious observance would be tolerated; that promise, as we have seen, came to nothing under a reactionary parliament. In those circumstances the emergence of a dashing young champion of the Protestant cause in the person of James, Duke of Monmouth, was greeted with some considerable enthusiasm in Somerset. The bastard son of Charles II by Lucy Walter, Monmouth had already toured parts of the county in 1680 and been gratified by the warm reception he received. The death of Charles and the succession of James II, a Catholic king, in the February of 1685 gave him his chance. Landing at Lyme Regis in Dorset on 11 June, a self-styled opponent of 'tyranny and Popery', he found hundreds flocking to his support; as he marched north to Shepton Mallet, arriving on the 23rd, more recruits arrived from Frome and the surrounding villages.

Monmouth's advance northwards was repulsed by the King's forces, and his army fell back to within six miles of Frome, at Norton St Philip: here, in the first real test of strength, the rebels in combat with the Royalist advanced guard achieved a tactical victory, shielded as they were behind protective hedges which flanked a deep lane leading into the village. Frome people – those who had not actually joined the fighting – were getting a ringside seat at an event of national importance; crowds gathered around the neighbourhood, labourers working at nearby Longleat for Lord Weymouth downed tools and joined the rebels, and in the heady atmosphere the Frome constable, Robert Smith, posted up Monmouth's proclamation as king in the market place. Frome was packed with rebels, armed with whatever they could lay their hands on, including scythes and pitchforks; ill-prepared rebels, alas, for they failed to resist the Earl of Pembroke, the Royalist commander, when he entered the town with all speed on 25 June. Pembroke tore down the Monmouth proclamation, forced the hapless constable to replace it with a statement that Monmouth was a traitor, and retreated back to Wiltshire.

There can be little doubt where the Titford family's sympathies would have lain: the champion of the Protestant cause against Catholicism would have been a man after their own hearts. What is perhaps mildly surprising is that no Titford joined Monmouth's army – or at least none appears in the voluminous lists of his troops and those who were later victims at the assizes. Perhaps they were either too young or too old: William was 40, Ralph 48, and the children hardly of an age to fight. So they must all have stood, impotently, and watched events unfold.

At dawn on 28 June, Monmouth and his army entered Frome in a fairly bedraggled state, as a contemporary account bears witness:

We marched . . . to Froome in a miserable rainy night up to the knees in dirt, almost to the destruction of our foot. Wee came to Froome about 8 in the morning being Sunday.[4]

Monmouth himself rode around the place, cheered by many – but when it came to tangible support, he was severely disappointed. Frome apathy had triumphed, and the young Duke claimed he lost two thousand men while he was in the town. Pembroke's earlier raid must have put the fear of God into many, James II had prudently granted a free pardon to all deserters, and when Monmouth departed two days later, having stayed too long and procrastinated too much, he was on the road to defeat at Sedgemoor, the last battle to be fought on English soil. Tracked down in Dorset after the fighting, sheltering in a ditch, '. . . hatless, hungry and in his pocket the Order of the Garter and a handful of raw peas', the hapless man was soon afterwards relieved of his head by Jack Ketch, the professional executioner.[5]

In the brutal aftermath of the fighting, as Judge Jeffreys began his 'Bloody Assize' and a period of what Macaulay has referred to as 'judicial massacre', 12 rebels were executed on Gibbet Hill in Frome, and their quarters were hung in public view, *pour encourager les autres*. The bitterness left behind by the affair ran deep and lasted long; when, three years later, another invasion threatened James II in the shape of William of Orange at the head of a well-equipped army, Somerset people were in no rush to rally around their King . . .

The 'Glorious Revolution' of 1688 and the arrival of a new monarch, William, and his wife Mary, daughter of James II, heralded good times for Frome and for the Titford family: these were to be their halcyon days – freer to worship as they chose, more prosperous than some of their ancestors might have dreamed of.

The Toleration Act was passed in May of 1689; Dissenters' meeting houses could now legally be recognised, providing they were registered with the bishop, archdeacon or Court of Quarter Sessions. Such registration was voluntary; it would cost the congregation sixpence, but in return there was an offer of some protection and exemption from local rates. Frome people took up the opportunity with alacrity, and Badcox Lane Baptist Chapel, which was to become the Titfords' spiritual home until midway through the 19th century, was officially founded in 1689.

More good news was on the horizon. The 1690s was not a happy decade for many, admittedly, but the slump in the wool trade which had affected Frome so deeply was on the way out, and times of prosperity were approaching fast; not based upon the traditional undyed broadcloth trade which had served places like Bratton so well in the past, but upon the manufacture of lighter, coloured cloths called 'medleys'. Good news, indeed, for dyers who could now find work in the town; good news for clothiers, who added to their fortunes; and good news for cardmakers and wiredrawers, who could share in the general cheer.

The fortunes of the Titfords, as so often, reflected the general economic health of the town in which they lived; so although William the Wiredrawer was paying rates of 4d. in Cheap Street throughout the 1680s (the average rate being about 3d.), the year 1693 saw a dramatic upturn in his fortunes. New prosperity meant more employment, more people – and they needed somewhere to live. The number of rateable inhabitants in Frome quadrupled during the period 1660 to 1695, but there was a limit to how many new properties could be crammed into the steep area immediately south of the river, with its narrow streets and winding alleyways. The town was under pressure to expand. Thus it was that the area known later as 'Trinity' grew up; what had once been fields – Katherine Close, Mill Close, Selwood Close, New Close – began to disappear beneath a very early form of planned industrial development. Rows of humble but solid terraced houses in a limited variety of styles began to encroach upon the erstwhile closes, most of them built as simple two-storey affairs with coursed rubble walls and stone-tiled roofs, one main downstairs room and a modest walled garden behind, also accommodating the privy. All this happened on what had once been

13. Frome, Somerset, from Cruse's map of 1813. William Titford's houses on Fountain
Lane can be seen above the words 'Coward's Batch'. He first acquired these in 1693. A
lease of 1699 which mentions 'William Titford, son of William Titford, wiredrawer' is
for a house on Long Street (misnamed 'Nail Street' on the map) opposite the opening
known as 'The Ope' (but left blank on the map). Thomas Titford occupied the bottom
two houses in High Street, on the left-hand side at the junction with Wine Street, from
1737 onwards. Charles Titford, cheesemonger, occupied a house and shop at the
junction of Bridge Street and North Parade from 1780 until his death in 1802.

the manor of St Katherine's, above the main sprawl of the original town and known alternatively as the 'Woadground', the 'Woodground', the 'Oadground' or the 'Oatground', taking its unusual name from the blue dye, woad.

But housing needs more than land – it needs capital and a developer. One of the principal businessman who stepped into the breach was Richard Yerbury, an absentee landlord from Wiltshire; he and others drew up a series of leases with a fixed duration of 99 years or three specified 'lives', giving the tenant one year in which to build a house and charging him an annual rent thereafter. In the event, many such leases never ran their full term, being cancelled or renewed on payment of a fine.

We are talking here about a very early example of planned industrial housing indeed. New Close was already being built on by 1665, and in 1693 the overseers' accounts inform us that William Titford had no fewer than eight houses 'in oad grounds', for which they were initially going to charge him 9d., but relented slightly and decided upon 7½d. There is a very marked increase in the number of ratepayers in 'Chep Street' at this period – in 1694 it reached 250 – and where an individual has taken up a house or houses in the Oad Ground, the fact is duly noted. Everyone who could afford to lease a new plot or two was

14. A wiredrawer practising his mysterious-looking craft. This was the trade followed by William Titford of Frome (1635-1717). From Sir Richard Phillips, *The Book of English Trades and Library of the Useful Arts*, 11th edn. (1823).

eagerly doing so. William's properties were not situated on the much-coveted flat ground; they formed the downward-sloping north-west corner of what would become Fountain Lane (later Castle Street), adjoining a triangular area known as 'Coward's Batch'. Subsequently, Titfords and their in-laws were to lease or occupy houses within this original row for over a hundred years.[6]

This is a quite dramatic jump in fortune for William Titford; it coincides almost exactly with the birth of the last of his children, but there is no very obvious reason why life should suddenly have decided to be so kind to him. Perhaps wire-drawing was on the up and up, and William a careful man; perhaps, like many a prudent Titford, he had married into money and an in-law had recently died. And things got better before they got worse: in 1694 the rates demand was 11d., still for eight houses under the overall 'Chep Street' heading, in a year when most people were paying from 3d. to 6d., with one exceptional sum of 3s. 6d. levied on a tycoon. William's neighbours were earning a living in a variety of ways, mostly connected directly or indirectly with the cloth industry – but rich and poor alike were co-existing in Frome, as elsewhere, very much cheek-by-jowl: there was Thom Smyth, clothier; Stephen Keeping, the local shopkeeper; Mr. William Wilkins the salter, and Edward Coward, who worked as a 'cardboard-maker'. Others included Joseph Papps, a barker; Nicholas Paine, Robert Smith and John Glover, all cardmakers; William Rogers, a saddler, and Charles Rogers, shoemaker.

In that same year, 1694, the overseers decided they would make as much capital as possible out of the rising tide of wealth, and began charging certain individuals under the heading of 'stocks'. William Titford escaped that year, but not subsequently; he was charged one penny in 1696 ('William Tidfurd') and is listed, though not charged, apparently, in 1696/7.

During the 1690s the overseers seem to have charged William variously 8d. or 11d. on his Oadground houses, almost at whim; but the rate amounts given against his name do not reflect the full extent to which he or his children were involved in property leases of one sort or another. So we find that on 10 April 1699 one of Richard Yerbury's indentures for a New Close property is issued on the lives of Thomas Lacy, John Lacy son of John Lacy, and William Titford, son of William Titford, wiredrawer. Thomas Lacy, moreover, was no ordinary leaseholder; as a carpenter and builder like others of his family, he had himself carried out the construction of many houses in the area, as well as having built much of Sheppards Barton and provided new galleries for St John's church.

The property here in question was on the east side of Blunt Street (alias Long Street) opposite the small courtyard called 'The Ope', and is still standing in the 20th century on what is now Selwood Road; it was built on a slightly more generous scale than the simplest houses, having a hall with a parlour behind, winder stairs against the chimney stack and two storeys – eventually increased to three in later years.[7] Whether it was Lacys or Titfords who lived there, they would have enjoyed a comparative degree of comfort. There was only one heated room, it is true, and that gave straight on to the street, but the house was sturdily built as one of a terraced row, with solid stone window frames and a rather generous garden at the rear, measuring 17 feet by 140 feet. William Titford would never be rated directly by name on this property, and when eventually the lease expired or was cancelled, in 1725, it was a certain Robert Lacy who handed it over to be added to the growing little empire of Avis Usher, widow. When she sold it again 25 years later, the garden was not what it had been – there were now two cottages on it. Everyone was sharing in the prosperous years.

Well, not quite everyone . . .

CHAPTER 9

Ralph the Pauper (1636/7-1708)

Frome, Somerset

THE PAUPERIZED BROTHER

Rattle his bones over the stones,
He's only a *pauper*, whom nobody owns!

T. Noel

It might seem at this stage as if we have forgotten the fourth brother – the youngest son of William and Mary, baptised Ralph Titford on 15 January 1636/7. Poor Ralph! Everyone does seem to have forgotten him – including, it appears, his plutocratic brother William.

We might like to think here of the parable of the talents: William the Wiredrawer started with a little and made it grow; but Ralph, the youngest son, seems to have started with next to nothing and made nothing out of it. He had two wives, the first, Susan, dying in 1662; his remarriage to Joan brought him three children: a Joan dying in infancy, a William (following the paternal grandfather naming pattern) and another Joan, dying at the age of fourteen. Son William married Joan Smith from the nearby town of Bruton in 1698/9, but they in their turn produced no males to father another generation of Titfords. Now poor unfortunate Ralph with his three children was not only less prolific at breeding than his elder brother William – he was also a good deal less wealthy. A lot has been written about the wonders of the extended family, and the closeness and mutual help that such a system can engender; that may be so, in theory, but when it came to siblings, more than one Titford seems to have believed that if charity begins at home, then the pauperized brother must have the family door slammed in his face. This certainly seems to have been the case with Ralph; while William was lording it with his eight houses in the grand style, the overseers' first really – organised list of paupers receiving benefit from the parish, made in March 1700, included Ralph Titford.[1] That situation continued through 1701 and 1702, payments of 2s. 6d. or 2s. per month being given out as a means of keeping a crust in the poor man's mouth and some kind of roof over his head.

Perhaps it behoves us to be a little more charitable towards brother William, after all. Unless a rigid means test were applied, whereby parish relief was refused to anyone who had any kind of relation with a few coppers to his name, there is no reason to suppose that Ralph did not take handouts from the overseers and also accept some help from William as well. It would be a strange person, poor or not, who would refuse any financial help if it were going free, even if the price Ralph and his family may have had to pay was the stigma of being seen around town with a pauper's badge on their clothing: the Settlement Act of 1697 stated that a large Roman 'P' cut in red or blue cloth and followed by the initial letter of the parish should be worn on the shoulder of the right sleeve of the uppermost garment, 'in an open and visible manner'.[2] The penalty for non-observance was as harsh as the regulation itself: the offender would be sent to the house of correction, there whipped, and condemned to three weeks' hard labour. By such means the overseers would try to restrict their payment of alms to worthy cases only, excluding 'loose idle persons' who might 'clamour for relief when they need none'.[3]

The overseers' task has a familiar ring to it: the needy must be provided for, but scroungers must be discouraged, and rates would have to be kept down to acceptable levels. The 1690s, for all that they brought material prosperity to many, saw a massive rise in relief expenditure generally as a run of bad harvests caused widespread destitution.

Ralph, were he still able-bodied, would have stood little enough chance of any alms whatever; a more likely explanation for his plight is that he or his wife Joan, or both, were not only advancing in years, but also ill. In the 1674 Hearth Tax assessment he had been the only Titford with two fireplaces, not one; now, as a new century was beginning, he was the one to fall into poverty. When the extant series of overseers' accounts ends rather abruptly in 1702 (to be taken up again in 1715), Ralph was still on the parish – and judging by other similar cases, he was probably there until he died, in 1708. There was a kind of inexorability about the Poor Law system of relief, for all its good intentions: once the vicious circle of poverty had set in, the victim's chance of ever escaping it permanently seem to have been slim indeed.

The 1715 poor list tells a different story: no sooner had the parish rid itself of Ralph, than there was his widow to support. The overseers did so to the tune of anything ranging

Two Weekly payer Anno April 23 1717	Anno Domini 1716	April	May	Juno	July
1-9	Elizabeth Tilley	0:0:7	0:0:7	1·9	3 2·4
	Widow Toope dead	0:2:0	0:2:0	8 0	8·0
3·0	Widow Tabor	0:1:0	0:1:0	1 0	4·0
3·0	Samuel Tailors child	0:2:0	0:2:0	6 0	6·0
	Alice Tanner	0:2:0	0:2:0	8 0	6·0
2·2	Widow Titford	0:1:0	0:1:0	4·0	4·0
2·5	Widow Thomas	0:0:9	0:0:9	3·0	3·0

15. Overseers' accounts, Frome, Somerset, 1716. Widow Tittford, pauper, is receiving regular handouts from the parish. (SRO D/R/fr.)

from 1s. 9d. to 3s. per month, helping out 'Widow Tittford' alongside about a hundred and sixty others in similar need. They had more to concern them that year than simply the provision of cash handouts to the destitute, however; an overseer's job was never that simple. The details of 'Exterordinary' disbursements for August, 1715, reflect the magnitude of the task they had taken on by virtue of their office. They needed a touch of liquid refreshment, of course, to get started: 'Spent at Taylors ye George & at Poopes: 16/9½d.'.

Then down to business. Help for the sick:

Robt. Sudden Senr x Junr haveing ye small pox.	79/8d.

– and yet, despite the massive medical fees:

pd. for his grave Robt. Suden.	6d.

Others needed a bit of expert help, too:

It. paid for Bleeding Sarah Gardner.	6d.
It. for a Blistering Plaster for Mary Hobbs.	6d.
paid for drawing Goody Rudlys tooth.	6d.

Then midwifery fees:

It. delivering Margt. Mere of a dafter child.	5/-.

Paupers to clothe:

– for one pair of Shoose for Jos James.	1/8d.

Bastards to support:

for keeping Tho Clarks Bastard.	2/3d.

And then the other side of their responsibilities – assisting the parish constable in the maintenance of law and order, and enforcing the settlement regulations:

It. paid for persueing crook to take him up.	2/-.
for a warrant to take up Jon Candy.	1/-.
paid for an order to carrie ann Smith into Glostershere.	4/4d.
It. carring An Smith into Gloster sheare.	43/-.

The 43s. it cost them to 'carry' Ann Smith out of town might have been better spent, we may argue; the overseers were only doing what the law required of them, but their expenses in this case could have provided up to two years' poor relief for the poor woman even had she stayed in Frome and become chargeable to the parish. And what of the quite massive cost they would incur in October of the following year – a resounding £9 14s. to convey Thomas Kingswood back to Kent?

It was a thankless task, then, in many ways, that of serving as overseer of the poor – unpaid as these men were, and frequently overworked. The strength of the system, as is clear from the Frome accounts, is that at least they were able to help people known to them personally. They could allow themselves the flexibility of modifying their practice to help those in real need, permit their discretion to determine their course of action. And through it all, just on occasions, there was time for a touch of thinly-veiled sardonic humour as they wrote up their accounts: '6th August, 1717: Pd. for a cofen for wdo Rodaway very deep & large. 7/-'.

CHAPTER 10

William the Emigrant (1681/2-1746)

Frome, Somerset, and Hawkhurst and Cranbrook, Kent

GO EAST, YOUNG MAN

We have arrived, then, at the dawn of a new century, to be called the Age of Reason and Enlightenment by some, but one which, especially towards its close, brought unmitigated misery to large sections of the population of England.

Queen Anne succeeded William III in 1702, and in the same year the country managed to embroil itself in that protracted struggle known as the War of the Spanish Succession. In 1709 Daniel Defoe, himself an acid commentator on that same war, had attempted a somewhat arbitrary division of the English nation into seven major groups:

> The GREAT, who live profusely; the RICH, who live very plentifully; the MIDDLE SORT, who live well; the WORKING TRADES, who labour hard but feel no want; the COUNTRY PEOPLE – farmers, etc., who fare indifferently; the POOR, that fare hard; the MISERABLE, that really pinch and suffer want.[1]

If we must take Defoe's distinctions as they stand, the Titfords of Frome at this period fit somewhere between the 'middle sort' and the 'working trades'; it might be more helpful, however, to follow the example of Gregory King, whose 1696 analysis had differentiated 'artisans' from 'labouring poor and outservants'.[2] William the Wiredrawer and his family were, in essence, an artisan family that had made good – a kind of 'artisan-with-leasehold-property' sub-category.

Ralph Titford – not marked out as a great survivor in this world, as we have seen – died in 1708, the year before Defoe drew up his social and economic categories, and both his daughter Joan and various of his grandchildren were buried in quick succession. That left William the Wiredrawer as the one surviving male Titford of his generation. Many of his neighbours were of a similar economic class to himself, some not quite so fortunate as he: the Town Tithing rate list for Frome in 1705 includes James Whitchurch, a cardmaker, with two houses; Geo. West, a 'shoomaker', had 'several houses', rated, like William's, at 6d.; there were the usual tailors, mercers, dyers – and Will Pope, ambiguously described as a 'twister' . . . Many were rated in the 'Stocks' list; William, by now, was not – he had probably retired gracefully.

So much for a snapshot taken in 1705; little seemed to have changed for the family, on the surface at least; but in reality, like it or not, the Titfords were almost over the summit of their prosperity, and the slope on the other side, gradual but inexorable, would take those of them left in Frome into poverty and illness before the century was out.

The first intimation that things were not so rosy comes in 1709: William is rated at 6d. as he had been over previous years, but now, rather abruptly, he is down to a total of only two houses – a situation which persists until his death eight years later. The state of William's finances must have been of concern to others as well as himself – not least to his two young sons, William and Thomas. Each had a very different fate lying in wait for him; between them they were to weather various storms, but both took the family forward into another generation – indeed, had they not done so, their present descendants would not be looking back inquisitively at them now . . .

Frome was a rough enough place in which to be living in the early 1700s. Some worthy folk may have exuded 18th-century reason and enlightenment in their demeanour, but they were under constant threat from a significant minority which got its kicks from drinking the infamous locally-brewed strong beer, thereafter launching spiritedly and more or less drunkenly into those nefarious activities in which the town specialised: fighting, bear-baiting, cock-fighting, single-stick combat – and even tripping up unwary travellers at night with iron crooks on long poles in order to steal their money. The profusion of pubs and the lively life-style of the town seem to have attracted a fair smattering of rogues and ne'er-do-wells from the surrounding district – much to the delight of the Frome publicans, we may be sure.

A bouncy place indeed, then, to welcome the Titford lads, William and Thomas, safely into adulthood. Both, it would seem likely, were apprenticed, possibly to their own father; the two of them would eventually become cardmakers, as would their sons after them. William himself hardly waited for his apprenticeship to be over before he upped and got married; Frome's singular importance as a market and trading centre had long attracted people and goods from a number of neighbouring villages, and the town boys were therefore luckier than most in their range of choice when it came to young maidens. William snapped up a bride from Great Elm, just north-west of Frome; he and Katherine Dicks were married there on 4 July 1703, William being just 21 years old.[3]

It looks as if William the father may have been delighted enough to provide his son and daughter-in-law with one of his batch of houses in Oadground, as in 1704 he is only rated for 'seaven' properties, not eight, at a cost of 6d. That figure of 'seaven' was to plummet to a mere two just five years later.

Frome was not to be a lucky place for young William; he was eventually to have healthy children who would outlive him, but here in the early years of the 18th century he was marked out for tragedy. An only daughter, Mary, died in 1705, just after her first birthday, and was soon joined in January of the following year by Katherine herself. Left a widower and childless by the time he was 23, William lost little time in marrying again – a bride two years or so his junior named Joan. And then – with a stroke of unpredictable originality which may surprise and impress us – he girded up his loins, took hold of his new wife and their little infant daughter Mary, got himself a settlement certificate which would act as a passport enabling them all to settle in a foreign parish, and promptly went off to live in Kent.[4] This was in the winter of 1711, close on the heels of a period of dearth which had seen the price of wheat rise to 72s. a quarter – a massive increase from the 46s. 3d. average price of the period 1706-10. Not only that, but the Titford property holdings, as we know, had recently taken a turn for the worse. Nevertheless, as an eldest son – mentioned, we may remember, in the Lacy family lease of 1699 – William would have had fewer reasons than many for uprooting himself in quite this dramatic manner in his early twenties.

The Kent village of Hawkhurst which would be his new home was, like Frome, a centre of the cloth industry, but it must have had a magnetic attraction we can only guess at in retrospect, to have taken him away from family and friends on a long winter journey across southern England. In the event, his decision to move would prove a wise one in terms of material prosperity: a year after arriving in Hawkhurst he was already selling his wool-cards to the overseers for the use of widows at 2s. 2d. a pair, and as years went by his, the senior branch of the descendants of William Titford and Mary Smyth, would fare much better than their poorer cousins left behind in Frome. We will meet the Kent Titfords again before the story is at an end.

William's departure left two male Titfords in Frome: his young brother Thomas, and his father, William the Wiredrawer. The old man appears as the recipient of 16s. 6d. parish relief in April 1717, a sure indication that all was then not well with him; in the December

Somerset
To wit. } To the Churchwardens and Overseers of the
Poor of the Parish of *Cranbrook*
- - - - in the County of *Kent* - - -
or whom else it may concern.

WE whose Hands and Seals are hereunto subscribed and
set, being the present Churchwardens and Overseers of
the Poor of the Parish of *Frome Selwood* -
- in the said County of *Somerset* - - - -
do hereby certify, own, and acknowledge *William Titford*
and Joan his wife - - - - ∙ ∙ ∙ ∙ ∙

to be - Inhabitants legally settled in our said Parish of
Frome Selwood —— In WITNESS whereof We have hereunto set our Hands and Seals, the *Thirtieth* —— Day of
July. - - - - in the Year of our Lord One Thousand Seven Hundred and *Forty five*

Signed and Sealed in the ⎱
Presence of us, who have ⎰
here-under subscribed our ⎱
Names as Witnesses. ⎰

} Churchwardens

} Overseers

Somerset
To wit. } WE, Two of his Majesty's Justices of the Peace for the
said County of *Somerset* - do allow of the above-
written Certificate ; and we do also certify, that *Thomas*
Titford - - - - one of the Witnesses to the said Certificate hath made Oath before us, That he did see the said Churchwardens and Overseers whose Names and Seals are to the said
Certificate subscribed and set, severally sign and seal the same.
And that the Names of the said *Thomas Titford* -
- and of - - - -
subscribed as Witnesses, attesting the said Certificate are of their
own proper Hand Writing. Given under our Hands the
- - - Day of - - -
in the Year of our Lord One Thousand Seven Hundred and

16. Settlement Certificate, 1745. William Titford (1681/2-1746) and his
wife Joan need a certificate from Frome in Somerset in order to settle in
Cranbrook in Kent. One of the witnesses is Thomas Titford. (KAO
P100/13/1/94.)

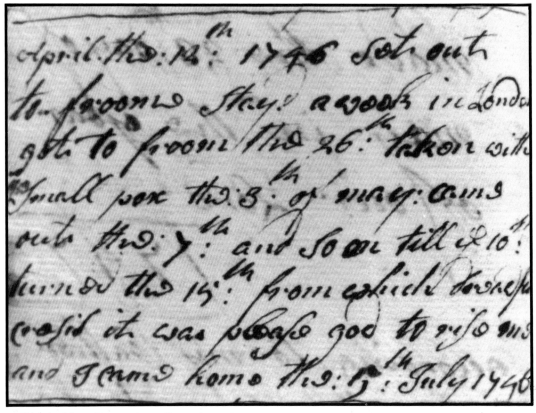

17. A visit to Frome, 1746. From the register book of Charles Titford (1717/8-1784) of Cranbrook
in Kent. 'April the 12th. 1746 Set out to Froome stayd a week in London got to Froom the 26th.
Taken with small pox the 3rd of May: came out the 7th. and so on till ye 10th. turned the 15th.
from which dreadful crosid it was please god to rise me and I came home the 5th. July 1746.'

of the same year he was buried at St John's church, with a last will and testament registered
at the Archdeacon's Court in the same year. What it contained must be left as a matter of
speculation: like so many other documents, it was destroyed at Exeter during the Second
World War.

One thing is certain: our man had lived through one of the most tumultuous periods of
English history. A mere lad when the Civil Wars began, a teenager when Charles I was
executed, an onlooker during the Monmouth Rebellion, in his fifties at the time of the
Glorious Revolution of 1688, he had outlived the Stuart monarchs and seen the throne of
England pass to the first Hanoverian. With his demise we move on one generation in our
Frome story: we must now get to know son Thomas.

CHAPTER 11

Thomas the Calvinist (1688-1771)

Frome, Somerset

THE GOSPEL OF DAMNATION

The *Calvinist* is taxt with Predestination, and to make God the Author of sin

John Milton

Thomas Titford, baptised in the year of the Glorious Revolution, was by 1718 the only male Titford left in Frome, following the departure of his brother William and the death of his father. As a cardmaker by trade, he would put to use the wire teeth prepared by the wiredrawers, making what one observer rather quaintly described as 'cards of labour and profit, not of pleasure and idleness'.[1] Cardmaking as a separate industry in its own right was a flourishing enough business in the early years of the 18th century, and it was said around 1716 that more wire cards were being made in Frome than anywhere else in the entire country.

There was money to be made, then, and as a consequence the town was beset by constant squabbles as to who should get what share of the pickings. The Frome cardmakers were in constant fear of being exploited by their arch-enemies, the clothiers. 1711 – the year William Titford the Emigrant left for Kent – saw a battle-royal between the two factions. On 21 January of that year the wiredrawers and cardmakers of Frome petitioned the House of Commons, complaining that the clothiers were making use of reconditioned cards, which the cardmakers claimed – naturally enough, as their self-interest was concerned – were 'too weak for the well carding of wool'.[2] To reinforce their case they also penned a 'Humble Petition' to Viscount Weymouth in the House of Lords, begging his support:

> . . . Such a bill would not onely be a generall good to the publick but of very great benefit to your Petitioners in lessening the rates to the poor of the said parish by keeping the greater part thereof imployed in the Manufacture of makeing New Cards.[3]

Sixty Frome cardmakers and wiredrawers signed this petition, plus the vicar, two church-wardens, three overseers of the poor and three constables. Strangely, no Titford was a signee: William the Wiredrawer was old by then, admittedly, but must have had an interest both as a craftsman and ratepayer; son Thomas was a cardmaker, and had similar interests. Maybe they weren't asked, maybe they couldn't write (though here were 60 people who could at least sign their names at the foot of the petition) or maybe they were felt to be too old or too young. But their fellow craftsmen did battle without them. To no great avail, as it turned out: after a flurry of claims and counter-claims in parliament involving petitions from various parts of the country, the bill failed on its second reading in the Commons and the *status quo* prevailed once more.

Whatever may have been the grievances of the cardmakers, there was obviously at least some work around for Thomas Titford; enough, certainly, to make him confident about taking a wife. At 27 – very much the average age for bridegrooms at that period – he married Elisabeth Franklin at St John's church on 19 August 1715, the year following the accession of George I. The baptism of two sons followed very soon afterwards: in 1717 there was William, named after his paternal grandfather (who was to die that very year); and then came Thomas, an exact contemporary of his cousin Charles, born in Kent as a son of William the Emigrant.

The churchwardens' accounts for 1723 show Thomas Titford paying a rate of 2½d. for 'a house', while 'Wid. Titford or oc.' was charged at 1d. for 'one house'. The entries reflect the legacy left by William the Wiredrawer to his son and widow: Thomas and his family were living in one of the original Titford houses on Cowards Batch with its attached workshop, while widow Margaret had the house next door.[4] It may all seem a far cry from the days of eight properties in the same street in the late 17th century, but many a Titford fifty years later would have been glad of the chance to pay rates on any houses at all.

Frome itself was veritably packed with people, and immigrants still came pouring in; a world atlas of 1721 speaks of the town in grandiloquent terms:

> Frome Selwood . . . is a very great town . . . reckoned one of the most populous in the West of England . . . very famous for the manufacture of broad and narrow woollen-cloths, in which it employs thousands of the poor . . .[5]

And thousands of poor there certainly were; five years later it was Defoe's turn to write that the town had '. . . so prodigiously increased within these 20 or 30 years . . . that it is now reckoned to have more people in it than the City of Bath'.[6] Not all the inhabitants in that year of 1726 were so happy with their lot in this most populous town, however, and weavers from Wiltshire and Somerset made common cause against the clothiers in Frome, accusing the latter of sharp practices and taking to the streets in protest. The dragoons were eventually called out – on Boxing Day – to restore order.

As the riots abated, so a new cause for concern dogged the last few years of the 1720s in the shape of inclement weather – wet springs and sickly summers – with high corn prices and a series of merciless epidemics, particularly those of smallpox. Thomas and Elisabeth's son John was buried in 1727, a week before George I died; their little daughter Mary followed her brother two years later, while in 1728 Margaret Titford, widow of William the Wiredrawer, was added to the long list of the dead who succumbed during those cruel years.

Thomas Titford, then, had lost two children and his own mother within a period of three years; not only that, but by early 1733 he had also been left a widower by the death of his wife Elisabeth. Thomas lost little time in remarrying: eight years earlier the original lease on the house in Blunt Street undertaken by Thomas and John Lacy together with 'William, son of William Titford, wiredrawer' had come to an end, and with wisdom as well as love to guide him, Thomas Titford married Thomas Lacy's daughter Sarah at St John's church on 5 February 1732/3.

The bad times were not quite over, nevertheless: within a few months of this marriage, Thomas's son Thomas – barely 15 years old – was buried.[7] It is difficult to say by whom exactly, as the rather effete vicar – the Hon. Henry Villiers, son of the Earl of Jersey, who had been handed the Frome and Marston Bigot parishes on a silver plate – was perpetually absent. And on the basis that while the cat is away, the mice will play, it should perhaps come as no surprise to find that the sexton, Thomas Baily, was habitually drunk and constantly mistaking one grave for another. Such chaos at St John's underlines all too clearly the fact that much of the mass defection to Nonconformity during the 18th century would not have been on purely theological grounds.

From the time of the marriage of Thomas to Sarah Lacey in 1732/3 we can see a pattern developing in the Titfords' fortunes whereby what was once family leasehold property finds its way into the hands of men who had been wise enough to marry Titford girls. Thomas's sister Ann had been married in 1715/6, his cousin Martha in 1723, and a further sister, Margaret, in 1731. Three new in-laws were thus welcomed into the Titford fold: there was Joseph Bedford, together with John Pollett (or Pollard) and his brother William, both originally from the isolated hamlet of Podimore Milton, near Ilchester.[8] These men, together with two later in-laws, Thomas Hinton (or Henton) and Joseph Elliot, all ended up leasing or occupying one or more of the original Titford properties on Coward's Batch or elsewhere as the 18th century wore on. The St Katherine's Manor half-year rental roll for Michaelmas 1735 finds 173 tenants occupying houses in the Trinity area, mainly labourers, tradesmen and craftsmen, together with 'ye lame woman', each paying a few shillings in rent. Thomas Titford is charged 4s., while the split-up of the eight original Titford houses is indicated by references to William Starr (11s. 6d. for 'Part of Titford's'), Goody Smith (1s. 9d. 'For Titford') and William Pollard (2s. 'For Titford'). The properties themselves may have passed into other hands, but the Titford name is perpetuated, at least in the rent and rate books of the period.

Within two years, Thomas was preparing to abandon the last of the Coward's Batch houses in Fountain Lane: John Pollard, his brother-in-law, had taken over one property from Widow Titford, while by 1739 Thomas himself had moved out of his own house and workshop next door, making way for Stephen Humphries, a Wiltshireman from Devizes. Humphries already had a property or two under his belt, and he was to acquire more as time went by; he was also, 10 years later, to marry Thomas's daughter Mary.[9]

What of Thomas himself? He was too canny to leave himself homeless, and he had made contingency plans before allowing young Humphries to take over.[9] On 24 June 1737 he took out a lease on a plot of ground on High Street – literally the highest street in the town – where he built two houses at its south-west end, abutting Wine Street. Soon he was assessed for a rate of 1½d. on what the overseers chose to call 'a house in Badcox Lane'. The land itself belonged to William Sheppard, a member of the influential family of clothiers, who were busy developing this new street in what had previously been the orchard of the *Sun Inn*. Thomas's plot, measuring 45 feet by 26 feet, gave him the space for a pair of substantial little houses; latterly knocked into one and numbered as 17, they still exist in the 1980s, forming quite a modest but handsome corner property with a pantiled roof.

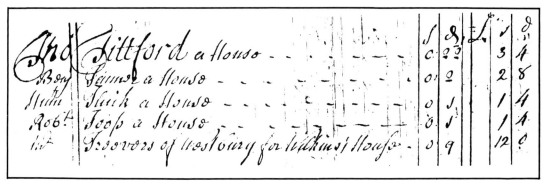

18. Overseers' accounts, Frome, Somerset, 1738-9. Thomas Tittford is paying rates on his house. (SRO D/R/fr.)

Life on High Street cannot have been unpleasant for Thomas while it lasted; perhaps he could lie in for an extra 10 minutes on a Sunday, knowing that a brisk walk down the street, followed by a right turn, would take him to chapel in double-quick time. And if there were neighbours to avoid, he could always take the alternative route – along Wine Street and down Sheppards Barton . . . Yet it was not to last for long; by 1744 it was Mrs. Sheppard, not Thomas, who was paying rates on his High Street houses, and they are described as being 'late Titford's'. Subsequently, by an arrangement of 1 January 1755, William Sheppard granted a 99-year lease on the properties – two tenements 'lately built by Thomas Titford' – to his brother John. The rent would be 4s. 4d. yearly.[10]

Thomas Titford may have given up his lease to become a tenant – an unusual arrangement, perhaps, and a theory which might be discounted; in the event, Thomas's disappearance from High Street remains a mystery. What is certain is that from 1744 male Titfords never again appear as ratepayers in Frome; there are plenty of references to properties 'Late Titford's', but somehow the family had let it all slip away.[11] The only consolation is that initially it was in-laws who occupied the houses. If we wish to find the family in the rate books later in the century, we turn to the lists of those entitled to benefit as paupers, not to those whose contributions were making the payment of such benefit possible.

In the meantime, Thomas Titford may not have been busy paying rates from 1744, but he was certainly not idle during the next two years, at least. It had been 34 years since his brother William had left Frome for Hawkhurst in Kent, complete with that requisite settlement certificate of 1711; but such certificates were specific to one named parish of sojourn, and in 1745 William and his wife Joan were in the process of moving house from Hawkhurst to Cranbrook, a few miles away. Now Cranbrook demanded a settlement certificate of its own, just in case the couple should become destitute and need parish support. In actual fact, far from hovering on the edge of pauperdom, William had already established himself as a Cranbrook ratepayer, and in the circumstances this demand from his new parish does seem a trifle pedantic, if not positively vindictive.

Still, the appropriate procedure had to be followed to satisfy the regulations, and in Frome Thomas Titford set about getting things organised for his brother. In August 1745 he was having a busy time – on Friday the 9th he paid a visit to the local J.P.s to sort out the certificate, and the following Thursday he was due for his half-yearly home visit from Thomas Hurne, the Badcox Lane Chapel pastor. Then came a hiatus, until someone arrived from Kent to collect the certificate.

This hiatus lasted until the following April, eight months later, and the 'someone' who made the journey west was young Charles Titford, son of William the Emigrant. Charles was one of three surviving children: he had a brother John and an elder sister Mary, who as a young child had accompanied her parents to Kent, and was herself to return to Frome in 1757 and live out the rest of her life there. This family appears to have taken emigration and immigration, together with journeys of some considerable distance, very much in its stride.

Charles Titford was 28 years old in April 1746; according to his father and mother's account he had been born on 6 January 1717/18 and duly baptised into his local General Baptist congregation in the October of 1740, as an adult in the twenty-third year of his age. A thorough man in many ways, we may be sure, he began to keep a register of significant family events in May 1747, entering retrospectively details of his journey to Frome the year before.[12]

He set out from Kent on 12 April 1746, staying a week in London and arriving in Frome on the 26th, a Saturday; exactly a week later, 3 May, his physical and spiritual resilience were to be dramatically put to the test by the onset of smallpox. An unforgettable experience for him, no doubt, and one which he later recorded in detail in his register; the disease 'came out' on 7 May, and continued unabated until the 10th; the turning-point came on 15 May, '. . . from which dreadful (crisis) it was pleased God to rise me . . .' and so the danger passed. In later years Charles would take no chances: in 1763 he had three of his own children inoculated against smallpox – a dangerous and unpredictable medical practice, certainly, but one which affected his children very little, as they '. . . had it very light and came home again very well (Blessed be God)'. The exercise cost Charles 11 guineas – an outrageous price, we might think, but no doubt money well spent.

So in Frome in late May, 1746, Charles Titford was on the road to recovery – time for a long chat with his uncle Thomas, who would be keen for news of his long-lost brother, but would also have local gossip of his own for young Charles to take back with him:

How was Hawkhurst then, Charles? Why the move to Cranbrook? Is your father's health holding up? What are you doing – a cardmaker? a woolcomber? – good old family trades, my boy!

You've seen St John's church just over there, where your father and I were baptised? Well, this wretched vicar called Villiers has just about brought that church to its knees – they can't even ring the bells, for fear of the steeple collapsing! Not that your aunt Sarah and I care – we're nicely settled at Badcox Lane Chapel; but the goings-on there, too – did you ever hear about this man called Roberts?

How do you like all our fine new buildings – I must show you that new inn just across the river – it has a Tennis Court – a *Tennis Court*!

You must have heard the news from Scotland – they've just finally defeated that awful man who wants to be king . . . 'Bonnie Prince Charlie' or some such name . . . your grandfather used to say that they couldn't wait to get rid of this Prince Charlie's grandfather (King James, you know . . .) after Monmouth was beheaded and some of the town's best men got their limbs chopped off in the fighting . . .

Do you know the chapel is having its very own burial ground? That's where Sarah and I want to go when we die – and all the children, too. No, I don't suppose you and your father agree with all my views on the Gospel, eh? You and your chapel friends in Kent – what do you call yourselves? General Baptists? They call us Particular Baptists . . . well, don't tell me you think everyone can go to heaven – not just *Anybody*? Surely not! Oh, well, have it your own way – I don't want to start an argument . . .

Have you heard about these Frome 'poets' as they call themselves? There was that Mrs. Rowe – she's dead now – and then this Dr. Samuel Bowden – you know, sort of: 'Fair be the morn, spotless the azure sky . . .' No, I can't stand it either; they say he read out that kind of stuff to old Lord Orrery at Marston last year sometime . . . don't believe it, myself . . . And all these newcomers! Coming in here causing trouble . . . we had some mobbing here over corn about six years ago[13] . . . they say we've got a population of about thirteen thousand – it can't be *that* many – I don't know where they get these figures from . . .

You know, I'll be glad to get out of this cardmaking business – leave it to you younger ones! Did you know they formed a 'Society of Cardmakers' here a few years ago? But my poor old hands aren't as nimble as they used to be . . . I can write all right – look at this fancy signature of mine on your father's certificate here – but I haven't got the strength I used to have.

I'm glad they defeated that awful Jacobite in Scotland – I don't want the likes of him having control over my life – it's bad enough owing your soul to these Sheppards, these 'clothiers' as they call themselves – in my grandfather's time they were cardboard-makers, you know, no better than the rest of us! . . . I meet 'em in chapel sometimes, and they put on a pleasant face, saying we're all brothers in Christ, but they're different from us, aren't they? They must be making a fortune now the slump is over – you know, they say that seven waggons a week leave Frome with cloth for Blackwell Hall in London – I expect you've seen them buying and selling there, haven't you? I've seen them load a 140 pieces on those waggons, worth I don't know how much . . .[14]

And so on . . . until Charles had to bid a fond farewell to his uncle, his cousins and his friends, and return home to Kent, arriving on 5 July. He may have narrowly escaped death while in Frome, but this was to be a tragic year for his immediate family; on 4 November his father, William the Emigrant, died just as the 8 o'clock curfew bell was tolling in Cranbrook, to be followed exactly a week later by Charles's brother John. Perhaps one or both of them had succumbed to that same disease of smallpox which Charles had managed to fight off just a few months earlier?

William the Emigrant's wife Joan outlived him by a mere three years, aged 64 at her death, as he had been; Charles, by then, had married Frances Ballard, second daughter of Isaac and Frances Ballard of Glassenbury, near Cranbrook, and was busy setting about producing a family whose descendants are still thick on the ground in the 20th century.

There we leave the Kent Titfords – but not for good – and return to Frome, where 1752 was to be a memorable year. John Wesley made his first – and rather stormy – appearance in the town, causing less of a furore, nevertheless, than that which followed the change from the Julian to the Gregorian calendar – 'Old Style' giving way to 'New Style'. The year was now deemed to begin on 1 January, not 25 March (Lady Day) as hitherto. How old would a person now say he was? When did his true birthday fall? Whatever had happened to those missing days – they had all lost the 3 to the 13 September 1752 completely!

During the month following those missing September days, Stephen Humphries 'of Devizes' married Thomas Titford's daughter Mary at St John's. The next year, Lord Hardwicke's Marriage Act was to ensure that all weddings were duly recorded in the parish registers as theirs had been; Hardwicke is one of the family historian's favourite characters for that very reason.

Stephen Humphries, the Wiltshireman, had finally been received officially into the Titford fold, then; and very appropriate too, we might say, since not only was he a member of Badcox Lane Chapel (baptised as an adult in 1751), but as early as 1739 he had taken over the lease on Thomas Titford's former house and workshop on Fountain Lane/Coward's Batch.[15] He died in 1781, though by then the Coward's Batch properties had passed out of his hands: Joseph Davies had them in 1770, followed two years later by Thomas Hinton (or Henton), a barber. The Titfords knew how to marry off their daughters as a way of getting a grip on their original properties, of course, and a certain Margaret Titford had led the said Mr. Henton up the aisle of St John's on 7 May 1764. No Titford gives up that easily.

Significantly, as we have seen, Titford in-laws managed to end up leasing or occupying various ex-Titford properties, sometimes to the exclusion of Titford sons themselves. And it is to these sons we must turn shortly, but not before closing the chapter properly on Thomas, the cardmaker, whom we must dub 'Thomas the Calvinist'. Thomas did not just make cards, sign settlement certificates, have children and take out leases – that is merely a catalogue of his secular activities; we would be doing him an injustice here if we ignored the spiritual dimension to his life. The links between Titfords and Nonconformity have already been mentioned in passing – now is the time to delve a bit deeper; through a detailed look at the chapel where Thomas worshipped, we can arrive at some understanding not only of his Christian creed, but also of the more general social milieu which helped to mould his life from day to day.

One of the luxuries enjoyed by 20th-century man is that, having once paid his rates and taxes, he is more or less free to choose those institutions which he wishes to join, those to which he will voluntarily pay allegiance or support with a regular subscription. Not only that, but there are few enough recriminations against those who no longer find the time or the enthusiasm to support the local Women's Institute, the Rotary Club, or the village Horticultural Society; institutions are very largely made for men – and women – and not the other way round.

How strange for us in retrospect, therefore, to contemplate that great and complex institution, the Church, with its ecclesiastical and administrative half-nelson on the lives of English people, be they never so famous or anonymous, throughout so many centuries of the nation's life.

Here there was no choice; or for those brave enough to dissent, there lay persecution and terror at worst, exclusion from public office at best. The Titfords of Bratton had felt the serpent's tooth of the mother church – hounded by churchwardens for a child born out of wedlock, 'presented' for non-attendance at Divine Service; how they must have longed to be untrammelled, to escape the grip exercised upon them by what amounted to a heartless bureaucracy posing as a brotherhood of Christian believers!

Here, surely, lay the roots of Nonconformity in English society from the 16th century onwards. We need not doubt the theological probity of many if not most Dissenters, but what they were dissenting from may well have been not an alien creed in itself, so much as an institution which encroached upon their everyday lives, which spied pruriently upon every aspect of their conduct, spiritual and secular.[16] In such circumstances, then, it is little wonder that a number of early Puritans adopted some form of congregationalism, and with it the chance of running their own affairs, free from an Established Church.

Even before Thomas Titford the Shoemaker was a target for the Bratton churchwardens in 1615, the sect which was to have such a significant impact on the lives of the Titfords of Frome had founded its first church on English soil. In 1612 a number of men known as Antipaedobaptists began the first Baptist church in Newgate Street, London; herein lay the origins of the General Baptist denomination, believers with an evangelical turn of mind who believed that Christ's saving grace was available to all men in general. By contrast, 21 years later in Southwark a group of bretheren seceded from the Independent Church and formed the first Particular Baptist congregation. Calvinistic in their outlook, these believed that only the Elect were candidates for salvation; that the power of the cross was available to a few who were chosen, that its application was particular, not general. At worst, such a creed could produce a singularly uncharitable 18th-century hymn which ran:

> We are the sweet selected few,
> The rest of you be damned;
> There's room enough in hell for you –
> We won't have heaven crammed[17]

The Particular Baptist sect, like many another, took very firm root in the West Country, and our special concern will now be one of its chapels: that of Badcox Lane in Frome.

The Badcox congregation dated from at least as early as 1669, in which year it sent a delegate to hear a case of discipline at 'Cliford', just north of Beckington. By no means the only Baptist assembly in Frome as the years went by, it can thus claim to be the oldest – and for all we know it may have counted Titfords in its number from the outset.

Times were hard for Dissenters, Baptists included, during the Restoration, as we have already seen in passing; ineligible as they were for national or municipal office except by the loophole of occasional conformity, many of them turned to trade, to craft or to commerce. Charles II's own declared desire that his reign should be marked by freedom of worship for those of 'tender conscience' was set at naught in the 1660s by the reactionary elements in Church and State, who forced through a series of punitive acts in a vain attempt to put Nonconformity firmly in its place.

Its place, of course, turned out to be underground; the root was hidden but healthy, and when better times came under William and Mary there was a great flowering of meeting houses up and down the country in the wake of the Toleration Act of 1689.[18] Badcox Lane was officially founded at this time, having its Confession of Faith established '. . . by the elders and bretheren of our denomination meeting in the City of London in the year 1689'.[19]

By 1712 the congregation had its own meeting house 'in the street leading from Catern Hill to Badcok's'; things must have seemed to be set fair – soon they were proudly self-styled the 'Congregational Church baptiz'd upon a personal Profession of Faith in the Lord Jesus Christ, now meeting in Froom-Zelwood . . . under the Pastoral Care of our Honoured and Beloved Brother John Sharpe . . .'[20] Here at last was the Congregationalism they had sought – they could govern their own affairs, be responsible only to themselves, free in so many ways from the grip of the Established Church at St John's just down the road and all that Anglicanism represented.

It would be nice for everyone's sake if the story could end there: happily ever after. In the event, however, the Frome Baptists' new-found liberty took them from the frying-pan into the fire; bad news always makes news, to be sure, and the Badcox Lane pastors made little attempt to cloak all their difficulties whilst writing up their chapel minute books, but we are left with a picture of 18th-century Dissenters torn apart time and time again by schism and back-biting, self-righteous justification and knives in the back. Flushed with success in the fight against Anglicans, it seems, they now found time to fight each other.

We must balance what we read of those battle-torn years by the likely assumption that many worshippers passed their time in comparative peace and quietness, saddened by the antics of some of their fellows and hallowing God in their lives and prayers. Yet some degree of turmoil would seem to be an inevitable complement to the dogmas by which the Particular Baptists ruled their lives. Jonathan Swift, author of *Tale of a Tub* and many another prose denunciation of 18th-century religious fanaticism, never tires of reminding us that Dissenters were charged above all with too much 'zeal' or 'enthusiasm' – qualities he talks of in deprecating terms. What this means, in effect, is that in seeking for the truth and trying to foist that truth upon others of a different persuasion, Dissenters could be guilty of a narrow-minded bigotry, choosing as their first enemies those in theory most close to them. It was an easy step, after all, from denouncing sin in general to railing against one's fellows; zeal and energy were so readily mischannelled.

Such fervour-turned-bitchiness, born no doubt of excellent motives and sincerely-held convictions, was inherent in the Particular Baptist creed. Badcox Lane had its own 'Particular Principles' of belief:

> As to election: we believe that God of his pure goodness and free grace did from eternity choose a certain number of mankind in Christ . . .
> As to the extent of redemption: We believe that all mankind in general are not partakers of the saving benefits of Christ's redemption, but only the elect of God.

When a new member made a covenant with the church, was baptised and entered the closed fellowship at Badcox, he or she – Titfords and their in-laws amongst them – had to answer an unequivocal question:

> Do you solemnly give up yourself to the Lord and to the church, to watch over, to be watched over . . .

The 'watching over' was crucial – legalised prying, we might term it, uncharitably; members made a solemn undertaking:

> . . . to be watched over by our bretheren and to be advised, admonished and reproved by them as there shall be need, and to take the same kindly and well at their hands. Matthew 18: 15, 16, 17.

Here, then, complete with scriptural justification, was a nosey-parker's charter which effectively paved the way for a situation as bad as anything Titfords had gone through in the Established Church at Bratton in the early 17th century, when neighbours noted and churchwardens and sidesmen presented the fact that wives were no longer living with their husbands, or that a lady at Dilton had given birth to a base-born child and had been 'seen in the act'.[21]

Nor was Badcox Lane Chapel unique in its rigid Calvinism: in the years 1715 to 1718 a Committee of the Three Dissenting Denominations established that the Particular Baptists made up 0.74 per cent of the population as a whole, as against only 0.31 per cent for the General Baptists. These General or Arminian congregations, in any case, were to weaken as the century progressed, many of their number eventually adopting a form of Unitarianism.[22]

Whether a group of believers adopted the Particular or the General tenets of belief depended to an extent upon the fashion of the locality: the former were stronger in the West Country, leaving the east and south-east to their General colleagues. In Frome, Badcox Lane Chapel was forever suspicious of its neighbouring congregation in Sheppards Barton, whose members were not even moderately Calvinistic by profession and would have joined a General Baptist Association had one existed locally – or so it was rumoured.

It is difficult, in retrospect, to view High Calvinism with very much charity. It was, paradoxically, part of the movement of radical Dissent, yet also very conservative and inward-looking. Buttressed by its dogmatic certainties, its members could view with equanimity the unequal distribution of wealth and happiness within society: was that not all part of God's plan for mankind?

It was precisely that kind of attitude that could lead to a commentator in 1708 declaring that:

> It is GOD's own Appointment, that some should be Rich and some Poor, some High and some Low.[23]

And even later in the century it was still possible for William Paley (1743-1805) to express the following views, apparently without a flicker of humour:

> How thankful . . . the poor should be that the very circumstances in which they are placed have such a powerful tendency to cherish the divine spirit of dependence and subordination.[24]

Not only that, but Calvinism has been called, with some justification, the 'Gospel of Damnation' – for just as surely as some were 'elected' to salvation, so others were marked out, chosen by the Almighty, to be damned. Little wonder, perhaps, that the Anglican Church, afraid of such theological extremes, is characterised in the 18th century by moderation in its flabbiest form – opting for what has been called 'decent mediocrity'.[25]

Nevertheless, a congregation committed to High Calvinism, for better or worse, made up the society in which Thomas Titford moved; this was his world. By the time he became a full member of Badcox Lane Chapel, he was already in his fifties; although he had been baptised as an infant at St John's in 1688, he and his wife Sarah (née Lacey) underwent a second baptism – or, in Baptist eyes, the first and only meaningful immersion – on Thursday, 15 April 1742. They were received into full communion and fellowship with the church the following Sunday – Easter Sunday: Badcox had to wait until 1763 to have it own 'baptistory', and the Titfords would have undergone the sacred ceremony at the hands of the pastor, Brother Thomas Hurne, at some convenient place where there was 'much water' – at Hapsford, at Mr. Henry Allen's at Pilly Hill, or at the dyehouse at Great Enox.[26]

Why did Thomas wait so long before becoming a full member of the Baptist community? The answer probably lies in the schisms which beset Badcox Lane from the 1720s onwards. Central to our story is a certain Mr. James Roberts, who was a leading light in a strong Baptist revival which took place in about 1725. At that period, according to Roberts's own account, no less than a hundred and fifty people were baptised in 'two or three and twenty months' – a glowing testimony not only to the fine reputation of the pastor, John Sharpe, but no doubt also to the charisma of the said Roberts himself. But those with charisma can turn off as many people as they turn on, and the net result of Roberts being invited to the co-pastorate of Badcox in 1725 was that 41 members left on the spot. Among them was a certain Elizabeth Titford, with an indication that she departed 'just after Mr Roberts's coming about the year 1726' but that she had been 'received by Mr Hendy's church' – in other words, dissatisfied with our friend Roberts for whatever reason, she had changed her allegiance to nearby Sheppards Barton Baptist Chapel. With her went her relations and in-laws, Joseph and Ann Bedford and Margaret Pollard; all four of them appear in a list drawn up for Badcox Lane Chapel in 1740 of those who had been 'Straggling upon sundry occasions without regular dismissions'.[27] By this later date Elizabeth Titford had died – her name is given the perfunctory addition 'dead' in the church book. We are looking here, it would seem, at Thomas Titford's first wife Elizabeth, née Franklin – and she, poor lady, appears to have worshipped at Badcox Lane without her husband, since the first time his name appears in the chapel records is 1742, the year of his baptism.

Thomas and his new wife, Sarah Lacey, had bided their time before committing themselves to the Badcox community; they had been married for 10 years – since 1732/3 – before taking the quite literal plunge, by which time James Roberts had departed from the chapel and the ageing and unwell John Sharpe had been replaced (in 1740) by a younger and more energetic man, Thomas Hurne of Crockerton, Wilts.[28]

In a sense, the couple had missed all the fun in the intervening years, though the goings-on at Badcox must have provided regular fuel for gossip-mongers in Frome pubs and on street corners. In June 1735 it had been decided to call the aforementioned Brother James Roberts to undertake some of the pastoral care of the Badcox Lane community; the request was couched in delicate terms for fear of offending the minister, poor old John Sharpe: the church meeting '. . . then also solemnly declared and assured our Brother John Sharp that we have no design or intention herein to his prejudice in the least wise . . .'. Roberts accepted, although several members disagreed with the majority verdict. Then trouble erupted; the church meetings broke up in disarray as factions for and against Roberts did battle with each other:

> 7th October, 1736: all other things omitted from entring upon the church book until the 25th February, 1736/7 by reason of the discord which did appear amongst us which rendered us incapable of doing business in an orderly manner.

The anti-Roberts camp triumphed in the end; with true Dissenting zeal they withdrew themselves from the 'abettors and adherents of Mr Roberts' together with the man himself, charging Joseph Partman with the thankless task of delivering a letter to that effect. The wording here is significant: the Chapel made it very clear that it never excluded anyone as such – instead, the victim was 'withdrawn from'. A nice distinction, indeed. These people could fight with the gloves off; they were never slow to bring charges, real or imagined, against anyone not of their persuasion; we see Roberts through their eyes, and maybe he was an unsavoury character in some ways. But he was driven out by virtue of a charge which was paradoxically both specific and yet unspecific:

> June 12th, 1737. Mr James Roberts was excluded from the communion of this church for his sin committed in the Meeting Room garret and his encouraging a disorderly company to make a division in the church, he refusing to give satisfaction for the same.[29]

So Roberts was up to no good in the garret, and had to go. He took 58 members with him.

Significantly, at precisely this period – in 1735 – there was another division, even more virulent, erupting at the Little Wild Street Baptist Church in London. Its pastor, Andrew Gifford, later to become a famous if not universally popular Baptist luminary, was in that year accused of 'sodomitical attempts' by a number of his church members. Titfords were numbered in Dr. Gifford's congregation in Eagle Street, Holborn, at a later date – in 1757 Mary Titford arrived at Badcox Lane bearing a letter of introduction from the great Doctor himself – but even in 1735 there was a Frome connexion with this seemingly distant squabble. Central to the homosexual charges against this London pastor was a set of four documents, three from the West Country (Gifford had been born in Bristol) of which one was 'a letter from Mr Sharpe of Frome'.[30]

Beset as he was with a power struggle on his own doorstep, John Sharpe found time to add fuel to the fire of a distasteful affair in London which would leave Gifford's reputation more or less scarred for the rest of his life. Overall, Sharpe's contribution to the Baptist cause in Frome was a signal one – but the unhappy events of the 1730s show all too clearly the weaknesses of the Elect and the covenant of watching over and being watched over . . .

Thomas Hurne's arrival as pastor must have seemed like a breath of fresh air after such troubled times. He accepted the call officially on 29 June 1740, being released from the chapel at Crockerton in Wiltshire, which was sorry to see him go. He found things at Badcox in a troubled state; in the wake of the Roberts affair and a grim few years under the care of an ageing pastor, the worshippers were low in number and no doubt dispirited:

> At the Lord's Table, August 31st, 1740. Called over ye members; ye list was 60 and there was but 31 presant.

It must be to Hurne's eternal credit that he built upon such shaky foundations with great success; membership increased steadily until it reached 104 in 1743, and he did his best to placate those who had defected during the Roberts affair. Many returned to the fold; others, like the redoubtable Avis Usher – she who had taken over a new lease replacing the one issued in the names of William Titford the Wiredrawer and the two Laceys – did not:

> August 28th, 1740. Avis Usher declares herself to be of Mr Roberts's party, who are withdrawn from.

Baptists were notoriously suspicious of their members marrying outside the chosen fraternity; hence it is no surprise that the names of members of Badcox Lane taken at Thomas Hurne's arrival, and then added to as appropriate, include those of families into which various Titfords married: Elliot, Lacy, Humphries, Coles, Carpenter, Pollard. We are looking here at a very close community within a somewhat isolated town – little wonder, in effect, that what were really storms in teacups had assumed epic proportions. The chapel, after all, was the focus of many people's very existence: not just a place of worship, but the centre of their social life, their entertainment, a surrogate battlefield – their own private world. Under Brother Hurne, however, more reconciliation was in the offing: on 4 February 1741 it was agreed to forge a union between Badcox Lane and the Baptist Meeting at Starve Acre, in order to 'advance the honour and strength of the Baptist interests in the town'.[31]

One name that appears among those of the 33 Starve Acre members who transferred at this time is that of John Pollard; he had married Margaret Titford at St John's in 1731, eight years after his brother William had celebrated his wedding to Martha Titford. The said Margaret Titford was quite probably Thomas's younger sister, and appears – as 'Margaret Polard' – in the 1740 list of those who had left Badcox Lane for Sheppards Barton Chapel in 1726; if she did indeed leave to escape the company of James Roberts, how strange for her husband, John, to have worshipped so long at a different meeting house, Starve Acre, at which place Roberts himself was a regular preacher! There may be some other explanation, but it was not unknown for husband and wife to worship at separate chapels and it does look on the surface as if the Roberts affair had created a divide between husband and wife.

Pollard was received into full communion and fellowship with Badcox Lane in 1741; thereafter he was to play a significant role in its affairs and seems, for example, to have been forceful or silver-tongued enough to entice the straying Sister Elizabeth Pobjay back to her place in church in 1742. He died seven years later, in 1749, having even been described in the interim as a 'minister'.

Thomas Hurne's liberal ways continued; the question of the propriety of singing hymns in church had often been raised in Particular Baptist circles – so in about 1688 the pastor of Goat's Yard Passage Chapel in Southwark was the first to allow such a practice, condemned immediately by others as 'a carnal formality' and leading to a rupture in the Church centred upon the said pastor, Mr. Benjamin Keach.

Nothing daunted, Badcox's new pastor took the bit between his teeth, and we read in the minutes of a church meeting on 8 July 1742, that it was '. . . agreed (after several months consideration) to admit of singing ye Praise of God after ye service Lord's Day evenings; several members being desirous of it and not one speaking against it'. And later that: '. . . Ye singars may have ye Liberty to sing at any Time after ye Rest of ye Service be Intirely ended'.[32]

Hurne, it seems, was slowly breaking down a few of the conservative ways of his flock. The entries so common in Sharpe's time, that members were 'concerned in liquor' or 'disorderly and overcome in beer' were now slightly less frequent, though the 'watching over' was still there, and in 1742 Sister Mary Aldaredge was accused of 'drinking to excess' and – worse – telling her fellows that she was keen to resume her place in Church, '. . . yet is said to have expressed some things, to others, very inconsistent with it . . .'.[33]

By contrast, perhaps, one of the most impressive aspects of Baptist church life was that there seemed to be a nationwide fellowship of like-minded believers; members would think nothing of travelling quite large distances to worship on a Sunday, and preachers in Hurne's time included a Mr. James of Upton, Mr. Oulton of 'Lemster', Mr. Pearsal of Warminster, and two visitors from the capital itself, Messrs. Dew and Dorks, in 1742. It must have been precisely this kind of quasi-Masonic network existing between chapels up and down the country that made Baptist Church members more mobile, if they wished to be, than their fellow Anglicans. The question of migration is one which often troubles family historians; but practising Baptists could quite likely make a move from, say, Frome to London, as more than one generation of Titfords did, certain in the knowledge that even if they had no relations to stay with, they would be sure of a warm welcome and perhaps a bed for the night from their Christian brethren. In the light of this, seemingly unlikely moves made by the various branches of the Titford family – to London or to Kent – can be seen as a fairly natural and rather less than daunting journey away from existing roots.

So Thomas Hurne's spell as pastor was a healing period. Life went on as it had to – a sermon on Sunday afternoons and evenings, a solemn recitation of the church covenant when new members were admitted, regular church meetings on Thursdays, a lecture given by one of the four ministers in the town on a Tuesday evening, and an official roll-call every six months. The singing of hymns continued, Watts' *Hymns* at 2s. 8d. being used for the purpose, and some members even accompanied the congregation and 'singers' on instruments in the gallery. Such was the week-in, week-out, experience of the Titfords and their Baptist brethren and relations in the 1740s.

Hurne took his pastoral role seriously enough to decide that each member ought to be visited by him on a regular basis in his or her own home:

> Jan 4th, 1744/5. Being concious to myself and troubled that through my many incomberances I have neglected visiting my people as my office required, I do purpose and resolve that I will for the future (if God will) make it my constant practice to visit at least four of my members every week and every member of my society that are in the near about the town twice every year, and those out of town that I cannot reach I will endeavour to get them to my house at least once every year which will be much the same in effect as visiting them at their own houses.

So it was that he visited Thomas Titford and Sarah, living within the town itself, twice a year during 1745, 1746 and 1747, once in early spring and once in the summer or autumn. After the January visit in 1748 he has added 'sundry' – perhaps the visits were to be less frequent; in any case he was only just over a year from his own premature death. Strangely, because of an error in his notes or for some other reason, he indicates that he visited Thomas Titford on 12 January 1748, but Sarah Titford a week earlier, on the 5th.

We are looking here at a conscientious man with a sincere concern for the pastoral welfare of his people. In the end, his energy and dedication took their toll; when he died in June 1749 he was barely 40 years of age. He had come to a dispirited and failing church, but at his death, having received over forty souls by transfer from Starve Acre in 1741 and baptised about forty more himself, he left a healthy chapel of a hundred and sixteen. A Methodist's rather uncharitable back-handed compliment on the man was that:

> He was a good man and a faithful preacher, as far as the peculiarities of his creed would permit: but he was so straitened and fettered by high Calvinism as rarely to address *sinners* in his public ministrations.[34]

The charge, in short, was that, as a Particular Baptist, Brother Hurne was quite literally preaching to the converted. Perhaps so, but his flock must have been grateful for the soothing power of his ministry among them – a power which might quite well have saved the chapel from extinction.

A new man arrived: Abraham Larwill of Bampton in Devon was able to take over a growing and robust church in 1750. A fresh list of members was taken in June 1751, which included Thomas and Sarah Titford, and the new pastor soon set about baptising others – seventy in all, over the next ten years. One such in 1751 was Mary Titford, Thomas's daughter, who was to marry Stephen Humphries of Devizes in the following year; another, baptised on 11 January 1752, was a lady by the name of Rebekah Coles. She was soon to play a significant part in Thomas Titford's life, as we shall see shortly.

Larwill, like Thomas Hurne before him, was to prove a successful minister: nothing like the Roberts affair plagued the chapel during his term of office, though the need to discipline recalcitrants was never far beneath the surface:

> 1752: Sarah Starr cut off for a base child . . . 1753: Robert Phillips cut off for drunkenness and profaneness after sundry admonitions . . . 1754: Brother Hall and his wife withdrawn from on a report that they have from time to time bought goods which they knew were stolen.

Plenty of 'watching over' in evidence here – and nowhere more so, perhaps, than in the case of Elizabeth Turner:

> Elizabeth Turner cut off for criminal conversation with a married man which she acknowledged and apprehended herself with child by him. August 20th, 1755.

Here, shrouded in pompous euphemism, is the long arm of discipline still very much at work. Old habits die hard.

It was Abraham Larwill's achievement overall to consolidate the good work done by his predecessor; at his death in 1760 the total chapel membership stood at a hundred and twenty-two. He had been with them 10 years, and they were quick to express their grief at his parting, committing themselves to paper in the church minute book:

> Whereas Our Beloved Pastor The Revd Mr Abraham Larwill was removed from us by Death the 6 Day of Sepr. 1760 (on Saturday abt. one a clock in the Afternoon) We the Distressed flock thought it our Duty for Various Reasons to take a New List of the Members . . .

This new list of members includes Thomas and Sarah Titford, but also another member of the family by the name of Mary. Mary Titfords are never easy to place – there have been a good few of them over the years – but we seem here to be talking of Thomas's niece, daughter of his brother William, who had accompanied her parents to Kent in 1711 as a babe-in-arms. She hadn't been in Frome very long at this time – a mere three years, in fact. We first come across her in London in 1756, at which time she became a fully-baptised member of the Eagle Street Baptist Church, meeting in Red Lion Square, Holborn:

> 19th September, 1756. Mary Titford and Sarah Thomas witnessed a good confession and the Conversation of all ye aforesd. haveing been sufficiently attested agreed they be admitted after Baptism.

Mary was baptised along with six others on 26 September of that year by the renowed Dr. Andrew Gifford, of whom we have heard already; he was himself a Westcountryman. But Mary was not to stay long in the capital: Gifford's own church minute book for 4 August 1757 reads:

> A letter from Froom Selwood in Somersetshire desiring a Letter of Recommendation of our Sister Titford to a church of ye same faith & order – a Letter was drawn up & signed accordingly.[35]

Mary, then, was duly recommended by one Particular Baptist church to another, and Abraham Larwill of Badcox Lane entered the fact in his church book: 'Mary Titford. Rec. by letter from Dr Gifford's church in London. August 15th, 1757'.[36]

1757 was a bad year to be going anywhere, let alone taking to the road on a hundred-mile trip to Frome. Britain was embroiled in the Seven Years War, and the recent Militia

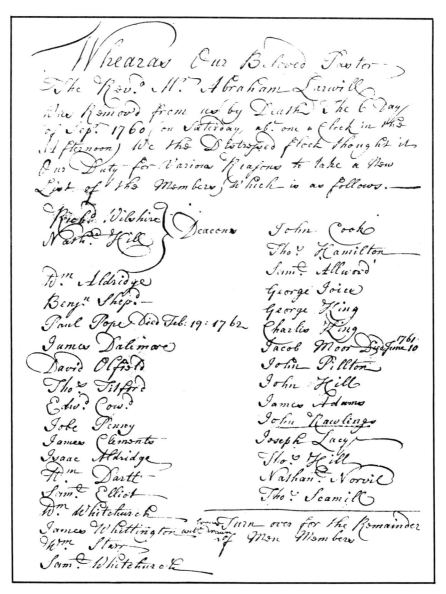

19. Minute Book, Badcox Lane Baptist Chapel, Frome, Somerset, 6 September 1760. The 'distressed flock' lament the passing of their pastor, Abraham Larwill. Members include Thomas Titford.

Act meant that any man chosen by lot would have to serve for three years or pay £10 for a substitute; widespread rioting occurred as a result. The unlucky lottery losers can hardly have been encouraged when, in March of that year, even so high-ranking a military luminary as Admiral Byng was shot on the quarter-deck of *H.M.S. Monarch* for alleged incompetence. And yet things were little better at home: wheat was to reach 55s. a quarter, and food riots broke out in Taunton, Exeter, Worcester and Frome itself in May. Colliers from Radstock had been the catalysts in the Frome uprising during April, and a shoot-out a month later resulted in five deaths.

Mary Titford, mercifully, had missed all that, arriving in the August. What would almost certainly have driven her on the road west out of London was the need to escape yet another threat rampant there that year: that of an epidemic of smallpox. She could hardly have taken refuge with her immediate family in Cranbrook, since the pestilence was raging there as well, with her brother Charles, as an overseer, soon to be out on the road visiting stricken settlements in the locality. So she appears to have set off to find shelter with her uncle Thomas. A fateful choice, as it turns out, because it was in Frome five years later that she found herself a husband, getting on in years as she was. She and Joseph Elliot, a shearman, went in for a Boxing Day wedding: 26 December 1762. It might perhaps have been a matter of some pride for Mary Titford that she could sign her name, albeit rather shakily, while her new husband was only able to make his cross.[37] One other literate person present, apart from the minister, was Uncle Thomas himself. Not only did he act as a witness, signing with his usual panache and style, but he also stayed on, just for good measure, and performed the same function for the next couple getting wed that day: William George and Hannah Pask.

Yet the occasion cannot have been one of unmitigated joy for Thomas: nine months earlier, on 8 March and barely a month after the couple's thirtieth wedding anniversary, his wife Sarah had passed away. As he sat there in his straight high-backed pew in chapel surveying the familiar scene, Thomas the widower would have found his eyes alighting more than once on a certain female member of the congregation: young Rebekah Coles. Well, he wasn't much of a catch: 74 years old, rather less well-off than he had once been, but a reliable sort of chap for all that, and not exactly destitute. So he'd give it a try – and it worked . . . Less than a year after Sarah's death he led his young bride up the aisle – his third wife, and the one who was to outlive him. Both could sign their names, though Thomas – perhaps more from excitement than incompetence – managed to leave a prominent ink-blot on the marriage register; Peter Mayson, the officiating curate and master of Frome Grammar School, probably went home mumbling something about a rabid Dissenter who couldn't even handle a nib . . .[38]

The marriage was on 7 February 1763; just over two months later the Rev. John Kingdon, having been at Badcox Lane Chapel since the previous November, was officially ordained as its pastor. He was 31 years old, and would minister to his flock – initially almost twice as many women as men, and numbering 143 in total – until his death in 1806. He was to bury many members of the Titford family in his time.

The new minister began a new church book, kept carefully and thoroughly all the years he held office. Further information about Badcox during his pastorate is furnished by a framed drawing now in the possession of the Bristol Baptist College. It shows what it describes as 'John Kingdon's Meeting House', a rather plain but serviceable building, later to be enlarged in the early years of the 19th century; added beneath is a sketch of its ground floor plan.

Nine years after John Kingdon's arrival, the story of one generation of Titfords was beginning to draw to a close. Thomas Titford, a grand old man of 82, died on 15 March 1771. He was buried two days later at the chapel's burial ground in Wayland's Close behind Catherine Hill, having survived his brother William the Emigrant by almost a quarter of a century.[39] William himself had been a leading light in General Baptist circles in the Kent area from at least as early as 1740 until his death. But our old friends the Particular Baptists had one more sting left in the tail for the Titfords of Frome. On 8 July

1774, just over three years after her husband's death, Thomas's widow Rebekah felt the full force of the chapel's wrath, and suffered that terrible fate: 'withdrawn from':

> At our Church Meeting this evening agreed to withdraw our communion from Eliz. Titford, formaly Coles, she being charged with dishonesty intemperance and falsehood.[40]

And on such a sour note ends the story of the long-lived Thomas Titford and his wives at Badcox Lane. Rebekah must have achieved at least a degree of reconciliation with her fellows, for it was at the chapel burial ground that she was eventually laid to rest; dying on 27 April 1776, she was buried on the 29th, described as 'Becky Titford'. In the grave, quietness; all charges of dishonesty, intemperance and falsehood far behind her. There we leave her in peace.

Not for the first time, we bid farewell to one generation and usher in the new; a simple enough process, in theory, but one which will prove to be more than usually difficult this time round, as we shall see. It would make sense on this occasion to begin with a young girl, leaving the males for a brief spell. All the evidence we have would point to the fact that, for all his advanced years at his marriage to Rebekah, Thomas the Calvinist nevertheless managed to father a child shortly after the wedding: Hephzibah, alias 'Hippy'. Her mother's death, of course, left her an orphan in 1776 – an unenviable postion to be in, to put it mildly. The following year the overseers were recognising her need, and were paying out 6s. per month for 'Titford's family'. But it was not their way to let such children fall into permanent pauperdom – that would be too high a charge on the rates; thus it is that payments ceased on 7 July 1778 with the annotation: 'Put App. to Thomas Millard'. So Hippy would serve a term of apprenticeship with the said Thomas Millard (or Miller), theoretically learning a trade and standing a chance thereafter of supporting herself. As for her master, the overseers might pay him a premium for his trouble, but were under no obligation to give him any choice as to which parish apprentices he would accept or reject.

Hippy, at fifteen, was fairly old to be apprenticed, though it seems unlikely that she would have been expected to learn a highly-skilled trade. Thomas, her new master, lived in a house in The Mint owned by a Mr. Cooper, where he worked as a shearman – that is, once the superfluous nap on cloth had been raised by being 'rowed' or brushed with teazels, he would chop it off using huge shears. A skilled and a heavy job, to be sure, and hardly one to be carried out by a young girl like Hippy; her role, then, might have been that of fetching the water which would be sprinkled on the cloth, or even work of a more general domestic nature around Mr. Millard's establishment. What was spoken of as the 'apprenticeship' of pauper children was often little more than a fiction for disposing of them in any way possible: many a child apprenticed to husbandry or housewifery would have been used as nothing far short of slave labour, in effect. Frequently a young female's entire working day would be spent serving her master, with no pay.

And yet things might have been worse for Hippy; at least she remained in town, working within a trade which involved minimal physical danger, rather than being sent far afield to rob her of her settlement in Frome. Not all local children were so lucky: in 1788 poor little John Woolly was apprenticed by the overseers, with the connivance of his mother, to serve a Bath 'chimney sweeper' by the name of Cray.[41] Better to be in the shearing shop in Frome than up some labyrinthine sooty chimney in the home of some fashionable Bath gentleman.

Not only that, but Hippy was a Titford, we must remember, and would have wanted to turn her situation to her own advantage. What better way to alleviate the boredom of the job than to court her master? She had to wait almost exactly ten years to win him as her husband, but she got there in the end. She was 26 by then, as one-time apprentice stood beside one-time master at the altar of St John's on 25 August 1788.

Various daughters of the union followed, all baptized at the Zion Chapel – Sarah, Ann,

Elizabeth and Mary – until poor Hephzibah, a wife of only eight years' standing, died.[42] She was laid to rest in the graveyard on Catherine Hill, sharing the same plot as her mother and father, together with her grandfather, Joseph Coles, who had been buried as a 99-year old pauper four years earlier. There, too, lay her little cousin Nancy Titford and sister-in-law Elizabeth. James Whiting, the sexton, duly entered the burial in his book: 'Hippy Millard. Bur. Nov. 13 1798. Grave no. 108'. She was aged only thirty-three. Thomas Millard himself remarried in April of the following year, his new wife being Mary Carr, and lived on until 1823, when he died, aged 66, in the workhouse.

Hippy, it appears, had been the only child of the union of Thomas Titford and Rebekah Coles, and one born so late in her father's life that she was almost contemporary with the next generation below her – the children of her half-brothers and half-sisters. But who were these half-brothers and half-sisters? Thomas himself may be smiling at us wryly even now, more than a little amused at the genealogical problems he has set us. It is the male line – the descent of the surname – which interests us principally. Even Thomas's first marriage of 1715 to Elisabeth Franklin provides us with unresolved problems: two sons followed, William and then Thomas, both of whom appear to have died young. And 'appear to have', unscholarly as it sounds, is the best we can do, given our present state of knowledge.

Elisabeth died, as we have seen, leaving Thomas free to marry Sarah Lacey in 1732/3; she was 22 at that time, more than twenty years her husband's junior. Their married life was to span 30 years : can it really have produced no children? Were we to rely solely upon the parish registers for Frome, we would believe just that; there were no Titford baptisms at St John's church from 1718 to 1763, no burials between 1733 and 1798 – almost as if the family had vanished from the face of the earth.

Vanished, no; gone underground as far as the Anglican Church was concerned, yes. That forces us, willy-nilly, to rely upon other documentary evidence in an attempt to create a credible pedigree. Not an easy task, as it happens: our one potentially informative will, of 1717 (that of William the Wiredrawer), went up in flames in a 1940s bombing raid, and no amount of diligent searching has unearthed significant manorial records for the principal manor of Frome for the relevant period.[43]

What other option then, if the attempt is not to be abandoned, but to turn to what should be fairly peripheral material – that which puts flesh on the bones, as it were – to help us create those very bones themselves? Thus it is that quite heavy reliance has been placed upon sources in which Frome is particularly rich: churchwardens' and overseers' accounts; leases; rentals; commercial directories; diaries; and, above all, chapel minute books and burial records.

The result has been the creation of a likely pedigree, but not a legally-provable one. Scholars would say – and ultimately, in a sense, they are right – that there is no such thing as a 'gap' in a family line; you keep researching backwards until you hit a brick wall, and there you stop. The brick wall we have hit here is an entire generation of men and women for whom no baptismal or birth records exist at all – and we can almost certainly see the family's Baptist affiliations as being responsible for that. These people were living, after all, according to their own lights, not with one eye on posterity.

The 'missing generation' are all very much in evidence once they have reached adulthood; it is their baptisms, and through that, their parentage, which eludes us. Who were they? If we focus upon the male line, there are four contemporaries – William, Thomas, Charles and John – all born between *circa* 1737 and *circa* 1751. They appear to have been brothers – and henceforward, for our story's sake, we will refer to them as such.

Who was their father? No existing records from Frome in the first half of the 18th century give us any reason to suppose that there was any other adult male Titford in town other than Thomas the Calvinist.[44] Heart in mouth, and lacking that final and incontrovertible proof which all family historians seek, we would propose Thomas and Sarah (*née* Lacey) as the parents of our four men.

The problems do not go away entirely: Thomas would have been 62 when the youngest of his sons was born, and his wife 40 – unusual, perhaps, but by no means unheard of. What does tend to corroborate the hypothesis, however, are the names, trades and places of abode of the putative sons themselves. William, Thomas and John – these are all very much Titford names, even if Charles is not; significantly, too, three of the brothers were cardmakers like Thomas himself and his brother William the Emigrant.

Not only that, but we can pick up clues by following the occupiers of properties in the town once leased by earlier Titfords. Thomas the Calvinist's house on High Street – possibly the very place where the four boys were born – was occupied by the eldest of them, William, in 1800 if not long before, leaving one of the original Coward's Batch houses – that taken over by Stephen Humphries after Thomas senior's move to High Street – to be lived in by Thomas, junior, from at least as early as 1785.

One piece of evidence remains – and an intriguing one, at that. Charles, one of the four brothers of whom we have spoken, was to have an eldest son, William Charles. This young man left Frome in the 1790s to join the descendants of William the Emigrant, who had by then moved away from Kent and settled in the City of London. There William Charles was to befriend a certain William Jowett Titford, great-grandson of the emigrant William himself. William Jowett was not only a great letter-writer – he also kept copies of most of his correspondence, copies which have survived to the present day. Writing to his mother in 1802, William Jowett talks of '. . . the father of our relation William Charles Titford', giving news of the older man's recent death. The reference to 'our relation' establishes at a stroke the fact that there is a connexion between the two branches of the family; that William Charles must have been descended from Thomas the Calvinist, just a surely as William Jowett himself was descended from that Thomas's brother, William the Emigrant.[45]

Such a connexion thus being established by a chance remark in a letter, if not by a complete set of parish register entries, we should be able to proceed with at least some degree of confidence. Let the four putative brothers of the 'missing generation' become brothers in fact, as far as our narrative is concerned – the surname is a rare one, the overall picture is clear in general outline, and our desire for definitive answers can temporarily give way to the challenge of living with a credible working hypothesis. The stage has been cleared ready for a new scene; enter William, the eldest brother.

CHAPTER 12

William the Cardmaker (c.1738-1801)

Frome and Lullington, Somerset

COLD CHARITY

Am I not Christopher Sly, old Sly's son of Burton Heath; by birth a pedlar, by education
a *card-maker* . . . by present profession a tinker?

Shakespeare: The Taming of the Shrew

William Titford, born in 1738-9, was a cardmaker, and a literate one, like his father; at his
marriage in 1762 to a young lady by the name of Euodias Stark, he signed his name, leaving
her to make her little cross. The name 'Euodias' itself was to prove a bit of a challenge
even to the literate: an unusual appellation at the best of times – a variation on 'Yved' – it
gave constant trouble to the parish clerk in Frome, who seemed to prefer the alternative
'Evadia'; on one occasion he even began writing the name in his register and gave up in
despair half-way through.

The occasion of her marriage was not the first time Euodias had been to Frome; nearly
twenty years earlier she had tried to put down roots in the town with a signal lack of success.
Born in the little village of Lullington, she was baptised there at the exquisite Norman font
in the parish church on 26 February 1737/8, daughter of Benjamin Stark and his wife Mary.
The mother died very shortly afterwards, leaving Benjamin with Euodias and her elder
sister, Jane, to raise as best he may. In the event, he made two decisions: he would marry
again – which he did, to a lady called Elizabeth – and he would leave the picturesque but
increasingly decrepit little village nestling against the northern edge of Orchardleigh Park,
seeking a better life in nearby Frome.

It was precisely such optimists as poor Benjamin Stark who were hit hardest by the
Settlement Act of 1697, still very much in use in the 1740s; William Titford the Emigrant,
we may remember, had needed settlement certificates in order to satisfy the overseers of the
poor of Hawkhurst and then Cranbrook that he would be looked after by his original parish
of Frome if ever he became destitute.

But a certificate of that sort was precisely what Benjamin Stark did not have; nothing
daunted, he crossed the parish boundary into Frome, taking his new wife and two little
daughters along with him. Given the way in which the settlement laws of England operated
at the period, it would have been less of a problem to cross the Pennines than to travel that
short distance into foreign parochial territory as he had just done. Overseers could smell
out a potential pauper a few miles away, let alone a family of four, it being their responsibility
'. . . to keep an extraordinary look-out to prevent persons coming to inhabit without
certificates, and to fly to the justices to remove them'.[1] They pounced on the Starks with all
speed – not because they were yet chargeable to Frome rates as paupers, but because they
were 'likely to become chargeable'. Only later – in 1795 – was the law changed to allow
intruders to remain wherever they had chosen to live until they actually became a burden
on the rates; here, in 1744, anyone without a certificate was subject to the indignity of being
escorted, not to say carried bodily, out of the parish by the overworked constable. The
Starks had to go.[2]

The bureaucracy was set in motion: Lord Weymouth, who would sign a settlement

County of }
Somerset } **to wit.**

To the Church-Wardens and Overseers of the Poor of the parish of _Frome selwood_ in the said County of _Somerset_ to execute and convey.

And to the Church-Wardens and Overseers of the Poor of the parish of _Lullington in the same county_ to Receive and Obey.

FOrafmuch as Complaint hath been made unto Us, whofe Hands and Seals are hereunto fubfcribed and fet, Two of his Majefty's Juftices of the Peace, of and for the said County of _Somerset_ (whereof one is of the Quorum) by you the Church-Wardens and Overfeers of the Poor of the said _parish_ of _Frome selwood_ — in the said County of _Somerset_ That _Benjamin Stark Elizabeth his wife Jane aged about ten years and three quarters, woodiah aged about six years his children by a former wife_

lately came and intruded into the said Parish of _Frome selwood_ — endeavouring there to fettle as Inhabitants thereof, contrary to Law, not having any Way Acquired or Obtained any Legal Settlement therein, and is _likely to_ — become chargeable thereunto: We do, upon due Examination, adjudge the said Complaint and Premifes to be true. And we do farther upon the Examination of _the said Benjamin Stark_

taken upon _his_ — Oath, adjudge, That the said _Benjamin Stark Elizabeth his wife Jane and woodiah his children were_ — laft Legally fettled, in the said _parish_ of _Lullington_ in the County — of _Somerset_ aforesaid.

THESE are therefore, in his Majefty's Name, to Require, Order, and Command you, the said Church-Wardens, and Overfeers of the Poor of the said _parish_ of _Frome selwood_ — or fome or one of you, forthwith to remove and Convey the said _Benjamin Stark Elizabeth his wife Jane and woodiah his children_ —

from the said _parish_ of _Frome selwood_ unto the _parish_ of _Lullington_ aforesaid, and _there_ — to deliver to the Church-Wardens and Overfeers of the Poor there, or to fome or one of them, (together with this Order or Duplicate, or true Copy hereof) who is, and are hereby required to Receive and Provide for _them_ — as the Law directs. And hereof you are not to fail, Given under our Hands and Seals the _twelfth_ — Day of _June_ — in the _18th_ — Year of the Reign of our Sovereign Lord _George the 2_ King of Great-Britain, &c. and in the Year of our Lord, One Thoufand Seven Hundred and Forty _four_

Weymouth

Hatway

20. Removal order, 12 June 1744. The Stark family are to be removed from Frome to Lullington.

certificate for William Titford of Kent a year later, was called upon to put his name to an official removal order. The churchwardens and overseers of the poor of the parish of Frome and the churchwardens and overseers of the parish of Lullington were informed that:

> Benjamin Stark, Elizabeth his wife, Jane aged about Ten Years and three quarters, Evodiah aged about Six Years his Children by a former wife . . . [were in Frome] . . . endeavouring there to settle as Inhabitants thereof, contrary to Law, not Having any Way Acquired or Obtained any Legal Settlement therein . . .[3]

The whole family had to be moved and conveyed back whence they had come; how dare they wander around the countryside without permission? How glad Euodias must have been, then, in 1762, to achieve an official settlement in Frome by marrying a parishioner, William Titford. Now no-one could evict her!

His new wife had brought slightly more to William than abject poverty as a dowry, nevertheless: her grandfather, another Benjamin Stark, had been a clothworker, and we find her, as his administratrix, involved in a transaction of 24 June 1789 whereby she and her husband William assigned a moiety of the middle part of a messuage called 'Stokes' in Lullington to George French of Frome, clothworker. Grandfather Stark, who died intestate, had himself bought the property in question in 1706 from a certain John Vigor of Hemington, yeoman; it had cost him £18.[4]

So William and Euodias were not penniless, at least up to 1789; poverty would take its time to get them in its clutches. Other problems than financial ones were to beset the newly-married couple, however; as the years went by, five of their children – Benjamin, William, Lucy and two others – were to die in infancy. Three had been baptised at St John's (two of them late baptisms), since William, like his brothers Thomas and Charles, was never quite sure how he stood in relation to the Established Church, and seemed not to want to take any chances. One of the infant children they lost died in May of 1771; by all accounts the winter and spring of that year had been brutally cold. On 16 January Parson James Woodforde, then at the Somerset village of Ansford, wrote in his diary:

> Extreme hard frost with a cutting wind. It was allowed by my Father and Aunt Anne this afternoon that the weather now is as severe as it was in the year 1740 . . .[5]

Things grew worse rather than better; as late as 11 April Woodforde notes: '. . . never such weather known by any person living at present'.[6]

The extremes of cold had already carried off Thomas Titford the Calvinist on 15 March: William's child was buried at Badcox Lane on 14 May, and Woodforde's own father, severely affected by the appalling conditions, died just two days later. Brutal times, indeed. The only other surviving child of William and Euodias was Sarah, baptised in 1763. She had been an eight-month baby herself, and when she married Joseph Starr in May 1785 it was to be only seven months before their first child, Mary, was baptised at St John's. Others followed, though by the time young George was baptised in 1793, they were at Rook Lane Meeting House. Many worshippers seem to have switched affiliations from chapel to chapel or from church to chapel almost as the whim of the moment took them, just as Joseph and Sarah did here.

Not all the Starrs' children survived, and we read in the Catherine Hill Burial Register of 'Willm. Titfords 1st and 2d grandc buryd May 6th 1790'. Soon to follow his own children into grave no. 80 was Joseph Starr himself; described rather disparagingly as 'Joseph Starr, Titfords son in law' (perhaps William paid for the burial?), he was laid to rest on 10 May 1796, only a few months before our old friend Hippy Millard.

The loss of loved ones was to be only one of William's problems: exactly 100 years after his ancestor, William the Wiredrawer, had improved his fortunes and acquired his eight houses in Fountain Lane, William the Cardmaker found himself on parish relief of 2s. a fortnight, starting on 27 September 1793. It was a doubtful privilege which he was to enjoy until his death. Wiredrawing had brought the family a degree of wealth in the past, and cardmaking had seemed a safe enough trade in the early and middle years of the 18th century. But as that century drew to a close, here was William, soon to be followed into pauperdom by his two cardmaker brothers, on the parish on and off until his weary body gave up the struggle. Only brother Charles, who was a shopkeeper and could raise his prices as his costs rose, managed to avoid the poverty trap – and even then, only just.[7]

There is no shortage of possible explanations as to why William Titford should have ended up in the parochial dole queue in the September of 1793. Harvests had been bad the year before, and 1793 itself was to be a year of international crisis: France declared war on Holland and Britain at the beginning of February, and news from across the channel – that Louis XVI had been guillotined, Marat murdered and the Reign of Terror was well underway – must have sent a frisson of horror down many an English spine.

At home, the closing decades of the century were cruel ones for all wage-dependent people as a '. . . vast flood of pauperism was beginning to engulf almost the whole of the labouring classes'.[8] Some artisans could just keep their heads above water, possibly by resorting to the dual occupations so much favoured by many of their 16th- and 17th- century forbears; Frome's James Trotman, for example, a cardmaker like William Titford, spread his risks by taking up a little side-line as a dealer in earthenware. For those not so enterprising or so lucky, accepting the parish dole was frequently the only alternative.

By 1781-2 and the passing of Gilbert's Act, it was becoming increasingly clear that the workhouses could never accommodate the sheer numbers of new paupers being created day by day; the new act entitled able-bodied men to parish relief for the first time – if only in augmentation of existing bread-line wages. The cash pension was thereafter to become the universal remedy to combat widespread poverty, as a statute of 1796 widened the scope of the Gilbert provision and overseers were allowed to order outdoor relief without applying the workhouse test. Not only that but, mercifully, paupers' badges need no longer be worn publicly, '. . . upon proof of very decent and orderly behaviour'.[9] When Sir Frederic Norton Eden visited Frome in the middle 1790s, he noted that the new legislation was being complied with:

> The poor are chiefly maintained at home, where it is thought they can be relieved at less expense to the parish than if they were sent to the workhouse.[10]

If Eden is right here, it does give an interesting slant to the problem, of course; in his view outdoor relief had replaced admission to the workhouse from motives of parish parsimony, not humanity . . .

So William Titford's situation as a parish-subsidised pauper must be seen against a fairly desperate local and national back-drop. Other personal factors may also have come into play: he may have been sick or injured – though the overseers would probably have noted the fact in their accounts; he may have been ready for what we should today think of as an old-age pension – it was nothing unusual for a man to 'retire' when he reached fifty, prematurely aged by a strenuous life, a limited diet and poor medical care. William, in the event, was aged 54, certainly approaching the end of his active working life. Yet if we look closely enough, we can find what may prove to be the most likely explanation for his enforced redundancy. In 1794 an ominous advertisement appeared in the *Salisbury Journal*: Rawlings, the firm of Frome cardmakers, were pleased to announce that they had now installed a card-making machine. There was still a host of cardmakers in the town at the end of the century, but very many fewer than there had been in the good old days of the early 1700s. At a time of slow but steady decline in the industry, and just as machines were being brought in to do the job, William may well have found, in his middle fifties, that his services were no longer required. All of that makes him, if true, an early victim of the march of technology which would eventually spell the final demise of clothmaking in the town during the next century, as Yorkshire with its modern methods cornered the market.

How William survived on a mere pittance of 2s. per fortnight we can only guess at: did he receive any further payment in kind, was there access to subsidised food, could his family and friends help out in any way?[11]

Five years later, in the May of 1798, William's wife Euodias joined her husband on the list of paupers; she was not to be there long. Her 1s. per fortnight benefit, a supplement to the 3s. he was by then receiving, stopped abruptly in mid-summer; the Catherine Hill sexton had another job to perform – 'Willm Titfords wife' was buried on 16 August, no longer a burden on the ratepayers. The overseers promptly reduced William's fortnightly benefit to 2s. 6d. on 21 August – no point in paying a man for a dependant he no longer had . . .

We might spare a thought for William Titford here in the summer of 1798; his plight was obviously not untypical, but hard enough for all that. Aged 60, a widower; five children dead in infancy, one daughter widowed; he himself trying to keep body and soul together on a mere half-a-crown a fortnight, his brothers nearly as poor as he, and prices rising month by month. His own end – mercifully, we may say – was not to be long delayed. By 1800 he was living in a house on the west side of High Street, owned by John Imber, a woolstapler – very probably that same house Thomas the Calvinist had built the year before William was born. Quite a short street, then as now, it consisted mainly of houses or houses and gardens, except for Thomas Imber's workshops on the same side as William.

Here William continued to receive poor relief; various amounts of 1s. 3d., 2s. and even 4s. were paid, according to need or the overseers' moods. By 1800 the end was already near, as payments became stablished at 2s. per week until 27 October 1801. Then, perfunctorily, 'Dead'.

It cost the parish 11s. 6d. to bury poor William; he was the first of the four brothers to go, and no doubt they mourned him, though Charles, at least, was already ill and very near his own death at the time, and Thomas was to live only two years longer. Perhaps the greatest indignity for William was that even in the grave there was no rest; nearly six years later, in the July of 1807, he and one other body were dug up to make room for a younger, 22-year old corpse, that of William's granddaughter, Mary Starr. What price the Age of Enlightenment?

CHAPTER 13

Thomas the Cardmaker (c.1740-1803)

Frome, Somerset

LEAN TIMES

We must not expend every last drop of sympathy on William Titford the cardmaker, for there are others who need some too; William's brother Thomas was one. Married to a sickly wife, then having to cope as a widower with a daughter who suffered fits frequently, finding work difficult to obtain, Thomas Titford must have felt he had enough crosses to bear for one lifetime.

His wife was Elizabeth Adlam, whom he had married in 1765; baptised in 1737, daughter of William and Ann, she came from a fairly prolific Frome family. Thomas and Elizabeth lost their first child five months after the marriage; the next, Nancy or Nany, was buried at Catherine Hill on 16 December 1773, the day of the Boston Tea Party. She was barely seven years old. One more child had died in 1768, shortly to be followed by the births of daughters Elizabeth and Mary. There were to be no male heirs for Thomas – indeed, he was to father only one robust child who would survive into old age, as we shall see shortly.

The delicacy of the children seems to have been passed on to them by their mother, and in any case a succession of pregnancies had very probably weakened her own constitution severely. As early as 1777 she was on parish relief of 1s. per fortnight, augmented 'during winter' by a further 6d. – for fuel, presumably. Increasingly it becomes clear that her plight was the result of her poor health; in addition to the regular help she was receiving, the overseers had the generosity to pay her various *ad hoc* amounts as the need arose, 'On acct. being sick'.

There was at least something to be said, after all, for a poor-relief system which was adaptable to suit personal need as it arose; for all the parsimony of parish overseers, careful guardians of the ratepayers' monies as they were, they were dealing with paupers whom they knew as people. Eventually the Frome overseers decided, and annotated it accordingly, that Betty Titford was a 'sickly woman'; and so she remained until her death. The poor book entry for 1783 helpfully gives us her age as 48, and she is variously described as living at 'Coniger', 'Cowards Batch' and 'Nail Street' – all within the Trinity area.

The family may well have moved around from street to street, but by 1785 they were settled in Fountain Lane, that most familiar of Titford haunts.[1] Thomas, as a cardmaker, was by no means the only person down the lane in that year who depended upon the wool trade for his livelihood: we find several shearmen, a scribbler, a weaver and a wiredrawer, with the added variety of a butcher and a baker, a tailor and a miller, John Moon at the *Lamb and Fountain Inn*, and a lady charmingly described as a 'widow bewitched'.[2]

Meanwhile, Betty Titford was clearly getting no better as years went by, and she must have had friends who realised only too well that 1s. a fortnight could hardly supply even her most fundamental needs. So, whether the overseers were aware of it or not, the members of Sheppards Barton Baptist Chapel set about helping their ailing sister with a bit of cash support of their own. They started off with a lump sum of 5s. in the January of 1778, followed by a similar amount a year later, and 10s. for each of the next two Christmases. They, too, listed her as 'sick', and it wasn't long before they were eking out her parish relief

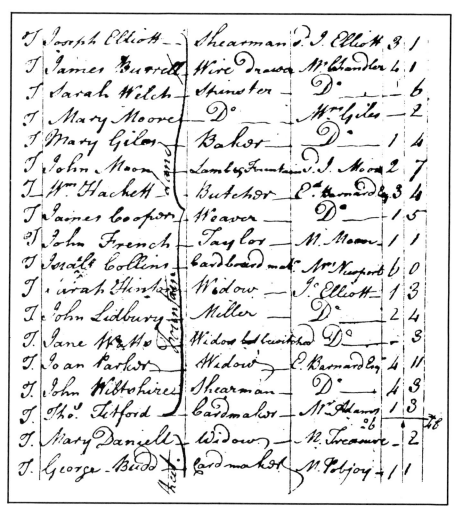

21. Census of 1785, Frome, Somerset. From a copy probably made by John Battle in 1789. Thomas Titford, cardmaker, is occupying a house on Fountain Lane owned by Mrs. Adams. The house is said to have one male and three females living within it.

22. Overseers' accounts, Frome, Somerset. Paupers receiving benefit, 1801-02. Mary Titford, a sufferer from 'Fitts' is receiving a helping hand, as is her father Thomas, who has 'no work'. (SRO DD/LW.)

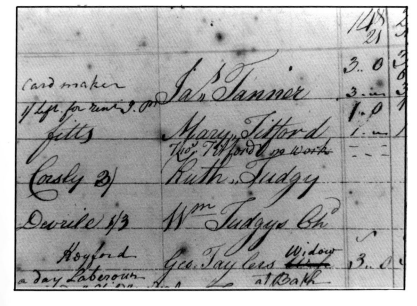

with a regular 1s. a month, starting in the March of 1783. What the chapel and the parish managed to ensure, in the last analysis, was that Betty's last few years were less harrowing than they might otherwise have been. With the usual lack of euphemism, the overseers enter the rubric 'Dead' against her name at the beginning of 1786; their accounts for 10 January indicate that it had cost them the grand sum of 3s. 9d. to bury three paupers: 'West Wife; Titford and Robbans'. Betty left this world with a one-and-threepenny funeral, supplemented only by the generosity of the chapel which had stood by her in time of need: 'Pd. for Betty Titford's grave: 3/6d'.[3]

She was buried on New Year's Day, 1786, at Catherine Hill; six years later, predictably, up came her remains to accommodate Joseph Coles, aged 99; and up he came, finally, in November 1796, to allow some space for Hippy Millard. The extended family were all moving over to make room for each other once this fleeting life had passed.

We should pause, as we did for his brother William, to contemplate Thomas Titford's state in 1786: a widower, with one 17-year old daughter who seemed healthy enough, one who was to be constantly gripped by fits, and at least three children previously dead in infancy. He struggled on, as he had to. Payments to him for his sick daughter Mary are included first in what are known as 'Church Extras', then in the main list of relief to paupers. The handouts are intermittent; the amounts vary, as does the regularity of payment. Sometimes we read of 'Thomas Titford'; sometimes 'Thomas Titford's child: subject to fitts' or 'fitts continually'; sometimes 'Thomas' is crossed out, and 'Mary' inserted instead.[4]

In 1800 Thomas was still living in the house on the north-west side of Fountain Lane, then owned by Mrs. Hellier. In the next year, one in which bad harvests had pushed up the price of wheat to 119s. 6d. a quarter, the overseers not only paid 1s. per week to Mary, but also found a further 2s. per week for Thomas himself from 26 May until 30 June on account of him having 'No work'.[5] Supplementary to Mary's allowance was '1s. for rent: J. Pobjoy'.

Two years later, having outlived brothers William and Charles, Thomas died. Immediately after his burial on 13 November 1803, poor Mary's benefit was doubled to 4s. a fortnight. Even that proved not enough to save her; less than a year after her father's passing, she finally succumbed to the illness which had beset her for so long, and was laid to rest at St John's.

Sister Elizabeth, then in her early thirties, was the only survivor of Thomas the Cardmaker's family, having outlived her parents and all her siblings. She was still in Frome, we may hope; if she had nursed her younger sister and helped her father through his years of loss, she had done well indeed. Now there were few options open to her; rather on the old side to be sure of getting married, she decided to do what most of those who wanted to survive usually did: she left Frome.

She was destined to remain a spinster, finding work as a domestic servant in – of all places – far-away Surrey. As if to make up for the early deaths of her sisters, she lived to a ripe old age, dying in the Almshouses at Dorking on 4 November 1855, aged eighty-seven. Her will included legacies of twenty pounds each to her Frome cousins, Mary and Sarah, the daughters of her uncle John Titford; she was not to know that Mary would die just two months before she did, though Sarah, as we shall see, survived for another five years, long enough to bless the generosity of her Surrey cousin.

We, too, should be grateful to Elizabeth; not only did she have the foresight to bequeath a will for posterity to read, she also had the good taste – so rare in the family, alas – to be buried beneath a headstone which would retain its legibility over the years. She lies in the churchyard in the village of Wootton, near Dorking: 'Elizabeth Titford. Died Nov 4th, 1855. Aged 87'.

CHAPTER 14

Charles the Cheesemonger (c.1749-1802)

Frome, Somerset

SCRAPING A LIVING: THE FRENCH THREAT

A nation of *cheesemongers*!
Louis XIV's description of the Dutch

'Charles the Cheesemonger' now moves to the centre of our stage; a very significant actor in the little drama, too, since he, and he alone of his generation of the Titford family in Frome, was to father sons who would in their turn pass the name down through the 19th into the 20th century.

Neither Charles nor his bride, Elizabeth Carpenter, could sign their own names when they married at St John's on 9 July 1770 – or rather, neither would admit to being able to do so. So they made their bold little crosses in the register and set off on their adventure.[1]

A marriage of Baptists believers, this: Charles, unlike his brother John, was never a full member of Badcox Lane Chapel, and he was even to play safe by having his children christened at the parish church; but it was to the Baptists he turned whenever there was a death in the family, and eventually he and his wife would find a last resting place in the chapel burial ground on Catherine Hill. The Carpenter family were themselves stalwarts of the said chapel, and Charles's bride is probably the Elizabeth Carpenter who was baptised there on 2 April 1760, then aged between 11 and 12 years old. Although various records of their activities exist in Frome itself, many of the Carpenter family lived in the nearby parish of Rodden. A certain George Carpenter was even hanged at Warminster in 1812 for the murder of a farmer called William Webb of Roddenbury Hill – but for the most part the Carpenters, like the Titfords, seem to have been law-abiding, not to say staid, folk. One thing that marks the Carpenters out is their uncanny fondness for incorporating the names of distaff families into their own; from the early days of the 18th century we can spot the Frome and Rodden Carpenters by their use of the name 'Thynn' as a first or second Christian name for boys, and even in the middle years of the 19th century a branch of the family in London called one son Starmer Thynne Carpenter. It would be tempting to assume that we have evidence here of some direct relationship with the Thynne family, Marquesses of Bath, at nearby Longleat; that may be the case, but an equally likely explanation could be that the family was involved in nothing more than a slightly sycophantic attempt to ingratiate itself in some way with the local aristocracy.

Back to the Titford/Carpenter marriage, then. Charles, the bridegroom, was in some ways set apart from his three brothers; for a start he appears to have been illiterate, whereas they were not, and also he was the only one who was not a cardmaker – or if he had learned the trade, he chose not to practise it. That was a wise decision in the event, for judging by the poverty of William, Thomas and even John, cardmakers were about to hit bad times. Charles was essentially a shopkeeper and pig butcher; he turned his waste animal fats into tallow candles – a foul-smelling process at best – to sell to those who chose not to make their own, and also kept up a bit of a sideline in cheese – a product for which the area was, of course, justifiably famous. Nothing very dramatic here, then, but at least he was in the buying and selling game, not a wage slave, and there can hardly have been a time when it was not easier to sell the odd pork chop or two than it was to convince an employer that he ought to buy your skills as a craftsman. The craftsmen in the family went to the wall: Charles just put up his prices and carried on.[2]

Elizabeth was pregnant very shortly after their marriage; a harrowing pregnancy, too, we may be sure, as that merciless winter and spring of 1770/1 set in. The child was born to what must have been exhausted parents, strained to their physical and mental limits, and it never lived to see another year; in the December of 1771 the nameless infant was buried on Catherine Hill – the first occupant of plot number 119, but certainly not the last.

A son followed in 1772; what should he be called? An examination of the naming patterns used by the Titfords of Frome would suggest at a cursory glance that every eldest son was named after his paternal grandfather, as a matter of course. In the event, perhaps there was a slightly different factor at work. It had been the custom from early times to name children after their godparents; precisely because the paternal grandfather was an obvious choice to fulfil such an office for the eldest-born son, the impression we often receive – wrongly, perhaps – is that a specific Christian name was perpetuated just because it was that borne by the male-line grandparent. But suppose the paternal grandfather were dead when the eldest grandson was born? This was precisely the situation in which Charles and Elizabeth found themselves in 1772; and we may surmise that they did what brother John was to do later – in the absence of Thomas the Calvinist, who had died just over a year previously, they honoured Charles's elder brother William by making him the godfather and giving the child his Christian name.[3]

So far so good, it seems; but what with brother William Titford and *his* son William, there was every chance that individuals with the same name might soon be confused with each other, leaving a whole host of Williams, Wills and Bills to confound the assembled company at every family gathering.

Charles and Elizabeth seem to have come up with an intelligent expedient: they would give the boy two Christian names – the first Frome Titford ever to enjoy this luxury – and he could be called 'William Charles' after his uncle/godfather and father respectively, though they would actually use the name 'Charles' in everyday conversation. Little wonder, as things turned out, that in adult life poor 'W. C. T.', as his cousin William Jowett Titford called him, found it very difficult to convince bureaucrats that he was really called 'William', though everyone knew him as 'Charles', like his father. Various documents later describe him as 'Charles Titford', with the 'William' entered later as an afterthought, or they settle for calling him 'Charles William Titford' instead.[4]

When W. C. T. was two years old his mother gave birth to his brother John; the pair of them were baptised together at the parish church on 21 January 1775. From then on, every two years or so, they were to acquire more brothers and sisters: Elizabeth; Mary, who died the year after her birth; then Sarah or Susanna, baptised along with a new Mary in 1784. All attempts by the parents to have a Lydia or a Charles would be doomed to failure: one Lydia just lived to see her first birthday – the first two years of life seeming to be the most dangerous by far for the poor little infants – and the next passed away at the age of three, baptised at St John's but buried by the Baptists of Badcox Lane. Similar fates were to befall those children called Charles: Charles Thynne Titford (the influence of the Carpenter family at work here in the choice of a second Christian name) survived for a mere 11 months, and a further Charles was dead and buried within three weeks of his birth.

Poor Mary, Charles's daughter who was buried at Catherine Hill in 1779, was to share a similar fate with many Titfords of the period – a fate we have seen before. The stolid sexton, James Whiting, had to find a bit more space in her grave to accommodate a certain Mary Humphries; we know her – she is Thomas the Calvinist's daughter Mary, *née* Titford,

Wm. C. Titford	Born September	8th	1772
John. Titford	" October	26th	1774
Elizabeth. Titford	" September	19th	1776
C Mary. Titford	" April	11	1778
Susannah. Titford	" April	11	1779
Mary. Titford	" June	20th	1780
Lydia. Titford	" April	14th	1785
Benjr. Titford	" Decr	15th	1786
Charles. Titford	"		
Lydia. Titford	" July		1796
Lydia. Titford	Dyed " August	6th	1786
Benjr. Titford	" February	25th	1816
Wm. Titford	— June	20th	1828

23. The children of Charles Titford, Cheesemonger. Family notes listing Charles Titford's children from William Charles onwards; the notes themselves were written many years after the events they outline – in 1860 or thereabouts. Details of exact dates of birth and death recorded here provide information not available in any public record.

24. Burial register, Badcox Lane Baptist Chapel, Frome, Somerset. Family notes reveal that Lydia Titford, daughter of Charles, died on 6 August, 1786. Two days later she was buried in the Badcox Lane Baptist Burying Ground by John Kingdon, the pastor, 'aged 1 year'. (PRO RG4/1550.)

No. 12. Arabella Pobjoy of Frome Aged 74 was buried in the said burying Ground July. 2nd.

No. 13. Lydia Daughter of Chas. Titford aged 1 year of Frome was buried in the said Burying Ground. August 8th By John Kingdon.

who had married Stephen Humphries of Devizes in 1752. So Mr. Whiting carefully entered in the burial register against little Mary's name: '. . . and diged up a gain and Mrs Humphries put in'. So aunt and niece lay together, Mary Humphries being buried 'in the same grave'.

One further male child survived this period of holocaust. Benjamin Titford – the name had always been a popular one with the Carpenter family – was born on 15 December 1786, and was baptised along with his ill-fated sister Lydia and brother Charles Thynne at St John's on 27 May 1792, Whit Sunday.[5] Charles the Cheesemonger was not averse to using the parish church to record the existence of his children, but on this occasion he may have been under more pressure than usual from the Anglican minister to arrange this triple baptism. Faced with the mounting cost of a war against the American colonies, the coalition government in Westminster had instituted a punitive and highly unpopular tax by the Stamp Act of October 1783: all registrations of baptisms, marriages and burials would be charged at 3d. a time – and so there was every incentive for local clergy, working on 10 per cent commission, to get around the parish and bring in the strays. Two years later the tax was extended to include Nonconformist registrations – a move petitioned for by the Dissenting churches themselves, who welcomed the official sanction of their records. Badcox Lane and Sheppards Barton Chapels in Frome began their burial and birth registers, respectively, in the October of that year, 1785, within three weeks of the new act being passed.

The tax on all registrations was eventually repealed in the October of 1794, but in the meantime Charles the Cheesemonger had had to hand over ninepence of his hard-earned money to have his little brood's details entered in the Anglican parish register, having already spent sixpence in the same way for Mary and Sarah in the October of 1784. If pig butchers kept piggy banks, his must have been empty once in a while during this period . . .

As the 18th century wore on, families could expect to see more and more of their children reach adulthood; nevertheless, the survival rate of Charles and Elizabeth's offspring – only six out of 13 reached their twenty-first birthday – is certainly nothing abnormal for the period. Being born and brought up next to a butcher's shop in a Somerset town in the closing years of the 18th century may not have been the healthiest start in life for a child, but those who saw out the dangerous first two or three years seemed to have stood a good chance of survival thereafter.

And compared to his three brothers, Charles was not doing too badly in the world, after all. Unlike any of them, he actually paid rates; not on any property as such, but on his 'stocks' – probably stores of pigs' carcasses, tallow, cheese and the like. In common with most of his contemporaries paying such rates, he was charged twice a year from 1783 onwards at a penny a time, though even he was excused in 1784 on grounds of poverty.[6]

It seems clear from the overseers' accounts for the late 18th century that two of the four adult Titford brothers were living as occupants of houses once held as leasehold properties by their better-off ancestors. William was in one of his father's two dwellings on High Street, while Thomas had taken over one of the original Fountain Lane/Cowards Batch houses built by his forefather William a hundred years before. The two younger brothers, Charles and John, had no such luck, and were forced to look for accommodation of their own; Charles found his on Pig Street – appropriately named, in view of his activity as a pig butcher – just north of Frome town bridge.[7] The Land Tax returns for 1780 show that John Prior, owner of the *Ship* public house at Oldford, held several properties which included '2 houses, Wid. Pains', then occupied by Charles Titford. Indeed, 'two houses' was probably a fair description of what consisted, in fact, of a dwelling house and an adjacent shop. They would pass into the hands of number of different owners over the years, but Charles Titford was to remain the occupier until his death in 1802.

So Charles and his family lived in the southernmost house and shop on the east side of the street, a fact confirmed by a deed of 1783 which defined the property in question as being immediately to the north of a stable, killing house and other buildings owned by Daniel Rossiter, clothier.[8] Having a slaughterhouse for his pigs next-door may have been very convenient for Charles, but it was a luxury he was soon to lose: The Frome Turnpike Trustees had decided to drag Frome into the modern world by demolishing Rossiter's buildings as part of a scheme to widen the road and ease the notorious bottleneck north of the bridge.

'On the north' the trustees wrote by way of explanation, 'is a dwelling house of Joseph Mintrim's now in the tenure of Charles Titford'; and from this dwelling house Charles and his family could have watched the demolition men at work. The census of 1785 confirms that the Titfords were still on Pig Street, not having been driven out by the noise of falling stone or splintering wood; not that noise would have been anything unusual for them – they already had Thomas Addams' blacksmith's shop down the street, and the ringing sound of metal on metal emanating from there must have mingled nicely with the constant clip-clop of horses' hooves as Henry Webley went about his business as the Bristol carrier a few doors away.

It was very much an artisan street this, but with a smattering of richer folk, too, so the shearmen, scribblers, shoemakers, carpenters and shop-keepers were neighbours to an attorney and two well-heeled clothiers – Thomas Clement, employing 11 scribblers and 12 shearmen, and Henry Sheppard, who even described himself as a 'Gentleman'. By 1785, Mary Gifford of *The Swan Inn* across the street had taken over the ownership of Charles's house. And pretty cramped it must have been there, too, with three males (Charles, described in the census as a 'shopkeeper', with son William Charles and son John) and five females (Elizabeth the mother, and daughters Elizabeth, Sarah, Mary and Lydia).

Ten years later, still in Pig Street, things were rather different: there were more children to cram into the same limited accommodation, but by the middle of 1795 they were motherless. Elizabeth, having given birth to 13 children and aged only 46, was buried at Catherine Hill on 19 June. Like all his brothers, Charles was destined to outlive his wife; and in a sense we may not wonder at that fact. We have seen what a struggle it must have been for men in the late 18th century to keep body and soul together – how much worse, then, for their womenfolk.

Things had improved slightly for married women since the patriarchal days of the feudal system, and few people in the late 1700s could have shared Luther's view that:

> If a woman becomes weary, or at last dead, from child-bearing, it matters not; let her only die from bearing, she is there to do it.

But to be forever in child-bed, surrounded by countless sons and daughters, many of them ill; to run a self-supporting household with endless heavy domestic chores; to be victim to a view that a woman's one means of self-fulfilment must be through the home – all that adds up to a state of affairs not to be envied. A rather chilling symbol of what we would now regard as the male chauvinism of the times is furnished by the wording and the sentiments contained in an Act of Parliament passed in the year Charles and Elizabeth were married, 1770:

> All women, of whatever age, rank, profession, or degree who shall, after this Act, impose upon, seduce, and betray into marriage any of His Majesty's subjects by virtue of scents, paints, cosmetic washes, artificial teeth or false hair, iron stays, bolstered hips, or high-heeled shoes, shall incur the penalty of the law now in force against witchcraft and like misdemeanours; and marriage under such circumstances, upon conviction of the offending parties, shall be null and void.

One can only hope that Charles Titford had chosen a wife for her lasting qualities, and was not 'seduced and betrayed' by a daub of lipstick and a set of false teeth; his marriage lasted – as, in a sense, marriages had to – and it bore fruit. But we can scarcely doubt, for all that, that Elizabeth must have gone to her death not a little exhausted by the duties of a wife and mother in hard times which found out the slightest weakness in every individual's constitution.

In a sense it is all too easy in retrospect to see what it must have been that hurried Elizabeth to that early grave. James Woodforde, ever a reliable source for the minutiae of late 18th-century life, wrote on 25 January 1794 that he could never remember having seen the barometer lower; a savage and relentless winter was setting in throughout Britain and the rest of Europe. Again, just as in 1771, Elizabeth Titford was pregnant when it struck; her last son Charles was born within a week of Woodforde's ominous comment about his barometer – little wonder, then, that the poor child was dead inside three weeks.

Inevitably a disastrous harvest followed – one-fifth below the average for those of the previous 10 years – and prices almost doubled. Wages did not rise in proportion, and by the Spring of 1795 there was the extensive distress and threat of mass starvation which led, in May, to the infamous meeting of the magistrates at Speenhamland in Berkshire, an event which would have such an impact on poor-law provision for the next few decades. By Easter heavy frosts had ended hopes of a good harvest that year, and in the summer and autumn food riots broke out in the country at large as the price of a quartern loaf – where one could be had at all – rose from 3d. to over 1s. And the cycle of bad weather, poor harvests, high prices and malnutrition looked all set to repeat itself. Caught inextricably in that cycle, with pregnancies to confuse and exacerbate the situation, Elizabeth Titford's body finally gave up the struggle in June; with tragic inevitability, we might be tempted to say, looking back with the advantage of hindsight.[9]

Charles, then, was the second brother to be left a widower, after Thomas; the domestic burden thus falling upon him and his remaining daughters must have been rather a daunting one, including the need to feed, control and educate young Ben, then only nine years old.

At least there was soon to be a bit of activity in the neighbourhood to distract the young lad's attention: in June of 1797 Charles the Cheesemonger was to achieve the singular distinction of being mentioned, *en passant*, in an Act of Parliament. The Frome Turnpike Trustees have returned to the scene; the powers vested in them by previous legislation having been insufficient to meet their needs, they were now given a helping hand on 19 June 1797, with:

> An Act for enlarging the Term and Powers of two Acts . . . for repairing and widening several roads leading to, through, and from the town of Frome in the County of Somerset; and for paving the Footways and lighting the Streets within the said Town.[10]

Certainly there was every need for a road-widening scheme: four years earlier, in the October of 1793, poor old Parson Woodforde had nearly come a nasty cropper on Frome Hill, when the chaise he was in had had an unfortunate encounter with a large 'heavily loaden' London waggon, complete with eight horses:

> . . . it being very narrow where we met it, the Driver of the Chaise in backing his Horses to avoid being drove over overturned his Chaise, but very providentially, blessed be Almighty God for it! we received very little Injury, Nancys Face was a little bruised. It was a wonder that we escaped so well, as we were afraid that the Waggon would have crushed us.[11]

After a walk back to the inn and a half-hour wait, they set off again for Bath, very much relieved that matters had not been worse.

The demolition of Daniel Rossiter's slaughterhouse in 1783, it seems, had just been an interim measure to ease congestion near the bridge; now the Trustees were to have the power to '. . . pull down and remove certain Houses and Buildings, now being in the Line of the said new proposed Road . . .'. The road in question was to be the new North Parade, and – just to be sure – the Trustees wanted permission if necessary to knock down almost the whole of Pig Street and a lot else besides, including:

25. (*right*) Commercial directory, Frome, Somerset. Showing 'Charles Titford, Chandler's Shop and Pig-butcher'. From the *Universal British Directory*, 1794-8, vol. 3.

26. (*below*) Act of Parliament relating to roads in Frome. Certain roads in Frome are to be widened: among the properties affected are '. . . a Messuage or Tenement, with the Outhouses, Yards, and Hereditaments, adjoining or near thereto, now or late in the Tenure or Occupation of Charles Titford . . .'. 19 June 1797.

IV. And be it further enacted, That it shall be lawful for the said trustees, or any Nine or more of them, and they are hereby authorized and empowered, to contract and agree with the several Owners, Proprietors, and Occupiers of, and Persons entitled unto, any Messuages, Cottages, Shops, Lands, Gardens, Grounds, Tenements, or Hereditaments herein-after mentioned, for the Purchase of the same, or of so much and such Part or Parts thereof as shall be necessary for turning, altering, widening, enlarging, and making more commodious and convenient to the Public the Roads included in the said former Acts and this Act; (that is to say,) With the Owner or Owners, Proprietors, and Occupiers of Nine Square Feet of the North West End of the Court or Yard of the *Frome* Alms House, on or near the said Bridge; a Messuage or Tenement, with the Stables, Gardens, Out-houses, and Hereditaments, adjoining or near thereto, now or late in the Tenure or Occupation of *John Adlam*; a Messuage or Tenement, with the Outhouses, Yards, and Hereditaments, adjoining or near thereto, now or late in the Tenure or Occupation of *Charles Titford*; a Messuage or Tenement, with the Outhouses and Hereditaments, now or late in the Tenure or Occupation of *Richard Singer*; a Stable and Hereditaments, now or late in the Tenure or Occupation of *John Neale*; a Workshop or Tenement and Yard, now or late in the Tenure or Occupation of *Thomas Adams*; a Messuage or Tenement, with the Stables, Gardens, Yards, Tennis Court, Dung Pit, and Hereditaments, adjoining or near thereto, now or late in the Tenure or Occupation of *Sarah Webb*; a Stable or Stables, with the Yards, Gardens, and Hereditaments,

Trustees may contract for Purchase of Houses, &c. to widen the Road.

> ... a Messuage or Tenement, with the Outhouses, Yards, and Hereditaments, adjoining or near thereto, now or late in the Tenure or Occupation of Charles Titford ...

And if Pig Street were to fall under the axe, there would be a real rag-bag of properties of every sort razed to the ground, including – from the sublime to the ridiculous – a tennis court and a dung pit:

> Courts, Messuages, Tenements, Stables, Outhouses, Yards, Workshops, Tennis Court, Dung Pit, Barns, Waggon or Coach House, Woodhouse, Press Shop, Orchard and Hereditaments ... [12]

In the event, at least in the short term, most of these multifarious properties would be safe: North Parade was cut east of Pig Street itself, with the result that Charles Titford's shop, already exposed on its south side in 1783, would now have a naked eastern flank as well, leaving it on a kind of promontory. Maybe it was all good for trade?

But Charles now had another little job to do: the new Act allowed for pavements to be laid in the town, with the proviso that:

> ... all and every Person and Persons, inhabiting within the Said Town where the said intended Pavements shall extend, shall sweep and cleanse, or cause to be swept and cleansed, the Footways in the whole Length of the Front of their respective Houses, Buildings, and Walls, once in every Week, upon Pain of forfeiting and paying the Sum of Two Shillings and Sixpence for every Neglect therein.

And those who couldn't afford a half-crown fine, but would rather wait until nightfall to sweep or cause to be swept their bit of pavement, must have been more than grateful that the Trustees would also kindly provide 'Lamp Irons or Lamp Posts to be put or affixed into, upon, or against the Walls or Pallisadoes of any of the Houses, Tenements, or Buildings within the said Town'.

Frome was being catapulted, despite itself, perhaps, into the world of the new century about to dawn. And the prospect of that new century, and with it the hope for a better future, was something the people of Frome, like the people of Britain itself, sorely needed.

It is easy – too easy, perhaps – to see the last decades of the 1700s as a time of unalleviated misery for a large part of the population of the British Isles. To attempt to bring up children in the 1780s and '90s was an unenviable task indeed – yet the number of such children was itself increasing by leaps and bounds. The population of Britain was to rise from between seven and eight million in 1760 to 15 million in 1820 – in other words, it doubled in a period of 60 years. Not everyone saw this as an 'explosion' as such, but those commentators who did, like the much-quoted Thomas Malthus, prophesied disaster if the growth couldn't be controlled; how was the country to survive when there were hundreds of thousands of extra mouths to feed every year?

The overseers of the poor in Frome must have asked themselves very much this same question; at one time or another something between a quarter and a half of the population of Britain were to receive parish relief in the late 18th century – and the £1,970 per annum it was costing for such relief in Frome in 1792 would rise to a staggering £11,723 per annum by 1831. To complicate matters still further, many parishes after 1795 began to adopt the Speenhamland system of making up wages to a minimum rate dependent upon the price of corn. That sounds humane enough in theory, and no doubt it saved many hundreds of families from starvation during the years of the French wars; but it positively encouraged employers to keep wages at rock-bottom levels, while anyone who wanted to do an honest day's work for an honest day's pay was subject, instead, to the ignimony of accepting supplementary alms in order to live. A man remained a pauper, in other words, even when he was in full work.

Things wouldn't have been so bleak, perhaps, if the dramatic rise in population had been brought about by healthier times and a consequent increase in life expectancy; in the event, many scholars would cite a different cause or causes for it – like the fact that the decline of the apprenticeship system meant that couples were marrying younger, and so increasing the number of child-bearing years per family.

For all the rise in the number of births, and despite some medical advances, potential causes of a premature death were lurking around every corner, or sweeping the country in periodic epidemics; especially vulnerable were the very young, the old and the infirm. Inoculation against smallpox had been practised since the 1720s, although it constituted a potentially lethal measure in itself and only achieved an erratic degree of success against a disease which probably claimed the lives of up to a quarter of the population throughout the century, and disfigured many of the survivors. Jenner had begun to make use of cowpox for human vaccination in 1798, but it would be a few years before its use was widespread, and 1840 before it was available free. In the meantime, it is likely that everyone had contracted the disease at some time or another in his or her life, and it proved fatal to those with the merest weakness whose bodies could not withstand its ravages. And if smallpox didn't get you, there was always diphtheria, scarlet fever, typhoid, typhus or consumption lying in wait.

In Frome, as elsewhere, a large proportion of the population lacked the general state of good health which would have gone some way towards combating these killer diseases. In their cramped and insanitary dwellings, often ill-fed as they were, the poor of Frome were constantly beset by outbreaks of typhus; known variously as 'Irish Fever' or 'Gaol Fever', it frequently picked off not only the inmates of the country's overcrowded prisons, but also the hapless judges who had to try the prisoners. Under attack on all sides, not least from the infant population which was itself unwittingly helping to spread disease through the narrow streets and alleys of the town, some Frome people found a temporary escape in one or other of the forty or more pubs which vied with each other for custom; drunkenness was commonplace, and many of those who didn't go to an early grave with some infection or other departed this life with a putrid liver.

All this would have been bad enough, even without another little trick nature had up its sleeve: the weather. The first half of the 18th century had seemed kind enough: improved climatic conditions and better harvests had combined with the disappearance of bubonic plague to help curtail the mortality crises which had beset Northern Europe up until then. But things grew a great deal worse as the century wore on. Severe winters, of course, hit the poor twice over: those who survived the effects of the frost and snow might well die of malnutrition as the resultant disastrous harvest reduced the amount of food available and forced up prices. The Titford family, as so often, was a mirror of the times; every major period of dearth in the 18th century is reflected in at least one family burial, and sometimes more. The late 1720s, the most brutal time of all with its bad harvests, high prices, and killer epidemics, saw off no fewer than six Titfords within two years; the period 1766/7 also claimed its victims in the family, as did the winter and spring of 1771, as we have seen; and the near-famine year of 1795, following hard on a winter which was said to herald something resembling a new ice-age, had brought the death of Charles the Cheesemonger's wife Elizabeth.[13]

The price of wheat is frequently used as a measure of degrees of economic hardship by historians of this period; not every family, it is true, was totally dependent upon wheaten bread, but the steep upward price curve which was to reach an undreamt-of high of 113s. 10d. per quarter of wheat in 1800 must be a fairly accurate barometer of the plight of the poor, especially in the 1790s.[14] Wages, meanwhile, were held down – or, at best, rose only very slowly; and it doesn't need a Mr. Micawber to tell us that the net result for thousands of families was a fluctuation in living standards bordering all too often on total destitution. 'In the past,' as G. M. Trevelyan put it, 'poverty had been an individual misfortune; now it was a group grievance'.[15]

What the country needed, we might say, was a compassionate and caring government, prepared to control the balance between wages and prices, and to attempt to regulate working conditions. In the event, it got nothing of the kind. The country's rulers were, after all, running scared: the American colonies had declared their independence in 1776 in dangerously democratic terms; the writings of Tom Paine were being disseminated far and wide; and, most threatening of all, there was every chance that the Jacobin ideas of the French Revolution of 1789 might take firm root in English soil. 'Life, liberty and the pursuit of happiness' and 'Liberty, equality, fraternity' were rallying-cries guaranteed to provide a few sleepless nights for many an English gentleman. Class divisions hitherto non-existent or only latent in English society were beginning to open up as the Agrarian and Industrial Revolutions gained momentum, and popular unrest was in the air.

Government was in no mood, in the circumstances, to give much priority to the plight of the poor. In any case, many of its members in the late 18th century, though not yet necessarily committed to a full-blooded doctrine of 'laissez-faire', were moving towards a political philosophy involving less, not more, government intervention in everyday affairs, leaving the 'natural' market forces of supply and demand to regulate the economy as best they may.[16]

From 1793 that economy was one of a country at war. Pitt, as Prime Minister, was ill-prepared for such a turn of events, and through years of hesitancy and uncertainty he watched a yet deeper impoverishment overtake many thousands of his fellow-countrymen. The government was quite content, in essence, to use inflation as a weapon of war: somebody had to bear the costs, and apart from those assessed for the new Income Tax of 1799, that somebody had to be the consumer. Prices were allowed to rise unchecked, hitting the poor worst of all and adding thousands to their number; parish relief, it was argued, woud provide for the true paupers, and the rest would have to be satisfied with the temporary increase in employment which the war brought with it.

Yet as the war years set in, the landed classes, together with the newly-rich manufacturers, had never had it so good; Napoleon has been called, not entirely without justification, 'The patron saint not only of farmers, but of landlords'.[17] And there are few enough references to international hostilities in the novels of Jane Austen, or signs of distress in the great landscape and portrait paintings of the age. Down in Brighton or Bath, it must have seemed, nothing had changed.

Elsewhere, however, from 1793 onwards the French war itself would vie with food prices as the most talked-about subject in town and country alike. There were those, of course, who wondered why England should be sending her brave lads across the Channel to fight against a country which seemed – the Reign of Terror notwithstanding – to be the cradle of a new and attractive democracy. Others – and the majority, no doubt – would wait anxiously for any news as a French invasion force was massing ready to launch itself against English shores. The two countries would be fighting each other, on and off, for 22 years; and there were those, like Benjamin Titford, born in 1786, who lived through nothing but wars and rumours of wars from the day they were born to the day they died.

Down in Frome they were preparing for the worst; on 23 February 1798 a meeting of the 'inhabitants of the town and neighbourhood of Frome' took place at the *George Inn*. As a result of this and subsequent deliberations it was agreed to form a local defence force consisting of 60 cavalrymen, who were to extend their protection '. . . as far as any adjoining town not exceeding 20 miles distance from Frome', together with 100 infantry. The Frome Military Association, later re-named the 'Frome Selwood Volunteers' had been born.[18]

Throughout the spring, talk of invasion was on everyone's lips; those who could help to fund the new military force did so, while others, providing they were householders or 'such other Persons as shall be recommended by two Householders', were invited to enlist at the

George Inn, '. . . where such persons as are willing to join the Frome Selwood Volunteers, either cavalry or infantry, are requested to attend and sign their names'.

All of this excitement – the meetings, the handbills, the brave volunteering – can hardly have escaped the notice of the Titford family down in Pig Street. William Charles, the eldest son, had only recently left town for good, off to join his cousins in London; young Benjamin was too young to be playing at soldiers, and Charles the Cheesemonger himself was a bit too old and certainly far too unhealthy to offer his services as a volunteer. So the mantle fell on the second son, John, then 23 years old; without more ado, he set off over the bridge into the Market Place, across to the *George*, and signed up for the infantry.[19]

It is not without significance, of course, that a young man of good Dissenting stock, with impoverished uncles, aunts and cousins, should nevertheless have chosen to stand up and be counted in a fight against a nation which, for all its extremes, represented some form of democratic republicanism. Can John really have been so politically conservative? The question is probably too sophisticated: after all, his own father was by no means destitute, and had at least something worth conserving. We must remember, too, that Dissenters in the 18th century were not the political revolutionaries they had been in the 17th – there was a sense in which the rabid Nonconformity of one generation became the established respectability of the next, and commentators like Halevy have suggested that it was precisely the innate conservatism of the new dissent, Methodism, which helped stave off revolution in England in the early 19th century – a real opium of the people, in effect. Not only that, but post-revolutionary France would have represented atheism at worst, Catholicism at best; little wonder that a good Baptist lad, fired by an upsurge of patriotism which temporarily united all Englishmen in opposition to a common foe, should have joined the struggle.[20]

In any case, Titfords have not exactly been famous for their military prowess over the centuries, so we should cherish young John's gesture. He had to provide his infantryman's uniform at his own expense – a deep-blue coat with matching lapels, and blue pantaloons with red edgings. A musket and other accoutrements were provided from Ordnance, and pistols followed at the end of the year. There was to be no pay, and yet any private who failed to attend for two hours, at least twice a week, for 'The Exercise' when the troops would '. . . go through the Evolutions together' would be fined two shillings. Admittedly the main duty of this force – if we may call it that – was ceremonial, but at a time when many of their contemporaries were off fighting in a real war, they must have looked at times like extras from a pantomime.

Why, then, was John Titford a member of this glorified Home Guard when, at the age of 23, we might have expected him to have joined the regular army or to have found his way somehow into the militia?[21] The answer is an all-too-simple one: by the time he courageously signed on as a volunteer infantryman, John was in the terminal stages of consumption. Having survived the early years of childhood, unlike so many of his siblings, he had been struck down by that other malady which afflicted a tragically high proportion of those who lived on into teenage years and beyond. As incessant rain lashed the town in late July, 1798, to be followed on the 28th of that month by one of the worst floods in living memory, John's health can hardly have improved – and who knows what bacteria he was daily picking up from his father's butchery?[22]

Frome itself was nothing if not lively that year; 170 of the North Gloucester Supplementary Militia arrived in June, en route to Plymouth, and then the Prime Minister himself passed through the town on his way to Burton Pynsent, accompanied by the Chief Speaker of the House of Commons. Plenty here for poor John Titford and his brother Ben to stand and gaze at.

The infantry went to church in their new uniforms for the first time on 9 September, and had the singular honour, a month later, of joining their fellows in the cavalry who were escorting the funeral cortège of the late Earl of Cork 'in slow and decorous movement suitable to the solemnity of the occasion'.

There was some good news, too: the harvest had been the best for over thirty years, and after much anxious waiting there was a victory to celebrate from the war front – Nelson had trounced the French fleet at the Battle of the Nile. Having sworn allegiance to the sovereign on 15 October, the Volunteers then had a special function to perform two weeks later: they were out in force at Divine Service on 29 November, forming a focal point for a day of General Thanksgiving for the glorious victories achieved by His Majesty's troops by land and sea. Immediately afterwards they had a grand Field Day.

And so the year 1798 drew to a close, and with it came another crippling winter in a decade of crippling winters. On 2 February 1799 Parson Woodforde, by then in Norfolk, wrote in his diary: 'Such severe weather has not been known for the last sixty years till the present'.[23] Heavy snow had fallen in Frome the day before that, the deepest since 1767, and conditions were dismal. It proved the last straw for John Titford; ill enough, no doubt, without the need to struggle against a winter to end all winters, his weary body gave up the ghost.

Edmund Crocker, the son of the master of the Blue Coat School just across the bridge from Pig Street, kept a diary during this period, and young John Titford's death did not escape his notice. An entry for 8 February reads:

> On the 2[d] instant died in a consumption J. Titford, aged about 4 or 5 and 20 years. He being a volunteer in our Infantry, he was this day interred with the military honours due to him.[24]

It can have been no easy journey for the funeral procession of mourners and military volunteers as they followed the coffin up the steep climb to Catherine Hill Burial Ground that bleak Friday in February with the snow thick on the ground. The Rev. John Kingdon, the Baptist minister, had two other ceremonies to perform that day, as he also officiated at the burials of Mary Whiting, aged 77, and a deaf and dumb girl of 45 years, Christiana Yerbury. He duly entered John's interment in his register: 'Aged 24; with Military Honours'. And so it was over.

As he left that all-too-familiar graveyard and tramped home through the snow, Charles the Cheesemonger must have thought that the century was drawing to an unpropitious end indeed. Yet back at Pig Street the diminished family – Charles himself, Elizabeth, Sarah, Mary and young Ben – had plenty to occupy themselves with, apart from a period of mourning and an attempt to keep warm. Five days later the snow melted, and on the morning of 11 February the second massive flood in seven months overtook them; it was all very well for the town directory to speak in glowing terms of the River Frome teeming with trout, eels, and all manner of fine fish – but to the inhabitants of Pig Street that wretched river too often spelt disaster and despoilation. How they must all have found curses on their lips, Baptists or not! And really it was no joking matter: across the bridge John Chapman, nephew to a Market Place shoemaker, went back to work in the shop too soon after the flood, caught a chill in the process, and died in the April, aged just twenty-one.

And as if the elements were ganging up on defenceless human beings, half the neighbourhood around the bridge was woken up at 3 o'clock on the morning of Sunday, 10 March by shouts of 'Fire!' as a stable next to Sheppards' workshops went up in flames. Thanks to the timely action of those living nearby – the Titfords probably among them – and the deployment of the town fire engines, the workshops themselves were saved. Edmund Crocker, the diarist, added his own laconic comment to his account of the episode: 'All was insured'!

Through all this period of turmoil the cruel winter was beginning to abate, but only very slowly; Woodforde in his diary was still lamenting conditions in April: 'Never such cold

French Invasion!

At a Meeting of the Committee of the FROME MILITARY ASSOCIATION, it was directed,

THAT a Book be left at the George Inn, in Frome, for the enrolment of Volunteers, where such Persons as are willing to join the FROME SELWOOD VOLUNTEERS, either Cavalry or Infantry, are requested to attend and sign their names.

THAT another Book be left at the Frome Somerset Bank, for subscriptions, from such Persons as do not give their Personal Service.

May 3d. 1798.

CROCKERS, PRINTERS.

27. Frome prepares for the expected invasion, 1798. John Titford responded to the call and signed up for the Volunteer Infantry. (SRO DD/LW.)

28. The diary of Edmund Crocker of Frome, 8 February 1799. 'On the 2d instant died in a consumption J. Titford aged about 4 or 5 & 20 years – he being a volunteer in our infantry, he was this day interred with the military honours due to him.' (SRO DD/LW.)

> February
>
> 1. Not many days since Friend Gregory, in conformity to the Scriptural injunction, Luke 14. 13v. gave a dinner to 14 old men of this place; the aggregate of whose ages was 1075 years.
>
> 8. On the 2d instant, died in a consumption J. Titford aged about 4 or 5 & 20 years. — he being a volunteer in our infantry, he was this day interred with the military honours due to him.

known by man'. And what he has to say makes it clear that young John Titford was not the only one to die in its grip:

> Very dismal accounts on the Papers respecting the last severe Weather – many, many People having lost their Lives thro' the inclemency of the same. Mail coaches &c. unable to travel . . . the long continuance of so severe cold Weather having scarce been known for the last Century. [17 Feb. 1799.][25]

Woodforde is certainly prone to a touch of hyperbole in such matters, but weather which even prevented him from getting to the outside privy ('Jericho') must have been severe indeed . . .

In Frome there was one more natural disaster to come before the year was out: the afternoon of September 17th saw 'One of the highest floods that has been remembered perhaps for these 20 years', according to Crocker. It was up two stairs in the Crockers' house, and level with many of the old women's beds in the Blue Coat School almshouses. One can imagine, in the circumstances, what havoc it caused in Charles Titford's house and shop across the bridge . . .

Perhaps we might have a look at things, at this stage, through the eyes of young Benjamin Titford, the youngest surviving son, left motherless at nine years old; waving his big brother William Charles goodbye as he set off for London soon afterwards; watching brother John cough himself into an early grave; listening to endless conversations about high prices, shortages, and a war across the channel; dragged out of his bed in the middle of the night to cries of 'Fire!' and 'Flood!'; struggling to keep warm every winter; watching his father die of a long illness – these experiences made his childhood, in modern terms, an awful, albeit a dramatic one. And, indeed, he must have been a tough little lad to have survived it all, though it was to take its toll on him eventually; by the time he died in far-away London at the age of 29 he had lived through some very harsh times indeed. Meantime, there was a lot happening just down the street to capture his attention, as troop after troop of soldiers passed through Frome on their way somewhere else: 300 of the Staffordshire Militia came in April of 1799, replaced by an equal number of the same later in the month; then the 300-strong Somerset Supplementary Militia arrived from Wells, complete with their own band, followed by the glorious Fifteenth Light Dragoons – 'It is supposed that these are the finest men and horses of any regiment in England'; and the next year no fewer than nine hundred men of the Seventeenth Regiment of Light Dragoons came at one go.[26] Ben must have been wide-eyed.

There were other goings-on to occupy his attention, too, not least the marriages of two daughters of the Titfords' Pig Street neighbour, Thomas Clement the clothier, within a three-month period. 'Mr Shatford's Company of Players' arrived in town in the July of 1800, consisting of Mr. and Mrs. Shatford themselves, together with 11 men, one 'Miss', five 'Mrs.'s' and someone described darkly as a 'young lady of Bath . . .'. Having regaled the population of Frome with 'Hamlet', 'Romeo and Juliet', 'School for Scandal' and a few other evergreens, they were soon off to take the same dose of culture to Shepton Mallet and Wells.[27]

Ben may not have been much of a theatre-goer, but he would no doubt have been fascinated by one unexpected visit in the June of 1801:

> Arrived here, for the inspection of the public, a basking shark, caught at Abbotsbury, in Dorsetshire, in the fishing seine of Hardy and Co., May the 4th. It measures 28 feet in length and 20 feet in girth; the tail from point to point is 8 feet. The body has contained 27 persons at one time, and its liver produced four hogsheads of oil . . .[28]

The so-called 'proprietor' of the shark, glorying in the name of 'Captain Wm. Boatswain', no doubt knew how to entertain an audience, just as the Shatford Players had done: '. . . after it was entangled in the net, it received seventeen musket balls from the Greyhound

Cutter' (Gosh!); '. . . it was dragged to the shore by seven horses . . .' (Well!); '. . . and three hundred men . . .' (Gadzooks! Odsbodykins! Zounds! etc. . . .) Life in Frome, for all the town's comparative isolation, can hardly have been dull.

Of course, and as we might expect, despite alterations made to the weir and hatches in the river below the town, another tremendous flood had arrived on 9 November 1800. The entire Market Place was underwater, and the road over the bridge was impassable from six in the morning until seven at night. Poor Charles the Cheesemonger can hardly have sold much in his little shop that day. In any case, the price of food in that year, in the aftermath of a very bad harvest, had soared abruptly: Charles Titford, your friendly butcher and cheesemonger, would be charging 7d. per pound for pork in March, 1800, as against 4½d. in January; his cheese would now cost you 7d. per pound, against 5d. in January.[29] He may well have lost customers; and even those he retained would no doubt have been despondent if not positively angry at what they were having to pay.

Further down the street, the local baker would be telling his hapless visitors much the same story as their butcher: the cost of wheat was out of all control, and he was as sorry as they were that his prices were up, while their wages had held steady. In January of the following year, a grand masquerade held at nearby Orchardleigh House served supper 'in the richest profusion', but 'from a laudable attention to the severity of "existing circumstances" the use of bread was entirely prohibited'.[30] Even the gentry, then, were having to eat pheasant without bread; what was the world coming to?

By 1800 the overseers' rate books indicate a few changes in the personnel living down Pig Street. Thomas Balne had acquired the *Swann Inn*, and was also Charles Titford's new landlord. Elizabeth Addams lived next door, Thomas Addams was still at work in his smith's shop, Thomas Burge had taken over as the Bristol carrier, and the Clement family were producing cloth for all they were worth in workshops at the end of the street.

As Charles stood in his doorway and looked around, he must have seen a bustle of activity and a variety of dwellings only possible before the days of clinical town planning. So although his neighbours opposite occupied houses with gardens, his side of the street had to work for a living: he would have been used to seeing the flame fanned by the bellows of the blacksmith, the steam rising from the sweating horses in the carrier's stables, and – we may hope – a line of customers waiting to be served in his little shop. The sounds, as we have already said, must have provided a constant cacophonous background to the daily round, while the smell of a street which included a butcher and chandler's shop, stables, a smithy, clothiers' workshops and a liberal supply of earth closets would be scarcely credible to modern sensibilities.[31] Flies, we can well imagine, must have had a hey-day in such an environment, and those attracted by the flesh and the dung of horses would have had to be whisked off Charles's meat – perhaps by boys with birch whisks specially employed for the purpose. Little wonder, in a sense, that so many children died in early infancy, or that those who survived would have built up a set of antibodies we might well envy.

Had Charles looked the other way – south, over the town bridge – we have a very good idea of exactly what he would have seen, thanks to a contemporary engraving by Abraham Crocker. There is the Blue House and the *Blue Boar*, the Market Place still divided by buildings across the centre of it, and the spire of the unrebuilt St John's church rising in the middle distance. A tranquil enough scene, we may say, once the squads of militia had departed and the floods abated.

Crocker's engraving was published on 1 June 1802; five days later, aged 52, Charles the Cheesemonger died. On 2 October of the same year William Jowett Titford, great-grandson of William the Emigrant, wrote to his mother in London: 'The father of our relation W. C. Titford died at Frome June 6th after a long illness'.[32] Charles joined his young nephew

29. Frome: Blue House and Lower Market Place. This engraving, showing what would have been the view from Charles Titford's shop in Pig Street, was published on 1 June 1802, five days before he died.

30. The Letter-book of William Jowett Titford. William Jowett Titford's copy of a letter to his mother of 2 October 1802, mentioning the death of Charles the Cheesemonger: 'The father of our relation W. C. Titford died at Frome June 6th. after a long illness'. From the letter book in possession of Mr. Tony Titford of West Horsley.

Joseph in plot no. 223 on Catherine Hill; there he lay in peace until 1811, when – and this should not surprise us by now – he was 'digd up again' while Betty Naish, 67, was put in.

One month after Charles's funeral, wasting little time, his eldest daughter Elizabeth, who had probably tended her father through his final illness and was by then the official occupier of the dwelling house next to his shop, upped and married by licence. She became the wife of James Baker, a saddler in the town who was also making his professional services available to the Frome Volunteers. He was to live on until 1832, when he died, aged 58, described as being of the Lower Market Place.

So it was 'all change' on Pig Street: Solomon Mead replaced Elizabeth Titford in the little dwelling house which had served the Titford family so well over the years, and Thomas Tuck began to see what kind of commercial success he could make out of the vacated butcher and chandler's shop next door. One male Titford of the new generation – William Charles – had left the town already; his brother Benjamin was soon to follow him to London; Elizabeth was now a married woman, with two as yet unmarried sisters, Mary and Sarah.

Charles the Cheesemonger's major contribution to the history of his side of the family was to ensure that the name continued; not in Frome, where Titfords were to disappear completely by the 1860s, but in London. The young males had left the nest and taken wing; within a couple of generations almost no-one would even remember these Westcountry origins – such is the way of things. But we know, and Henry James Titford, a great-great-grandson of Charles the Cheesemonger, born in 1875, could still remember in the 1960s having heard it once said that his surname came from Frome. How right he was – folk-memory was not quite dead, after all.

CHAPTER 15

John the Cardmaker (c.1750-1828)

Frome, Somerset

NO BREAD FOR THE BAPTIST BROTHER

The story of the Frome Titfords properly ends with the youngest of the four brothers whose fortunes we have been following; his children were to be the last Titfords in the town, and he himself outlived William, Thomas and Charles.

John Titford was a more ardent Baptist than any of the others; he alone of the males of his generation was ever a fully-baptised member of Badcox Lane Chapel:

> Tuesday, March 7th, 1780. John Titford came before the church & made a profession of his faith to their satisfaction.[1]

He was baptised by John Kingdon in the chapel's own 'baptistry' on Friday 5 May 1780 and officially received into the church two days later.

John was by then an adult, of course, aged about thirty, and also a married man. All four of the Titford brothers of this generation were in their early twenties on their wedding day – a reflection in itself of the fact that the average age at marriage for men was falling as the century wore on; that average in the early 1700s had been as high as twenty-seven. John was 21 years old when he married Ann Oldbury on 15 June 1771, three months to the day after the death of his father during that most vicious of winters.[2]

There are just the odd hints here and there that John and Ann did not always see eye-to-eye on religious matters. She appears not to have worshipped alongside her husband at the chapel; he was a full member, and his daughters would later follow in his footsteps, but Ann never committed herself in quite that way. Then there is the baptismal entry at St John's on Christmas Day 1773: 'Sarah Titford, daughter of Ann'. This might be an illegitimate birth of some kind, as it seems to be, or possibly just evidence of John and Ann's first child. John himself would hardly have deigned to enter the parish church with a child of his, and may have sent his wife instead: 'If you want her baptised, dear, you go and do it . . . I'm having nothing to do with it . . .'. At all events, John was singularly successful in the long run at turning his back on everything that smacked of Anglicanism; he alone of all the Titford brothers managed to cold-shoulder St John's church for everything except his marriage.

John's other children consisted of two boys, William and Joseph, and four girls – one of whom, Elizabeth, born in 1787, would eventually broaden the family's chapel affiliations by being registered as an adult church member at Rook Lane Independent Meeting House in 1837.[3]

John was a cardmaker, and yet it was his good fortune to have depended on parish relief rather less often than some; he and his family needed a brief period of support in the famine period of 1801-2, when they were allowed 2s. a week, later reduced to 1s., until payment stopped on 9 March 1802. Only in 1817 do we encounter them again, in a list headed 'Our Paupers', when first Ann ('70 years old . . . Behind the Hill') and then, in 1821, John and Ann ('70; Behind the Hill') pick up amounts varying between 5s. and 10s. per fortnight. Parish authorities generally were constantly reviewing their ideas about what constituted a minimum acceptable subsistence payment during this period.

If we pause briefly and attempt to list the possible reasons why an individual or a family might have needed parish relief in the late 18th and early 19th centuries – sickness, unemployment, the needs of one-parent families or of orphans or young children, support in times of local or national economic crisis, old age – then we have now found Titfords in every category. Betty Titford, Thomas's wife, received help because she was sick; Thomas himself was out of work in 1801, and qualified for relief both on that score and because he was the head of a one-parent family which included a sick daughter; Hephzibah, the little orphan, had been helped and then apprenticed by the overseers, and finally John and Ann, briefly subsidised during times of economic dearth, eventually survived long enough to collect a very modest old-age pension.

The couple had lived for many years on a narrow pedestrian street known quite simply as 'Behind the Hill' (later Paul Street), a useful little short-cut between Palmer Street and Catherine Hill. The 1785 census finds them there, two males and four females in a house owned by Mr. Muir. Catherine or St Catherine's Hill itself constituted a Pandora's box of small-town trades and occupations at the time: everything from a gingerbread maker to a hairdresser, a staymaker, a breechesmaker, Charles Tucker the coalminer, John Golledge the blind schoolmaster, Mrs Allen at the *Castle* public house, and even John Ward, who seemed to be able to support himself by practising the noble art of a 'horse jockey'. The Titfords' little house nestled among others occupied by these larger-than-life characters – John was, after all, merely a humble and humdrum cardmaker. In 1800 the family's landlords are given as 'Muir and Wayland', and the property itself is described as 'House and Garden'. By 1802 John Wayland – a member of a famous Frome family, some of whom were to be very eminent in Baptist circles in America – was the new owner, and rates on it cost him 4d.; lucky old Mrs. Muir, then, who had taken over by 1804, and was only charged half the price . . .

John Titford was never what we would call a leading light at Badcox Lane Chapel – he seems to have been reliable, but perhaps not dynamic. Even so, he was called upon to sign documents on occasions, as when a conveyance relating to the chapel and its land was prepared in 1805 and his name as witness ('John Titford, Cardmaker') appears alongside those of John Lacey, shoemaker, Richard Butler, weaver, and James Browning, clothier; together they form a nice little thumb-nail sketch of the kind of men who were 'Chapel' rather than 'Church' at this period.[4]

Eight years later, on 21 May 1813, a set of proposals for the enlargement of Badcox Lane Chapel was drawn up – signed by the deacons, the minister, subscribers and seven members, including John Titford.[5] The new meeting house opened its doors for worship almost exactly a year later; it had cost £3,366.

Though his name appears on various lists of members of the chapel, John never became a deacon and never involved himself deeply in church affairs. His three spinster daughters, whom he had not registered at the parish church in any way, were all baptised as adults at Badcox. Mary, the youngest, was the first to commit herself, in June 1810:

> The following persons related their religious experience before the church: Eleanor Cullen; Rachel Rowe; Emma George; Mary Titford – who were all baptised on the Sabbath morning, June 10, and admitted in the afternoon.[6]

Ann followed suit in 1815, and Sarah in 1816, though all three sisters had actually attended the chapel for some years before becoming full members: a seating list for April 1807 shows us that Mary was in Mr. Porter's 'Dark Gallery', with Ann and Sarah sharing Mr. Coomb's 'Light Gallery'.

Ann, the mother, as we have seen, refrained from sharing those galleries with her daughters or from sitting next to her husband in chapel on Sundays. Yet Badcox Lane must have regarded her as a member of their congregation in the widest sense, at least in spirit;

when she died, aged 79, and was buried at Catherine Hill on 18 May 1826, the chapel entered the fact in its register. A visiting minister performed the burial service, a man who was lending the chapel a helping hand during the interregnum which came between the departure of Samuel Saunders and the arrival of Thomas Fox Newman. And Ann, till the very end, seems somehow to have been a member of no chapel and yet of every chapel; here she was, being afforded a burial service by courtesy of the Badcox congregation, yet being laid claim to at the same time by a neighbouring Dissenting church: Sheppards Barton Baptist Chapel registers include the entry: 'Anne Titford. Frome. May 18th, 1826. Aged 79. In the Burial Ground on Catherine Hill. W. A. Murch, Minister'.

John outlived his wife by just over two years, dying on 5 June 1828. His old friends the overseers did him proud to the very last: in their generosity they provided him with a 14s. funeral.

John had been the last of his generation. There were now to be fewer and fewer Titfords in Frome as time went by; many had died, some had left town for good. The daughters of Charles the Cheesemonger were still very much around, however, and as the offspring of a man in trade and one who, despite his early death, had enjoyed quite a full working life, they were fairly well-breeched compared to the daughters of their Uncle John.

Charles's daughter Sarah had made a prudent marriage, and quite late in life, too: the ceremony at St John's had taken place on her thirty-fifth birthday, with sister Mary as witness. All four of Charles's children who married were to do so by licence; that suited two of them – Elizabeth in Frome and then Benjamin in London – who were in a bit of a hurry, but in Sarah's case there was maybe a hint of Nonconformist protest against having banns read out in a church which she did not attend. Her new husband, William Chinnock, had affiliations with the Zion Chapel on the corner of Catherine Hill and Whittox Lane, and had been baptised there as an infant in 1789. A wheelwright at marriage, he had subsequently made a successful career in the building trade, and by the 1830s was rated on no fewer than six houses in Gore Hedge – almost a third of the street.

Sarah's sister Mary was to remain the spinster of the family, but seems to have been equally comfortably-off; when times were hard and shops were perpetually falling vacant through lack of trade in the 1820s, Mary dodged around from one location to another like an enterprising little businesswoman. She was running a milliner's shop in the Market Place as early as 1822, thence to King Street, along from the *Three Swans Inn* and the infant school, followed by a brief spell in Cheap Street, where she was paying a rate of 9d. and an additional amount for 'Stocks' by virtue of her fleeting partnership with someone called Grant. Then off to North Parade in 1833, where two 'Miss Titford's' followed the same business as milliners, the other, Elizabeth, being almost certainly Mary's niece, daughter of her brother Benjamin who had died in London in 1816. Finally a return to King Street in 1836; eight years later Mary died at her sister and brother-in-law's house in Gore Hedge, aged sixty-four.[7]

Mary and Sarah's comparative affluence was by no means typical of conditions in Frome in the 1820s and 1830s, however. William Cobbett, visiting the town in 1826, the year John Titford's wife Ann died, talked with a perverse kind of delight about the 'irretrievable decay of the place'; four years later it was the turn of a Bridgwater grocer, Thomas Clark, to write of Frome in his journal in the following terms:

> . . . a dreadful distress prevailing and consequent depression . . . the people are working for a very pittance – 5000 persons on the poor book in Frome – very inadequately relieved . . .[8]

Among those on the poor list were the daughters of John Titford; their brother William, a mason of Whittox Lane, had died in 1822, and by the November of 1824 his widow, Sarah, was being paid 2s. a fortnight by the overseers. In 1826 she was joined by her sisters-in-law,

Sarah and Ann, who had just lost their mother; the poor relief 'Extras' list granted them 1s. or 18d. a week for at least the next three years.

So John Titford's daughters, like himself and his wife, needed the parish dole in order to survive. Young Sarah stayed on in her parents' house behind the hill, only one of a number of poor people in that humble street.[9] In 1835 she teamed up with two other pauper girls, Eliza Johnson and Ann Yerbury, and between them they occupied three tenements belonging to Thomas Edwards on Naish's Street. The Trinity Area, a serviceable enough place to live in the 17th century, was fast becoming a slum for the destitute. Whittox Lane was, if anything, poorer than Naish's Street, and it was here that John Titford's eldest daughter, Ann, moved in 1828 – probably to join her sister-in-law, Sarah. All three Titford sisters – Ann, Sarah and Mary – were together in Whittox Lane when the census man called in 1841, and all three, poor relief or not, were engaged in some kind of gainful employment as 'wire dappers' or 'wire setters'. Ten years later it was a slightly different story: only Sarah and Mary appear in the census, Ann having died that very year, aged sixty-nine. Times must still have been hard down Whittox Lane, though nearly all its inhabitants seem to have been employed in some way or another – most of them in the clothing trade, alongside Mr. Middleditch, the Badcox Lane Baptist minister, and Charles Dyer, 23, a coal miner. The Titford girls were on the east side of the street, on the right-hand side going down from Badcox.[10]

But Sarah and Mary were growing old; by May 1855 Badcox Lane Chapel was taking upon itself the responsibility of arranging home visits to Mary, who was sick with diarrhoea, and were paying 1s. per month to help her out. Her cousin Elizabeth of Dorking's £20 legacy was to arrive just too late to be of any comfort to her, and she died in the September, aged sixty-five.

Sarah, left alone, had the dubious distinction of being the last of all the Titfords in Frome. A family line which had begun with a marriage of 1625, seen good times and bad times, sent its bright young sons to London and married its daughters into many a Frome family was seeing here, in Sarah, its last torch-bearer. Poor Sarah, as she lived into her seventies, can hardly have felt like much of a torch-bearer; during her childhood in the 1780s and '90s Titfords had been thick on the ground – as had many families she now saw no more. Those days had passed, and she only had the Chapel for consolation; even they, alas, got her name wrong – were the three sisters so alike that no-one could decide who was who? – and when sickness payments to her started in November, 1857, she was erroneously entered as 'Mary'. By February of 1859 they had rectified their mistake – but by then Sarah was past caring. The last Frome Titford died at Whittox Lane on 18 October 1860, aged 76, and a chapter in our history closes with her.

CHAPTER 16

W. C. T. (1772-1828)

Frome, Somerset, and London

SILKEN PURSES AND SOWS' EARS

There was also the magnet of London and many families had adventurous members who moved into the capital during the period from about 1775 to 1825, some considerably raising their financial and social status in doing so.

Gerald Hamilton-Edwards: *In Search of Ancestry*

If this were a study in local history we should now, of course, be looking ever more closely at the ups and downs of everyday life in Frome. But our focus is primarily upon people, not places as such; the male survivors of the next generation of Titfords succeeded in wrenching themselves away from the town which had been home for their ancestors for over a hundred and seventy years – and we have no choice but to follow them.

What is in many ways remarkable is that the family had stayed in Frome as long as it had. Even more remarkable, perhaps, that this branch of the Titfords was to make only two significant moves from one place to another in the entire 400-year period from 1547 to 1947: first leaving Bratton for Frome in 1625, then settling in London from the late 1790s onwards.

The population of the capital grew dramatically in the 18th and 19th centuries, just as it had done in the 17th, and despite the fact that its death rate was higher than the national average. Even the most cursory examination of the census returns for London from 1841 onwards will reveal the extent to which those born in country towns or villages chose – or were forced – to seek employment or advancement in the big city.

Those who made the journey to London might have done so for a variety of reasons. Most significantly, the impact of the Agricultural Revolution and the extensive enclosures in rural parishes during the late 18th and early 19th centuries drove the young and healthy away from home in search of work and the possibility of keeping body and soul together. The lucky or plucky ones got out, leaving the older generation, all too often, to see out their days as paupers on the parish.

Poverty was not only rampant in the country villages, though, as we know only too well. Almost an entire generation of Titfords in Frome was increasingly destitute from the 1780s onwards; in a town which had depended heavily upon the wool industry for its prosperity for so long, the innate conservatism of the local clothiers left them unable to respond to changing times and new technology. Cardmaking was a declining trade, savage winters and poor harvests had sent prices soaring, and England was eventually trying to cope with the ravages of a war-time economy.

This is the background against which we must see the departure of William Charles Titford for London. His own father, Charles the Cheesemonger, was neither a cardmaker nor a pauper, and we can hardly suppose that any loss of common rights through enclosures had had any direct impact upon his family as it had upon so many others. Nevertheless, the lad had reasons enough for his departure: by the late 1790s his mother was dead, his father solvent but none too rich, and his aunts, uncles and cousins all paupers or on the verge of becoming such. Had he stayed, there was every chance that he might have been forced eventually to join the Militia – a thing few Titfords would face with relish; but most significant of all, perhaps – apart from his obvious inner resilience and entrepreneurial spirit – he had the singular advantage of having well-off relations to latch onto in London.

A journey to the capital in the late 18th century can scarcely have been as harrowing an affair as that made to Kent by William the Emigrant in 1711. A fast stage-coach could now cover over a hundred miles in a single day, good roads and weather permitting, though comfort was not necessarily to be looked for and there was an outside chance of ending up with a foul-mouthed and drunken coachman for the length of the journey.

Assuming he could not afford the luxury of a high-speed post-chaise, William Charles may have taken one of the coaches which left the *George* in Frome for the *Bell Sauvage* in Ludgate Hill on Sundays, Tuesdays and Thursdays at 3 o'clock in the afternoon. That would have cost him £1 7s. Alternatively, he could always have chatted up one of the drivers of Middleton & Co.'s waggon, asking if there was a bit of spare room for an extra body when they left for the *King's Arms* in Holborn on a Sunday evening or a Monday morning. Failing that, perhaps Webb's would take him to the *Castle Inn* in Wood Street, if he spoke to them nicely?

Speaking to people nicely may well have been William Charles's greatest worldly asset, one which would enable him to make a living in the great metropolis, for all his lack of more specific skills. His story as it unfolds is at times scarcely credible when we think back to the way things were in Frome in the 1790s. By 1798 he was already comfortably settled as a linen draper within the hallowed precincts of the City of London, and had the fact entered in the commercial directories accordingly; Titford and Barwick might be consulted for your drapery needs at 77 Bishopsgate Within, situated at the end of Suttons Court opposite the Marine Society Offices. The man who collected the sewer rates in Bishopsgate was quick to notice a change of ownership at no. 77; striking out 'Joseph Ready' in his book, he substituted 'Titford' instead – that would cost W. C. T. 6s. 8d. per annum, whether he liked it or not.[1]

At 26, then, young William Charles ('Call me Charles . . .') had magically catapulted himself into the lower echelons of the Establishment – all achieved, we may suppose, with the help of a good head for business, a degree of energy and flamboyance and an ingratiating style with customers, especially ladies?

Could we have seen W. C. T. at work in his shop, we might well have appreciated the importance of a silver tongue. Two foreign visitors to London in the late 18th century spoke with wonder of certain City shops with their 'shop-fronts with large glass windows and a glass door'.[2] Maybe William Charles's premises were designed in that style? Inside, Titford and Barwick could apply the soft-talk while lining their elegant pockets with silver. One account of an 18th-century visit to a draper's talks of the proprietors as being '. . . positively the greatest fops in the kingdom'. The customer was confronted by three partners; two of them '. . . were to flourish out their silks', while the other was to be 'gentleman usher of the shop', complete with the necessary patter:

> This, madam, is wonderful, charming. This, madam – ye Gods! would I had 10,000 yards of it! . . . Fan me, ye winds, your ladyship rallies me! Should I part with it at such a price, the weavers would rise upon the very shop. Was you at the Park last night, madam? Your ladyship shall abate me sixpence . . .[3]

Perhaps W. C. T. was never quite up to this level of verbosity? He must have had charm, nevertheless, not to mention a broad Somerset accent which may have added to his own special brand of eloquence.[4]

Some drapery establishments were plain, if expensive: Parson Woodforde, paying a call on one in Southampton Street in the October of 1786, was £13 6s. worse off after he had paid for '. . . table linnen, muslin, a piece of Holland, cravats, etc.'.[5] At the upper end of the scale came those shops which bewildered members of the public – those who could

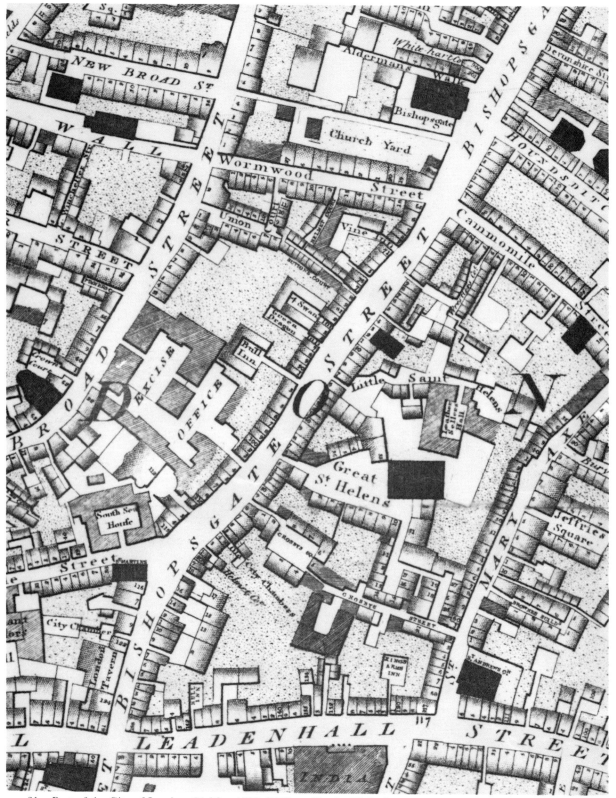

31. Part of the City of London, 24 May 1799. William Charles Titford ran his linen draper's business from 77 Bishopsgate Street, at the end of Sutton's Court between the *Vine Inn* and the *Four Swans Inn*, from 1798 to 1806.

afford it all – with an astonishing range of merchandise: Dutch ratteens, duffles, frizes, beaver coatings, kerseymeres, forrest cloths, German serges, Wilton stuffs, sagathies, namkeens, Silasia cambricks, Manchester velvets, grograms, double allapeens, silk camblets, barragons, Brussels camblets, princes stuffs, worsted damasks, silk knitpieces, gattias, shagg velvets, serge desoys and shalloons. And was there anything else, Madam? . . .[6]

Titford and Barwick, let us guess, ran an altogether more humble establishment than that . . . Nevertheless, however humble the business, the City did not take kindly to outsiders trading within its boundaries; William Charles had a bit of bureaucracy to sort out before he could feel safe and settled. He needed, essentially, to become a Freeman of the City of London – and the most direct route for him, considering he had served no appropriate apprenticeship, was to buy himself into a livery company first. The Weavers' Company would do as well as any other in the circumstances, especially since his cousins, as silk weavers, were already members of it.

So we read in the minutes of the Court of Assistants of the Worshipful Company of Weavers, London, for Tuesday 2 January 1798: 'William Chas. Titford of Bishopsgate Street, Linen Draper, was made free by Redemption on the Recommendation of Mr Lum'.[7] Dear Mr. Lum – who had been admitted to the Weavers' Company himself in 1787 – had agreed to recommend his friend William Charles Titford, and the deal went through as a freedom by redemption – that is, by virtue of payment – rather than by apprenticeship or patrimony. Wiliam Charles was then half-way there; the next stage was to take along a piece of paper certifying this aforesaid freedom, and present it to the Chamberlain's Office as part of the procedure for achieving full freedom of the City. The whole thing didn't take very long; just over a year after his freedom of the Weavers' Company had been approved, William Charles Titford, Linen Draper, 'Son of Charles Titford of Frome, Somersetshire, Cheesemonger', became free of the City, '. . . paying unto Mr Chamberlain for this City's use the Sum of forty six shillings and eight pence'.[8]

William Charles's sponsor was no less a gentleman than 'Robert Peckham Esquire this City's Justice for the Borough of Southwark', who was allowed to present three men to the said honour. Well, Peckham may have recommended him, but it fell to the new Freeman himself to pay his own 46s. 8d. And that should give us food for thought; while his uncle William in Frome, amongst others, was receiving poor relief at the rate of between 1s. and 4s. per fortnight, here, in the same year of 1799, the nephew-made-good was handing over what amounted to about a year's dole payments to join an exclusive club in the metropolis. The order of the Court of Aldermen to admit William Charles to the City freedom is dated 15 January 1799; just over two weeks later his brother John, the brave little Frome volunteer, died of his consumption back home.

Further privileges lay in store for W. C. T. as a member of the Weavers' Company – though nearly every entry in his name subsequently is confused by his double Christian names: even the document granting him his Freedom of the City had to insert 'William' in front of 'Charles' with a caret mark, and as far as the Weavers were concerned, he was really 'Charles William'. So 'Charles William Titford' joined the Livery of his company, being 'cloathed' on 14 July 1801, and promising to 'pay the fine' (a resounding £10). Four years later, in 1804, we find that 'Charles William Titford and Daniel Slamp . . .' were elected to be two of the Company's stewards,

> . . . to find and provide one third part of the entertainment on next St James' Day each unless they shall severally pay the usual fine of £15 each in lieu of serving the said officer at the next court . . .[9]

We are talking here, of course, about amounts of money that the uncles, aunts and cousins back in Frome could only have dreamed of. William Charles had very definitely arrived on the scene.

How had all this opulence come our young man's way? There are essentially two reasons,

32. Minutes of the Court of Assistants of the Worshipful Company of Weavers, Basinghall Street, London, 2 January, 1798. 'William Chas. Titford of Bishopgate St. Linnendraper was made Free by Redemptn. on the recommendation of Mr. Lum'.

33. *The Gentleman's Magazine*. A list of 'Marriages and Deaths of remarkable Persons' includes the marriage of William Charles Titford and Anne Edgar on 21 June 1799.

1799.] *Marriages and Deaths of remarkable Persons.* 527

more, sister of T. B. esq. of Briggins, Herts.

1b. Richard Oliver, esq. of Leyton, Essex, to Miss Brassey, eldest daughter of the late Nathanael B. esq. of Lombard-str. banker.

13. The Rev. Mr. Disturnell, rector of Worms-hill, Kent, to Miss Cranke, daughter of Henry C. esq. of New Bridge-street, Black friers, auditor-general of Bridewell and Bethlehem hospitals.

15. William Fowle, esq. of Durrington, Wilts, to Miss Everett, eldest daughter of Thomas E. esq. M. P. Bedford-square.

17. Mr. Wm. Smith, merchant, to Miss Bagshaw, both of Burton-upon-Trent.

18. At Bath, John Upham, esq. of Exeter, to Miss Elizabeth Chapman, daughter of George C. esq. mayor of Bath.

20. At Easton, near Grantham, James Raymond Johnstone, esq. of Alva, co. Stirling, to Miss Mary-Elizabeth Cholmeley, third daughter of Montague C. esq. of Easton, co. Lincoln.

21. Mr. William-Charles Titford, of Bishopsgate Within, to Miss Anne Edgar, of Gough-square, Fleet-street, youngest dau. of the late Jos. E. esq. of Yately, Hants.

23. John Savill, esq. of Bocking, Essex, to Miss Webb, of Norwich.

24. Jonathan Raine, esq. of Lincoln's-inn, to Miss Price, of Knightsbridge.

26. At St. James's church, Thomas Heathcote, of Embly, co. Southampton, esq. eldest son of Sir William H. bart. M. P. for that county, to Miss Freeman, only dau. of Thomas Edwards F. esq. deceased, late Member for the Borough of Steyning, and grand-daughter of Thomas Edwards F. of Batsford, co. Gloucester, esq.

27. At St. Andrew's, Holborn, William Keating, esq. only son of the late Col. K. to Miss Cameron, only daughter of Mr. and Mrs. C. who keep a boarding-school for young ladies at Enfield.

At Enfield, Mr. Taylor, school-master, of Hammersmith, to Miss Morris, youngest daughter of the late Mr. M. school-master, of Cheshunt.

of which he had passed on that island, John Graham, esq.

24. At Woodlands, Demerara, G. Robertson, esq.

April 22. At Mr. Griffin's, in the Strand, aged 16, Mr. Joseph Adams, youngest son of Mrs. Joseph A. of Ware, Herts, and brother to Mr. A. goldsmith in the Strand.

May . . . At Totteridge, Herts, the Rev. Mr. Paget, chaplain to the late Lord Rodney, and his private secretary during the greater part of his active services on-board the fleet in the West Indies and at St. Eustatia; from the emoluments of which employments, the share of prize-money, and the appointment of distributing it to the ships companies under the Admiral's direct command, he made a competent fortune, and secured the favour of his patron to his death. Though very much deformed, he was remarkably active, both in body and mind, and particularly distinguished himself for laborious equestrian exercises. His extraordinary testamentary disposition would not have been noticed here, had not one of his friends communicated it to a similar Miscellany of last month. His not surviving the lady with whom he had passed 20 years in happy union, laid him under a necessity of discovering that she was his *wife without the ceremony,* &c. He has left a son and two charming daughters, in the happiness and education of whom he was unceasingly employed.

At Hereford, Mrs. Skinner, relict of Mr. S. prebendary of that cathedral.

2. This day Mr. Ritchens, an opulent farmer at Biddestone, Wilts, aged 97, was hastily conveyed away from his own house to Bristol, where it was soon after said he had died, and was brought back for interment on the 25th; but some suspicion arising, his body was dug up; and, on examination, supposed to have been poisoned.

3. At Leeds, in his 86th year, Mr. Mar-

of which the first is the munificence of W. C. T.'s London cousins. Just as fate had been unkind in many ways to those Titfords who had stayed in Frome throughout the 18th century, so it had been a firm friend to the descendants of William the Emigrant after his arrival in Kent. This branch of the family had had all the material success which their poor Frome cousins lacked, together with the necessary altruism to help out as best they could. Well, it was mainly altruism; to an extent the relationship they had with William Charles, the poor relation up from the country, was a symbiotic one. The London Titfords made silk in Spitalfields; and a draper cousin could help sell it for them.

The silk trade itself had hit very hard times in the mid-1790s; a contemporary ballad reflects its catastrophic decline:

> For in Spitalfields and Shoreditch, likewise Bethnal Green,
> Such decay and distress was seldom ever seen,
> Wives and many children, their mouths to be fed,
> Some forc'd to sell their furniture, and even their bed,
> Some gone for soldiers, some the streets they parade,
> In a low occupation, by the loss of their trade.[10]

Within a few years a temporary revival was on the way, however, and William Titford, grandson of William the Emigrant, was achieving a fair degree of success as a partner in the silk-manufacturing business of Cotes, Titford and Brookes, then operating in Union Street, Bishopsgate. He was already a person of some eminence in Nonconformist circles, too; he and his Methodist wife had enjoyed the distinction of being married by John Wesley in 1774, and by 1799 he was himself a deacon in the General Baptist movement. His own son, Richard, was contemporary with William Charles, and William senior was also acting as a surrogate father for his brother Isaac's son, a certain William Jowett Titford. Three 'cousins' in the broadest sense – W. C. T., W. J. T. and Richard – thus formed a kind of 'Titford trio' in the City.

So much for one reason why William Charles had had the wherewithal to prosper so quickly in his new surroundings; but there was another, just as vital to his continuing success – he had made a prudent marriage. The *Gentleman's Magazine* for 1799 was pleased to announce the wedding of 'Mr William Charles Titford of Bishopsgate Within to Miss Anne Edgar of Gough Square, Fleet Street. Youngest daughter of the late Jos. Edgar of Yately, Hants.'. Gough Square was no backwater – Dr. Samuel Johnson had lived there a few years before – and a Gough Square lady must have been a good catch for an impecunious cheesemonger's son. The formalities were gone through – including, in this case, the obtaining of a marriage licence; the bachelor of St Ethelburga's parish made an allegation that he knew of no lawful impediment why he should not marry the girl from St Dunstan's in the West, and it was there that they became man and wife on 21 June 1799.[11]

So 1799 was a signal year for W. C. T. in more ways than one: he was now a respectable businessman with a respectable wife, and a Freeman of the City to boot – what can they have thought of all that back in Pig Street, Frome?

Any account of William Charles's doings in the City during the early 19th century would be incomplete without some mention of his illustrious cousin, William Jowett Titford.[12] No ordinary man, he; with a good education behind him, coupled with a strong religious fervour, he would eventually achieve a degree of fame by compiling a treatise on the botany of North America, called *Sketches towards a Hortus Botanicus Americanus*. His father, Isaac, a gentleman with more than a little of the rogue about him, was in Jamaica during the closing years of the 18th century, taking refuge there, it would seem, after a bankruptcy of 1779. Styling himself 'Dr. Isaac Titford', he had been commissioned surgeon (not by any means so prestigious a profession then as now) in the first battalion, Sixtieth Royal American Regiment, and had lived for a while in Virginia; he was also giving his enterprising spirit

SKETCHES

TOWARDS A

HORTUS BOTANICUS
AMERICANUS;

OR,

COLOURED PLATES

(WITH A CATALOGUE AND CONCISE AND FAMILIAR DESCRIPTIONS OF MANY SPECIES)

OF

NEW AND VALUABLE PLANTS

OF THE

West Indies and North and South America.

ALSO OF

SEVERAL OTHERS, NATIVES OF AFRICA AND THE EAST INDIES:

Arranged after the Linnæan System.

WITH

A CONCISE AND COMPREHENSIVE GLOSSARY OF TERMS, PREFIXED,

AND A GENERAL INDEX.

By W. J. TITFORD, M.D.
CORRESPONDING MEMBER OF THE SOCIETY FOR THE ENCOURAGEMENT OF ARTS, &c.

LONDON:
PRINTED FOR THE AUTHOR, BY C. STOWER, HACKNEY:
Published by SHERWOOD, NEELY, and JONES, Paternoster Row; J. HATCHARD, Piccadilly; J. RICHARDSON, Cornhill, and all Booksellers in the United Kingdom.
1812.

34. Title page, William Jowett Titford's *Hortus Botanicus Americanus.* From the copy now in the possession of Mr. Tony Titford of West Horsley.

full reign out there in the West Indies, fathering the odd quadroon or two, dabbling in the slave trade, a postmaster at Spanish Town, a partner in a firm of druggists in Kingston and the owner of a coffee and pimento plantation.

In 1802 William Jowett was to sail to Jamaica to help sort out his father's affairs, having acted until then as an accountant for his uncle William at Cotes, Titford and Brookes. Shortly after his arrival in Spanish Town he wrote to his cousin William Charles, informing him that: '. . . some of your shawls sold for 200 and 300 per cent profit . . .', but adding:

> . . . before they were all sold, a quantity of the same sort came up to town at half the price, so that the rest remained on hand. This is to request that you will send me no more goods unless ordered.

Just a friendly letter between cousins . . .

Being undersold out there in Jamaica was to be only one of William Charles's problems as time went by: after a period of increasing success as a linen draper and mercer, he was eventually beset by financial problems, occasioning a move northwards from Bishopsgate to Finsbury Place, Finsbury Square (on the corner of Chiswell Street), together with a reproof from William Jowett, who lost no time in admonishing his cousin in a letter to Richard Titford from Jamaica, dated 28 April 1806:

> Sorry for W. C. T., but thought three things dangerous to merchants and tradesmen, too much and too long credit, borrowing too much on discount, and extending the trade too much and going out of depth.

Sound advice, indeed.

W. C. T. had been busy in other ways too, fathering a series of children; three at least were to die young, and he took them for burial to his cousins' Baptist Chapel at Worship Street, Shoreditch. There the register-keeper was well and truly confused, since he not only referred to children of '*Charles William* Titford, Linen Draper, Bishopsgate Street' – a nomenclature which we are used to by now – but also made an error when it came to wife Anne's name – she appears as 'Mary'. A degree of bewilderment is perhaps to be expected, after all: in 1805, for instance, there were two Charles Titfords buried at Worship Street – the one, son of Richard and Mary Ann, the other, son of Charles William and . . . well, 'Mary' would be a forgiveable error?[13]

Of the surviving children of William Charles and Anne, five were baptised together on the same day (10 July 1817) in their father's original parish at the miniature City church of St Ethelburga, Bishopsgate. There were two sons: John, the elder, became a solicitor's clerk, dying as a bachelor in Lambeth in 1862, while his brother Joseph, a house painter settling in Hoxton, assured the continuity of the Titford line by having a number of male children by his wife Elizabeth, *née* Griffiths.[14]

Two of the three daughters of William Charles were to find husbands for themselves. 1841 saw the marriage of Mary to Samuel Wates, a clerk from Greenwich, at the Denmark Place Baptist Chapel in Lambeth. Sarah, with a similar taste for a Nonconformist ceremony, took on an engineer by the name of William Parfitt at Westminster Congregational Chapel in 1846. Their wedding was conducted by the Rev. Samuel Martin, father of Charles Trice Martin, who himself was later to achieve fame by writing that most valuable of reference works, *The Record Interpreter*. Rev. Samuel himself, son of a Woolwich shipwright, had chosen to work in Westminster, then '. . . one of the most socially unregenerate districts of the metropolis', where his 'eloquence and steady devotion to his work attracted a large congregation'.[15] Not only was Sarah Titford's wedding celebrated in a 'socially unregenerate' part of London – it also featured a bride who gave her place of abode on the marriage certificate, ominously enough, as 'Millbank Prison'. Not, we may hope, as a guest of Her Majesty?

The last of William Charles Titford's children, Emely Sophia, born in 1819, nearly saw the 20th century. A spinster in her seventies and employed as a housekeeper at the time, she died in Bishopsgate Street on 17 April 1898. Her will makes a careful list of most of her very ordinary possessions; perhaps the most valuable, sentimentally and financially, goes to Samuel Wates, in the form of 'Uncle John's silver watch' – possibly the last remaining momento of her deceased brother.

Emely Sophia had outlived her father, William Charles, by almost seventy years. When we left him he was a linen draper and furniture warehouseman in Finsbury Square; by 1818 he had made his final move to Windsor Terrace, an elegant row of houses on City Road, having by then become a silk manufacturer like his cousins. He died 10 years later, on 20 June 1828, in nearby Wellington Street – just two days short of his twenty-ninth wedding anniversary, and a mere two weeks after the death of his pauper uncle, John Titford, in Frome. He was buried at that most busy of London churches, St Luke's, Old Street, leaving a widow who would run a little milliner's business in Soho before dying, 23 years later, in Westminster.

An appropriate valedictory comment on W. C. T. might be that he underwent a dramatic rags-to-riches transformation, conveniently abandoning the Dissenting zeal of his ancestors in the process. It does look, after all, as if respectability posed the greatest of all threats to the survival of Nonconformity; the son and grandson of Baptist believers as he was, cousin to a family of ardent devotees of the Worship Street Chapel, William Charles appears to have paid little more than passing lip-service to the cause. All the evidence seems to indicate that he had become a half-hearted Anglican – perhaps that was a safer way, after all, of establishing yourself as a respectable tradesman than anything which smacked in any way of revolt or radicalism? Or maybe he picked up good trading contacts from Chapel and Church alike, just as it suited him? Whatever fire he may have had in his belly, it hardly seems to have been the religious fire of his Frome forbears. The pure flame of radical Christianity, we might say with the example of the Titfords before us, would be lucky indeed if it burned brightly for as many as three generations.

William Charles had no doubt been a success in his own terms, for all that. He had also enjoyed a longer life than his father; his younger brother Benjamin, to whom we now turn, was not to be so lucky.

CHAPTER 17

Ben the Outrider (1786-1816)

Frome, Somerset, and London

SHOREDITCH WORKHOUSE

. . . When the humble *outrider* astride his saddle bags, goes his rounds for fresh orders, to dealers and chapmen in the country . . .

from the *Oxford English Dictionary*

It is high time we renewed our acquaintance with young Benjamin Titford, William Charles's younger brother. When we met him last he was a mere lad down in Somerset, gazing in wonderment at troops of militia, itinerant theatre companies and a larger-than-life basking shark. His was, in many ways, an inauspicious start to life: an 18th-century guide book could say of Frome:

The situation of the town is pleasant; the surrounding country being agreeably diversified with hills, valleys, large enclosures, and fine woods; and having the seats of many nobility and gentry . . .

but that has a touch of the rose-coloured spectacles about it; Wesley was not so impressed with the town when he first preached there in 1753 in what he called a 'dry, barren, uncomfortable place'.

Young Ben Titford was born and raised in smelly, noisy Pig Street – a lively enough corner of the world, perhaps, but not the healthiest of places for all that. No fewer than seven of his siblings had died there – five of them before their first birthday. He had lost his mother before he was 10, seen the departure of William Charles for London shortly afterwards, then witnessed the death of his consumptive brother John, followed by that of his father. By the middle of 1802, as the family house and shop passed into other hands, Ben was left alone with only sisters for company; Elizabeth, the eldest, had very recently married, and little brother must have been in imminent danger of succumbing to the petticoat government of Mary and Sarah. If that didn't ensnare him, then the Militia might, as he grew older: there was a brief hiatus in the war with France from 1801 to 1803, but by the following year Napoleon was massing his army of invasion on the cliffs at Boulogne. The Military Training Act of 1806 – the year after Trafalgar – was to provide for 200,000 troops to be raised by ballot, a measure which prompted serious riots in Frome seven years later. This Act of 1806 may well have given young Ben the final push he needed: in that or the following year he packed his bags for good, waved his loving sisters a fond farewell, and set off for London, fame and fortune.[1]

As it happens, he wouldn't be arriving at the best possible moment: William Charles, 14 years his brother's senior, was finding his own fame and fortune rather on the wane just at that time – he didn't need those supercilious letters from William Jowett in Jamaica to remind him of that. Nevertheless, it looks very much as if he was able to help young Ben out a bit: probably by employing him as a commercial traveller in his own drapery business. Ben is described variously as a 'merchant's clerk' and as an 'outrider', itself a dialect term used extensively in Somerset and elsewhere to describe a tradesman's travelling agent – a meaning it still carried in New Zealand, for example, well into the 20th century.[2]

No doubt this draper's 'Rep' would have cut a bit of a dashing figure in the big city in his way, replete with some of the family charm and salesmanship which we have assumed

35. 'Ben The Outrider' (1786-1816). Artist's impression by Richard Scollins, 1983.

to be one of the hallmarks of William Charles himself. His would not have been the only provincial accent to assail the ears of Londoners at the time, but at least it would have lent his speech a touch of bucolic appeal, with its rolling Somerset post-vocalic 'r' sounds and a liberal sprinkling of 'v's for 'f's and 'z's for 's's.[3]

All of this was enough to attract one person in particular: a London girl, seven years his senior, called Elizabeth Hasted. He may have met her while doing business with 'her father Robert, a tea dealer in Crutched Friars, or her brothers, who were all coopers in Stepney; sales talk for the men, but softer words for the lady – one who was shortly to become his wife.

The very mention of Stepney and Whitechapel to a 20th-century ear suggests cramped housing, urban poverty, the cheapest property available on the 'Monopoly' board. Yet it hadn't always been so. Stepney in the late 18th century was becoming what the Northern Heights – Highgate and Hampstead – became later, namely, an early form of London suburbia. In the closing years of that century the eastward spread was beginning: there was already some development east of the Tower of London, including the later-notorious Ratcliff Highway and the docks area at Wapping, Shadwell and Limehouse. That apart, Whitechapel Road and Mile End Road ran into open fields, and the ancient parish church, St Dunstan's, was in an entirely rural setting. From 1800 the street pattern which lasted in essence until the blitz ofthe Second World War was rapidly growing. The austere but imposing Hawksmoor tower of St George's in the East rose above its riverside parish and the bustling London Docks, and to the north St Mary Whitechapel rubbed uneasy shoulders with the Union Street Independent Chapel, both standing opposite the Whitechapel work-house and down the road from the London Hospital and the famous Whitechapel Bell Foundry.

It was to this area that the Hasteds had come at the very beginning of the 19th century; previously their home had been in the City, in the parishes of St Katherine Coleman and St Olave, Hart Street, but like many of their contemporaries they made the pilgrimage east. A short pilgrimage, to be sure: John Frederick and Thomas Hasted set up in business as coopers in Well Close Square and, later, in nearby Princes Square.[4] Well Close Square was elegant and private, fed by Shorter Street in the north and Neptune Street in the south, but with narrow alleys leaving it diagonally at its four corners. The houses, many of them partly timber in construction, were fine products of the rising artisan class, to which class the Hasteds undoubtedly belonged.

Before making this move east into Stepney, John Frederick Hasted had married in 1803 a young lady by the name of Sarah Hunt, with his sister Elizabeth acting as a witness; the ceremony took place at the City church of All Hallows by the Tower (also known as All Hallows Barking). Elizabeth was to return to the same church for her own wedding five years later; she and young Benjamin Titford were married there on 24 January 1808.

Matters had not proceded entirely without the odd hitch or two for the young couple – mainly because the bride was heavily pregnant with a child, one conceived during the long dry summer of 1807. Ben and Elizabeth found themselves doing what many others did in a similar predicament – rather than wait for banns to be read, they married by licence. For him it meant a brief wait until he was of the appropriate age of 21, in December 1807; barely a month later he was off to Doctors' Commons in St Paul's Churchyard to sign an allegation '. . . that he is of the Parish of All Hallows, Barking, London, a bachelor . . .' and '. . . that there is no lawful impediment . . .' before being issued with a licence by the Archbishop of Canterbury's Faculty Office. Thence to the church, two days later.[5]

Standing at the corner of Great Tower Street and Seething Lane, in the very shadow of the Tower of London, All Hallows must have been as impressive a building then as it is today: one of the oldest parish churches in the City, it has always had close links with the Tower itself, and was used as a place of burial for many an unfortunate wretch executed

KNOW all Men by these Presents, That We *Benjamin Titford of the parish of All Saints Barking London Gentleman and John Thomas* are holden and firmly bound to the Most Reverend Father in God, CHARLES, by Divine Providence, Lord Archbishop of CANTERBURY, Primate of all ENGLAND, and Metropolitan, in the Sum of Two Hundred Pounds of good and lawful Money of GREAT BRITAIN, to be paid to the said Most Reverend Father, or his certain Attorney, Successors or Assigns: To which Payment, well and truly to be made, we bind ourselves, and each of us by himself for the Whole, our Heirs, Executors, and Administrators, firmly by these Presents. Sealed with our Seals. Dated the *Twenty Second* Day of *January* in the *Forty eighth* Year of the Reign of our Sovereign Lord *George the Third* by the Grace of God of the United Kingdom of Great Britain and Ireland, King, Defender of the Faith, and in the Year of our Lord One Thousand Eight Hundred and *eight*

THE Condition of this Obligation is such, That if hereafter there shall not appear any lawful Let or Impediment, by Reason of any Pre-Contract, Consanguinity, Affinity, or any other lawful Means whatsoever; but that the above bounden *Benjamin Titford a Bachelor and Elizabeth Reed Spinster of the said parish* may lawfully solemnize Marriage together, and in the same afterwards lawfully remain and continue for Man and Wife, according to the Laws in that Behalf provided: And moreover, if there be not at this present Time any Action, Suit, Plaint, Quarrel, or Demand, moved or depending before any Judge Ecclesiastical or Temporal, for or concerning any such lawful Impediment between the said Parties: Nor that either of them be of any other Parish, or of better Estate or Degree, than to the Judge at granting the Licence is suggested, and by *him* sworn to

And lastly, if the same Marriage shall be openly solemnized in the Church or Chapel in the Licence specified, between the Hours appointed in Constitutions Ecclesiastical confirmed, and according to the Form of the Book of Common Prayer, now by Law established; and if the above bounden *Parties* do save harmless the above mentioned Most Reverend Father, his Commissary of the Faculties, his Surrogates, and all other his Officers whatsoever, by Reason of the Premises; then this Obligation to be void, or else to remain in full Force and Virtue.

Sealed and Delivered
in the Presence of

J. Tustock

B Titford

36. Marriage bond, 1808. Issued by the Faculty Office of the Archbishop of Canterbury in London. Benjamin Titford's probably-fictitious fellow bondsman is a certain 'John Thomas'.

on the nearby scaffold. It had been lucky enough to have survived the ravages of the Great
Fire of 1666, when its tower acted as a vantage-point from which Samuel Pepys could stare
in horror at the extent of the blaze. William Penn, who founded Pennsylvania, was baptised
at All Hallows, and John Quincy Adams married there in 1797; he was later to become
the sixth president of the U.S.A.

At least John Quincy Adams left the clerk his personal details after the ceremony, unlike
one couple married there in 1650, who went away and '. . . gave not their names'. In the
circumstances, Benjamin Titford might have been tempted not to leave his name in the
parish register, either, as his bride came gingerly down the aisle bearing his as-yet-unborn
son and heir. One may imagine William Charles tut-tutting in the front pews: 'To think
that young brother o' mine, Ben, would disgrace us all by getting Bob Hasted's daughter
in the family way . . . silly young shaver . . .'.

Charles the Cheesemonger had signed his marriage certificate with a cross – a common
enough occurrence, in the event, even among those who could read and write if they put
their minds to it. But one of Charles's achievements was to ensure that all his children who
reached adulthood, male or female, could at least sign their names; his daughter Elizabeth
had produced a most business-like signature at her marriage in 1802 and, here at All
Hallows, Benjamin signed with a flourish, above the rather more demure attempt of his
new wife. Witnesses were Joseph Morrice, the register clerk, and Dorothy Sebbon, but no
Hasted signed except the bride. Were her family offended at this shot-gun marriage? Hardly,
one would think, since such occurrences were by no means rare at this period, and in any
case they came to the rescue in every possible way. A few years later it would be Elizabeth's
brother Samuel who would step into the breach at a time of crisis, as we shall see, but in
1808 it was Thomas Hasted, as the newly-weds skirted round the northern edge of the
Tower and established themselves just inside the parish of St Mary Whitechapel.

Thomas, Elizabeth's eldest brother, was then living at 11 Chambers Street, Stepney, an
18th-century thoroughfare consisting of about seventy houses in all. Those on its northern
side had ample yards or gardens abutting Great Prescott Street, which itself gave onto
Goodman's Fields. It all lay a stone's throw from the Tower and the docks, and the housing
in the surrounding area was punctuated by small workshops, timber yards and warehouses,
along with the East London Theatre just across Rosemary Lane, and the Royal Mint to the
south-west.

The lists of names of those assessed for the Whitechapel sewer rates for the period – yes,
there was some rudimentary sanitation! – reveal the extent to which immigrants into the
area consisted not only of young lads up from Somerset, but included, amongst others,
Jewish families for whom East London would be a place of shelter, away from persecution
elsewhere. In nearly every street in Whitechapel there was a Levy or a Cohen, an Abrahams,
Moses or Grossman – sometimes living together in one area, sometimes striking out on their
own. In Chambers Street in 1810, for example, Mr. Isaac was nicely settled in alongside
the very English-sounding Chas. Taylor, Geo. Bannister, Richd. Morris and our man
Thomas 'Halstead' or Hasted.[6]

It was here in Chambers Street that Benjamin and Elizabeth Titford were living –
probably, we may guess, as guests of brother Thomas at no. 11 – when they took their little
son for baptism at St Mary Whitechapel in the March of 1809, a few days short of his first
birthday. He had been born just over two months after the marriage, and they named him
Charles Benjamin after his paternal grandfather and father respectively.[7]

By the time another male child followed the first, almost exactly a year later, it was time
to perpetuate the maternal grandfather's Christian name. Robert Hasted must have been
more than usually proud, then, of his daughter Elizabeth's second son, Robert Titford.
Born on April Fool's Day 1809, young Robert was destined not to be baptised until he was

13 years old; his sister Elizabeth, the next of Ben and Elizabeth's little brood, was similarly left unbaptised until six years after her birth in 1811. She had entered the world in the January of what would prove to be a notorious year down in Stepney: a series of brutal murders was to take place on Ratcliff Highway, a major road which ran to the south of Well Close Square and right past St George's church itself. It must have been a worrying time for Titfords and Hasteds alike, not to mention the rest of the inhabitants of the densely-populated riverside parishes; the victims of the killer – or rather the remains – were laid to rest in a corner of St George's churchyard, while the murderer himself, who eventually committed suicide, was buried with a stake through him at the top of Cannon Street where the newly-built Commercial Road crossed.[8]

Violence at home, terrible as it was, could be seen as little more than a reflection of what was then happening on foreign shores. From 1812 to 1815 Britain was fighting a war on two fronts, against what were essentially two cradles of a new democracy: France and the former American colonies. Bad harvests, meanwhile, had once again forced wheat up to famine prices, and the 'outbreak of peace' after the Battle of Waterloo in 1815 was to herald what C. P. Hill has referred to as 'one of the grimmest periods in modern British History'.[9]

The population of England and Wales was undergoing a further massive increase – nothing short of a fifty per cent rise in the years from 1801 to 1831 – and the effects of the recent Agricultural and Industrial Revolutions hardly needed a post-war depression to make matters even worse for the poor. Yet a depression there was, with a vengeance, as the labour market was flooded with returning soldiers and sailors and prices fell dramatically. The Government could scarcely have been more out of touch with the people at large, and was still, in any case, terrified that Jacobinism might even then give rise to a revolution at any moment. Keen above all to protect the interests of the country's farmers, and abandoning the doctrine of *laissez faire* in a period of crisis, parliament moved with alacrity to pass the Corn Law of 1815. With grain prices kept at an artificially high price thereafter, the further impoverishment of those already poor was the inevitable result.

Down in Stepney, Benjamin and Elizabeth Titford's last child was born shortly before the end of the war, on 10 October 1814. Time, at last, to call a baby boy after father himself, so this was to be Benjamin Titford, junior – destined to become a silversmith by trade, and a bit of an entrepreneur like his uncle William Charles.

Just as the post-war economic depression set in, so it signalled its own personal tragedy for the Titford family: on 25 February 1816, Ben the Outrider died, aged barely 29. By then the couple had moved east to Chapman Street, part of the new housing development in the neighbourhood of St George's in the East; it was here at the nearby parish church that Benjamin was buried five days later, the ceremony being conducted by the rector. No cause of death is given, but we may make an informed guess, for all that, that a man whose elder brother had been carried off by consumption was himself the victim of that 'white plague' which accounted for one-third of all deaths in the early years of the 19th century.[10]

Cause of death would have been of purely academic interest to the deceased man's widow. Elizabeth was in an unenviable position: here she was, at the age of 36, with young children on her hands and no husband to provide the necessities of life, at a time when Social Security was undreamt of and the country was in the grip of an economic crisis. Things could hardly have been worse for her. The only minor consolation was that prices had fallen just after the war, though that situation was not to last long. The general climate of the times was all too apparent as riots broke out in Spa Fields in London in late 1816, followed in due course by the March of the Blanketeers, the Pentrich Rebellion in Derbyshire, the Peterloo Massacre and that desperate attempt to kill the entire cabinet known as the Cato Street Conspiracy.

Elizabeth Titford must have thought that a London in which mobs could go on a looting spree in the City was no place to raise her young daughter. She had enough on her hands trying to bring up the boys, and the simplest expedient would be to get the little girl down to Frome, where her deceased husband's sister and brother-in-law, William and Sarah Chinnock, could provide her with a decent upbringing. So it was duly arranged, and Uncle William and Aunt Sarah took their little niece for baptism at their recently-rebuilt Zion Chapel in Frome in 1817, just across the road from the Badcox Lane Baptists. The chapel register records the birth, registration and christening of six-year old Elizabeth Titford, '. . . daughter of Benjamin and Elizabeth Titford of St George's in the East, Middlesex'.[11] In times of crisis, as we have already seen when Mary Titford arrived in Frome from London in 1757, families or individuals could be quite surprisingly mobile.

Elizabeth's sons could stay with their mother, at least for the time being. They were all still at Chapman street in April 1818, when Benjamin junior was baptised at St George's, after which Elizabeth upped and left for Shoreditch and the parish of St Leonard's, where at least one of her brothers was then living.

The Hasteds no doubt did what they could to help their bereaved sister, though their best turned out to be insufficient to save her as time went by. One brother of her's, at least, rallied to the cause – Samuel Hasted, younger than his sister, who was a cooper living in Bermuda Street, Stepney, a small row of eight houses just off Commercial Road. In 1822 Elizabeth's son Robert was baptised at the Mile End Old Town Zion Chapel on Union Street, built by devotees of Lady Huntingdon's Connexion; the young boy, then 13, may well have been staying with his uncle Samuel at the time, the latter having married three years previously.

The Countess of Huntingdon's Methodist Connexion, founded in the mid-18th century, was yet another Calvinistic organisation, we may note with interest; what with Robert Titford being baptised at one of their chapels, and his sister Elizabeth having been registered with the Zion congregation in Frome, Calvinism seems once again to have cast its shadow across the family, even into the 19th century.

Elizabeth Titford, the mother, must have needed a bit of Christian faith herself as she grew older and struggled to live through the hard times which were a mark of the 1820s with its long and painful inflation. By hook or by crook, and with the assistance of her brother Samuel and her in-laws, she had provided for her children in times of personal and national distress. But the struggle must have taken its toll on her, until the time came when she needed help herself. Any chance of aid or succour from her brother-in-law, William Charles Titford, would have been swept away by his death in 1828; but two years earlier than that, Elizabeth's name appears in the registers of Shoreditch Workhouse.

The English Poor Laws, first effective from the late 16th century and radically revised in 1834, had always proved a headache to those who administered them. The problem has a modern ring to it: how do you balance the necessary provision of aid to those really in need with the risk of supporting malingerers on the parish rates? The more populous the parishes became, the more diffuse the community grew, the more acute the problem: no longer did the overseers or the ratepayers know everyone receiving relief, and it was then far from an easy task to sort out the needy from the charlatans. The workhouse – institutional rather than 'outdoor' relief – was one way of controlling the help given to paupers; but demands that such institutions should pay for themselves had a hollow ring to it – many of the inmates were there because their skills were not needed in declining industries, so they could hardly be set to work profitably once they were taken within its walls.

Yet despite Charles Dickens *et al.*, workhouses were not all the dark satanic mills of legend. They acted as hospitals for the sick and the elderly; as houses of refuge for widows, like Elizabeth Titford; as a maternity home for unmarried mothers; and as a place of respite for men temporarily unemployed. Above all, they educated and eventually apprenticed

NAME.	Age.	Ward.	ADMITTED.	DISCHARGED.	REMARKS.
Tierney Jane	7	12	July 18. 1826	July 22 1826	To Enfield
Tierney John	4	12	" " "	" " "	" do
Tierney James	2	13	" " "	" " "	" do
Tarling Eliz^th	70	19	" 27 "	Novr 22 "	Absconded
Taylor Jeffry	50	8	" 28 "	Decr 5 "	Himself
Trotman Ephriam	20	8	Augt 17 "		
Tarr Sarah Ann	19	22	" 18 "	Augt 22 1826	Absconded
Titford Eliz^th	48	16	" 22 "	25 "	
Thompson Fred^k	15	8	" 26 "	Augt 28. 1826	To the H^o of Cor for refusing to work
Tennant John	21	6	Septr 4 "	Novr 11 "	Absconded

37. Admissions Register, Shoreditch workhouse, 1826. Elizabeth Titford, aged 48, spent just three days in the workhouse during the August of 1826. She would return ... (GLRO P91/LEN/1336.)

young paupers, ensuring in theory that they themselves should not in turn need poor relief in adulthood; thus Shoreditch had a so-called Nursery at Enfield specifically for the care and education of destitute children.

Elizabeth's stay in 1826 was a short one; admitted on 22 August, she was discharged three days later, on 25 August. Discharged, perhaps, but not for good.[12] Her presence in the workhouse in itself seems an odd occurrence; it was hardly as if she had no-one to turn to – any one of her brothers must have been in a position to help when help was needed. She might have had a brief illness best treated outside the home, or it is possible that the balance of her mind was disturbed in some way. But another quite plausible explanation presents itself: here was a lady whose role in life was changing, whose function as a mother and whose status – if we may call it that – as a widow were becoming things of the past. To be a spinster was one thing; to be a married woman with or without children, or a recently-bereaved widow, all were recognised and acceptable roles in society. Yet Elizabeth had been a widow for over ten years, and her children were very nearly off her hands; it is quite possible that her brief sojourn in the workhouse was part of an attempt to give her life a new direction and meaning – perhaps she was there as a helper, a visitor, a counsellor to those in need, or even as a missionary spreading the gospel of Christianity in general or that of the Lady Huntingdon's Connexion in particular. The fact that she would return to the same workhouse 10 years later was in itself not untypical; many genuine helpers in such institutions may have had it in the back of their minds that one day they would become the cared for, rather than the person doing the caring, as old age took its toll.

Old age did, eventually, take its toll on Elizabeth; she was on the Shoreditch Workhouse register again by March 1837 – and a very populous place it was by then, too, in the wake of the 1834 Poor Law Amendment Act. The 1841 census lists five hundred or so inmates, including Elizabeth Titford, who is described as being a needleworker.[13] Eight years later she was still there, by then paralysed and helpless, as a virulent epidemic of cholera swept through London. It was the paralysis which caused her death in the end, or so the doctor was to certify; she died there in the workhouse, aged 70, on 12 September 1849. Her lifetime had spanned five reigns.

CHAPTER 18

Robert the Mariner (1809-1839)

London

DEATH IN HONDURAS

Now longe moot thou saille by the cost, . . . gentil *Maryneer!*
Chaucer: *The Prioress's Tale*

Elizabeth had done all she could in the circumstances to provide the best possible start in life for her sons once her husband had died. There were some risks to life and limb, however, over which she had no control; how could she ever have guessed that she would outlive her son Robert by almost exactly 10 years? Robert Titford's life was destined, like that of his father, to be a tragically short one; the boy from the dockside parish whose early years must have been spent in an atmosphere redolent of the sea and ships, old tars and tales of high adventure, chose to make his living on the ocean waves. And it was those waves which were to carry him, steadily and inexorably, to a far-distant grave.

By 1832, and then aged 23, Robert was already a mariner, living at John Street, Stepney, with his wife Eliza; they had married the previous year in his mother's adopted parish, St Leonard's, Shoreditch – he a bachelor and she a widow. Robert's own Christian name, as we know, had come from his maternal grandfather, Robert Hasted, and he passed it on to his second child, Robert Edward; thereafter the same name would continue in that branch of the family until well into the 20th century.

The marriage lasted only a few years, cut short by the death of Eliza; when Robert returned to the same altar at St Leonard's in January of 1837 as a widower, he must have had more than a flash of *déjà vu*. His new bride, a spinster in her thirties called Elizabeth Shaw, would bring him one further child before being left a widow.

A new character must enter the drama at this stage: not a human being, but a ship: the *Orynthia*. She it was who would carry Robert half-way around the world on more than one occasion, until, in the end, she returned without him. The *Orynthia* was a bark of 318 tons; built at Chepstow in Monmouthshire in 1823, square-rigged and with three masts, she measured 100 feet in length, and 27 in breadth, with one and half decks and a square stern. She was carvel-built with flush planks, and – as a *pièce de résistance* – she sported a woman's bust as a figurehead. Quite an impressive sight, we may suppose, as she pitched and tossed in full sail across the Atlantic with fifteen or so mariners on board.[1]

The 1835 Merchant Shipping Act stipulated that agreements and crew lists be filed with the Register Office of Merchant Seaman; the master was to make a list of his men, and submit it within 48 hours of returning to a U.K. port. Thus it is that we know as much as we do about the *Orynthia* and her voyages in the late 1830s.[2]

Robert Titford was already a member of the ship's company when the *Orynthia* docked back in England in mid-December, 1836. And he had a bit of business to attend to: within three weeks he was in Shoreditch – getting married, as we have seen. Just time for a quick honeymoon followed by a few fond farewells, and the intrepid sailor was off again on board his old ship on 17 February, leaving his second wife to look after her newly-acquired step-children, Elizabeth Eliza and Robert Edward, in his absence. A neat arrangement, to be sure, from his point of view, as he returned to his all-male environment once more.

John Lawton was master for this voyage, fresh from another ship but prudently bringing his own cook with him: it fell to Robert Titford to be first mate. There were 15 men on board, ranging in age from 17 to 54, and all English: five ordinary seamen, a steward, a boatswain, two apprentices, a carpenter and a sailmaker, alongside the master, his two mates and the cook. These were not all strangers to Robert: four had previously served aboard the *Orynthia*, including the second mate, William Tilson, nine years his senior. The destination – as so often with this ship – was Honduras in Central America, quite a rich source of exports to England at the time, including the mahogany which was used for so much 19th-century furniture. Captain Lawton and his men seem to have had a fairly trouble-free time of it, because all 15 of them were duly discharged back in London after the seven-month voyage.

But ships are too valuable to lie idle for very long, and Robert barely had a month in which to re-acquaint himself with his new wife and pat his young infants on the head before he was leaving John Street and Stepney again – through Limehouse into Poplar and aboard the *Orynthia* in West India Dock. The master had changed: William Cox, the oldest man aboard at the ripe old age of 54, was not merely the ship's captain – he also owned a half-share in her. Five ex-*Orynthia* men, including Cox himself, feature in the crew of 16, while among the newcomers was young George Groves, a 15-year-old Portsmouth lad on his first voyage. They all did what they had to do – a trip to Honduras again, via Madeira – and were safely back home on 11 June 1838.

Robert seems to have had a special affection for the *Orynthia*; whereas many mariners came and went as the whim took them, he stuck to his old ship. Anyway, there was promotion in it: when we next come across him, less than a year later, he has risen to the giddy heights of master, taking over from William Cox.

And so Robert Titford, Master Mariner, took over his first command. There were 15 crew members, as usual, but they were a bit of a mixed bag this time, including a Scot, an Irishman, a seaman from Nova Scotia and a character born in 'Zamalia' by the name of John Saula. Five of the crew had remained loyal to the *Orynthia*, though Robert only had one mate to rely upon – and that was a situation which would be little short of a recipe for disaster, as things turned out.

We can make a pretty fair guess as to how much the ship's crew were paid on such a trip as this: a surviving Schedule 'A' Crew Agreement for the same ship four years later reveals that a seaman could expect to earn £2 per month, the cook and steward slightly more, the carpenter £5 10s., and the first and second mates £6 and £4 10s. respectively.[3]

The Times for the morning of Wednesday, 29 May 1839, announced that the *Orynthia* was cleared outward with cargo for Demerara and Honduras; the woman's bust figurehead was leading her brave boys away from home on the long voyage south-west. The Atlantic crossing was over by 12 July and the *Orynthia* had arrived in Demerara, a one-time Dutch settlement which had been absorbed into British Guiana in 1831. Here a coastal lowland is backed by a belt of forest before the ground rises to the Guiana Highlands. But any charm the scenery may have had was lost on one member of the crew: James McKeatling was taken sick in the far-from-healthy climate, and was left on shore. Worse was to follow.

They were still at Demerara two weeks later when the cook was drowned; the next day – by ominous coincidence or not – John Saula, the man from 'Zamalia' was thrown into prison. We can only guess whether inter-racial bickering – or even rows over bad food! – might explain such a bizarre two days' events. Whatever may have been the cause, the whole thing was all too much for 18-year old Francis Burke, the youngest man on board: on 31 July he left the ship, thus reducing its crew to 11 men.

Robert Titford, we may imagine, must have wondered what he had done to deserve all this. After some uneventful voyages over the years, and at least seven previous masters, the

38. Crew list, the *Orynthia*, 1839. A chapter of disasters here culminates in the death of Robert Titford, the ship's master, at 'Rattan' off Honduras. (PRO BT98/376.)

Orynthia seemed to have turned into a hornets' nest. There was nothing to do but carry on, severely reduced in numbers as they were, and without a ship's cook. They set off along the coast of Venezuala and Colombia, south to Panama, past Costa Rica and Nicaragua, until finally they reached Honduras, their intended destination.

The independent republic of Honduras had been created a year previously, in 1838, having once been part of Spanish America; its fertile coastal plains surround a mountainous interior, rich in forests, and it just manages to have a 40-mile strip of southern coastline on the Pacific to complement its much longer Caribbean seaboard. It was to this Caribbean coast that the *Orynthia* came – or limped, perhaps. It was an unhealthy enough place to be even at the best of times, swampy and malaria-ridden; any Europeans trading there would have been only too aware of the risks involved, and the depleted crew of the *Orynthia*, overworked and probably ill-fed, must have been as vulnerable as they could possibly be. Just off the northern coast, on the island of Roatan in the Islas de la Bahia group, lay one of the country's northern ports. And here, thousands of miles from home and loved ones, the master of a ship in a state of disarray, Robert Titford fell sick of a fever and died. He was 30 years old.

A total of five extra crew were taken on board over the next three months, including a new master, Edward Barker; he found a ship's company of nine men – Robert Gray, the steward, having died a day after Robert Titford. One more man left on 4 November, but Barker managed to bring the rest back home, arriving on 1 February 1840. The *Orynthia* had been away for eight months; and only one member of the returning crew, we may not be surprised to hear, decided to risk a voyage in her again – George Groves, the boy apprentice.[4]

The *Orynthia* lived on, despite it all – off to Honduras again in March, 1840, where this time it was the cook who ended up in prison: William Rhodes took her out to Fernando Po, Ascension and India in 1841, and William Cox was master again on a voyage to the Cape and Burma in 1843, in which year he sold his half-share to Henry Johnson, a City merchant. In 1845 she was re-registered in the names of a ship-owner, a farmer, a master mariner and a sailmaker, and began a new life in Newcastle upon Tyne.

Family tradition – that fund of oral folklore which passes on half-garbled stories, legends and rumours to succeeding generations – has it that one Titford died as a pirate. We might be doing Robert Titford's memory a disservice to imagine that his disastrous voyage to South and Central America – his first and last as a master mariner – had any such sinister backdrop. But the crew agreements for merchant ships involved men in an undertaking '. . . to conduct themselves in an orderly, honest, careful and sober manner . . . and to be obedient to the lawful Commands of the Master . . .'.[5] Something, somewhere in the story of that series of events in 1839 give us cause to doubt whether the *Orynthia*'s crew obeyed such injunctions to the letter. Suspicions of foul play or insurrection must remain, if only as suspicions.

But we must return to Stepney, and Elizabeth Titford, *née* Shaw. Her lot had not been a happy one: the husband whom she had only ever seen for a few precious weeks in all since their marriage had now left her a widow, without support and with a child and step-children to fend for. In Frome in the late 18th century, we may remember, the women had died young, leaving their bereaved husbands with youngsters to care for; here in London that burden was to fall on young widows instead.

It was to be Samuel Hasted the cooper, that most bountiful of men, who would come to the rescue of a lady who was, after all, only his niece by marriage. The census of June 1841 finds Elizabeth living in Uncle Sam's house in Bermuda Street, together with her stepson Robert Edward, and her own daughter Selina.[6] By ensuring that young Robert Edward would live to father the next generation of Titfords, Elizabeth had made her contribution to the survival of that branch of the family. When her daughter Selina married Alexander Cowley, an optician, she found lodging with them, earning money as a dressmaker; it was in their house in Skidmore Street, Mile End, that she died in January 1873, aged sixty-seven.[7]

CHAPTER 19

Benjamin the Silversmith (1814-1879)

London

THE VICTORIAN SELF-MADE MAN

That me spute with gold smythis, and *silver smythis* . . .
Wyclif. *Wisd.* xv.9

In the December of 1844, shortly after his thirtieth birthday and five years after the death of his brother Robert, Benjamin Titford had his portrait painted in water-colours by G. J. Adkin. There he sits at a table, a confident and debonaire man-about-town, a bachelor with even a touch of the dandy about him. He stares out at us with steely blue eyes, his hair neatly twisted into one dark curl on his forehead; he's sporting a smart black frock-coat with a neatly-buttoned waistcoat and a full cravat anchored down with an ornate jewelled pin and chain.

Here, then, seven years into the young Queen's reign, with the national economy on the upturn, is the typical aspiring Victorian gentleman bearing all the outward signs of success. He was by no means unusual for his place and time: there were not a few London families in the mid-19th century who were busy accumulating all the paraphernalia that seemed to give them a gilt-edged claim to middle-class respectability – the portraits, the studio photographs, a family bible, ornate gravestones, even the odd crest and Latin motto. Benjamin's modest but handsome little portrait seems to want to relay a message to us: I may not be blue-blooded, it says, but please don't for a minute put me down as any kind of manual labourer – I belong to the established and rising ranks of the artisan middle-class. And so he did.[1]

The accumulated bric-à-brac of status which graced many a Victorian family parlour, tucked away on a mahogany table behind the aspidistra, was so often important to the owners precisely because they felt rather less than secure about their own ranking in an increasingly volatile and uncharted class structure. There were other reasons for insecurity, too: no matter how much material prosperity had come a family's way, there was still every chance that illness or a premature death might send them all back down a snake at a much faster speed than they had been able to climb up a ladder.

It takes three generations to make a gentleman, they say; but the sons and daughters of impoverished immigrants into London in Victorian times were only one remove from their humble roots elsewhere – every reason, therefore, to collect around themselves the trappings of grandeur. Everyone who could was playing this confidence trick on his neighbour – a sophisticated pretence that one's family was, or had been, one of the noblest in the land.

Supreme in this field were the members of another branch of the Titford family, at that time recent arrivals in London from their home in Wylye, Wiltshire. William Titford, furnishing undertaker, funeral-carriage master and featherman, would provide his clients with a first-class funeral for the princely sum of £29. For that – according to one of his advertisements of 1867 – you would get a hearse and two coaches with four horses each, plus all the necessary equipments, shell, lead coffin, outer case (handsomely finished) covered with velvet or fine cloth, with enamelled furniture. And William and his family sported the Titford arms, listed in Burke's *General Armory* as: 'Gules. Three lions heads erased or. Crest: A demi lion rampant or'. A Latin motto completed the package, though the family could never decide which sounded better – '*Cui debeo fidus*' or '*Suscipere et finire*' – and ended up using either according to taste.[2]

This William Titford then, surely, must have been a scion of one of England's noblest houses? Not so. He had his little ancestral secrets, as follows: his great-grandfather, also a William, had been buried as an 80-year-old pauper in Wylye in 1806 after a lifetime spent as a humble shepherd, and his own father, James, was to die in St Pancras Workhouse in 1862 at the end of a lively career which had included being an agricultural labourer, a french polisher, a clothes salesman, a catsmeat dealer – and a pauper. None of that prevented father, like son, being buried beneath the imposing family crest and a resounding '*Suscipere et finire*'. It behoves us to be sceptical, then, about Victorian genealogical status symbols; frequently there is an inverse proportion between the degree of pomp and the humble nature of the ancestry.

Benjamin Titford, we must say, was not quite as elevated socially as he appears to be in his water-colour portrait; or rather, he had only recently become so – which was good enough, after all, for any Victorian member of the *nouveaux-riches*. Benjamin's mother was lying paralysed in Shoreditch Workhouse even as the portrait was being executed, and he himself had only been saved from abject poverty after his father's premature death by the generous good offices of his uncle, Samuel Hasted.[3]

And so we return to that familiar Good Samaritan, Uncle Sam. He had come to his sister Elizabeth's rescue in her time of trouble, contributing almost beyond the call of duty; he had already done what he could to help his young nephew Robert – now what of Benjamin? In 1829, as the lad approached the age of 14, decision time was coming; if Benjamin had any yearning to go to sea like his brother, he seems to have kept it quiet, but there was every need to find him a safe and secure job with prospects. And so it was that he gained his passport to that respectability which lay so easily on his shoulders by the time his picture was painted: he would be apprenticed. For seven years he would live in Bloomsbury, learning a trade from Daniel Jones of Broad Street, pawnbroker, silversmith and general salesman. His master would provide instruction, sufficient meat and drink, lodging and other necessaries, leaving Uncle Sam to find wearing apparel and to organize washing and mending. The terms sound harsh, not to say positively feudal: Benjamin was to serve his master faithfully, keep his secrets, gladly obey his every word. He should neither do damage to Mr. Jones, nor be slow in warning him of any impending danger; fornication, marriage, gambling and the haunting of taverns or playhouses was strictly proscribed, and generally a monastic restraint was to be observed in all things.[4] Yet all turned out for the best: on 20 July 1836, Daniel Jones returned Benjamin his indenture, only too pleased to inscribe on the back of it the fact that he had appreciated the boy's seven years with him, and making him a generous gift of five pounds in the process.

Craftsmen with an eye to the future like Benjamin would be quite likely to make fairly late marriages – there would be a lot of saving up to do first, and the better established one was, the better the chances of attracting a lady of some substance. So at the beginning of 1846, 10 years after his apprenticeship had finished and then aged 31, Benjamin Titford was still a bachelor – but only just. He was practising his trade as a silversmith, living in Cornhill in the City. The street was full of goldsmiths and silversmiths and their assistants and apprentices at the time: Messrs. Cook, Ive, Sarl, Hyams and others all appear in the commercial directories for that year, along with the tobacconists, Fribourg and Treyer, whose shop in Haymarket has persisted almost as an anachronism into the 1980s.

It was high time for Benjamin to get married then – he had waited long enough. His choice was a certain Elizabeth Augusta Josephine Parkes, daughter of Ebenezer Parkes of

39. (*right*) Benjamin Titford, silversmith (1814-1879). From a watercolour by G. J. Adkin, 16 December 1844, in the possession of the author.

40. (*below*) Benjamin Titford (1814-1879): Apprenticeship Indenture. Young Benjamin is apprenticed to Daniel Jones of Broad Street, Bloomsbury ('Pawnbroker, Silversmith and General Salesman') for seven years, 18 February 1829.

This Indenture Witnesseth, That Benjamin

Titford by and with the consent of his Uncle Samuel Hasted of Bermuda Street Commercial Road in the County of Middlesex Cooper (testified by his executing these presents) doth put himself Apprentice to *David Jones of Broad Street Bloomsbury in the said County of Middlesex Pawnbroker Silversmith and General Salesman* to learn his Art; and with him (after the Manner of an Apprentice) to serve, from the *day of the date hereof for and during and* until the full End and Term of *Seven* Years from thence next following, to be fully complete and ended. During which Term, the said Apprentice his said Master faithfully shall serve, his Secrets keep, his lawful Commands every where gladly do. He shall do no Damage to his said Master, nor see it be done of Others; but that he to his Power shall let, or forthwith give warning to his said Master of the same. He shall not waste the Goods of his said Master, nor lend them unlawfully to any. He shall not commit Fornication, nor contract Matrimony within the said Term. He shall not play at Cards, Dice, Tables, or any other unlawful Games, whereby his said Master may have any Loss. With his own Goods or Others, during the said Term, without Licence of his said Master, he shall neither buy nor sell. He shall not haunt Taverns or Playhouses, nor absent himself from his said Master's Service Day nor Night unlawfully. But in all things, as a faithful Apprentice, he shall behave himself towards his said Master, and all his, during the said Term. And the said *David Jones in consideration of the Services of the said Benjamin Titford as aforesaid doth for himself his executors administrators and assigns covenant and agree*

his said Apprentice, in the Art of a *Pawnbroker Silversmith and General* which he useth, by the best Means that he can, shall teach and instruct, or cause to be taught and instructed; finding unto his said Apprentice, sufficient Meat, Drink, Lodging, and all other Necessaries during the said Term. *except wearing apparel washing and mending And the said Samuel Hasted doth for himself agree to find and provide the said Benjamin Titford with good and sufficient wearing apparel washing and mending during the term of his said apprenticeship*

And for the true Performance of all and every the said Covenants and Agreements, either of the said Parties bindeth himself unto the other by these Presents. In Witness whereof, the Parties above named to these Indentures interchangeably have set their Hands and Seals, the *Eighteenth* Day of *February* in the *Tenth* Year of the Reign of our Sovereign Lord GEORGE the Fourth, by the Grace of God, of the United Kingdom of *Great Britain and Ireland*, King, Defender of the Faith, and in the Year of our Lord One Thousand Eight Hundred and *Twenty nine*.

B.

Sold by
W. G. & WH. WITHERBY,
Stationers,
No, 9, Birchin Lane,
London.

Sealed and Delivered (being first duly stamped) in the Presence of

Benjamin Titford

Sam Hasted

Fetter Lane, a brass-rule maker for the printing trade. Quite a nice catch for him, we might think, though who was catching whom exactly may not be so easy to determine – many a man, according to a rather cynical 19th-century doctor, was 'bounced into marriage'.[5] What does seem strange in retrospect is the choice of church the couple made for their wedding: the Parkeses had strong Nonconformist tendencies, though they had baptised young Elizabeth in an Anglican church, St Dunstan's in the West. But the marriage of Benjamin and Elizabeth took place neither there, nor in the City where he was then living, but back in the parish where he had been born: St George's in the East, Stepney. Things had changed slightly down there, however; a new parish, that of Christ Church, Watney Street, had been carved out of the ever-more-populous St George's, and it was at this recently-dedicated Christ Church that the couple were married on 22 March 1846.

This was indeed an odd location for Benjamin and Elizabeth to choose: there were, to put it mildly, more fashionable places in London to celebrate one's wedding. Dickens, writing in 1850, has this to say about the district around Watney Street:

> The houses in the Eastern St George's are almost all small, and the streets and alleys form a sort of labyrinth – a tangled web of dingy structures – ins and outs, and twisted meshes of lane and alley, having only one feature in common, that feature telling of poverty . . . not always squalid . . . but ever displaying the presence of a population of the humblest means – one in fourteen of the whole population of the parish are paupers. Surely such a spot offers few inducements for its selection as a place of permanent abode . . . an area of Jews, thieves, rags, filth, foul smells, and wretchedness.[6]

Deliberately choosing to marry in an area full of paupers – Benjamin might just have well have been in Frome! There were those, however, who decided by a quite conscious effort of will to involve themselves in the day-to-day life of such humble if not squalid areas of London; one such man was Rev. William Quekett, about whom Dickens was here writing in his article, 'What a London curate can do if he tries'. William Quekett was living in fashionable Well Close Square in the 1840s – a few doors away from John Frederick Hasted, Benjamin Titford's cousin – but his real work lay in the poor courts and alleyways of the parish at large, where his dedication and Christian charity had made him a legendary figure.[7] He it was who had pressed for the creation of Christ Church parish, and he became its first incumbent; Benjamin and Elizabeth had the singular distinction of having him officiate at their marriage – poor surroundings, then, but in the presence of a minister of great reputation.

Filling in the details on the marriage certificate may have proved a problem for Benjamin: his mother was now past hope in the workhouse, and his father had died when he himself was less than two years old. What to put for 'Father's profession'? Possibly Mr Quekett came to his aid: it would be a simple matter to consult the parish registers for St George's until they found the bridegroom-to-be's baptism in 1818, son of Benjamin Titford of Chapman Street, 'Outrider' – and so the entry reads on the marriage certificate.

A new Benjamin and Elizabeth Titford were, in a sense, rising out of the ashes of the old; they and their children – Benjamin James, William, Henry Joseph, Charles Frederick and Emily Jane – will be our companions on the next stage of our journey.

We have made mention in passing of mobility within the context of a family's history: both the ups and down of social mobility according to circumstance, and the more obviously-apparent geographical moves people made to ensure their own survival or to better their lot. Benjamin Titford had managed to clamber up the social ladder, as we have seen – rising, in the process, higher than his impoverished cousins in Frome had done. But he was also exceptionally mobile in territorial terms, too, albeit within the confines of London itself. For thirty years after his marriage Benjamin hardly let his feet touch the ground before he was on the move again – giving us over a dozen different addresses for him during his lifetime. Those moves themselves were very probably not unrelated to the family's general social mobility – the two would co-exist, especially for an entrepreneur like Benjamin, who would seek to better himself whenever and wherever he could. Whether he was changing his job, dabbling in accommodation suitable for lodging houses or seeking a larger or smaller house to suit an expanding and then a contracting family, the silversmith-cum-general salesman-cum-lodging-house keeper-cum-commercial clerk-cum-clerk to a manufacturing jeweller-cum-collector to a goldsmith-cum-writing clerk never seemed to settle for long in one place.

Benjamin and Elizabeth's first home was in a rather unusual location for them: Titfords in general rarely seem to have favoured areas of London south of the Thames as a place to live, but here was a brief exception. Benjamin James, the couple's eldest child, was born at 5 Liverpool Street, Walworth – in the parish of St Mary Newington, then in Surrey.

The Victorians, of course, for all their virtues, had an edge of prudery which made them condemn in public that which they were busy practising in private. Births in a family which pre-date a marriage or follow it by only a very few months were increasingly common and apparently quite acceptable in the late 18th century; here in Victorian London, however, the suspiciously early arrival of little Benjamin James (on 11 December 1846 – rather less than nine months after the marriage) was regarded, it seems, with a touch of disquiet. At least, it was so by those who were to write up family notes at a later date: the year of birth would be coyly laundered to read '1847', thus ensuring that a rather harmless skeleton stayed in its cupboard for a while.

Whatever may have prompted Benjamin and Elizabeth to pay this visit to Walworth – a chance of staying with some of the Parkes family, perhaps? – it was not to last long. They would feel happier north of the river like everyone else; Islington seems to have been their favourite suburb, and that was where they had moved to by the time the next child arrived, three years later. William was born on Monday 9 April 1849 – the only one not to bear a middle Christian name, but then, of course, there had been William Titfords galore back to the 17th century, so the boy was in good company.

A rapid look at *The Times* newspaper for this Monday in April might give us just the slightest inkling of the minutiae of English life on a most ordinary of ordinary days: Dickens was completing *David Copperfield*; Bass's India Pale Ale could be had for 33s. per 18-gallon cask; Hampshire Breakfast Bacon would cost you 7½d. by the half side, while Captain Reid's 'Walls End' coal was 19s. a ton. And the Royal Institution of Great Britain in Albemarle Street was that day announcing that there were to be eight lectures given by Mr. Faraday on Static or Franklinic Electricity, to commence on 21 April.

Nothing very special here, then, to herald the arrival of little William; but just as that year brought in the new, so it took away the old: Benjamin Titford the Outrider's widow Elizabeth, 70 years old and paralysed, died in Shoreditch Workhouse on 12 September. We have noted already the fact that her passing coincided with a most virulent attack of cholera: no fewer than two thousand people in London succumbed to it in one single week in that September of 1849. Suggested cures were legion, and one correspondent wrote to the newspaper concerning the closure of the graveyards at Spa Fields, St Botolph Bishopsgate and St Thomas, Golden Lane, suggesting that the ground in each case be covered in quicklime. In the event, St Bride's Burial Ground was closed, along with a nearby well contaminated by the sewer in Bride Lane: as the said well, used by soda water manufacturers, was not very deep, there was every fear that 'the solution of dead men's bones would be more concentrated and injurious to health'. An understatement, indeed.[8]

Mercifully, Islington was not the disease-trap that nearby Shoreditch was, and the Titfords were spared the fate of many of their fellow citizens. In any case, they had moved from their Islington address – 14 James Street, St Peter's Street – to 140a High Street, Hoxton Old Town, by 1852, in which year a third son, Henry Joseph, was born.

Hoxton was thriving with small businesses, and Benjamin was showing the first signs of a schizophrenic uncertainty about what his official professional title should be: the commercial directories for 1853 list him as a General Salesman, while Henry Joseph's birth certificate plays safe with 'Silversmith'.[9] Of course, a birth certificate allowed a man to be a bit flamboyant, while the directory, which might bring him trade, needed to be perfectly honest about what he was up to . . . In general, apprenticed originally as a silversmith as he was, Benjamin would always return to this professional description when all else failed.

There was a certain entrepreneurial spirit about our man; he seems to have had an eye for the main chance, and at no time more so than in 1854, when he left behind the delights of Hoxton and begun a brief flirtation with the idea of running a lodging house. And he did so at what must have been a very fashionable address: 36 Wilmington Square, Spa Fields, peopled with Esquires and seemingly rather an unlikely location for such an enterprise. In 1852, two years previously, there was a certain Samuel Baker Morris, Esq., living at no. 36; by 1856 it was occupied by Charles Hilton Lawrence, Esq. But in between Benjamin Titford was offering beds for the night to paying guests.[10]

It may well have been fun while it lasted, but we might guess by now that the Titfords would not stay long in Spa Fields, any more than they had anywhere else. Just long enough, in the event, to baptise William and Henry Joseph at St Andrew's, Holborn (in the September and October of 1854 respectively), before returning to Islington and altogether less salubrious surroundings. Number 4 Brays Buildings, Lower Road, Islington, was the decidedly seedy-sounding location for Benjamin's new enterprise: 'Miscellaneous Repos' . . . Can it really have been much more than an up-market doss-house?[11] Their immediate neighbours were Joshua Burn, a grocer, at no. 6, and James Bradnam, butcher, at no. 5; one can only hope that Mr. Bradnam kept his slaughterhouse at a decent distance from his retail premises – the very special aromas of a butcher's and a grocer's shop must have been enough to discourage many a potential guest at Miscellaneous Repos, without the sound of dying cries from butchered beasts.

Number 4 had not always been a lodging house; just as several families, like the Titfords, were constantly on the move from place to place, so many an individual house or shop would see a very rapid turnover of occupants. George Benjamin Coaffee, a dyer, had previously shared 4 Brays Buildings with William Bolding, a fringe manufacturer; later, in 1851, George Cowton was running a milliner's business there with three assistants. Yet the kind of premises favoured by small-time craftsmen look as if they were not so suitable for a spot of Miscellaneous Repos; by the October of 1856 the Titfords were on the move yet again, this time to 15 Penton Street, Clerkenwell. From then on the family would continue to take lodgers to help supplement its income, but very much on an *ad hoc* basis and on an altogether more modest scale.

Nevertheless it had been at Bray's Buildings, stench or no stench, squeals of slaughtered beasts or no squeals, that one of the most fascinating of Benjamin's children had entered the world. On 17 April 1856, shortly before they left for Clerkenwell, Elizabeth gave birth to a boy whom they named Charles Frederick. His life would take him far away from Bray's Buildings as the years went by, searching for adventure on the high seas, visiting in reality places his parents could only have dreamed of.

Charles's birth was registered fairly late in the day: a certificate wasn't issued until 3 October, by which time Elizabeth was pregnant for the fifth and last time. If they were wishing for a girl by then, their prayers were answered: Emily Jane was born in Penton Street on 31 May 1857. Father was then 42, mother thirty-five.

Over the next few years, as the children grew up, Benjamin and Elizabeth began amassing their typical Victorian store of family momentoes. Chief amongst these would be the photographs which could be displayed in ornate frames for all to see, or tucked away more discreetly in leather-bound, gilt-edged albums. Each member of the family had his or her picture taken at least once: there, recorded for posterity, is father Benjamin, leaning back comfortably in a chair just as he had done when sitting for Mr. Adkin all those years before, still wearing his favourite ring on the little finger of his right hand. Young Charles Frederick, photographed while still in his teens, seems generally ill-at-ease as he poses in what appears to be a borrowed long coat. He is making a commendable effort to appear nonchalant and relaxed, despite the oversize top hat in his hand and the obtrusive stunted tree and rustic stile provided by the photographer, Mr. G. Diviani, in his Holloway Road studio opposite the Caledonian Church. Later photographs of Charles and his brother William would show two men-about-town in their twenties. E. C. Russell, also in business in Holloway Road, managed to catch the confident suavity of the pair of them, and this time Charles is in full frock coat and waistcoat, with the merest hint of a beard on his face, as he rests his arm with a convincing air of relaxed dignity on an animal skin rug. Young teenagers were growing into young men.

So much for the photographs. Another essential item then very much in vogue was the family bible; the Titfords duly acquired one, ornately gilded and standing in its own glass-topped case, and proceeded to enter births, marriages and deaths as they occurred.[12] At about the same time, however, there was someone, somewhere, who was more than usually interested in chronicling Titford family details from past generations: a sheet of pale blue paper watermarked '1860' was covered with names and dates by some mysterious hand, and eventually found its way into Benjamin's own papers. One side of the sheet lists the children of Charles the Cheesemonger, starting with the birth of William Charles in 1772 and appending a few dates of death for good measure. There is no mention anywhere of the fact that these were brothers and sisters, nor that they were born in Frome; that has been for us to establish later. On the reverse are details of the marriage of William Charles to Ann Edgar at St Dunstan's in the West, together with their offspring. Who had gone to the trouble of making such notes? The most likely candidate seems to be Benjamin's cousin John, son of William Charles. He was 55 years old in 1860, living in Lambeth as a bachelor – perhaps with nothing much else to interest him at the time? A few scribbled legal notes are crossed out at the top of the paper – and John was a solicitor's clerk, after all. Benjamin must have been more than a little interested by all the information this sheet of paper contained, principally because he had scarcely known his own father, who had died before he was two years old. We, too, are eternally grateful to the compiler – would that more people had followed his (or her?) example![13]

The 1861 census gives us the chance to meet Benjamin and Elizabeth at yet another new location: 7 St Thomas's Street, Islington. He was then 46, a clerk to a manufacturing jeweller, while Elizabeth was only thirty-eight. Benjamin James was a young teenager of 14, William 11, Henry Joseph eight, Charles four and Emily Jane three.

Their new abode was in a small, intimate street of 26 houses; the Titfords in the male line were second generation immigrants from Somerset, but their neighbours there in Islington consisted of families who had been born anywhere other than London – a cosmopolitan mixture of Geordies, Lancastrians, people from Essex, Suffolk, Shropshire, Kent, Wiltshire, Somerset and Norfolk. These people followed a variety of occupations: there was a G.P.O. messenger, a solicitor's clerk, a manufacturer of waterproof leather, a lithographic printer, and a comb manufacturer. A few houses in the street even boasted servants. At no. 6 lived Anne Knight, a widow born in Horningsham, Wilts., where, by coincidence, a number of Titfords had been baptised in the mid-17th century; no. 8 contained the Tomlinson family, a hay salesman's bookkeeper from Norwich; George Childs at no. 10 described himself grandly as a 'Landscape Painter', and at no. 14 a lady called Mary

Archer was in business as a private lodging-house keeper, assisted by Eliza Wade, her 17-year-old servant from Stepney.

One man further down the street was a Somerset-born commercial traveller for a draper – very much like Benjamin's father, Ben the Outrider – and Henry Budeler at no. 13a, assistant to a law stationer, had been born in Frome almost exactly at the time when Ben, senior, was leaving that town for London.

The Titfords, it seemed, had not given up the Miscellaneous Repos business for good: an unmarried Scottish lady in her sixties, Jessie Grieve, was staying with them as a lodger; what little she may have paid in rent would have been very useful, no doubt, as a means of eking out the family income.

The year 1861 ended on a sombre note for everyone; in December Albert, the Prince Consort, died at the age of forty-two. Although he had been a sobering and restricting influence in a Germanic way upon the Queen, she took to wearing black immediately after his death and, in a sense, appeared never to cease mourning for him until the day she died. Within a few days of Prince Albert's death, young Henry Joseph Titford, aged nine, fell ill with tubercular bronchitis. In an age before antibiotics, any doctor must have felt particularly helpless in such a case; the situation worsened during the winter months and into the spring, until in late April peritonitis and meningitis set in. Within six days, on 3 May 1862, the young boy died, Benjamin declaring as he applied for a certificate that he had been present at the death.

What, then, of life and death in a typical Victorian family, compared with the way things had been a hundred years previously? What we already know of the Titfords can serve as a model: Charles the Cheesemonger in the late 18th century had 13 children, seven of whom died in infancy; his grandson, Benjamin the Silversmith, had reduced the number of offspring to five, and would live to see all but one reach adulthood.

The conclusions are obvious enough: that there was a tendency among some Victorians to have fewer children where they could arrange it that way, and that improved medical care, hygiene, sanitation and living conditions generally were improving life-expectancy and helping to eradicate infant deaths. These remarks, as they stand, are sweeping generalisations based upon the narrowest of samples; nevertheless we know with the wisdom of hindsight that the trends in question were definitely there in the 19th century and would become even more obvious in the 20th – that families woud be smaller, and that the survival rate would improve dramatically. In so far as it was possible to control the number of children they had, a significant number of Victorian parents were beginning to do so – if only because of the simple fact that the fewer sons and daughters there were, the more could be done to give each of them a good start in life. They would be better fed, better clothed – even better educated – while their parents were alive, and better pleased with their legacies once those parents were dead.

Having fewer children, of course, gives rise to a situation which so many 20th-century parents will understand only too well: that one minute there are young babies in the house needing constant attention, while the next, in the twinkling of an eye it seems, Derby and Joan are staring around an empty house and having to re-learn the art of living with each other all over again. This was the case with Benjamin and Elizabeth. The 1861 census enumerator had caught the family at the height of its expansion; 10 years later they were down to two children, one of whom would be leaving home very shortly.

Of course there had been time for two moves in the interim. First to 31 Richard Street, off Liverpool Road in Holloway – rarely, we note, did the family flit any great distance – and then to more modest accommodation at 12 Lennox Road, Stroud Green Lane, Upper Holloway. The census for April 1871 gives us Benjamin, aged 56, 'Clerk to a silversmith'; Elizabeth, aged 47, Charles Frederick, then 14, and Emily Jane, thirteen. The Titfords were sharing the house with William Parker, a 28-year-old warehouseman with a Manchester and Bradford merchant, born in Devon, and his wife Louisa, aged 21, from Greenwich.

Where had the two other Titford boys gone to by 1871? Three years after the death of little Henry Joseph, in January 1864, William had been put apprentice to a gold-engraver in Clerkenwell, while Benjamin James, the academic star of the family, had gone off to Cheltenham two years later to train to be a teacher. That left Charles Frederick at home with Mum and Dad – but not for long; by the end of 1871 he, too, was serving his apprenticeship in Haymarket with a goldsmith. This was the artisan middle-class family consolidating itself: make sure that the boys learn a craft or enter the professions, marry the girls off as well as you can – give them all, as they say, a better chance in life than you ever had yourself.

Benjamin must have been well-pleased with his little brood: Benjamin James and William were both married by 1872, and soon brought him a series of grandchildren. Charles Frederick was the odd one out in this respect – his feet were far too itchy to allow him to settle down into any sort of domesticity, and he would prove the fact in a dramatic enough way by sailing off around the world as soon as the opportunity presented itself.

By June 1879 Benjamin the Silversmith was terminally ill with cancer of the abdomen; in the earlier part of the century that would have meant admission to the workhouse or protracted and difficult nursing at home. A mark of how things had changed was that there was now a hospital to which he could be admitted: there in the University College Hospital in Gower Street he made a will on 7 October witnessed by his old friend Edward Humberstone. He left his monies in the New 3 per cent Bank Annuities and the London Provident Savings Bank, Moorfield, together with the proceeds from the sale of his household furniture and effects, plate, linen, china, books, pictures and other chattels to be divided equally between his four children. The total estate came to just under six hundred pounds.

Benjamin died there in Gower Street on 10 October 1879, death from cancer and exhaustion being certified as the cause by J. M. Briggs, M.R.C.S. Consistently inconsistent to the end, he is given as a 'Silversmith' on the will, but as a 'Writing Clerk' on the death certificate; just for good measure we are also given a final address for him to add to our collection: 355 Edgware Road. It fell to William, the only son left in London, to prove the will, which he duly did on 22 October at the Principal Probate Registry; the body was laid to rest at Abney Park Cemetery, Stoke Newington, grave no. 66,417. A year later William Titford, our old friend the undertaker from Wylye in Wiltshire, would be buried in the St Pancras Cemetery at East Finchley. Here, in the suburbs of the Metropolis, members of the extended family whose ancestors had parted company down in Wiltshire as long ago as the late 16th century found neighbouring resting places.

Benjamin Titford's material and social success during a lifetime spanning 65 years could not match that of William the Undertaker, but he had done very well for himself, for all that. No freehold property is mentioned in his will, but his goods, chattels and savings constituted quite a nice little nest-egg for his sons and his daughter – and was not ambition for one's children one of the marks of a Victorian middle-class man?

Whatever social class we ascribe to Benjamin the Silversmith will be open to some degree of misinterpretation; it has been said that 'The sixty years of Queen Victoria's reign were above all the sixty years of the middle-class man', and we could apply that statement to our man's ability to consolidate and improve upon his standing in society.[14] We can but suppose that he practised the middle-class virtues of Samuel Smiles – those of hard work, thrift and sobriety – and embodied the very quintessence of what we would speak of today as the Protestant Work Ethic. Benjamin was clearly an ambitious and careful man, neither dissolute nor spendthrift, and was probably very conservative in every way; he had made himself respectable in Victorian terms, generating enough of a cash surplus by a lifetime of hard work and good fortune to build up that stock of 3 per cent Bank Annuities and accumulate a healthy balance with the London Provident Savings Bank. Few of his Frome ancestors had ever been so lucky, and nor had his father; if death or disease did not rob a 19th-century artisan of his earning power, he had, as we see, the luxury of earning more than he needed to spend.

Middle-class values and a middle-class bank balance do not in themselves guarantee a man any specific social status, however. It would seem more useful to reserve that much over-used tag of 'middle-class' for those higher up the social and financial scale than Benjamin – those who lived in larger houses with servants, who sent their children to public schools and could afford a day at the races or a night at the opera, suitably dressed. Benjamin and Elizabeth and their family belonged, in effect, to what we might choose to call the 'comfortable working class'; they benefited from the general rise in Britain's prosperity in Victorian times – cheaper food and clothing, better sanitation, faster transport, more substantial housing – but their money still had to be earned, had to be worked for.[15] Benjamin's income came from any one or more of a series of sources, as we have seen: at times he earned wages as a silversmith or a clerk; he also dabbled in the retail trade as a general salesman, and picked up some spare cash from his boarding houses. All of that placed him very safely above London's poor manual labourers – but it should not persuade either him or us that he had achieved social parity with the genteel and leisured classes.

The name of one person, we may notice, was conspicuously absent from Benjamin's 1879 will: that of his widow, Elizabeth. She may have had some capital of her own, though many a wife in Victorian times was little better off as one man's wife than she had been as another man's daughter:

> Until the passing of the Married Women's Property Act the husband's marriage vow, 'with all my worldly goods I thee endow', was ironic. In fact the reverse happened. A newly-wed husband legally acquired all his wife's real and personal property, and he could dispose of it exactly as he thought fit.[16]

There are numerous examples in English wills throughout the centuries of men who were careful to make provision for their widows by insisting that children who inherited some property would allow their mother to stay somewhere comfortable for the rest of her life. Where such stipulations were not heeded, a Chancery case might well follow, if the wronged party could afford such a luxury. Benjamin Titford, by contrast, must have trusted his children to see that Elizabeth was fairly dealt with – and his trust appears to have been justified.[17] Benjamin James was away in Somerset, and William had a family to accommodate, so the two unmarried children, Charles Frederick and Emily, set up house with their mother at 50 Cumberland Street, Barnsbury.

Most of the neighbours were craftsmen of one sort or another – a shoemaker, a signwriter and a builder appear in the commercial directories for 1881 – though at least one master mariner was using Cumberland Street as his land-base at the time. The Titfords were a little different – Charles Frederick had decided to use his share of father's estate to set up a modest retail business, one which his mother and sister could contribute towards when he was in London himself, and one which they could perhaps handle efficiently without him when he departed on his sporadic travels around the world. The 1881 census tells the story: Charles F. Titford was a 'Potman and Tobacconist', with Emily as his 'Assistant Tobacconist' and mother as a general 'Assistant'. To help matters along, boarders had been resorted to once more: a warehouseman from Hammersmith and a wheelwright from Norfolk were helping the Titfords pay the bills. One widow and four unmarried people were sharing the little house, and still they had to find room for the customers who wanted an ounce of tobacco or a portion of snuff.

We shall tell the full story of Charles Frederick Titford in due course; enough for now to say that he would be outlived by his widowed mother, who was 80 when she died at 24 Warner Street, Lower Holloway, on 4 March 1902, 'Widow of Benjamin Titford, Commercial clerk'. She was buried, like her husband, at Abney Park Cemetery.[18]

CHAPTER 20

Benjamin James (1846-1905)

London and Curry Rivel, Somerset

THE VILLAGE SCHOOLMASTER

Where there's muck, there's brass, as the saying goes – and there was plenty of brass around during the early years of the Industrial Revolution in England for those with the skills and the enterprise to go looking for it. Mucky hands and a fat bank balance would be a way of life for the first generation of *nouveaux-riches* manufacturers; but with a bit of care the brass itself could be used to buy their children out of the world of muck altogether. There were ways of consolidating and improving upon the status acquired by being a rich and successful industrialist – like providing a solid and traditional education for one's sons, and a prudent marriage for one's daughters. In a rather odd way, 19th-century public schools were just as ideally suited for the fathers of gentlemen as they were for the sons of gentlemen. In other words, three generations might take a family from hard toil through private education to gilt-edged respectability.

All that was fine as far as it went, but it would often mean, as the 19th century wore on, that work associated directly with industrial processes tended to be looked down upon. In Germany, by contrast, technical education was well advanced, and Napoleon had had the foresight to create institutions of excellence which would provide France with its future engineers, agriculturalists and the rest; but many an English self-made man would want to see his offspring succeed in altogether 'cleaner' and more respectable fields, making their mark as doctors, lawyers, Oxford classicists or even politicians. For that reason alone some historians would even argue that Britain's decline as a manufacturing nation was already underway within a generation of the onset of the Industrial Revolution itself.[1]

The Titfords, as we know only too well, were very far from being rich and powerful tycoons; nevertheless, the trend we have just outlined was at work in a much more modest way even in their fortunes as time went by. From the moment the family moved to Frome in the early 17th century and gave up being subsistence farmers with a complementary craft skill or two under their belts, they had been involved in one way or another with the world of industry – be it as manufacturing craftsmen or as retailers.

Now, with Benjamin James Titford, the eldest son of Benjamin the Silversmith and Elizabeth, we encounter a craftsman's son who would establish himself as a member of the professional classes – by becoming a schoolmaster. The training undergone by aspiring teachers in the 19th century was of a fairly rudimentary kind, and the financial rewards at the end of it all were nothing like those accorded to successful lawyers or doctors. Nevertheless, the job was beginning to carry its own very real status; Benjamin James would be the first member of his branch of the family ever to have a 'career' in anything like the modern sense of the word. Not for him the path of apprenticeship followed by his two younger brothers – at least, not quite.

He had started off in a modest enough way as a schoolboy like so many others – but at a time when education had not yet become compulsory; what he did have was both the brains and the parental support to turn his flair for learning to good effect. In the year in which he had been born, 1846, the Secretary of the Education Committee – a certain James

Kay-Shuttleworth – had introduced a system of apprentice schoolmasters; the trainee had to be at least 13 years old, be able to read with 'fluency, ease and expression', write neatly and accurately, and understand the essentials of arithmetic and the system of weights and measures. If he was based at a school governed by the Church of England, then the Catechism would have to be recited, and some examination by a priest would be necessary. This was an attractive scheme, not least because both the pupil-teacher and the headmaster or headmistress were paid for their trouble, and was very probably the route which Benjamin James followed. At the age of 19 he sat the Queen's Scholarship Examination, which he would have to pass if he wished to pursue any form of teacher-training after the initial apprenticeship. All went well, and he was duly admitted to St Paul's College in Cheltenham from the Islington Trinity National School, having been awarded a Queen's Scholarship, second class.[2] The Cheltenham course was one he completed to the College's satisfaction, and as he left as a qualified master his first thought was to return home to North London, at least for the time being. For a brief spell he worked as headmaster of the Cattle Market School, St Luke's, Holloway. That gave him the chance to exercise one of his talents, as a teacher, but he was also a bit of a musician, and soon established himself as the organist at the parish church in Holloway. Whatever might his Frome ancestors have thought of a Titford playing for Divine Service in an Anglican place of worship!

Teaching and organ-playing gave Benjamin James (hereinafter simply 'Benjamin' for the sake of conciseness) the wherewithal to leave one place for another if he wished to – they were skills more marketable over a wide area than those of his father, for example, who presumably relied upon local contacts and reputation in order to earn a decent living. There was probably nothing particularly distasteful about working at Cattle Market School in Holloway – despite its rather down-to-earth title – but Benjamin sought greener pastures, nevertheless. In 1868, a mere two years after he had first begun his course in Cheltenham, he left London and his family again – for good, this time.

Many Titfords over the years, we know, have uprooted themselves from one place to go and settle elsewhere. Benjamin's case, though, was subtly different: for the most part family emigration seems to have been prompted at least as much by the need or the desire to leave one place as it has been by the yearning to live somewhere else. Bratton was abandoned because making a living there was proving increasingly difficult; William Charles and Ben the Outrider left Frome partly because it was fast becoming a town in recession. Yet already, with Benjamin the Silversmith, we have noticed a change: he moved around London as often as he did not because life was proving difficult where he was, but because customers or lodgers might be more easily found just round the everlasting corner. Finally comes Benjamin James, the professional man with a career to build. Teachers seeking advancement have traditionally had to be mobile – much more so than their legal or medical colleagues; there is everything to be gained by arriving as an unknown quantity in a new school – promotion will usually attend such a move, and all the unfortunate errors perpetrated in one's early years can be left far behind. Benjamin James Titford may or may not have made his fair share of mistakes as a young teacher; but when the chance came of running his own show in a conducive environment, he took it with alacrity.

Family historians very soon become aware of the rather bizarre and uncanny way in which people's lives can bring them circling back to places which have strong connexions with their own forgotten ancestry. Certain locations can evoke in us a very strong sense of 'belonging', of *déjà vu*, almost as if the spirits of our long-since-departed forbears still walked the streets. It should hardly surprise us, then, that Benjamin decided to settle in Somerset: not in Frome, admittedly, but in Curry Rivel near Taunton, where he replaced Charles Thomas Price as headmaster of the village school. That brought him within a mile or two of Stoke St Gregory, down the steep incline and on to the Levels, where a family of Titfords had once made their home as long ago as the end of the 16th century. Almost certainly unwittingly, Benjamin was returning to the land of his far-off kindred.[3]

Curry Rivel sits on a low ridge nearly two hundred and seventy feet above sea level; not high ground, to be sure, but high enough to afford panoramic views all around over the low-lying Somerset Wetlands. To the south there are the Dorset Heights looking over Hamdon Hill and the Windwhistle Ridge; to the west stands the Wellington Monument, almost on the Devon border; northwards there is a fine view of the Quantock Hills with the Brendons to their left and the Mendips to their right; eastwards lie the Wiltshire Downs and a view of King Alfred's Tower at Stourton. On a clear day the Black Mountains of Wales can even be made out to the north-east. Seductive country, then, to charm a young London schoolteacher away from the semi-rural but crowded northern suburbs of the capital.[4] Benjamin, we may say to his credit, seems to have taken to Curry Rivel like a fish to water, and would stay there until the day he died.

Other forms of seduction were also at work on him as it happens, and on 1 October of the year of his arrival in the village he married Edith Mason, youngest daughter of Henry Rice Mason of Godmanchester, Hunts., a cabinet-maker. Benjamin was then 23 years old, described on the marriage certificate as the son of Benjamin Titford, 'Jeweller's Assistant'. The rather handsome Perpendicular church of St Andrew in Curry Rivel where the ceremony took place was soon to become a familiar enough place for Benjamin, as he took over as its organist to complement his work as the local headmaster.

North of the churchyard itself lay the Old School Room, built in 1828 at a cost of £127 8s. 4d.; it served its purpose very adequately until the passing of the 1870 Education Act, at which time decisions about the future had to be made. Elementary education was to be provided for all children in England and Wales; now did the village want a new church school, or would it prefer a board school, one which would be secular and undenominational? Debate in Curry Rivel became heated on the issue; so much so, that a committee of villagers, including Benjamin James Titford himself, was appointed to decide what to do. They discussed and they reached a conclusion; as a result a new church school – Curry Rivel Parochial School – was built in Church Street in 1876, the year in which the first of two Acts was passed making school attendance compulsory. Described in the commercial directories as a 'voluntary school' and doubling up as a Sunday school, it was intended for 180 children, and sported Benjamin James as its first headmaster. He would teach the senior pupils with the aid of an assistant mistress, leaving the little ones lower down the school to learn their early lessons from children older than themselves – this was the 'monitor' system, widely adopted and potentially very successful.

By 1883 the Titfords were living at 2 Mount Terrace, Curry Rivel, where Benjamin was supplementing his income – a trick he had learned from his father? – by acting as an insurance agent for the 'Lancashire'. Even professional men, it seems, would dabble in a bit of commerce if it helped pay the bills.

The new school suffered from a degree of excess capacity for quite a number of years: by 1894 the average attendance was 109, Miss Harris acting as assistant mistress; she was shortly replaced by Benjamin's daughter, Minnie Titford, and they were joined by Miss Maud Reading, the infants' mistress, as the average attendance rose to a hundred and twenty.

Benjamin and Edith were to have no fewer than nine daughters in all, three dying in infancy, and just one son. Not only was the boy outnumbered in this predominantly female household – he had the additional problem of having to contend with a rather cumbersome and unusual first Christian name: Marwood James Henry Titford had presumably been named as such by way of homage to the vicar of Curry Rivel, the Rev. Charles Marwood Speke Mules. It was typical of Benjamin James, as it happens, to go in for such a touch of

41. Benjamin James Titford (1846-1905) with his wife, Edith, and six of their children. Curry Rivel, Somerset.

harmless sycophancy to please his friend the vicar; he had very soon become, as we might have guessed, a respectable pillar of the Curry Rivel establishment.

A Titford family photograph taken in the early 1890s shows husband and wife with five daughters and young Marwood, the girls in neat smocks or severe black dresses, the son in an Eton collar, and every one of the group looking his or her most miserable Sunday best. Those photographers who made a speciality of enticing young ladies to say 'prunes' and 'prisms' to bring out their charming dimples, called 'watch the birdie!' with much gusto or tried 'cheese!' in the hope of a smile would have had a rough time indeed with severe-looking Benjamin James and his wife and children. Victorian studio portraits, of course, rarely show us smiling or happy subjects; but as master of the local school, church organist, registrar of births and deaths, secretary to the Women's Friendly Society, stalwart of the Langport branch of the Ancient Order of Foresters and the local cricket club, Benjamin James must have felt the burden of responsibility resting heavily on his shoulders – and it shows in his face. Were he to defend himself, no doubt he would surprise us all, but the overriding impression we get of him in retrospect is that he had fallen all too readily into the role of the squire's man, the vicar's buddy, the stern schoolmaster. Such is the price a silversmith's son may have had to pay to achieve respectabiity in a Victorian village community.[5]

As things turned out, Benjamin just lived beyond the Victorian era and into the Edwardian: on Sunday 3 September 1905 he was in church about to play the organ for a children's service when he collapsed. The vicar managed to catch him before he fell to the floor, and he was removed to his home, where he died on the Friday morning, 8 September. A moving obituary in the *Langport and Somerton Herald* declared that '. . . no death within recent years has created such a universal expression of regret'. He was clearly very highly regarded in the district, and his funeral was even attended by a representative of the London Titfords in the person of Ernest William, the deceased's nephew, son of his brother William. They had not entirely forgotten him back home, then, although he had been away 37 years.

A brass plaque was duly struck in Benjamin's memory and mounted in the church near the organ, where it may still be seen:

> In Memory of Benjamin J. Titford. 37 years organist and schoolmaster of this parish. Died, September 8th, 1905. Aged 58

Even as this story is being written, in the 1980s, one man can still remember that far-off funeral of 1905, though he was only five at the time:

> Coo! I remember sneaking from school to watch old Titford's funeral procession and standing under the chestnut trees and thinking how beautiful the singing in church sounded.[6]

No doubt it did. And so impressed was this man by the occasion that, having lived away from Curry Rivel for many years, he returned late in life to be re-married there – because of his cherished memories of the village in all its beauty on the day 'Old Benny Titford' was buried.

More mundane events followed that moving funeral: the deceased had died intestate, and Letters of Administration were granted to Edith, the widow, on 25 September, there being £130 in effects. Edith was to live on until 1928, dying in Bath.

Benjamin had just lived long enough to see the first of his children married: Ella Frances May Titford's wedding had taken place on 26 August 1905, in that very church in which her father was to collapse eight days later. What kind of men were a village headmaster's daughters marrying at that period?

Ella's husband, John Miles Smith of Wick, near Curry Rivel, was an engineer, the son of a signalman. Twenty years old as she was, Ella had beaten her big sisters to the altar: Alice Maud, the eldest, waited a further two years before marrying Frank Foote, a clerk in Godsell's Brewery in Stroud, Gloucestershire, in which town she herself had served an apprenticeship with a ladies' hairdresser in High Street. They named their eldest son Benjamin, after his maternal grandfather, and she would tell the young lad when he grew up of how she had been taught piano and organ by Benjamin James her father, there in that big house in Curry Rivel where they used to hang hams or sides of bacon in the huge chimney piece.[7]

The next sister, Elizabeth Marian Edith ('Bessie') married Alf Davidge, a silk-buyer trained at the 'Cavendish House' department store in Cheltenham, who then took up employment at Debenham's in London, near St Paul's. Alf and Bessie lived in Cricklewood, and would receive visits from time to time from Bessie's sister Minnie who, having worked alongside her father at Curry Rivel School for a while, later became headmistress of a similar but smaller establishment in Newton St Loe, Somerset. There she lived in the school house and had charge of a little brood of no more than eight or nine children. Never very healthy, she nevertheless managed to live on well into retirement, and was 74 years old when she died at Alf and Bessies's house in 1951.

That leaves two sisters. Octavia Gertrude ('Gertie') went rather farther afield for a husband: to Norwich, in fact, where she and Frederick William Foxwell, manager of the *Livingstone Hotel*, Orford Hill, were married at St Peter Mancroft church in 1911. She was

OBITUARY.—Death has deprived Curry Rivel of one of its most useful and respected residents in the person of Mr. Benjamin James Titford, which took place at his residence on Friday morning of last week, after only a few days' illness. For several years past Mr. Titford had enjoyed unusually good health, with the exception of a slight illness last Christmas, and no one, not even his nearest relative, was prepared for the sudden collapse which ensued. He transacted the several duties connected with the positions he held as headmaster of the Curry Rivel schools and organist at the Parish Church up to the very moment he was seized by his last and fatal illness. It was while on his way to preside at the organ for a childrens' service held in the church on the afternoon of Sunday, the 2nd inst., he had a seizure. He had only just reached the sacred edifice when it was noticed that something unusual had happened, and fortunately, the Vicar, the Rev. H. Speke, who was near the porch, caught him before he fell on the floor. The Vicar immediately ordered his removal to the Vicarage, which is close by the church, where he was medically attended by Dr. R. H. Vereker. Later in the afternoon Mr. Titford was removed to his residence, and he remained in a semi-conscious condition up to the early hours of Friday morning, when, in spite of all that medical skill could do, he passed peacefully away. No death within recent years has created such a universal expression of regret. The deceased gentleman was the eldest son of the late Mr. Benjamin Titford, of Islington, London, in which place he spent most of his younger days. He chose a scholastic career, and at the age of 19 went to Cheltenham College where he qualified himself as a first-class master. His first appointment was the headmastership of St. Luke's Schools, and organist at the Parish Church, at Holloway, London. In the year 1868 he came to Curry Rivel to fill similar positions, and it is needless to say that during his thirty-seven years residence in the village, he has carried out his duties both as organist and schoolmaster to the satisfaction of all concerned. He married Miss Edith Mason, youngest daughter of Mr. H. R. Mason, of Huntingdon and London. He has also filled the offices of registrar of births and deaths and secretary to the Womens' Friendly Society. As a member of Court "Portcullis" A.O.F. (Langport), he took an untiring interest in everything that tended to promote the welfare of the Court, and was C.R. at the time of his death. Up to within recent years he was one of the most enthusiastic members of Langport Cricket Club, and a player of no mean ability. Deceased, who was 58 years of age, leaves a widow and seven grown-up children, for whom the greatest sympathy is felt in their unexpected and heavy bereavement.—The funeral of the late Mr. Titford took place in Curry Rivel Churchyard, on Wednesday afternoon, and was largely attended. The cortège left the late residence of the deceased gentleman about three o'clock, the coffin being carried on a bier by Messrs. J. Baker, W. Tilley, H. Towning, A. Reed, G. West, and G. Pippin, who acted as bearers. The mourners following in carriages were the widow, Miss Titford, the Misses M. Titford, B. Titford, G. Titford, L. Titford and Mrs. Smith (daughters), Mr. M. Titford (son), and Mrs. Huuton (sister-in-law). Among those in the procession were Mr. E. Davidge, Mr. E. Titford (nephew), Mr. J. Holbrook, the Rev. F. Mules (representing the Rev. Speke-Mules, formerly vicar of Curry Rivel), Mr. Milliton (president of the Teachers' Union), Mr. Lilley (representing the Teachers' Union), Dr. R. H. Vereker, Mr. R. S. J. Spilsbury, Mr. W. Munckton, Mr. S. Stacey, Mr. T. Lock, Mr. J. Eames, Mr. J. Lang, junr., Mr. W. Dyer, Mr. C. H. Cadwallader, Mr. C. Mathams, Mr. F. Meade, Mr. H. Pittard, Mr. F. J. Cox, the members of Court "Portcullis," A.O.F., (Langport), and Court "Earl of Chatham," A.O.F. (Curry Rivel), the children attending the schools of which deceased was headmaster, and a large number of the principal residents in the district. At the entrance to the church the mournful procession was met by the Vicar (the Rev. Hugh Speke) and the surpliced choir. The school children lined the pathway, and after the opening sentences had been read, the choir sang

"Peace, perfect peace," as the procession slowly wended its way into the church. The first portion of the burial service having been impressively read by the Vicar, the mourners, on leaving the church, were preceded by the clergy and choir singing the hymn, "Now the labourer's task is o'er," the Rev. E. Honsfield (curate) presiding at the organ. The Vicar officiated at the graveside, and the choir rendered the Nunc Dimittis. Mr. H. Pittard read the Foresters' ritual. The coffin, which was of elm, with brass furniture, had the following inscription on the breastplate:—"B. J. Titford, died Sept. 8th, 1905, aged 58 years." The beautiful floral tributes, which numbered about 40, included the following:—Cushion heart, from his sorrowing wife; gates ajar, his deeply grieved children; harp with broken string, all at 61, Stad Road, Stroud; sheaf, Miss Lawrence and Mr. Bigg, London; harp, the choir of St. Andrew's Church, Curry Rivel; wreaths from Mrs. Harris and family, Bridgwater; his brother and sister and family, London; National Union of Teachers; Mr. and Mrs. H. E. Martin, Huish Episcopi; Mr. and Mrs. Eaves, Curry Rivel; Mr. and Mrs. W. Cole, Langport; W. and E. Tilley and family, Curry Rivel; Dr. and Mrs. Vereker, Curry Rivel; Mrs. Cousins and family, Curry Rivel; E. Cousins, Curry Rivel; Mr. C. H. Cadwallader, Langport; Mrs. Pope and family, Curry Rivel; E. Bickle and family, Curry Rivel; Mr. and Mrs. Mitcham and family, Curry Rivel; Mr. and Mrs. Smith, Wick; Mrs. Wheller, Somerset Villa, Curry Rivel; Mr. and Mrs. W. Lang and family, Curry Rivel; the teaching staff at the Curry Rivel Schools; Miss A. Maude, Midelney House; from all at Heale House, Curry Rivel; Mr. C. C. Lock and family, Curry Rivel; the members of Curry Rivel Institute; Miss Buckle, Weston-super-Mare; Mr. and Mrs. Rose and Mrs. Bird, Bath; the Rev. and Mrs. C. M. Speke-Mules, London; crosses from Mr. and Mrs. S. Stacey, Curry Rivel; friends at 66, High Street, Weston-super-Mare; Mr. and Mrs. Hole, Langport; Miss A. Smith, Wick; all his schoolchildren; Mr. F. Foxwell, Norwich; the Rev. and Mrs. Weldon Kirby, Beaconsfield; Mr. and Mrs. J. Eames, Curry Rivel; Mrs. Matterson, Langford Manor; and anchors from Auntie, Percy, and Minnie, London; Alf and Nell, Langport. The funeral arrangements were satisfactorily undertaken by Mr. C. Stacey, of Curry Rivel.

42. The obituary of Benjamin James Titford. From the *Langport and Somerton Herald*, 1905.

later to run a ladies' outfitters in nearby Gorleston, on the Suffolk coast. Lillian Victoria was the last to marry; she had found her way down to Cobham, in Surrey, where she became the wife of Wilfred Arthur Edlin, a widower working as a dairyman.

So we have the nine daughters of Benjamin James Titford: three died young, one remained a spinster, three were Edwardian brides, two married during the early years of the reign of King George V. Their lives would take them far apart from each other and from Curry Rivel itself – yet they would remain a close-knit family, for all the physical distance which separated them. Twentieth-century developments in communications – be it the faster postal service, the telephone, telegrams or improved road conditions and means of transport – would enable far-flung relations to keep in touch with each other with an ease at which their ancestors might have marvelled.

Only one of Benjamin James's children would prove more than usually difficult to communicate with as time went by: young Marwood James Henry, a strangely elusive character in many ways. He surfaces in different places from time to time: there he is at St Mary's church in Finchley, North London, witnessing the marriage of sister Bessie and Alf Davidge in 1907, then appearing as if from nowhere to perform the same function for Gertie and Frederick Foxwell in Norwich in 1911. Four years later, like so many of his generation, he was sucked into the tragically wasteful conflict of the First World War, serving – for reasons best known to himself – as a soldier in the Canadian Army. He had the singular good fortune not to die in the trenches, but the experience undermined his health severely for all that. More than a hundred years after John Titford, the Frome volunteer, had died of consumption, Marwood was afflicted with the same disease under its more modern and bland title of 'T.B.'. Medical advice suggested he should live in a drier and sunnier climate – so he did. As the war ended he got himself married in Long Ditton, Surrey, to a girl named Madeline Fowler, daughter of George Fowler, a traffic manager. Time at last to rid himself of the name 'Marwood' for good and all: he told the officiating minister, Alfred Martell, to write him down as 'James Henry Titford'.[8] His mother and sister Ella were there to act as witnesses.

It was to be fond farewells all round. The newly-weds were to live further from home than any Titfords on their side of the family had ever done before. This chapter began with a young teacher from London moving to Somerset; it ends with his son and daughter-in-law seeking a new life in California. Marwood James Henry was the only male descendant of Benjamin James, and he and Madeline were to have no children; only through Benjamin James's brother William would the Titford name continue in this particular branch, and his story comes next.

CHAPTER 21

William the Gold-Engraver (1849-1918)

London

A STEADY INCOME

His eyes are like the over-tired eyes of an *engraver*
Dickens: *Our Mutual Friend*

William Titford's elder and younger brothers were each well-travelled in their own ways: Benjamin James had settled in Somerset soon after his brief spell in Cheltenham, and Charles Frederick was to see more of the world than almost any Titford before or since. William himself, by comparison, seems to represent a remarkable degree of geographical stability: he was born and died in Islington, seems to have travelled but little, and apparently lacked either the desire or the need to move house every few years as his father had done. In a sense he was the fixed point around which others revolved.

Benjamin the Silversmith provided young William with the same kind of solid foundation in life from which he himself had benefited: on 7 January 1864 an apprenticeship was arranged with Frederick William Ashdown, a gold-engraver of 1 Green Terrace, Clerkenwell. For five years William would be instructed in the art of ornamental gold-engraving; Mr. Ashdown's side of the bargain was to provide meat, drink and lodging, leaving the boy's father to find wearing apparel and arrange for washing and mending to be done. Further, in consideration of £20 paid to his master, William was to be allowed a modicum of pocket money: 6d. per week for the first year, 1s. a week for the second, 2s. a week for the third and 3s. a week for the fourth. The indenture was duly signed by all parties and witnessed by Edward W. Humberstone of Leather Lane, Holborn.

William completed his five-year stay in Clerkenwell successfully; by the time it was over his brother Benjamin James was already down in Somerset and Charles Frederick was coming up to the age when he, too, would become an apprentice. William's best plan now would be to get himself established in a job, save up a bit of money, then get married and move into his own little house. He must have been an eligible enough bachelor: the son of a fairly prosperous artisan family, trained as a craftsman, and quite a handsome chap into the bargain. Neither William nor Charles Frederick had quite the severity of countenance which one associates with Benjamin James: William in his twenties had a pleasant and confident face, with a full mouth which he would allow to be overgrown by a drooping and slightly unkempt moustache in later years. His hairline at that age was receding at the parting, giving every intimation that he might be bald one day; not so, in the event – photographs of him as an older man show clearly that same hairline, looking very much the same as it had in the days of his youth.

For all the choice of possible brides he may have had, William picked one very near home indeed: when he married in 1872 at St James, Clerkenwell, it was to his own cousin, Mary Ann Keziah Parkes, daughter of James Parkes, brass-rule maker – himself the brother of William's mother Elizabeth. Mary was then an attractive dark-haired lady, slightly plump, with swept-back hair falling into ringlets – full in the face, and quite striking in appearance. Her third Christian name was, of course, a good Nonconformist one with a

43.   William Titford (1849-1918).   44.   Mary Ann Keziah Titford (1849-1930).

biblical pedigree, that of the second of Job's daughters – but then Mary Ann Keziah was, after all, the granddaughter of the impressively-named Ebenezer Parkes.[1]

William was aged 22 at this time, with his wife a year younger; they began their married life in that same rather elegant location that Benjamin the Silversmith had chosen for his early forays into the boarding-house business: Wilmington Square, Clerkenwell. By 1875 they had moved around the square from no. 2 to no. 24 – a rather conservative little change of home which was maybe typical of them. And William was a very careful man, we may be sure: while they were still at 24 Wilmington Square, and he was still only in his twenties, he had the foresight to arrange for a Titford family grave at Abney Park Cemetery in Stoke Newington. Burial in a churchyard was becoming a thing of the past in central London from the 1840s onwards; space was too precious, and the task of burying the dead was taken over by non-denominational cemeteries run largely on a commercial basis.[2] Abney Park in

45. Abney Park Cemetery, Stoke Newington. From Rev. Thomas B. Barker, *Abney Park Cemetery (London)* (1869). Many Titfords from a number of family branches found their last resting place at Abney Park.

46. Burial certificate, Abney Park Cemetery. William Titford had paid five guineas during the 1870s for the exclusive right of burial in his chosen plot.

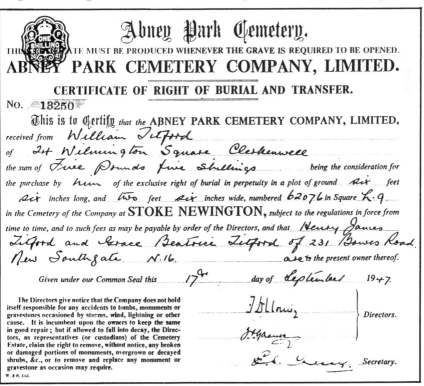

North London was a convenient site for the Titford family – fairly close to home, extremely spacious, and with a certain degree of Nonconformist tradition. The only slightly unnerving experience for any Titford mourners attending a funeral there would be the prominent sign dominating the entrance which read: 'Titford and Co. Undertakers'. The cousins up from Wylye were doing a brisk business at Abney Park.

William paid his five guineas to the Abney Park Cemetery Company, Ltd., in exchange for 'exclusive right in perpetuity' of burial in a plot of ground 6′ 6″ by 2′ 6″ – no. 62,076, square L9. Members of the family would be buried there until the 1940s, thanks to William's generous gesture.

No man as prudent as William Titford would have paid out good money for a family grave unless he had some firm evidence that there would eventually be some bodies to put in it. Well, there were: by the time they left Clerkenwell William and Mary Ann had already produced four out of their five children – all boys. Little Horace Charles was carried off by pneumonia at the tender age of eight months, but Ernest William, Henry James and Herbert George were healthy young children crawling or toddling around those rooms in Wilmington Square. The last child, Grace Beatrice, would not be born until the family had moved to 17 Brunswick Place, but once she had arrived we cannot but notice an almost uncanny similarity between William's family and that of his father: each consisted of four boys followed by a girl, with the third child dying in infancy. Certainly there are no profound conclusions to be drawn from that fact, except to note that various forms of contraception were beginning to be practised from the 1870s onwards, with a steady decline in the national birth-rate apparent during the following decade. William was only 34 when his last child was born, while his father had been 43; perhaps some form of contraception did account for William and Mary Ann stopping short at those four children? Either that, or they may have practised the oldest and surest method of them all for preventing unwanted pregnancies – abstinence from sexual relations. That is their secret, and will remain so; it behoves us not to pry, only to speculate in passing.

The family move to Brunswick Place, near the junction of City Road and Old Street, took place in 1879 – but just before, rather than after, the death of William's father Benjamin. The Titfords were more than lucky, in a sense, to have picked up their legacies from Benjamin's will in that year, since the nation as a whole was suffering from a period of deep depression following a boom which had peaked six or seven years before. Charles Frederick, we know, had used his capital to set up his little tobacconist's business in Cumberland Street; Emily Jane probably used hers to swell her bottom drawer, and William . . . well, in a moment of cavalier abandon, he dabbled in running a chandler's shop there in Brunswick Place. An odd move, to be sure, at a time when prices were falling – and in a rather smart street, too, where such a venture would not be guaranteed to make him instantly popular with the neighbours, as customers came in one door and noisome smells came out of another. Of course it was only an experiment and didn't last long: by 1884 the Court Directory for London lists William as an engraver once more – this generation of Titfords seemed to lack the heart for such enterprises, which had been the speciality of their father, Benjamin the Silversmith.

Brunswick Place itself was definitely rather an up-market location, as the 1881 census makes clear. Admittedly there was more than a hint of urban overcrowding two doors away from William at no. 21, where a glove cutter, a walnut-veneer repairer and a book finisher were living with their families – but that was exceptional. The Titfords' immediate neighbours boasted domestic servants: two of them to look after a boot manufacturer and his wife at no. 15, and just the one to attend to the needs of a photographer and his step-daughter who were living on the other side. William and Mary Ann Titford enjoyed no such luxury – but then they were among the youngest people in the street, and their daughter

The undermentioned Houses are situate within the Boundaries of the

Civil Parish [or Township] of	City or Municipal Borough of	Municipal Ward of	Parliamentary Borough of	Town or Village or Hamlet of	Urban Sanitary District of	Rural Sanitary District of	Ecclesiastical Parish or District of

In Loving Memory

OF

ELIZABETH AGUSTA JOSEPHINE TITFORD

Who Died 4th March, 1902,

AGED 80 YEARS.

INTERRED AT THE ABNEY PARK CEMETERY.

47. 1881 census: Brunswick Place, City Road, London. William and Mary Ann Titford are living with their family at no. seventeen. (PRO RG/393.)

48. Loving Memory card for Elizabeth Titford (1822-1902). The printer has had problems with the spelling of 'Augusta' . . . .

Grace Beatrice, born in 1883, would have been the only baby crying down Brunswick Place in that year – much to the consternation of the local worthies, no doubt:

> I rue the day these wretched Titfords ever came to live down here – couldn't they have stayed over in Wilmington Square? I can't sleep at night for that baby crying, I can't breathe in the daytime for that stench of tallow coming out of their back door – and one of his customers brushed me into the dusty street the other day . . .

A final comment on Brunswick Place in the 1880s would need to mention its peculiarly equivocal position as regards local government. There would have been a time when most small city streets would have come clearly within the jurisdiction of one parish; nothing so simple for Brunswick Place – it lay within the civil parish of St Leonards, the municipal ward of Hoxton New Town, the parliamentary borough of Hackney, the urban sanitary district of Hoxton, and the ecclesiastical parish of St John's. Come back the old English parish, all is forgiven . . .

We began by saying that William Titford moved house comparatively infrequently, and within a fairly limited area; he and Mary Ann found new accommodation only once more in their married life together – as the children grew up and left home the parents moved to 48 Freegrove Road, Holloway, just off the Caledonian Road. They were settled there as early as 1899, and it was from that address that the only one of their children to marry – Henry James – set off on his wedding day, 8 September 1902. Indeed, he could almost have walked the short distance to Arundel Square Congregational Chapel, as could his bride, Margaret Archibald, from nearby Ringcroft Street. William and Mary Ann were there in all their glory, as we might expect: he with a spotted waistcoat and flamboyant flowery buttonhole, she with an expanse of fur on her head and around her shoulders.

William lived on for a further 16 years after that, into the reign of George V and the First World War. That war, like its successor in 1939, had its civilian as well as its military casualties, and William Titford was one of them. He was 68 years old in the early months of 1918, when the experience of living through an air-raid proved too much for his system and he suffered a stroke. He was admitted to Islington Infirmary, unable to speak, and yet desperately trying to convey a message to his daughter-in-law Margaret. He kept stroking his own hand, then bursting into tears at his inability to communicate; was it, as Margaret supposed afterwards, that he was trying to say that he had a second bank-book which they needed to find? If so, they never found it; William died intestate on 4 March and Letters of Administration were granted to Ernie, the eldest son; the gross value of the estate was just over £564, with the net value of the personal estate standing at £43 12s. 4d. Well, perhaps there had been a second bank-book, after all?

William, we may remember, had thoughtfully provided himself with a burial plot many years before: so square L9, grave no. 62,076 it was, as he was laid to rest at Abney Park. Once again a widow was to outlive her husband – how very different from the experience of those 18th-century Titford wives, worn out after years of child-bearing and dying in their fifties if not before! Mary Ann settled back into widowhood in Freegrove Road, this time at no. 17 with her two unmarried sons and one unmarried daughter. Sometimes they would all venture out to visit Henry James and Margaret in Bowes Road, New Southgate, where the grandchildren would try to suppress their giggles at hearing the mixture of voices as the grown-ups sang round the piano – 'Come, Birdie, come and live with me', 'Just a song at twilight', 'Down by the mill' and other contemporary favourites. Mary Ann had a beautiful voice even into her seventies, Ernie and Henry James both sang in choirs, and Bert played the piano and the violin: between them, then, they had all the raw material necessary for a good evening of typical early 20th-century home entertainment.

Granny's visits to Bowes Road would always be very much appreciated by her little granddaughter Doris, if only because of the teatime treats which would attend such occasions; as she took the old lady upstairs to dispose of her coat, Doris would whisper: 'We've got blackcurrant pie today because you're here; we only ever have it when you come . . .'.

These visits to New Southgate were, of course, reciprocated as the grandchildren paid a visit to Granny in Freegrove Road; stopping off at Beale's on Holloway Road for chocolate fingers on the way – a great treat – they would go to the side entrance of no. 17 and ring the bell. 'Who is it?' would come a voice from the passageway within, as Granny called through the grating: 'Walk in, please . . .'. Then would come tea up in the parlour – winkles, usually, extracted with a pin – as the young visitors gazed around the cluttered but tasteful room with its ubiquitous red plush and velvet and its ruby glass and ornaments with glass-drop clusters.[3]

Mary Ann was blind during the last few years of her life, and it had the quite understandable effect of making her very emotional; she only had one set of grandchildren, and she made such a fuss of them: 'My Siddy', she would say, as she stroked her young grandson's cheek with tears in her eyes. 'Siddy's' fiancée, Beth, would cut and set her hair for her in the late 'twenties, but by the time the couple married in June, 1930, Granny was very near the end. She died in the December of that year, joining her husband in the family grave; many letters of condolence were received by Ernie at Freegrove Road, including one from Cousin Alf Davidge of Cricklewood – the husband of Benjamin James's daughter, Bessie. That link with Curry Rivel was still not quite forgotten.

The role of memory and reminiscence in family history research should never be underestimated. The case of Mary Ann Titford, *née* Parkes, is fairly typical in this respect: her grandchildren, still alive in the 1980s as this story is being written, remember her well, though she had been born as long ago as 1849. Human memory in this case carries us, in a way, over a span of history lasting nearly a hundred and forty years. Whatever can a person like Mary Ann, born in the early years of Victoria's reign, have thought of England in the 1930s? Cultural and social eons had passed, in effect, and William Titford himself, also an early Victorian, could never have predicted in his wildest nightmares that his death would be hastened by bombs dropping from the sky. It must be a tribute to the resilience of these people that they lived so long and survived through it all.

CHAPTER 22

Charles Frederick (1856-1899)

London

FOOT-LOOSE AND FANCY-FREE IN THE DAYS OF EMPIRE

Family historians should not play favourites – or out of the window goes any objectivity. Yet despite ourselves we cannot help warming to some characters who make up our story more than we do to others; these were people, after all, not just historical data, and there will be those long since dead for whom we develop a special affection, just as we have similar predilections when it comes to men and women we meet in our everyday lives.

The reader may notice, then, that the author has a soft spot for the youngest of Benjamin the Silversmith's sons, Charles Frederick. He appears, in any case, to have been everyone's favourite: the favourite uncle ('Charlie') of his nephews and niece, as he bewitched them with tales of far-off places, and the favourite son, one suspects, of his mother, who presented him late in her life with a hand-painted miniature of herself in colour and on bone, 'taken when six years of age'. Elizabeth had carefully written her name on the reverse: 'E. A. J. Parkes, born 15th February 1822', followed by a simple dedication: 'For Charles'.

Charles was hardly a mother's boy – he was far too independent for that – but he would have seen more of her than he ever did of his father, especially in later years during her widowhood. It was nothing unusual for a boy in Victorian times to live in the same house as his parents for no more than 14 or 15 years – that is, from birth until the start of an apprenticeship. This proved to be the case with Charles, who had even less continuous contact with his elder brothers than he did with mother and father: he was only seven when William went away to begin his apprenticeship, and witnessed the final departure of Benjamin James just two years later.

For a brief spell Charles was left at home with sister Emily Jane, then he, too, was off to learn a craft and live in his master's house. On 1 November 1871 he was apprenticed to a silversmith and goldsmith by the name of George Lambert of Coventry Street, Haymarket; one copy of the indenture was kept by the family, as was the custom, while the other was retained by the Chamberlain's Office in Guildhall. The usual stipulations applied: the apprentice was not to commit fornication, contract matrimony, haunt taverns and playhouses nor gamble during the said term. George Lambert was to provide meat, drink, apparel, lodging and other necessaries for his 15-year old apprentice, and the arrangement was to run for seven years – two years longer than brother William had had to serve. Benjamin, the father, always enigmatic when asked to name his profession, decided that for the purposes of young Charles's indenture he would be a 'Collector to a Goldsmith'.

There was probably little enough temptation for Charles to break the conditions of his contract with Mr. Lambert by getting married – that, after all, was a bit of an expensive business. But fornication may have been a different matter – what red-blooded young male working in Haymarket at that time could have failed to notice the female flesh on offer at every street corner? This was the centre of London prostitution at the period – English girls rubbing uneasy bare shoulders with continental ladies of easy virtue, many using the streets off the Haymarket to find rooms they could rent by the hour as they went about their nefarious business. One commentator writing of the area in the 1860s said that it

... literally blazed with light from such temples as the Blue Post, Barnes's, The Burmese, and Barron's Oyster Rooms . . . night houses abounded, and Rose Burton's and Jack Percival's were sandwiched between hot baths of questionable respectability, and abominations of every kind.[1]

Of course we should never dream of impugning the reputation of young Charles by suggesting that he saved up his coppers for an hour's fun round the corner in Panton Street, but there might well have been nights when he lay in bed listening hard to what was going on below, intrigued if not tempted.

Their boy Charles, then, was probably having a broader education than his parents had bargained for. Yet somehow the young lad was not altogether fulfilled in life as he slaved over a goldsmith's bench; Haymarket by day and by night may have been lively, but he craved even greater excitement. Whatever safe and secure future was being planned for him by others, he had ideas of his own – and a wanderlust which needed to satisfied. He would travel the world!

And so he did. Shrugging off the trammels of apprenticeship before even five years had passed, our young adventure-seeker waved a fond farewell to friends and loved ones, and set off on one of the longest journeys in the world – all the way to Australia. In April of 1876 a letter sped its way from

49.   Charles Frederick Titford (1856-1899). A photograph dating from the period 1878-90, during which time the photographer, Edward Russell, was in business at 276 Holloway Road, the address given on this *carte de visite*.

Upper Macedonia in Victoria, Australia, to Melbourne, thence by the Up Train to Sydney, addressed to 'Mr C F Titford, c/o W Sanderson, Young Men's Xtian Assn, 125, King St, Sydney'. Quite what message this letter had to convey we cannot tell, but the envelope found its way into Charles's personal collection of momentoes of his varied life – a collection containing enough envelopes, together with the occasional letter and postcard, to enable us to chart his movements as he criss-crossed the oceans of the world in the 1870s and eighties.

Australia no doubt held its attractions for Charles, and this was to be by no means his

50. Charles Frederick Titford (1856-1899): Apprenticeship Indenture. Charles is to be apprenticed for seven years to a Haymarket goldsmith, 1 November 1871. One half of the full indenture was enrolled at the Chamberlain's Office at the Guildhall; this half was kept by the apprentice himself.

last voyage to the Antipodes; but he was a traveller, not an emigrant, and before the year was out he had crossed another of the world's great oceans and was seeing what pleasures the great city of San Francisco could afford. We have no record of his reaction to the place, but it could hardly have been less than favourable, one suspects, since a place advertised even in the 1980s as 'America's Favourite City' must have been a jewel ideed before the age of the skyscraper, when the outline of the rolling hills on which it is built would have been clearly in evidence, and the major earthquake still lay some years in the future.

A postcard awaited Charles in California, addressed to him at the San Francisco Post Office ('Mr Chas Fredck Tidford'), from his friend Charles Smith, then in Healdsburg, Sonoma County, and dated 3 September. The writer just wanted to inform his friend that he finally had employment in Healdsburg, but that as soon as the wet weather set in he would get a job on the Panama Central American Steamers; the card had a bit of a business ring to it, too, as the enterprising Mr. Smith foresaw the prospect of picking up some postage stamps down in Central America, and asked Charles to leave a forwarding address so that they might start up a kind of mutually-beneficial agency between them. Such a suggestion presages Charles's own life-long interest in philately which he was to pursue with great gusto once he was finally settled back home in England.

In the October of 1876 a British ship of thirteen hundred tons called the *Cartsburn* had recently arrived in San Francisco after a somewhat troubled voyage from Dundee. Three crew members had been left behind in Plymouth on the way out, guests of Her Majesty in the town's gaol; not only that, but ships' cooks, it seems, were vulnerable to ill-fate of a different kind. Robert Titford's ship, the *Orynthia*, we may remember, had lost its cook in Demerara in 1839, 'Drowned'; now a similar fate had befallen young William Stewart, 22 years old, aboard the *Cartsburn*.

The accident has elements of tragedy and farce commixed: the sea had been smooth and the vessel proceeding at a stately three knots when William had felt the need to pay a visit to the primitive ship's lavatory – the 'heads'. There, drunk or sober as the case may be, he somehow lost his footing and fell from the head rails, tumbling into the ocean which gaped below; the *Cartsburn* put about once the alarm was raised, but although it re-traced its route burning a blue light, neither sight nor sound of young William Stewart was ever had again.

This had happened on the 1 June, with the ship off the coast of South America; now in San Francisco it was time to set on a new cook – a Frenchman – and also to replace nine members of the crew who had deserted once the shop arrived in port. This gave young Charles Titford his chance to work his passage home; stating that the last vessel on which he had served was the *Australia*, and satisfying the Vice Consul in San Francisco that he understood the conditions of service, he signed on as an ordinary seaman aboard the *Cartsburn*.

One can only hope that the new cook was less accident-prone than his predecessor; he would feed the crew according to a specified menu: one pound of bread per day; one and a half pounds of beef and one and a quarter pounds of pork respectively on alternate days; one and a half pounds of flour a week, and various amounts of peas, tea, coffee, lime juice, lemon juice and sugar.

The fare seems to have done no lasting damage to Charles; he arrived back safely in Liverpool on 5 March 1877, claimed his £3 balance of wages owing, and was home in time for his twenty-first birthday on 17 April.

Abroad, Rutherford B. Hayes was inaugurated as President of the U.S.A. – Charles was later to obtain a copy of this gentleman's autograph – and in the East, a week after Charles's birthday, Russia declared war on Turkey and invaded Rumania; the Russo-Turkish had begun in earnest. This might be an exciting time, then, to set off around the world once more, albeit at a safe distance from the war zone? Charles was ready and willing, and we can take the opportunity to follow his next voyage in some detail, because it was to hold danger and drama in store for him in a way that could hardly have been foreseen at the outset.

To Australia once more, then; there would be lachrymose farewells at home, no doubt, as freshly-laundered clothes and other necessaries were packed ready before the boxes were finally corded up for dispatching, and then Charles was off to the London docks ready to be aboard by 10 a.m. on 21 January 1878.

This time there was the comparative luxury of being aboard a steam-powered ship – the *Chimborazo* of 3,847 tons, iron-built at Govan in 1871, screw-driven and generating 550 horsepower; her 384 feet of length included three decks and an awning deck. This was to be Charles's floating home for the next few months, one that he would share with a number of passengers and a crew of men mainly in their twenties and thirties; some were fully-fledged sailors – others, like Charles, were engaged as 'servants' at a wage of £3 per calendar month and could expect a fairly bumpy ride if it fell to their lot to minister to the needs of those unfortunate passengers travelling 'steerage'.

The first short leg of the voyage east would be calm enough, however – just as far as Gravesend, then a busy little riverside town, where Charles found time to buy two small photographs taken by F. C. Gould, a local photographer – one of the *Chimborazo* itself, the other of her larger companion ship, the *Aconcagua*. Both vessels were named after extinct volcanoes in the Andes (one in Ecuador, the other in Argentina), and both had originally been built for what was then the largest steam shipping company in the world, the Pacific Steam Navigation Company, known as the 'Birkenhead Navy'. Seven months before Charles joined the *Chimborazo*, the P.S.N.C. had entered into a partnership with the newly-formed Orient Steam Navigation Company and begun regular sailings to Australia in competition with the P. & O. Four ships took it in turn to travel out round the Cape of Good Hope and back through the Suez Canal; the *Lusitania* (no, not *THE Lusitania*!) had started off the enterprise in the June of 1877, reaching Melbourne in just 40 days, and returning from Adelaide to Plymouth in forty-one. At an average speed for actual steaming time of just under 13 knots, she had broken the previous record for the voyage by a margin of 10 days. Her sister ships followed her at monthly intervals: the *Cuzco*, the *Garonne* and the *Chimborazo* itself. It was vessels like these which were to speed up the mail service throughout the British Empire, taking passengers along for good measure; sailing ships, in exceptionally good conditions, could match these steamers for speed, but were necessarily much less reliable and predictable, totally at the mercy of the vagaries of the weather as they were. In the event, the *Chimborazo* was playing it safe by sporting sail as well as steam; as late as 1947 a correspondent was writing to the nautical magazine, *Sea Breezes*, with memories of sailing aboard her in 1890:

> The *Chimborazo* was a clipper-bowed ship with a stump bowsprit, fully rigged as a barque. She was fitted with patent rolling topsail yards, and on one occasion, when steering westward through the Gut of Gibraltar before an easterly gale, we reefed the fore and main topsails. I am probably one of the few suriving mariners who ever reefed topsails in a steamer . . .[2]

As a mere servant on board, perhaps Charles Titford was doing nothing quite so dangerous or skilful as reefing a topsail in a gale?

And so on Wednesday 23 January 1878, as the British Fleet was being sent to Constantinople to help the Sultan of Turkey, a more humble vessel departed from Gravesend with our 21-year-old traveller on board. Through the straits of Dover they steamed, and so on to Plymouth to collect passengers for the voyage, Captain J. Vine Hall in command. Two hundred and two first-class, and 213 second-class passengers joined the ship, along with a full general cargo and 20 sacks of mail for Australia and New Zealand. On the Saturday, 26 January, everything being in order, they duly set off – first stop: St Vincent, to load up with coal.

They soon had a snow storm to contend with – this was not the ideal time of year for a voyage, perhaps – but were eventually in warmer waters, anchored off St Vincent by 2 February, on which day Greece joined the turmoil in the Mediterranean by declaring war on Turkey. Weather was fine on 3 February, and better still on the 4th, by which time they were level with Gambia in West Africa.

The passengers on the *Chimborazo* were generously provided with a regular little magazine or news-sheet as the voyage progressed. *The Neptune* No. 2, on 5 February, was veritably brimming with information: a special telegram from Colonel Glover declared that the Russians were now close to Constantinople and that peace was expected – 'Turks want to shake hands, Russians don't: Turks have invited Russians to dinner: Russians will stay to

The Neptune

No 2   Chimborazo   5th February 1878

St Vincent

One of the Cape de Verd group. Lat 16° 54' 45" N Lon 25° 1' 10" W Portugese own it. Can boast of a Custom House, Town Hall and Palace. The only product is coal, which is imported. The color of the natives is that of coal. They seem to enjoy it. The chief industry is diving for sixpences and loafing, principally loafing. Population 3000 —

War News

Special telegram p Colonel Glover. Russians close Constantinople preliminaries peace expected signed Thursday Adrianople. Looks like peace.

Phonograms

Turks want to shake hands - Russians don't. Turks have invited Russians to dinner. Russians will stay to tea, bed and breakfast.

Wanted

2 Pajamas - clean - B1
A Hammock   2

Found

Church Hymns   3

Lost

Bundle of rugs, straps have brass plate - Please examine cabins and oblige   4
A rug - contains air cushion, Beetons annual.

Dramatic Club

Members will please meet at port capstan 10 am today

Book Club

Books will now be received by Mr Leicester. Please let him have them today.

Mfu   mpwof
Espuifsmz   dhouy ovf
Instructions E.P. tonight. New applicants must produce diplomas or be vouched. P.C. on Wednesday, 7 pm punctual.   Fidelity.

51. 'The Neptune' news-sheet issued aboard the R.M.S. *Chimborazo*, 5 February 1878. A full-scale war was raging between the Russians and the Turks – and the news-sheet regales its readers with 'War News'. Charles Titford was a 'servant' on board.

tea, bed and breakfast'. With a touch of xenophobic arrogance, the editors announced that the 'color of the natives' in St Vincent, one of the Cape de Verd Islands, 'is that of coal. They seem to enjoy it. The chief industry is diving for sixpences and loafing, principally loafing . . .' Such opinions, no doubt, were commonplace on board a ship travelling to and from distant parts of the empire on which the sun never set.

Life on board seems to have been teeming with activity: the Dramatic Club would meet at 10 a.m. at the port capstan: the Book Club was underway, and the Second Grand Marine Ball of the season was due to take place on the port quarter deck on Thursday evening at 7.30. A Masonic Lodge was meeting for those who were 'vouched', clean 'pajamas' were wanted, a hammock had been found, church hymns had been lost. There is a riddle to which, frustratingly, we are not given an answer: 'What's the difference between a church bell and a church organ . . .?', while the correspondence column gives replies to letters of enquiry, the original contents of which we can only guess at: 'Annie: Captain Hall is married – so is we – sorry' or 'Boyer: We don't know – you must consult the surgeon . . .'.

The fare-paying passengers aboard enjoying themselves at the Marine Ball or passing the time pondering the answers to cryptic riddles were no doubt as out of touch with life below decks as some families on land were ignorant of goings-on below stairs; *The Neptune* magazine probably didn't see fit to report the fact that Thomas Boyd, a 27-year-old fireman from Armagh, had died on board on 6 February and been buried at sea, his effects 'destroyed, being filthy' . . .

The Equator was crossed – time to initiate greenhorns into the wonders of King Neptune – and they headed for the Southern Ocean. There would have been a few marvels to behold as time went by – most journals which give details of voyages to Australia at this period talk with wonder of the flying-fish, porpoises and albatrosses, as well as the bold beauty of the Southern Cross in the sky on a still dark night.

And so on eastwards to Australia – a country we tend to think of today as a single indivisible unit; in 1878, however, it consisted of six separate colonies, each independently subject to the British Crown. The first fleet of transported prisoners had arrived at Sydney Cove, a few miles from Botany Bay, in 1788; these convicts together with their uniformed overseers were to found the oldest Australian state, New South Wales. Victoria was carved out of it in 1837, and Queensland was created later, in 1859. Transportation had ceased 10 years before the *Chimborazo* reached Australian shores in 1878; nevertheless, the contrast that Charles and others would have experienced between sophisticated London and this vast and fairly primitive land in the Southern Hemisphere must have been marked indeed.

They arrived at Melbourne on 13 March, completing a 52-day voyage from London; no problems so far, and no doubt those passengers who disembarked did so with a smile on their faces and a word of thanks to Captain Hall. They would all be safe enough in Melbourne itself, though any incautious foray into the interior might bring them face-to-face with the notorious Ned Kelly, who formed his gang of lawless bushrangers in that very year.

What the passengers and crew aboard the *Chimborazo* did not know as they steamed out of Melbourne four days later was that greater perils awaited them at sea than were facing their companions left on shore. Captain Hall may have run a happy, sociable ship, but his Achilles' heel was a certain incompetence when it came to navigation. At 11 o'clock on the morning of 15 March the *Chimborazo* was approaching Point Perpendicular near Jervis Bay, en route for Sydney; the sea was calm, but a thick mist hung in the air, and the rocks at Point Perpendicular merited a very wide berth. Alas, they didn't get one; Captain Hall and his crew somehow succeeded in steaming full-speed into the jagged promontory, cutting a great hole in the ship's bows. In the scarcely-controlled panic which ensued, the engines were thrown immediately into reverse, and everyone on board ran aft. There was 'intense

52. The *Chimborazo* strikes the rocks near Jervis Bay. From the *Australian Town and Country Journal*, 23 March 1878. Charles Frederick Titford was aboard at the time.

excitement and confusion, particularly amongst the ladies', according to the *Australian Town and Country Journal* of 23 March, and 'the whole of the ship's crew came promptly into action, and the steady and quick way in which orders were attended to spoke of excellent nautical discipline'. Within ten minutes the ship was re-floated, and the sailors and others eventually managed to carry the women and children through the slight surf on to a little beach and so to safety. The news of the alarming incident, it is said,

> created a profound sensation in Sydney, especially among those who were on that day expecting to congratulate friends and relatives on the termination of a pleasant and remarkably speedy voyage.

Perhaps the Titford family, after all, were unlucky sailors? The sea could scarcely have held more perils than it did for Robert Titford the Mariner, yet here was his nephew Charles living through an exciting but rather harrowing experience on board ship nearly forty years later. Charles kept a cutting from a local newspaper in his scrapbook: 'View of the Chimborazo when striking the rocks near Jervis Bay' – it shows the ship in full steam, though with all sails furled, and a strangely inquisitive gaggle of people at the bow, watching it all happen as if in slow motion.

The ship was brought back to Melbourne for major repairs once it could safely be moved, but the entire incident was bad news for Captain Hall in more ways than one: he was found guilty of careless navigation and had his certificate suspended for six months. The magnates of the Orient Steam Navigation Company quite probably never forgave him.[3]

Charles Titford and the *Chimborazo* both lived to fight another day. Charles managed to pick up the odd letter or two shortly after the wreck had happened – one posted in West London on 12 February and despatched by the next Orient Line sailing to arrive in Melbourne in late April, and another, one of his own letters returned to him on board ship in Sydney, courtesy of the Dead Letter Office. The inside flap of the envelope informed him rather less than helpfully:

> The enclosed letter not having been delivered for the reason assigned thereon, was opened here by the officer appointed for that purpose, and is now returned to the writer. General Post Office, Sydney.

Charles had been away longer than he might have anticipated; it was mid-August by the time he landed back in London, collecting £10 8s. 2d. in wages owed to him, and returning to the bosom of his family with more than a few hair-raising stories to tell. Not that he was home for good, but there was a certain amount of unfinished business to attend to before he could set off on a further voyage with a clear conscience. Principally there was the matter of his unfinished apprenticeship; not that he ever seems to have had any intention of becoming a goldsmith, but perhaps father had put a bit of pressure on his errant son with a 'Get yourself some qualifications, my boy' kind of heart-to-heart?

At this point George Lambert, Citizen and Goldsmith, Charles's ex-master, seems to have come to the rescue by being prepared to perjure himself in a rather public fashion. From all the available evidence it seems unlikely that Charles ever completed even a full five years of his apprenticeship in Haymarket, yet the good Mr. Lambert was prepared to swear on the oath he took at the time of his own Freedom of the City of London that his one-time apprentice had served seven years with him from 1 November 1871, and had neither married nor received wages during that time.[4] This was enough to satisfy Francis B. Howard, Warden to the Chamberlain's Court of the City of London, and Charles Frederick Titford was duly granted the Freedom of the City of London on 4 June 1879, by dint of having (supposedly) served his due term of apprenticeship. The appropriate certificate was drawn up and handed to the new Freeman, issued during the mayoralty of Sir Charles Whitham.

George Lambert, then, was a friend indeed; it is nice to note that many years later, in 1892, he was still sending Charles a Christmas card worthy of being stuck in the young man's album, complete with gilt printing and an ornate crest. The two of them must have had quite a degree of affection one for the other – Charles, everybody's favourite, all over again . . .

A man who had lived through a shipwreck would now be game for anything, of course; Charles had previously left London as a war was raging between the Russians and the Turks – now he would arrive at his next chosen destination, South Africa, just at the end of the Zulu War, which had run its course from January to July, 1879. Perhaps he arrived just too late and was disappointed? In any case he was down there as early as December 1879, in which month the Transvaal Republic was proclaimed – hot times, indeed.[5] Having landed in Durban, he contacted Schenk's Forwarding Agency in West Street, arranging for his portmanteau and a box to be sent ahead to Petermaritzburg. Schenk's printed receipt diplomatically disclaimed any responsibility for his property, whether it might be lost because of water or vermin, or else destroyed by wet weather, bad roads, or by any other unavoidable accident.

Charles arranged to pick up his mail from the General Post Office in Petermaritzburg, and then set off for a bit of sight-seeing. His album contains photographs of places he had visited: Cape Town, with two

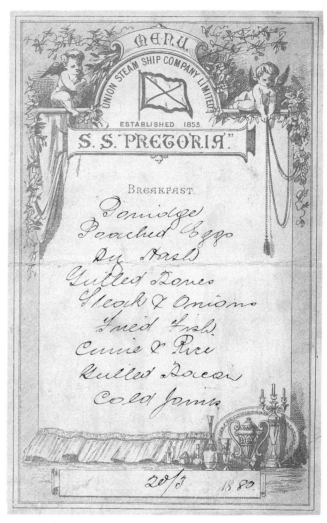

53. Breakfast menu, S.S. *Pretoria*, March 1880. Charles Titford was aboard the *Pretoria*, en route from South Africa to England.

old tars taking a rest and with a host of sailing ships in the background, the distant mountains covered in cloud; the monument to the Natal Carbineers, erected in the early 1870s; the Howit Falls in Natal, and a small photograph purchased from B. W. Caney of Durban, showing a group of natives attired in loincloths, posing with their mongrel dog against a grass hut.

Back to the Post Office in early February 1880, to collect the mail: a letter from the Shipping Master, Port Elizabeth Cape Colony, marked O.H.M.S.; one from Natal in a rather ornately-cut envelope – and, ominously, a missive from London posted on New Year's Day in a black-bordered envelope. One look at the envelope alone would have told him all he wanted to know: his father had died. The holiday in a hot climate far from the fogs of London was brought abruptly to an end; by late March he was headed back home aboard the S.S. *Pretoria*, a schooner of 3,199 gross tons with two decks and a spar deck, built in Dumbarton in 1878.[6] It operated along with 13 other ships on the Union Steamship Company's Cape of Good Hope, Natal, Zanzibar and East African Royal Mail Service route.

The *Pretoria*, master Mr. Owen, produced its own rather grand hand-written menu cards. For breakfast on 20 March there was a bewildering choice of gastronomic goodies: porridge, poached eggs, dry hash, grilled bones, steak and onions, fried fish, 'Currie' and rice, grilled bacon or cold joints. After such a spread the passengers must have prayed for a smooth crossing . . .

Back in London Charles was to receive news that in his absence his grandfather, Ebenezer Parkes, had died on 10 January, leaving Elizabeth Titford both a widow and fatherless within three months. Whether she implored her favourite son to stay at home and forget his foreign travels we do not know, but if so it was to no avail. Having set up his little tobacconist's business in Cumberland Street in the twinkling of an eye, Charles promptly set off again as if nothing could disturb his series of round-the-world tours; this time, for variety, he went west.

He certainly does look like a man in a hurry; in the October of 1880 he bought himself a large album – a sort of glorified scrap-book – in which to stick all the momentoes he had collected and would hope to collect. Though he was still in Cumberland Street on census day, 3 April 1881, we find him far away at 65 Walton Street in Toronto, Canada, just over two months later. There he received a postcard from a gentleman in Montreal, signing himself 'J. L.', whose idea of a friendly message seems to have consisted of filling every available space with religious exhortations and biblical texts. If such correspondence was in any way typical of that which Charles was receiving, he was in touch with a very fervent set of evangelical Christians indeed. Many of his later letters and cards, by contrast, are more mundane in nature.

The new album was soon put to good use, and quickly filled up with page after page of neat photographs of Canadian scenes – Ottawa, Montreal, Quebec and Toronto, juxtaposed with other pictures and ephemera from Charles's earlier travels. Clearly what impressed him the most during his stay in Canada was his visit to the Niagara Falls; one newspaper article which he cut out and kept warned the unwary visitor not to attempt to swim the rapids (think of Captain Webb, who had perished . . .) and to be on the lookout for swindlers: 'Most visitors do not go twice, and they are made the most of whilst they are there'.

Who, after all, could fail to be impressed by Niagara – nearly four thousand feet across, with fifteen hundred million cubic feet per minute of water careering over the drop of 167 feet? Charles underlined phrases of breathless hyperbole attached to a photograph of the falls: '. . . magnificent in volume, dazzling in radiance, stupendous in its breadth and awe-inspiring in its ceaseless roar'. He also marked off comments by Charles Dickens:

> I felt how near to my creator I was standing. The first impression and the lasting one of this tremendous spectacle was – PEACE – great thoughts of an eternal rest and happiness!

His stay in Canada may well have whetted Charles's appetite for yet more travel in North America, but when we next meet him two years later he was paying yet another visit to his old favourite, Australia, where he eventually found work abroad the S.S. *Garonne*, an Orient Line sister ship of the *Chimborazo* and almost identical with her in size and power, the pair of them having been built together at Govan in 1871. Charles must have felt very much at home. He joined as a 'General Servant' in Sydney on 24 September 1883, agreeing to a wage of £3 per month and to the ship's rules and regulations, which included the wearing of the company's uniform (to be purchased on board) and a preparedness to be held liable for lost plate, linen and cutlery. Swearing and profane language were strictly proscribed, and the company ruled that no sheath knives were to be allowed on board.

The *Garonne* called in at Melbourne and then Adelaide during October before setting off for English shores once more. Letters fit to be saved for his album were meanwhile chasing Charles as he moved from one Australian port to another; he had already suffered a repeat performance of the trouble he had encountered five years earlier, with a letter returned from the Dead Letter Office, addressed to him at the General Post Office, Sydney, and dated 28 August 1883. Another missive for 'Mr C F Titford, Steerage Steward, S S Garonne', from the Australian Gas Light Company, arrived without problems.

But not all mail reached its destination so easily, and no-one could accuse the Australian postal service of shirking its duty in trying to track down an elusive sailor who might have moved almost anywhere, with his ship or·without it. One particular letter which Charles received bears eloquent testimony to the dogged determination of those charged with delivering the mails. Posted in London 'N. 26' on 21 August 1883, it bears a sixpenny lilac stamp, plate 18, overprinted with '6d.' – an issue of 1 January 1883. It was addressed to 'Charles F. Titford, Atelestone Post Office, Adelaide, South Australia – to be left until called for'. Arriving at Adelaide on 1 October it was dispatched to Atherstone (the sender having misspelt the address) where, rather than leaving it until called for, the authorities endorsed it: 'S.S. Garonne: Sydney, Melbourne'. And so it set off for Melbourne, where it was postmarked 6 October, thence to Sydney by 8 October.

At this stage, alas, the hapless letter and Charles Titford were travelling in opposite directions! Charles was steaming westwards, while his letter was busy heading east. The poor thing was passed from pillar to post, festooned with postmarks and as many varied frankings as could be crammed on to both sides of its 4″ by 3″ format: 'Bought back: 15/-'; 'Try Melbourne Post Office'; '2d to pay'; '2d more to pay'; 'Advertised – unclaimed'. Twice it was postmarked 'G.P.O. Sydney'; on 22 October Mr. J. Greasworthy added: 'Not known and refused by Gibbs Bright & Co.' – although quite why Gibbs Bright and Co. might ever have wanted the much-travelled letter in the first place is hard to determine. Then, like many good things in the Antipodes, it settled itself down in Sydney: shell-shocked and battle-weary, it waited patiently for its intended reader, taking a final battering on 13 November in the shape of one last 'Sydney E' postmark. And there it might have waited in vain – because by 13 November Charles Titford was within five days of arriving back home in England aboard the *Garonne*; quite how he eventually received his letter is not clear, though one thing is certain – its contents could never have matched the fascinating appearance of its envelope.

Charles, like his letter, had had a good run for his money: he had girdled the world in his travels, had made friends and seen exotic places – perhaps now was the time to head for home and enjoy an early retirement, regaling his nephews and niece with stories of lands beyond the seas. He had kept a few easily portable artefacts: a shiny brown bean with matches inside, a striker on the base and a neat silver shield with 'T' engraved upon it; then, to fox and even shock the Victorians back in London, there was a small black and cream straw sphere, hollow inside and with a hole in its base, which he would swear was used by the male natives of a certain tribe to decorate their more intimate parts. Perhaps most interesting of all, he had his rich red and gold album into which he would stick not only souvenirs of his voyages, but also – using, alas, a very brittle, messy glue – a range of postage stamps including a penny black and an imperforate twopenny blue. One memento of his sojourn in the Southern Hemisphere was a small photograph showing two Fijian huts in a forest clearing, sold by F. H. Dufty's 'Royal Victorian Studio' at Levuka, Ovalau, Fiji, 'Under the patronage of His Excellency Sir Hercules Robinson, K.C.M.G., Governor of New South Wales'. The Empire in all its finery . . .

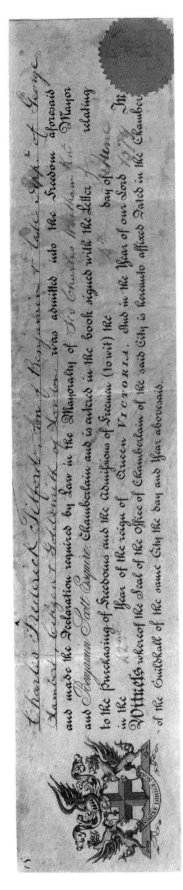

54. Certificate granting Charles Frederick Titford the Freedom of the City of London, 4 June 1879. This is a Freedom by Apprenticeship.

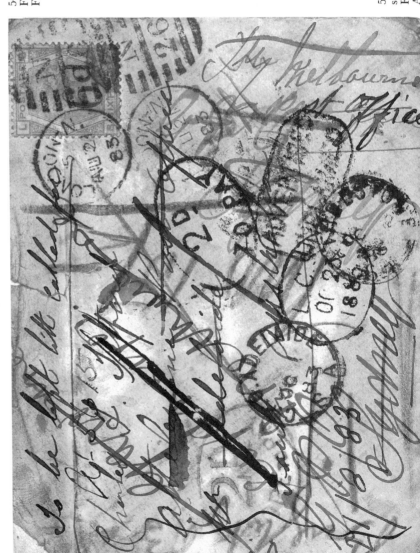

55. A much-travelled envelope. This envelope spent several months during 1883 in pursuit of Charles Frederick Titford as he moved around the coast of Australia.

And so Charles worked his passage home aboard the *Garonne*; that would mean suffering once again the heat of the Rea Sea and the 93-mile haul through the Suez Canal, opened in 1869. There is one particularly striking picture in Charles's collection taken near Ismailia by a photographer by the name of F. M. Good; it shows the sandy desolation of the canal area itself, with what one traveller described as one of those '. . . flat roofed, sand or concrete built houses of one storey . . .' which were springing up along the banks.[7]

How tame Barnsbury must have seemed by contrast when he arrived home! He would perhaps have shared the slight astonishment of many a foreign traveller that so little appeared to have changed in his absence. Once again he appears in the Directories as a tobacconist at 50 Cumberland Street, almost as if he had never been away. He was home in good time to attend the wedding of his sister, Emily Jane, in the March of 1884 – she married Walter Frederick Mullett, a warehouseman, at St James's, Holloway, with brother William acting as a witness. The details of her father on the marriage certificate now had to read: 'Benjamin Titford, Clerk, deceased.' She was then aged 26, while Charles the traveller, home from the back of beyond, was just short of his 28th birthday.

How did Charles occupy himself for the rest of the 1880s and nineties? He was still a tobacconist in 1885, but eventually, and rather anti-climatically, he found employment as a gardener. Such an apparent come-down in the world, along with his decision to cease his globe-trotting, may well be explained quite simply by illness – but of that, more later.

In any case, Charles was the kind of man whose employment seems to have been subservient to his hobbies; long after his gardening would be forgotten in the mists of time, he left behind a storehouse of minutiae for posterity. He was an obsessive collector, a hoarder; while his brother William bequeathed children to future generations, Charles's contribution was different – his immortality lies not in any act of procreation – not as far as we know! – but in the papers and the objects, some mundane, some quite rare and valuable, which he never threw away.

We already have evidence of his interest in philately; as well as accumulating a host of British and foreign stamps in a rather ornate red and gold album with printed pages ('The Imperial Postage Album') he also kept several examples of postal stationery – that is, cards and envelopes with an embossed or printed stamp. Among the more interesting items are a copy of the first printed English postcard with a lilac 'stamp' of 1870, and an example of a rather unhelpful two cents postal envelope from Ceylon: 'District Letter Envelope . . . this envelope will not pass through more than one Post Office, will only be delivered when called for, and will not be re-directed'. You can't say fairer than that . . .

2 July 1890 saw the Post Office Jubilee of Uniform Penny Postage and the issue of a special commemorative card and envelope, printed in a tasteful light blue. The envelope shows 'The North Mail making for Highgate, 1790, at eight miles an hour' along the top edge, matched below by: 'The North Mail, 1890, approaching Carlisle at forty-eight miles an hour'. Here were the Victorians, rightly proud of their up-to-date technology, celebrating the glories of the railway age. A postman of 1840 is pictured in top hat and frock coat, the current rates of postage then being: 4d., 8d., 1s. 2d., 2s. 6d. Opposite him stands his 1890 counterpart in a plain uniform and cap – postal rate: '1d.'. Inside, a card bears a likeness of Rowland Hill, with the caption: 'He gave us Penny Postage'.

Prior to 1840 the English mail service had been efficient but expensive, and letters needed to be endorsed on the envelope by a person of some eminence; Charles's philatelic interest dovetailed with another passion of his – autograph collecting. He bought envelopes going back as far as 1816, each with some kind of pre-postal franking, and signed by such luminaries as Sir Robert Peel, Lord Melbourne, Joseph Hume, the Duke of Richmond and Henry Grattan, the Irish M.P. Other autographs he either bought or solicited were those of C. H. Spurgeon, the famous Baptist preacher, Lord Palmerston, Lord Salisbury, Admiral Charles Beresford, Lord Sherbrook and W. P. Frith, the wealthiest painter of his day.

Any inveterate collector like Charles, of course, would naturally add bank notes to his list of interests: he acquired a very nice example of an early British £5 note, issued by the Carmarthen Bank in 1828, together with some interesting but not-so-rare examples of U.S. Confederate money, and two early American notes, one issued by the State of North Carolina in 1866, the other by the Corporation of Fredericksburg, Virginia, in 1861.

We can now meet Charles again five years after his return to London, in 1888; on 28 April his sister Emily had a daughter, Emily Elizabeth, who would later marry Tom Wood and live on until 1963. Charles duly entered the birth in his own list of family events – family history seems to have been another of his little passions, and he carefully noted facts of interest: 'Parents married at Christ Church, Middlesex, by Mr Quekett, 22nd March 1846'; 'The Reverend Daniel Parkes. Oil painting dated 1770', and so on.

One prize that Charles clearly sought as early as 1888 was the autograph of Queen Victoria; he had been fortunate in that year to obtain nice specimen signatures from George, Duke of Cambridge, a grandson of George III, and Randolph S. Churchill, father of Sir Winston and one-time Chancellor of the Exchequer. But the Queen herself was a different matter: his tactic was simple – he would write to Her Majesty with a mundane and even fatuous enquiry: had she published a *Life of the Prince Consort*? She would reply in her own fair hand, providing a lovely little item for his album.

Well, queens, of course, are not so easily hoodwinked, and in any case are surrounded by minions who prevent such trivial matters bothering their daily routines. Charles's letter was intercepted by one such minion, Sir Henry Ponsonby; it was he, and not her Gracious Majesty, who penned a reply – no, Her Majesty begged to inform Mr. Titford that she hadn't published any Life of the Prince Consort. Charles did get an envelope with a very ornate wax seal – that of the Privy Purse Office – on the back, but not the autograph he was after. Once bitten, twice shy, he eventually had to content himself with buying what he wanted: he obtained a Commission Certificate issued in 1890 to J. Bell, a Second Lieutenant in the 1st (Cumberland) Volunteer Battalion, The Border Regiment. Her Majesty invested Lieutenant Bell with all manner of responsibilities – and signed his certificate in the top left-hand corner; so that was the way to get autographs – join the Army.

Our intrepid collector was more fortunate, some years later, in inveigling an autograph out of America's First Citizen; in a very civil reply typed on blue ribbon (ah, the wonders of American technology . . .), President William McKinley was delighted to provide Mr. Charles Titford with a specimen of his signature. Poor McKinley's generous nature was to avail him very little in the long run: on 6 September 1901 he was shot by an anarchist at Buffalo and died eight days later.

In 1889 Charles was living at 22 Lesly Street, Barnsbury, a street to which he would later return; the autographs came pouring in – John Bennett sent his respects from 65 Cheapside; George Augustus Sala, the satirist, wrote to him from Westminster on Whit Monday; the Earl of Derby's autograph came from St James' Square, and Lord Fife tendered his respects from Cavendish Square on 9 July.

1890, too, was an interesting year – Charles was now at 34 Ellington Street, still in Barnsbury, where he received a postcard posted on 19 May bearing a special Penny Postage Jubilee postmark from the Guildhall. His correspondent, R. Holmes, had to inform him that '. . . the Special Cards are all sold out and are bringing 21/- each'. Charles did later obtain one of the said cards, whatever he may have had to pay for it.

He seems to have had a special respect for H. M. Stanley, the great African explorer, and managed to get himself an invitation to a meeting at the Mansion House, chaired by the Duke of Fife, on behalf of the Stanley Fund. In that year, 1890, Stanley was to be married, and Charles, nothing daunted, wrote for and obtained the man's autograph; nine days before the wedding the bride-to-be, Dorothy Tennant, took the time to reply to a similar request from her address at Richmond Terrace in Whitehall.

On the principle that everything comes to those who are cheeky enough to ask for it, Charles lost no time in getting an invitation card to the wedding itself on Saturday 12 July, at '2 o'clock precisely'. He was to enter Westminster Abbey by the West Cloister Door at 1.30, and had a seat in the nave; the marriage service itself was followed by an anthem, 'The blessing of the Lord', then the address, then a marriage hymn: 'Father of Life, confessing Thy majesty and power . . .'.

Perhaps in some ways this was one of the great luxuries of life in Victorian England, especially for a bachelor with time on his hands – that one could achieve a degree of reflected glory by witnessing the activities of the great and famous.

In 1891 Charles was at 16 Cornelia Street, Barnsbury, but then back to Lesly Street – this time number 15 – by 1897, when he was sent a specimen of a postcard printed specially for the Queen's Diamond Jubilee, 1837-97.

All of this adds up to a pleasantly-diversified lifestyle for our Barnsbury gardener: interesting mail arriving almost daily, and the rich pattern of Victorian London life to be enjoyed, even if only as an outside observer. It seems very likely that Charles was sharing a house with his mother at this period – maybe an attachment to her had kept him unmarried? That is one possibility, as is the fact that illness may have prevented him from forming a permanent attachment – but perhaps he was living such a varied and entertaining bachelor life that thoughts of marriage never crossed his mind. As things turned out, however, his single status and independence were to be the indirect cause of his death.

And so 1899, the penultimate year of the century, arrived; Charles was still at 15 Lesly Street, and his brother William lived within easy visiting distance at Freegrove Road. Plenty of opportunities to buttonhole the nephews and young Grace and recount for the hundredth time the wreck of the *Chimborazo*, the glories of Niagara and the exquisite beauty of San Francisco . . . The year was to see a strange mixture of events: there was the death of Johann Strauss and the births of Noel Coward and Charles Laughton; aspirin was invented, Tolstoy wrote *Resurrection*, and Elgar composed 'Enigma Variations'. Much of this may have been of little concern to Charles, though he probably had more than a passing interest in other news – that of the growing conflict in Africa, for example, which erupt into the Boer War before the year was out. Nearer to home within London itself, February would see Barnum and Bailey's Circus entertaining the crowds at Olympia, and J. N. Maskelyne was enthralling audiences with his illusions and 'Animated Photographs'.

On Monday 17 April Charles celebrated his forty-third birthday at Lesly Street; the next day H. J. Scott wrote to him from Buckingham Palace Road, thanking him for 10s. received to settle his account to date, and saying he had a nice card signed by the Prince Consort which Charles might have at a reduced price of 10s.: 'Shall I send it for you to look at? . . . It is a nice specimen'. On the Thursday Lord Garnet Wolsely, Commander-in-Chief of the Army, signed his name for Charles at the War Office.

The following Sunday, 23 April, was St George's Day: what a problem for the Victorians, then – to celebrate England's Patron Saint, or hold to their quiet and sedate sabbath observance? Late Victorian sabbaths were increasingly less austere than they had been in the past, and maybe some of the Titfords had gone out for a stroll or to visit friends for a natter. Charles was left alone at Lesly Street; had he been visiting friends or receiving visitors himself that day, events may have turned out very differently. As it was, on his own and with no-one to save him, he suffered an epileptic fit, suffocated and died.

Death had come to a man in his prime, active and involved, living a full and varied life. Given the circumstances a *post mortem* was undertaken, with an inquest on 26 April supervised by the London Coroner; suffocation during an epileptic fit – 'misadventure' – was the verdict. In a sense such a diagnosis poses as many problems as it solves; we could be cynical and say that many doctors of the period were perhaps only too happy to conduct autopsies on the bodies of comparatively young men and women: useful practice for students, masquerading as legal necessity . . .

Had Charles suffered before from any kind of epilepsy? He could hardly have endured the fairly taxing life of a sailor and a foreign traveller if he had been beset by recurrent attacks of the disease over a long period of time, though his decision to return to England for good may have been prompted by the onset of such an affliction. In any case, what may appear to be an epileptic fit could have had a variety of causes – *Grand Mal* itself, syphilis, or trauma following a blow on the head, perhaps sustained years previously. In the absence of blood tests at that period, we can perhaps forgive the coroner's verdict for remaining somewhat vague.

Charles's was the last Titford death registered in England and Wales in the 1800s a dubious distinction indeed. 'Loving Memory' cards were sent out by the undertaker, J. T. Bragg of Liverpool Road, bearing the text : 'God have thee in His keeping till we meet again'. The body was laid to rest at Islington Cemetery, Finchley, in a quiet spot behind grander and more ornate graves.

The deceased's goods and chattels were collected together by brother William and his family, including a final autograph – that of J. C. Liverpool, signed on 3 May, 10 days after Charles had died. William had the good sense to keep the essential items from his brother's many collections – and to pass them to his son, who passed them to *his* son, who passed them to *his* son . . . Had this not been the case, a sobering thought might strike us. Were we to rely solely upon Civil Registration records, census returns and the like, our story would have been a very different one indeed: 'There was once a man called Charles Frederick Titford, a tobacconist and gardener, who was born in Islington and died in Barnsbury . . .'. Only chance and good fortune have left us with any evidence at all that our man travelled much further than his front doorstep; how many other individuals in our story, we might wonder, have we sold short in that way? If we have, those ancestors are probably grinning knowingly at us from the great family reunion up in the sky . . .

CHAPTER 23

Henry James the Goldmounter (1875-1967)

London

BORN IN THE REIGN OF ONE QUEEN, DIED IN THE REIGN OF ANOTHER

The next generation of Titfords presents us with a different set of challenges. Here are men and women still remembered by those alive today; we are now less dependent upon archive material with its often churlish lack of detail, and can record memories and perceptions to help flesh out the bare facts. Modern family history, then, should be very easy for us to write, and in a sense it is; but memory is fallible, just as perception itself is fallible, and not every individual who reminisces about the old days tells a story consistent with the accounts of others – or even with known documentary evidence. Cherished stories quite understandably undergo modification and elaboration as the years go by; we would be unwise to equate the 'evidence' of oral history with any notion of total and unequivocal truth. Here, then, is the story of the children of William the Gold-engraver, as compiled from written and oral sources, including the author's own recollections of his grandfather, Henry James, who died in 1967 at the age of ninety-one.

The members of this generation of Titfords were very much Victorians by birth, but outlived the old Queen herself. At her death there were twice as many people in England and Wales as there had been fifty years before, and yet – the earlier fears of Malthus notwithstanding – the population was neither totally destitute nor on the brink of social revolution. We can have very strong reservations about the achievements of the Victorians, but in so many ways they had cleared up some of the grubbiness bequeathed to them by the 18th century. England was for most people a cleaner and better place to live in than it had ever been before; the physical environment had improved beyond measure for the majority, and the general standards of decency in everyday life had left some of the rumbustious but seedy habits of the 18th century far behind. The Victorians may have been hypocrites, but that hypocrisy in itself was the other side of the coin of the high standards of public morality they set themselves.

Victoria's death in early 1901 was lamented with hyperbole beyond measure:

> The golden reign is closed. The supreme woman of the world, best of the highest, greatest of the good, is gone . . .

So sobbed the *Daily Telegraph*, to be taken up in the same style by the equally ingenuous *Observer*:

> From savages in Africa who say they will now look out at night for a new star in their heavens, to monarchs on their thrones who will miss the sympathy of which a modern throne needs so much, all feel thay have lost a friend.[1]

'Savages' in Africa, of course, had more immediate things to occupy their minds than the passing of that distant and diminutive monarch, and so, we may say with a certain degree of bathos, did the Titford family down in Freegrove Road, Holloway. Ernie, Harry and Bert were possibly getting ready for one of their lively parties at home on that Tuesday in January when the good Queen died. All the evidence we might need that the position of women had not improved so very much by the early years of the 20th century could be furnished by their young sister Grace's role in a family which tended to be dominated by these three big brothers. For much of the time she had no bed of her own and had to make do with the settee to sleep on, and when it came to party time up in the parlour she would be like Cinderella down in the basement, cleaning the silver, getting everything ready and clearing up afterwards. Her relationship with her brothers seems to have been a happy enough one in the early years for all that, but there can be little doubt as to who ruled the Freegrove Road roost.

The Titfords' economic situation was a strange one, in a way; here was Gracie with no bedroom, and the Freegrove Road house was only rented.[2] Yet there was a freehold property in the family – a three-storey dwelling in Sonning Street, opposite Pentonville Prison, which was eventually sold by Henry James at auction; fully let as it was, it had become a burden to him, and the sitting tenants afforded him little joy. Nevertheless, at a sale price of £300, the builder who bought it very definitely picked up a bargain. Apart from that, the family managed somehow to support two non-earners for many years in Freegrove Road: Bert, who rarely if ever went out to work, and Grace herself, the unpaid domestic mainstay of the household.

This chapter really belongs to Henry James, but a word or two about his brothers and sister would not come amiss. Ernie, the eldest, never married – though he had what was known at the time as a 'lady friend'. A smart, dapper man throughout his working life, he was the clerk who did the books for the Pouparts Jam Company in Covent Garden. When he wasn't dating his lady, he found the time to attend the Upper Holloway Baptist Chapel, and left them £15 in his will. It was to be 10 years after that will was made that he met his untimely end. At the age of 73 he fell down at home and fractured some ribs; he was taken to St Mary's Hospital, Islington, where broncho-pneumonia set in and finally proved fatal on 5 April 1946. A post-mortem confirmed that death had been 'accidental', and he was buried in the family grave at Abney Park shortly afterwards.

By some odd quirk of fate Ernie, the outgoing and lively character that he was, managed to avoid being conscripted to serve in the First World War, leaving his withdrawn and more nervous brother Herbert to serve in the Royal Army Ordnance Corps. Joining the army was in many ways the making of Bert, who had always run the risk of being a mother's boy; the experience brought him out of his shell to some extent, though he remained a very retiring man until his death in 1936, when the Letters of Administration granted to his brother refer to 'Herbert George Titford – a bachelor without parent'. He, too, could be accommodated in the grave so thoughtfully provided all those years before by William, his father, and he was buried there on 13 March 1936.

Then there was Grace; taken for granted rather too often by the others as she probably was, she sustained herself much of the time by indulging in her favourite hobby – that of fighting a running battle of nerves with brother Ernie. The antagonism was mutual – Ernie had a strong streak of misogynism in his make-up, and the pair of them would write each other rude notes and pin them to the door as a challenge or a warning; a pastime of dubious value, we might say, indulged in by two unmarried people with the need for a bit of excitement in life. Ernie could fight with the gloves off, too, and give as good as he got: when Grace would come to see him in hospital bearing a conciliatory bunch of grapes, he'd mutter: 'Here she comes . . .' with weary forbearance under his breath. He had no intention whatsoever that his sister should be more pleased with him once he'd shuffled off this mortal coil than she had been while he was alive: finding a spare hymn sheet one day and having an odd moment to kill, he scribbled out a note for his executors on the back of it:

> If anything should happen to me and I should be cut off from life, my sister Grace Beatrice Titford is *not* to follow my body to the grave *or to provide flowers*, by request.
> P.S.: I have written this on account of her cruelty and indifference to me in life.

Nothing daunted, Grace did turn up at the chapel of rest to see his body – out of respect or curiosity – though when she went to Somerset House to check his will, there were no surprises: her name was conspicuous by its absence.

Freegrove Road proved to be too restricted a territory to accommodate a feuding brother and sister, and Grace eventually moved out – a woman as she was, and with few enough rights – leaving Ernie, once he had retired, to traipse around the streets like a vagrant, to the point where passers-by even offered him a bit of cash to help him out . . .

Grace took rooms in Tufnell Park Road, where she lived until she was taken into an Old People's Home towards the end of her life. Her great friend Ethel Walsh left her some money, but she was defrauded of this and any other capital she had by pseudo-spiritualists with their phoney séances. She had become blind in one eye as the result of a detached retina, caused by the constant jolting she suffered putting linings in spectacle cases for the optician who had become her employer; that semi-blindness itself only made things worse for her as the fraudulent séances conjured people from her past out of thin air. There was Ethel Walsh, come to greet her – and even brother Ernie, too, pleading: 'Grace, I never really meant to be unkind to you . . .'. Well, maybe he didn't, and maybe thinking so set her mind at rest, but her cash was flowing out as fast as the trickery was flowing in.

Poor Grace was born to be disappointed, it seems: nothing from Ernie's will; little enough from brother Bert when he died intestate, and nothing from the estate of their cousin, Emily Wood, whose bungalow in Essex Grace had counted on as her nest-egg one day. Her brother Henry picked up a fair proportion of what little there was available from the Emily Wood affair, so Grace then fell out with him, too. The one person she kept in touch with over the years was her niece Doris, to whom she gave her beautiful red leather family photograph album; inside were pictures of her relations back as far as her grandfather, Benjamin the Silversmith – a much-treasured Titford momento which is now in the possession of the present author. One person is not featured at all in the collection, hardly surprisingly: there is no photograph of brother Ernie . . .[3] Grace lived on until 1973 – the last of her generation; she was in the Dorinda Lodge Home in Lough Road, Islington, when she died of cardiac failure and senility at the age of eighty-nine.

Henry James, the author's grandfather, was the only brother to be married – and yet he, of all of them, had suffered special problems as a child. His mother had had one son before him, Ernie, but then wanted a girl; something inside her wouldn't let her admit that she had temporarily failed in such an enterprise, and she treated her second son for many years as if he were the daughter she had yearned for. He had to suffer the indignity of having his hair long and in ringlets up to the age of five or six; eventually, when the crisis was over, these locks were cut off and kept as an ornament under glass.

Yet he was an adventurous little lad: once he got lost and wandered around the streets of Holloway before being brought home by a small posse of policemen. And then there was that parrot down in the basement at Freegrove Road – what a temptation, to put one's hand in the cage! So he did – and promptly had the top joint of his finger nearly bitten off by the indignant bird; an operation to save what could be saved of his finger was carried out without anaesthetic – and his mother claimed she could hear his screams right out in the hospital grounds. For the rest of his life he had a kind of horny claw where he should have had a fingernail.

Other memories of his childhood included walking down the road past the horse trams to get a bowl full of milk at the General Stores; there was cream on top of the milk in the jug, and flies on top of the cream – but no-one seemed to heed that very much, except for the sensitive young boy with the bowl.

Henry James was the one son to follow in his father's professional footsteps; in 1899, at the age of 24, he was awarded a City and Guilds Certificate, First Class, for goldsmiths'

56. Henry James Titford (1875-1967) in 1902.

57. Henry James Titford: original birth certificate, 1875. Registered here in the name of Henry, but always known as 'Harry'.

Certificate of **Birth.**

Pursuant to the Acts Anno Sexto et Septimo Gulielmi IV. Regis,   Cap. LXXXVI. et Anno Primo Victoriæ Reginæ, Cap. XXII.

(Page *32*) Book *41.*

1875   BIRTH in the District of *Anwell*   in the County of *Middlesex*

No.	When & Where Born.	Name (if any.)	Sex.	Name and Surname of Father.	Name and Maiden Surname of Mother.	Rank or Profession of Father.	Signature, Description, and Residence of Informant.	When Registered.	Signature of Registrar.	Baptismal Name, if added after Registration of Birth.
160	Thirteenth May 1875 24 Wilmington Square	Henry James	Boy	William Titford	Mary Ann Keziah Titford formerly Parkes	Engraver	W. Titford Father 24 Wilmington Square	Twenty third June 1875	F. Tupper Registrar	

I, Registrar of Births and Deaths for the District of *Anwell* in the County of *Middlesex* do hereby certify the above to be a TRUE COPY of the BIRTH REGISTER, Entry No. *160* And I further certify that the said REGISTER BOOK is legally in my custody.

Witness my hand this *23rd* day of *June* 1875   F. Tupper   Registrar.

By the Statute 6 & 7 Will. IV., c. 86, s. 35, it is enacted "That every REGISTRAR, REGISTERING OFFICER, and SECRETARY, who shall have the keeping for the time being of any REGISTER BOOK OF BIRTHS, DEATHS, or MARRIAGES, shall at all reasonable Times allow Searches to be made of any Register Book in his keeping, and shall give a COPY CERTIFIED under his Hand of any ENTRY or Entries in the same, on payment of the Fee hereinafter mentioned: (that is to say,) for every search extending over a period of not more than One Year the sum of One Shilling, and Sixpence additional for every additional Year, and the sum of Two Shillings and Sixpence for every single CERTIFICATE." (Including the Stamp the "Certificate" is Two Shillings and Sevenpence.)

work, following a course he had attended at the Northampton Institute in London. Thereafter he would practise goldbeating and gold-engraving all his working life.

He was well on his way to being an established working man, then, by 1899 – time to look around for a wife. There were a few raised eyebrows when he started off by dating his own cousin – not that mother and father could say too much about that, of course, since they were cousins themselves. But we may feel, and he may have felt, that it was high time the Titford pedigree was boosted by a bit of Scottish blood. Luckily young Margaret Archibald had long set her sights on our Henry, praying every night that he might choose her as his bride – and she came of solid Scots stock; although she had been born in Islington, her parents – Robert Archibald, an engineer, and Mary Morn (*née* Smith) – had been married in Crown Street, Aberdeen, and had their first child there. Margaret Willox Archibald had acquired the maiden surname of her maternal grandmother, Penelope Willox, as had her elder brother, leaving another sister to struggle on with the name Jane Penelope Cruickshanks Archibald. Ah, the Scots knew how to perpetuate those family Christian names and surnames!

Sister Jane would be a witness at the Titford-Archibald marriage

58. City and Guilds Certificate in Goldsmiths' Work awarded to Harry James Titford in 1899.

when it finally took place, along with the bridegroom's brother Ernie. We have already made reference to the wedding in passing: it took place on 8 September 1902, at the Arundel Square Congregational Chapel in Islington. Here is evidence of a new streak of that Nonconformity which had been very much lacking for three generations or more. Many Congregationalists liked to think of themselves as constituting the respectable end of the spectrum of Dissenting churches – rather middle-class and very certain of their own well-deserved salvation. Moving to New Southgate in later years and finding no convenient Congregationalist chapel to hand, Henry and Margaret were to worship for forty years at the Bowes Park Methodist Church – second-best, perhaps?

We have been calling our man 'Henry' – but only because his birth certificate calls him that; no-one ever knew him as anything other than 'Harry', however, and it was to cause him a bit of a problem eventually. Forty-five years after his wedding, in the November of 1947, he needed to be sure of inheriting what was due to him from brother Ernie's will –

59. The marriage of Henry James Titford and Margaret Willox Archibald. The couple were married at Arundel Square Congregational Chapel, Islington, on 8 September 1902. At the back, centre and right, are the bridegroom's brothers Bert and Ernie; to the right of the bride are William and Mary Ann Titford, while to the left of the bridegroom stand his new in-laws, Robert and Mary Morn Archibald; on the front row between the Titfords is their daughter Grace Beatrice, and between the Archibalds is their daughter Jane Penelope Cruickshanks Archibald. An inquisitive neighbour – or is she a guest? – peeps over the garden wall on the right.

and in the process he had to request that the original marriage certificate be amended to read 'Henry Titford', his legally-correct Christian name.

This 1902 wedding, meanwhile, had been an impressive one in its way. The group photograph shows all the participants at their sartorial best, all the more striking because they are posing in a rather scruffy back yard. Flanking the bride and groom are both sets of parents – William Titford and Mary Ann on one side, Robert Archibald and Mary Morn from Ringcroft Street on the other – with Ernie, Bert and the best man at the back in top-hats, and the girls, including Grace, ranged at the front with large sprays of flowers. Over the head-height brick wall on the right a nosy neighbour makes sure she gets herself in the picture, too. The bride looks cool and graceful, as befits her role in the proceedings, while one is struck, on this occasion, by the facial similarity between the bridegroom and his father.[4]

The happy couple decided to live in rented rooms in Yonge Park, off Seven Sisters Road, from which address they sent friends and relations dainty chunks of wedding cake. Two sons would be born at this house – the first, Harry Charles, being an eight-month baby, much to the embarrassment of his mother with her delicate sensibilities. Sidney Horace followed in 1904, and Doris Grace two years later.

By 1908 there had been one move of house – to 50 Ronalds Road, Highbury – and there was shortly to be another. Harry's earnings were sufficient to allow him to take out a 99-year lease on a house in New Southgate; it would cost the princely sum of £320, made up of a £20 deposit and a mortgage to cover the rest. And so it was that the family settled down in the house which would be Harry and Margaret's home for nearly sixty years: 225 Bowes Road, New Southgate, later renumbered as 231. Interviewed years later for the local newspaper, Harry would say that the things he missed most about the old days in Bowes Road were 'the cows and the rabbits'. He may have lived in a semi-rural suburb, but he had to commute to work: having been employed for a short while before his marriage by a firm called Phillips and Grove, he soon began his mammoth stint with Cropp and Farr, manufacturing jewellers of Hatton Garden. He was there for a total of 58 years, until the day he retired.

Life was not easy for the family during those years, however, and at times the mortgage must have seemed like a burden which would never be lifted. The most fraught time of all was during the First World War: Harry never actually joined the hostilities, but back home regular employment was hard to come by, and he found himself on piece work. He ended up redeeming his life-insurance in a last-ditch attempt to see his children through school, and set to with a pair of pliers to earn extra cash in the evenings as a wiredrawer – not the first Titford, we know, to do that for a living . . .[5]

The management at Cropp and Farr and his erstwhile apprentices would remember Harry with affection: '. . . the perfect gentleman, always kind, cool and friendly, a very grand and fine character indeed'.[6] Nor was that just a bland and conventional accolade: Harry Titford was gregarious, where his wife was very private and home-loving; he had charm and geniality in abundance, though like many such charmers his *bonhomie* towards outsiders might annoy his wife if he had been particularly objectionable at home!

Although he would describe himself as a 'jeweller', he was properly-speaking a 'gold-mounter' – that is, he made articles all of gold (not set with precious stones) such as brooches in the shape of dogs or hunting horns, or the handles of riding crops. One of his more demanding commissions was to make the christening brooch for Princess Margaret; he was sent a photograph of Glamis Castle, with instructions to incorporate the building into the design, and to inscribe 'M' on one side and 'R' on the other, for 'Margaret Rose'. The Palace, which was pleased enough to have a young Princess born in Scotland after so many years, was also pleased to send Harry Titford a letter of thanks for the quality of his

60. Bowes Road, New Southgate, London, 1909. Henry James Titford and his wife Margaret had recently bought no. 225, a new house in the far block.

workmanship. There were other more mundane jobs in hand, of course – like cleaning the Lord Mayor's chain, which was so heavy that Harry had to wear it while he set to work wiping off the soup stains.

Working in gold must have always posed its temptations over the years; one employee at Cropp and Farr, so Harry would say, would run his fingers regularly through his greasy hair during the daytime, then go home at night and wash out all the gold dust to sell. Another character of dubious honesty was away ill when a box of stolen gems was found under his bench during his absence. Choosing competent but honest staff must have been a difficult task for jewellers then, just as it would be today. And certainly the craftsman in gold would never make himself rich by his earnings alone: when Harry Titford retired he had only 10s. a week from the Silversmiths and Goldsmiths to live on (later raised to £1) plus his modest pension from Cropp and Farr. Not that anyone was deliberately cheating him – but the days of the generous index-linked pension lay far in the future.

For the present author, Harry and Margaret ('Granfer and Nan') themselves were inextricably associated with the house in which they lived; in retrospect the place seemed to be redolent of much that was Edwardian, if not Victorian, with its walnut bookcase full of ornately-bound tomes (*Josephus*, *The poems of Eliza Cook* and the rest), its deep-red frieze tablecloth and uncomfortable chaise-longue. Tall vases stood on veneered tables, and the walls were bedecked with seascape watercolours and a black-and-white copy of an engraving – 'Well Done!' – courtesy of 'Bovril', over the piano.

This was the house in which, some years previously, Harry had liked to place his chair beneath the gas lamp so that he could feel its warmth on the top of his head; where any tall person would regularly collide with the brass gas-fitting when getting up out of a chair in a hurry; where 'Murders' would be played in the dark at Christmas time, and Uncle Ernie had once paced around the house with such slow, heavy footsteps during the game that his poor nephew Sidney had quite literally fainted away with the horror of it all.

Harry and Margaret had acclimatised themselves to the post-Victorian era, but only just, it seemed. She would never touch alcohol, and was mortified when the law eventually required that the alcoholic content of drinks be printed on the label – with the result that she discovered, too late, that Stone's Ginger Wine, her favourite tipple, did in fact contain traces of the dreaded intoxicating substance.

She allowed Harry his little luxuries – dried bananas soaked in water, an occasional smoke, a visit to the Springfield Golden Link Club; she was the quiet but forceful partner, when all was said and done, and he would say later in life that 'She has been my mainstay and the reason I am still here'.

Our story properly finishes in 1947, but it was some years after that that the author remembers his fortnightly visits to Bowes Road, with salmon sandwiches for tea ('Oh, Nan, you *shouldn't* – it's so expensive . . .'), a harmless game of 'sevens' round the table, with grandfather benignly winding his Geneva gold watch with a key, and grandmother taking her only grandson into the kitchen for that mock-secret ceremony – the giving of hard-earned and hard-saved coppers to the young boy by way of supplementary pocket money: 'Come and see Nan in the kitchen . . .'.

It was in part the respect he felt for this elderly couple, together with a similar respect which he had for his parents and his Titford uncle and Titford aunt, that made the present author turn, some years later, to the task of reconstructing his family story. Grandfather had hoarded documents covering his own and the two previous generations in a tin top-hat box – genealogical notes, 'Loving Memory' cards, apprenticeship indentures, photographs, scrapbooks and the like, together with the family bible which he eventually gave away, and his photograph album which was lost to the junk-man when the house was cleared. And then all those theories, some true, some far-fetched, which he had picked up from the deeper wells of oral folklore: 'The family name comes from Frome in Somerset'; 'One ancestor was a Freeman of the City of London'; 'The Titfords are impossible to trace – they all went to America'; 'One forbear invented the wooden blocks they used to use for paving roads'; 'One of our people was a vicar of St Clement Danes'. Even in more recent times Margaret Titford would purvey Titford family rumours to her daughter Doris: 'There's one Titford just round the corner in Ollerton Road . . . wrong side of the law . . . brush with the Police . . . you're NEVER to speak of it . . .'. Lucky the family historian, then, who has grandparents who have been hoarders, who have never thrown anything away, who have had stories to tell and family legends, however unlikely, to relate.

Harry and Margaret lived on well after our closing date of 1947: although it was she who had been ill for a long while, it was Harry who died first, on 17 February 1967. In the Old People's Home in Southgate afterwards Margaret would say: 'I'm tired, Dear; I want to join Dad'. Her wish was granted the next year; she joined him as she had longed to do, on 8 July 1968.

The pair of them had lived to a ripe old age, through no fewer than six reigns; they were both tired, and they had both earned that rest they eventually sought.

CHAPTER 24

Sidney Horace the Company Secretary (b. 1904)

London

WAR: DEPRESSION: WAR

While this story is being written in 1983, all three of the children of Harry and Margaret Titford are still very much alive: 'children' no longer – Harry has just celebrated his eightieth birthday, Sidney and his wife have been married for 53 years, and Doris is a constant fund of family memories and momentoes, whose letters are worth publishing in their own right!

The closer a person is to us in relationship and in time, the more difficult it can be to make any kind of objective judgment on his or her life and character. Nor should we even attempt such a thing; it would be invidious to subject living relatives to the harsh spotlight of social analysis, and our best course is to let those still with us tell their own story. We will let Sidney speak for all three members of his generation; he will isolate his own milestones, decide as he looks back which are the memories which have lasted with time, which events in his life have had real significance. We will simply say in passing that his middle Christian name, Horace, came from that little brother of his father's, Horace Charles, who died in infancy – a classical name, of course, first introduced into England in the 16th century. We could also add that Sidney Horace was a man who, like Benjamin James the Schoolmaster, would join the professional classes (as a company secretary), though his own father was one of the many Titford skilled artisans. Not that Sidney wanted to work in the City – he has always had the flair of the graphic artist, and would very much liked to have followed in his father's footsteps as an engraver had not that father himself dissuaded him from doing so.

Harry Charles, the elder brother, has always had a touch of devilish wit and a twinkle in his eye, as he would no doubt be the first to agree. He, too, worked in London – as a textile salesman for Calico Printers, a job which would take him on trips to Manchester from time to time. He was married to Dorothy ('Dorrie') Drew in 1934, and the pair of them lived for a number of years in the same house as Dorrie's mother, brother and sister-in-law in Edmonton. Tragically, Dorrie lost her first baby through a miscarriage, and they remained childless, though full of affection for their Titford nephew. On the day of Harry Titford senior's funeral, in February 1967, Dorrie was severely affected by the cold wind; she had suffered from angina for a number of years, and was taken ill when she arrived home. She was rushed off to hospital, but died in the ambulance before it could get there. Harry has lived on his own in Palmers Green ever since, now a widower of 16 years' standing.

Doris has a very special place in the author's affections; on the day he first left hospital as a new-born baby, it was she who took mother and child back home in a taxi. Thereafter she would delight in taking her nephew up to London by tube to see the bright lights on a Saturday evening – and must have had a knowing smile on her face when the little lad once said to his Grannie: 'I love you, and I love my Auntie Doris; but I love Auntie Doris more, 'cos she's *newer* . . .'.

Doris had suffered a fair amount of ill-health as a child, and would eventually have an operation to remove an extra rib; but it fell to her lot to stay at home and help look after

61. The three children of Henry James Titford and Margaret. Left to right: Harry Charles (born 1903); Sidney Horace (born 1904); Doris Grace (born 1906).

her mother and father, working during the day as a clerk for the Air Ministry. She might have seen out her days in that way, and perhaps she and others expected that she would; but Doris had a trick or two up her sleeve. She was into her fifties when keen observers began to believe that there was a man-friend somewhere around in the shadowy mid-distance . . . Doris would go out for the evening, say there was nothing untoward or special happening – when in. fact, there was. She had renewed her acquaintance with a widower whom she had once known when they worked together at Standard Telephones and Cables in Southgate: Teddy Mills, a man of maturity and charm, a lover of the good life who still had the knack of courting a lady. Doris was 53 and he was 64 when they finally ended all the speculation and were married at St Mary Magdalen church, Whetstone, in 1960. Doris had become the first Titford in her branch of the family ever to marry a Catholic – and an ardent and intelligent Catholic he was, too, who would make her an excellent husband just as she made him an excellent wife. Their life together in the house they shared with Teddy's son Arthur was as happy as it was short-lived; Teddy died of a heart attack in 1963, having shared with his wife the sweetest years of her life.

Sidney comes last, but not least, because Sidney is the author's father and has performed the unenviable task of writing down his own memories. The last word must rest with him, and he takes our story to 1947, the end of its four-hundred year span. Here, then, is his own account of his life:

On 27 August 1904 my mother gave birth to me at Yonge Park, Holloway, London, N.7, some 15 months after the birth of my brother Harry Charles. My sister Doris Grace, the last of the children, followed some two years later on 17 August 1906. In 1907 we moved to a newly-built house, number 225 (later renumbered 231) in Bowes Road, Bowes Park, London, N. 11, one of five terraced houses built by a man named Keene. In those days the view in front of the house was of the estate of Lord Inverforth – beautiful fields stretching away to the parish church, Christ's Church in Waterfall Lane. At the top of the road beyond what is now Arnos Grove Underground Station the road narrowed and the trees from the dense woods spread their branches almost completely across the road. The woods were full of rabbits and in the spring bluebells were abundant.

I have very little memory of my early years. At the age of two I had a small operation on my tongue and I have a vague recollection of the revolting smell of chloroform, and then at the age of seven I had an operation for hernia. All three of us children started our schooling at the elementary school in Bowes Road – the school looks the same today in 1983 as it did in those days. The headmaster of the boys' school was a Mr. Richardson, whom the boys called 'Rocker'. On one occasion the mother of one of my school mates called him 'Mr. Rocker' to his face. At 'Bowes' I seemed to be accident-prone, and on one occasion I remember falling off my 'horse' (another boy) whilst playing 'flying horses', and removing the skin completely from one cheek of my face. It was at this school that I first got to know my very good friend Louis Crerar, who left England for Canada in 1924, and with whom I corresponded until he died in May, 1981. My father was a regular churchgoer (Mother went occasionally in the early years) and he attended Bowes Park Wesleyan Church. We kids joined the Sunday school, and when older went to church morning and evening as well. In my teens I joined the Literary Society, and on one or two occasions Harry and I did a bit of singing in shows.

In 1917 I passed the entrance examination for Southgate County Grammar School – Harry was already at Wood Green Grammar School, and later Doris went to St George's College. Within the first year I obtained a Junior County Scholarship, giving free schooling and a grant. This scholarship was a real blessing to my father, who at that stage was paying school fees for all of us, and during the war business in the jewellery trade was very bad. My father brought home the materials for wire-drawing, and this he did in the evenings in order to add to his earnings; not an easy job, after a day's work at the bench. Very soon he was to be called upon by the government to work on munitions, and ultimately he had his call-up papers to join the army, which instructed him to report at 11 a.m. on the 11th November, 1918, the exact time and day of the signing of the armistice. Needless to say, he did not present himself . . .

During the war we were quite often awakened from our sleep by the wailing of the sirens, and if we heard the sound of the guns or the exploding of bombs we would all get up and gather under the stairs for protection. On such occasions I would use the time to add a bit more to my homework. The raids were carried out mainly by zeppelins, and the nearest bomb to us that fell was on a house at the top end of Totteridge Lane. I will never forget the excitement when two zeppelins were brought down north of London. The first was brought down at Cuffley by an airman named Leefe Robinson, for which he received the V.C. It was a misty night, and the whole sky in the front of our house was lit up by a brilliant glow. The second one that was destroyed was a far more exciting and spectacular affair. My Mother first saw the zeppelin from her bedroom window with the searchlights on it, and a small light on the front of it. She called down to us and we went to the front door, and from there we saw the zeppelin dropping in flames from the sky. Because of the fields opposite we were able to see the gasbag almost to its final destruction. All the neighbours flocked from their homes to watch, and cheering was coming from all around. Such a morale booster! In 1918, at about the time of the end of the war, a terrible epidemic of a killer influenza spread across the country, and with so many people weary and underfed the death toll was very large. My father's best friend, George Bond, succumbed to the virus, leaving a wife and two young children. He had been working extremely hard on munitions, and was often in our house. His death upset my father very much.

Throughout the years our playground was Broomfield Park. This was and still is a beautiful park, well tended with a man-made yachtpond, two natural lakes, and a fine old house dating back to the time of Elizabeth I, which today houses a very good museum. Through this park I cycled daily to the grammar school, travelling through Powys Lane and Derwent Road. When we first lived in Bowes Road, Powys Lane was pretty well a country lane with a small bridge crossing the Pymmes Brook, a pound at the top of the lane, and a sizeable farm on the left-hand side, from whence a herd of cows would emerge from time to time. At school I played soccer at outside left for my house (Red) and also enjoyed cricket, although I did not excel at the latter. In my studies I did pretty well, and kept a position mostly in the top half-dozen. About every week or so we were to partake in cross-country running, which was compulsory unless one could produce a medical certificate. I was no runner, and chasing all around Southgate and Winchmore Hill was not my idea of enjoyment.

I was one of a gang of four, consisting of Jock Atkinson, Ronald Hughes, Johnny Webb, and myself, and we were great mates. We had two main interests, namely two girls, Doris Pearce (in my class at school), and her friend Esther Smart, and playing tennis on the courts in Broomfield Park. Doris fancied Jock, and Esther, Ron, but that did not stop us all enjoying each other's company. All four of us played a reasonable game of tennis, so that the games were enjoyable. I have heard nothing of any of these lads or lasses for many years now. Our very good friend Jo Pierce (then Joan Burdge) was with me at Southgate School, but originally in a lower class, being a year younger. In due time the General Schools University of London examination came up, and all the masters gave me the thumbs-up. Alas, migraine, which used to plague me in my earlier years, chose to join forces with the nervous tension, resulting in my getting a General Schools Certificate only, with credit in arithmetic, elementary mathematics, and heat, light and sound.

So in the summer of 1921 I left my *alma mater*, and started thinking about getting a job. Around about that time I took on the job of acting as treasurer of the Band of Hope at the New Southgate Wesleyan Church, being at that time a non-drinker. This was a job I quite enjoyed. By way of exercise I joined a football club called Conway Athletic. We played on a pitch in Grovelands Park, and I was at outside left. My old mate Jock Atkinson and Jo's brother Reg Burdge were in the team.

My father wanted me to start work in Barclays Bank, which could be arranged through my Uncle Bob (Archibald). However, I did not want to work in a bank, and applied for a job advertised in the press as a counting-house clerk in a tailors' trimmings merchant in Warwick Street, in the West End of London. I got the job and was then out into the world at last. It was not a large business, with only about half a dozen staff. The company was named Frederick Thomas & Co., and the owner, Mr. Frederick Thomas, was a white-haired and bearded man in his seventies who actually lived in Maidstone Road, Bowes Park (the same road which housed my third cousins Leonard and Arthur). I kept the company's books, and each day Mr. Thomas and I would price the invoices together. This was an ordeal for me, for although I was quite good at figures, the boss, with years of experience of doing the job, was so very quick. The manager of the firm was a Mr. Dawkins, a short stocky man with a blustering manner and tendency to bully. After about a year in Warwick Street the firm moved to much larger premises in Saville Row, off Conduit Street – premises which were once the Tailors' Reading Rooms. After about 18 months I realised that this was not the job for me, partly due, I think, to the fact that I did not like the manager. So I started writing off to banks (despite what I had said previously) and insurance companies in the hope of getting taken on. Things were not very good in those days, and jobs were not all that easy to get. However in March 1924 I received offers of interviews on the same day from both the Swiss Bank Corporation and J. Henry Schroder & Co. I decided to go for the latter, and as a result was offered a job at £100 *per annum*, providing that I took on some evening classes in German. In the first week at the bank one of the staff came to me and told me that his name was William Beaton Titford, and would I please ask my father if we could possibly be related. My father said that there was no way in which we could find out, but now from the searching carried out by my son John I know that he was a distant cousin, a descendant of 'William the Emigrant'. I was put into the Clearing Department of the bank, which was the starting place for all new entrants. At that time the bank received enormous incoming mails from Germany and South America. Those of us in the Clearing Department had to arrive at 8 a.m. to open and deal with the letters in time for the arrival of the people concerned with them who started work at 9 o'clock. Before leaving the office each night we had to agree our books, and then go to the mailing department and deal with the equally large outgoing mail. From the Clearing Department I was later posted to the Collections Department, and from there to Foreign Exchange, in which department I served for 16 years.

Early in 1924 I was walking out with a girl named Betty Stiff from Noel Park, but this ended very abruptly when, on her birthday, I called at her house with a gift of a box of chocolates and was informed by her mother that she was out with another bloke. On Sunday evenings during the summer a band played alongside one of the lakes in Broomfield Park, and the path around the lake became a 'monkey parade' where the girls would walk around arm-in-arm, and the boys would eye them up and down. On a Sunday in September 1924 my school-mate Jock Atkinson and I were doing some eyeing, and eventually found ourselves talking to two young sisters who had come from Finsbury Park to visit the park. Jock paired up with the elder sister Alice (nicknamed Bal) and I with Ethel (nicknamed Beth). Bal was 19, and Beth seventeen. We spent the evening together, and then took the girls back to Finsbury Park on the bus. Beth told me of her serious frontal sinus trouble, and feeling very sorry for her I arranged to meet her again. From this developed a regular courtship, and in December, 1926, we became engaged. During these years Beth spent many weeks in hospital and underwent many operations. In 1929 we decided to have a holiday at Montreux, on Lake Geneva, Switzerland. Both Beth and I remember so vividly the time when we approached the lakeside in the train. We stood in the corridor staring with wonder at the beautiful mauves, purples, and orange in the sky and around the lake as the sun was setting. The following year, on 26 June, we were married at St John's church, Finsbury Park. We spent our honeymoon at Wycombe House, in Shanklin, Isle of Wight. On our return we set up home in a first-floor,

62. Ethel May Titford (*née* Buckler) as a teenager.

three-roomed flat at 94 Ridge Road, Stroud Green, for which we paid 23s. per week. The house owner, a Mr. Davis, lived in the flat below with his wife, a son and a daughter. We stayed there for two years and then bought a new house – no. 41 Chanctonbury Way, in the Woodside Park Garden Suburb – at a cost of £840 plus road charges, and after 53 years we are there to this day. In the beginning money was tight, for we had married on my salary of £245 per annum. I gave up smoking, and made myself a crystal wireless set. However we were happy, and I worked on the garden. At about that time I had all my teeth extracted because of pyorrhoea. It was six months before my dentures were fitted, and my friends nicknamed me 'Gummy'.

In 1936 Beth and I decided to have a holiday in the Black Forest. We crossed over by boat from Dover to Calais, and caught the train to Köln. In Köln we had not booked a hotel, but were given a bed for the night by a young German couple whom we had met on the boat coming over, and in their flat we slept four in one large double bed! The following morning we left for Coblenz, where we took a steamer down the Rhine to Assmanshausen. Here, after rather too much wine-drinking, we stayed the night, and in the morning we took the train to Heidelberg. We looked over the

63.   The marriage of Sidney Horace Titford and Ethel May Buckler at St John's, Queens Drive, Finsbury Park on 26 June 1930. The bridegroom's parents, Harry and Margaret Titford, are on the left of the group, with the bride's parents, Arthur and Annie Buckler, on the right. Next to the bridegroom stands his new brother-in-law Arthur Buckler, while the bridesmaids, left to right, are Doris Titford and Vera Buckler.

university and the town and pushed off the next day to Donaueschingen (the source of the Danube). Our next stop was at *Hotel Mündiger* in Freiberg. Whilst roaming around the beautiful countryside we came across a dream of a village in the Höllenthal valley called Himmelreich (Kingdom of Heaven), and here we called for a meal at a farm catering for visitors. The establishment was run by a widow by the name of Ketterer. Amongst the staff were several members of the family, including her daughter, a charming girl of 22 named Greta. When we told Greta that the day was in fact our wedding anniversary we received V.I.P. treatment. Beth and I decided that we could do no better than stay here for the rest of our holiday, and we had a very happy week, which included helping the family with haymaking in the surrounding fields.

In the following year, 1937, we decided to go back to Germany, but this time to Horn, near Füssen in Bavaria. This time we crossed over by steamer from Harwich to the Hook of Holland, and from there on by train. We stayed at a guesthouse called *Die Alte Freiewelt* recommended by an office pal,

Eric Fuchs, and it proved to be first-class. The proprietor and his missus, Herr and Frau Leo Hütter, were charming people, and for the taking of photographs dressed us up in native costumes. The surrounding country is really beautiful, with lakes and mountains all around. The two old castles of Neuschwanstein, built by the mad King Ludwig, and Hohenschwangau are within walking distance. One of the coach trips worthy of mention was to the village of Oberammergau, where the Passion Play is performed every 10 years. It is wonderfully situated amid the Bavarian Alps, and although we were not there during a year in which the play was staged, one could see many of the actors walking about the streets, including Fritz Lang who played the part of Christ for many years. A tour of the theatre with the extensive dressing rooms was most revealing, and the view of the Kofel mountain seen from the inside of the theatre through the roofless stage was superb. We enjoyed our German holidays so very much that we decided that we would go yet again in 1938. Alas, this we were unable to do, for that was the year of Munich, and the Second World War was already in the air.

On 3 September the following year, 1939, Britain declared war on Germany. The winter of 1939-40 was a severe one, and there was little activity on the western front, so much so that it earned the name of the 'phoney war'. In 1940 came the collapse of France and Belgium and the retreat of the British forces from Dunkirk, who, by a miracle, managed in the main to get back safely to our shores. At this time I joined the Civil Defence Service as an Air-raid Warden (A.R.P.), and had, as patrol colleagues, Jock Beath and Jack Gilbert. We were on call every other night, and on these occasions walked the estate when the sirens sounded. As we were in close proximity to the Mill Hill Barracks and a large ammunition dump in Partingdale Lane, the Germans gave us a fair bit of attention, and a large number of big bombs were dropped in the fields surrounding the estate, as well as one house being demolished by a delayed fuse bomb, with two set on fire. Our main danger as wardens, however, came from our own anti-aircraft shells which showered down their splinters on the streets and rooftops.

In 1941 I volunteered for a commission in the R.A.F.V.R., and was called for an interview at Adastral House in the Strand. I passed at the selection committee interview, but failed the ensuing medical test, being deemed 'not physically fit'. At the Bank there was very little business indeed, but at that time I was in a reserved occupation. However in April 1943 I was called up and instructed to report to Cardington, Beds., for duty in the R.A.F.V.R. on airfield control. Three days later, much to my dismay, I was back in civilian life, having to re-register and take another medical. This time I was graded three, and resultingly had no further calls for service in the forces.

The bombing of London in 1940 was horrific, and each day on arriving in the City for work one saw the results of the onslaught of the night before. At the office, there being no work in the Foreign Exchange Department, I was transferred to the Investment Trusts Department under Frank Dingle, which then dealt with the affairs of Arlington House, a luxury block of flats in St James's Street W.1. owned by Schroders, and the books of The Continental and Industrial Trust Limited.

The war dragged on. The Japanese brought the Americans into the war by their treacherous attack on Pearl Harbour, and the massive attacks by American and British planes on Germany both by night and day were well underway. Then came the first of the flying bombs (doodlebugs) which did a lot of damage. These were followed by a far more sinister weapon, the V2 Rocket, which – unlike the V1 – could not be heard. This weapon, had it been used earlier, could quite possibly have undermined the morale of the British people, but fortunately the opening of the second front eventually brought about the defeat of the Germans, and then the Japanese after the dropping of the atom bombs on Nagasaki and Hiroshima.

In 1944, after many miscarriages and operations, Beth again became pregnant, and on a freezing cold night in the following January she was taken by ambulance to The Royal Northern Hospital in Holloway, and on the 21st John Stuart saw the light of day. In the summer of that year we went with our friends May and David Baxter for a fortnight's holiday to May's cottage in Llanidloes, Wales. John, after being fed by Beth, started the habit of bringing up his food, and as a result Beth spent a week with him in Mothercraft, on Highgate Hill, as it was thought that he might be suffering from *pyloric stenosis*. However, the little beggar had apparently learnt the habit in order that he could have his food twice! From then on he progressed well.

In 1947 I bought a Morris 10 (1932) car from Frank Dingle. It was a very icy winter that year, and during much of the time that my brother-in-law, Nev., was teaching me to drive, I could not see a kerb because of the frozen snow. I passed my test on the second attempt. Beth started to learn with the help of our neighbour Stan Newsom, and passed her test on the first go! In the summer of that year we took my Mother and Father with us to Holland-on-Sea for a fortnight's holiday. We rented a bungalow, and it was during our stay there that John frightened us out of our lives by poking a knife taken from the table into a 15 amp socket in the pantry to produce a large bang with a vivid purple flash. Fortunately the knife had a bone handle and John got away without injury.

He now tells me he is writing up the family's history ...

CHAPTER 25

John Stuart (b. 1945)

London

THE END OF THE RAINBOW

Our four hundred years of Titford history closes in 1947 – very conveniently for the author, for he was only two years old in that year, and is consequently spared the task of recounting his own life story. John Stuart had been 15 years in the making; after a number of miscarriages, his mother finally gave birth to a healthy child against all the odds. He arrived prematurely, just to be awkward; there had been snow on the ground over Christmas, and it was still cold in January when he decided his time had come. Hoping and praying the air-raid sirens wouldn't sound, mother got herself as fast as she could to the Royal Northern Hospital in Holloway, and the baby boy arrived there at half-past ten in the evening on 21 January 1945. If the nurses had had their way, he would have been called 'Robin'; in the event it was John Stuart – whatever had happened to the paternal grandfather naming pattern!

Godparents
Miss Doris G. Titford.
Auntie Doris.

Mr. Harry E. Titford.
Uncle Harry.

Mr. David Baxter.
Uncle David

*Present at
the Reception*
~ 16 ~

Miss J. P. E. Archibald,
Mr. & Mrs. D. Baxter,
Mrs. A. Brodie,
Mrs. A. Buckler and Jill,
Mr. & Mrs. E. Childs,
Mrs. E. Nevill,
Mr. & Mrs. W. Pratt,
Miss D. G. Titford,
Mr. & Mrs. H. J. Titford
and of course
Mum & Dad.

64. The christening of John Stuart Titford, 13 May 1945. The event took place at St Barnabas church, Finchley; here the details of those present are entered in a book of childhood events by the baby's father.

In the   County of Cambridgeshire and Isle of Ely

Petty Sessional Division of   North Witchford (MARCH)

To   John Stewart TITFORD

of   7A The Avenue, MARCH

in the   County aforesaid

INFORMATION has this day been laid before me, the undersigned Justice of the Peace, by   Roy Alan MILLER Police Inspector

.

that you, on the   4th   day of   July   19 69,

at   MARCH

in the   County   first aforesaid, during the hours of darkness, at

.   11.35   in the   after   noon, unlawfully did [cause] [permit] a

certain vehicle, to wit, a   Triumph Herald   car

to be on a certain road, called   The Avenue

.

which vehicle did not then carry [two lamps each showing to the front a white light] [and] [two lamps each showing to the rear a red light] [each] visible from a reasonable distance and kept properly trimmed, lighted and in a clean and efficient condition and properly attached thereto, contrary to sections 1 and 12 of the Road Transport Lighting Act, 1957.

YOU ARE THEREFORE HEREBY SUMMONED to appear on

ues day, the   12th   day of .   August

19 69 , at the hour of   10.0   o'clock in the   fore   noon,

before the **Magistrates' Court** sitting at   The County Hall, MARCH

Cat. No. L.M. 4.

Road Transport Lighting Act, 1957, ss. 1 and 12.

Motor Vehicles (including bicycles with sidecars, motor bicycles with sidecars, and motor tricycles) not having proper lights.

Summons.

LONDON :
SHAW & SONS Ltd., Fetter Lane, Fleet Street, E.C.4.

in the   County   first aforesaid, to answer to the said Information.

DATED the   23 d   day of   July   19 69.

J H Billingham

Justice of the Peace for the   County   *first aforesaid.*

65. John Stuart Titford: Summons for a traffic offence, 1969. The wheel comes full circle . . . In 1578 Thomas Titford, alehousekeeper and husbandman of Steeple Ashton, had been fined by the Justices of the Peace for the County of Wiltshire. Here, nearly four hundred years later, John Titford is about to suffer the same fate at the hands of the Justices in Cambridgeshire. And not so much has changed, after all: the legal jargon, the Royal Arms, the use of Black Letter or Gothic type – all are redolent of an earlier age. And still the clerk has difficulties when it comes to spelling – 'Stewart' in place of 'Stuart' . . .

Just one final reflection of a genealogical nature might close this chapter: if we had come across a first child born 15 years after his parents' marriage in the parish registers of earlier centuries, would we have been prepared to believe it? Or could we have accepted that John Stuart's Aunt Doris had really waited until she was 53 before getting married? When we become bound by our expectation that couples will marry in their twenties and have the first child within a year or two, we might like to think how people can give the statistics the lie when they really put their minds to it.

And so our story itself is at an end – or at a pause, rather, since life and lives will go on. The acknowledgements which introduced the story of the Titfords began with a quotation from Montaigne, and we could do worse than close with a further thought from that wisest of men: 'When I play with my cat, who knows whether she isn't amusing herself with me more than I am with her?' In theory the author of this tale has been surveying the lives and times of his antecedents – that is the cat with which he has been amusing himself. But in the last analysis, we might ponder, who exactly has been looking at whom . . .?

Conclusion

If a man will begin with certainties, he shall end in doubts; but if he will be content to begin with doubts, he shall end in certainties.

Francis Bacon

History properly begins with details, not generalizations; one of the great luxuries enjoyed by family historians is that they can set about collecting genealogical raw material without the need to fit it all into any ideological or *a priori* scheme of things. Conclusions can be drawn later, patterns established, material analysed and then synthesized with the acquired wisdom of hindsight. We have attempted to include some degree of analysis in our story as it has gone along; now, in conclusion, one or two threads can briefly be drawn together.

Peter Spufford has said with a degree of tongue-in-cheek wisdom:· 'The mobility of ancestors is the most common problem encountered by genealogists. It is surprising rather that anybody ever manages to trace his ancestors'. (*Gen. Mag.*, Vol. 17, No. 10, June 1974, p. 539.) Mobility has been one vital and central feature in the Titford story as it has evolved; not just geographical mobility, either – alongside that has often gone some degree of social mobility as well.

At times the Titfords have appeared to be less mobile than many of their contemporaries: the family's stay in Frome, for example, despite the departure of a number of young males, lasted in total from 1625 to 1860, while their cousins from Wylye in Wiltshire lived in that village from 1622 until the mid-1820s. These are long periods to remain in one place – though the Titford cardmakers in Frome and the Titford shepherds in Wylye may well have thought that regular employment in a place they knew was preferable to a step into the unknown elsewhere.

Not everyone preferred the known to the unknown, however, and more often than not incontrovertible documentary proof exists of the moves which various individuals made around the country. The parish registers of Steeple Ashton in Wiltshire, for example, helpfully inform us that Thomas Titford the Alehousekeeper really did find a wife in Shipton-Under-Wychwood in Oxfordshire before returning to his home village in 1598; a settlement certificate of 1711 confirms us in our belief that the William Titford of Hawkhurst in Kent had come there from Frome; a Baptist Chapel minute book of 1757 states quite clearly that Mary Titford had recently arrived in Frome from London. Similarly unequivocal evidence makes us confident in saying that one of the Kent Titfords, William, was apprenticed in London in 1766; that William Charles Titford, Freeman of the City of London, was the son of a Frome cheesemonger, and that the Elizabeth Titford baptized in the Frome Zion Chapel in 1817 had come there from Stepney. The family's mobility, in other words, is there for us to discover in primary sources, not merely a figment of our imaginations.

Why did individuals and families move around in the way they did? More often than not there would be an underlying economic motive. A falling-off in the fortunes of the wool trade probably drove the Titfords of Bratton elsewhere in the early 17th century, though their arrival in Bratton in the first place, as we have indicated, may have been the result of their making a move alongside a new Lord of the Manor. Those Titfords who left Frome or Wylye in the late 18th and early 19th centuries would have been escaping the poverty which was daily besetting their friends and relations during and after the Napoleonic Wars. Economic hardship, then, would force out those young and healthy enough to make a journey away from home, most never to return.

Nor should we discount the need to escape from disease and pestilence as one of the strongest motives of all which encouraged people to make a speedy departure from an afflicted region. Some never escaped in time, of course: Henry Titford of Southwark succumbed to the plague in London in 1665, and Titfords and their in-laws in Frome were hit hard by successive outbreaks of disease throughout the 17th and 18th centuries, their predicament frequently exacerbated by bad weather and malnutrition. A fortunate few survived by virtue of a temporary or permanent migration: Thomas of Steeple Ashton fled from the Great Sweat which had carried off his wife in 1597 – the first widespread rural epidemic since the 1550's – and lived to fight another day; Mary Titford, leaving London for Frome in 1757, managed to put a safe distance between herself and the smallpox epidemic which would claim three thousand victims in the capital that very year.

Mary's case is an interesting one in that it indicates the kind of factors which would facilitate any attempt at migration: that is, she had relations in Frome who would look after her, and as a Baptist believer she could be assured of a warm welcome in a chapel many miles away from London. Not all prospective migrants can have been so lucky.

For many Titfords geographical mobility would carry with it the possibility for social mobility, too. Charles Titford and his brother Ralph left Leigh-Upon-Mendip in Somerset in the mid-17th century to seek their fortunes in London – and both became property-owning men of wealth, the successful *nouveaux-riches* of their generation. William Charles Titford left impoverished relations in Frome in the 1790s and prospered as a silk mercer in the capital, while his namesake, William of Wylye, traded the poverty of a humble Wiltshire village for life as a fashionable undertaker in North London. Both men, in the process, also exemplified yet another kind of mobility – abandoning, as they did, the Nonconformist church affiliations of their fathers for a safe Anglicanism.

We began our story by talking of the family as victim, and victims there have been – of economic hardship, poor health, disease, old age, inclement weather – and simple bad fortune. Yet every century we have passed through has offered rewards for those with the innate resilience to take risks – that, plus a degree of good luck. Some never had real opportunities in life; others had them and failed to respond; a few grabbed their chances and reaped the rewards. As these acquired money and property, so they made some advancement in the social structure; significantly, in nearly every case, it was their initial geographical mobility which facilitated their social mobility.

Properly speaking, the so-called social ladder which some people manage to climb is more often like the capricious wheel of fortune; rags-to-riches stories are often matched by others which move from riches to rags. Elizabeth Titford, wife of Ben the Outrider, for example, came from a prosperous family of coopers, but nevertheless died in Shoreditch Workhouse in 1849; and the Frome Titfords who leased eight houses in the 1690s were to have a string of pauper descendants just a hundred years later.

Nevertheless, the family we have chosen to follow has survived through it all over the four hundred years of our story. During the 16th century they were dual-occupation husbandmen and craftsmen; in Frome they became wage-dependent skilled artisans, moving eventually into the retail business; in Victorian times they tried out a blend of craft and retail, and this century has seen them established in the professions. An ordinary family, to be sure, and one whose experiences must have been shared by countless thousands of their contemporaries over the years.

It has been an exciting and fascinating experience for their descendants to have travelled through time and space with these people; one can only hope, in a modest way, to have ensured just a small touch of immortality for them all.

Addenda

The Titford Family, 1547-1947: Come Wind, Come Weather was completed towards the end of 1983. In the Preface we claimed that the book could do nothing more than offer a mid-way snapshot – that if research were to continue we would hope that 'something will turn up which will add to its findings, point out its errors, or at least modify some of the hypotheses we have proposed'. Research has indeed continued, extra information has come to light, and inaccuracies have been spotted. That, we believe, is as it should be.

Where we have unearthed extra facts which materially affect the story, modifications have been made to the text itself. The fact that Thomas Titford the Alehousekeeper of Steeple Ashton was involved as a defendant in a case in the Court of Star Chamber has meant some revision of Chapter 3; the discovery of the original family register of Charles Titford of Cranbrook in Kent has allowed us to state with confidence that its writer did indeed travel from Cranbrook to Frome during April 1746; and records in the keeping of the Memorial University of Newfoundland have made it clear that Charles Frederick Titford was not making his maiden voyage aboard the R.M.S. *Chimborazo* in 1878, as we had at first thought.

Not all new discoveries, however, necessitate a revision of the text; here we include, by way of addenda, some new facts, ideas and theories based upon further research, arranged chapter by chapter.

And still, God willing, further investigations will continue . . .

Introduction

1. Sir William Teford and Sir John Tefford: bearers of the arms later ascribed to Titford

Further research has not clearly identified these two individuals. There was a Sir Robert de Tetford and a Sir Gilbert de Tetford in Lincolnshire in the 13th century, however:

> Robert and Gilbert de Tetford, knights, who presented to the chapelry of Tetford in 1248, were, I suppose, the sons of Robert, son of Gilbert de Tetford. [*Lincs. Notes and Queries*, vol. 4 (1894-5), p. 229 (by W. O. M(assingberd).]

A certain Sir Philip de Teford is also much in evidence in Lincolnshire during the same century:

> Sir Philip de Theford (or Teford) knt. who presented to the moiety of the chapelry of Tetford in 1284, and to the Church of Tetford in 1296, was probably a son of Sir Gilbert. He was a witness to Sir Simon fitz Ralph's grant of land in Walmsgate to William son of Herbert de Walmesgare, circa 1280-1290. [W. O. Massingberd, *History of the parish of Ormsby-cum-Ketsby, in the Hundred of Hill and County of Lincoln* (Lincoln, n.d.), p. 188.]

We might identify this Sir Philip with a man of the same name who is given as a knight of Edward I in 1296:

> Sir Phillip de Theford. Summoned to serve against Scots, 1 Mar. 1296, and again as having £20 lands in Notts. & Derb. 7 July 1297. (Parliamentary Writ.) Presumably a knight. [*Knights of Edward I, vol. 5*, Harleian Society, vol. 84 (1932), p. 16.]

The only other individual with the surname 'Tiford' or its variants who has a title to his name is Lord Robert de Tifford of Hacunby, Lincs., who presented John Wade to the church of Hacunby in 1347. [*Lincs. Notes and Queries*, vol. 1 (1889), p. 177. (By W. Boyd.)]

So Sir William Teford and Sir John Tefford remain elusive; in 1336 and 1340, John, son of William de Tetford and William de Barkworth presented to the moiety of the chapelry of St Bartholemew of Teford. Perhaps this is the William and the John we seek, minus the prefix 'Sir'? [*Lincs. Notes and Queries*, vol. 4 (1894-5), p. 229.]

2. *The origin of the name Titford*

Bardsley and Harrison seem to be in agreement in deriving the name from Tetford in Lincolnshire. Another author, Robert Ferguson, tells a different story. Ferguson's book *Surnames as a Science* is not, to be fair, always taken very seriously by surname etymologists. He would have us believe that a number of Anglo-Saxon men's names were based upon local place-names and that these in turn have given rise to some modern surnames. So he claims that a place called 'Titferthes geat' gives us the Anglo-Saxon male name 'Titferth', leading to the English surname 'Titford'. [Robert Ferguson, *Surnames as a Science* (1884), p. 98.]

Ferguson here takes his place-names from a work by J. M. Kemble, *Codex Diplomaticus Aevi Saxonici* (1839). Kemble gives two references to 'Titferthes Geat', both in the year 939, and both in the area of Wansdyke, Wilts. It would be an intriguing possibility, to try to link such an early Wiltshire place-name with the presence of the Titford family in Wiltshire from the mid-16th century, but we may well be looking at nothing more than a coincidence, after all.

A radical reappraisal of the origin of the name 'Titford' may be necessary following the discovery of the following entry in Thomas Frederick Kirby's *Winchester Scholars: A list of the Wardens, Fellows, and Scholars of Saint Mary College of Winchester, near Winchester, commonly called Winchester College* (1888), p. 35.

Scholars: 1407: TUTFORD, Richard. [Born at:] Tutford, Winton Dio. *Ad religionem.*

Here, 140 years before his namesake first appears in Bratton, Wilts., in 1547, is an earlier Richard Tutford, a scholar of Winchester College who became a monk (*ad religionem*) and was born, intriguingly, in a place called 'Tutford' in the diocese of Winchester.

Scholars at Winchester in the early 15th century who were not founders' kin were apt to be '*pauperes et indigentes*' of good manners, towardly, apt for study, and proficient in reading, plainsong and Latin grammar. They were not to be admitted under the age of eight or over the age of 12, and upon attaining the age of 15 every scholar had to take the oath of fealty and secrecy enjoined by the statutes, and receive his first tonsure a year later. The College saw its function as that of preparing its pupils for New College, Oxford, or for Holy Orders.

But where is 'Tutford' in the diocese of Winchester? Very probably we are speaking of the small hamlet now called Totford, near Northington, Hants., and about seven miles north-east of Winchester. Maybe this hamlet, after all, is the origin of the surname 'Tutford', first in Hampshire then in Wiltshire, giving way to 'Titford' in the late 16th century? A very large proportion of Richard Tutford's 15th-century fellow-scholars were named after their place of birth: we have Henry Faryngdon from Faryngdon, Lancs., John Tychfeld from Titchfield, Robert Dorkyng from Dorking, and many others. Perhaps our young scholar arrived at the doors of the College with no surname as such and was ascribed one according to his place of birth? We might expect that Richard Tutford, as a monk, fathered no offspring, but perhaps his newly-acquired surname was adopted by his siblings or even by his parents?

Just as Tetford in Lincolnshire gave rise to a family or families called 'Tetford' or 'Tiford', so Totford in Hampshire spawned the surname 'de Totford'. The *Registrum Henrici Woodlock Episcopi Wintonienses* [Canterbury and York Society, vol. 44 (1941)] includes references to '*Johannes filius Roberti de Totteford*', who took his first tonsure in the year 1306, and '*Robertus de Totteford*', listed amongst the *acoliti* for 1309. The *Victoria County History* for Hampshire, vol. 3, gives us more details in its article on the hamlet of Totford. William de Totford witnessed a charter to Hyde Abbey in 1191; Robert de Totford witnessed a grant to Roger,

Abbot of Hyde (1248-63) and had a son John living in 1262. Members of the 'de Totford' family held part of the land now known as Totford; late in the 13th century the whole of Totford, consisting of five hides, was held by Philip de Totford, Philip Butler, Peter de Fraxino and Henry le Frankelyn by service of one knight's fee to the Abbot of Hyde. Philip de Totford's two hides were probably inherited from him by Robert de Totford, who was living in 1272. In 1314-15 John de Totford paid scutage for two hides in Totford, and was succeeded by his son John de Totford, whose daughter and heir, Christine, was taken into the Abbot's custody in 1349 when she was only four years old. Totford itself had passed to the Tichborne family by the 16th century.

Did the family which eventually became 'Titford' move north-east from Hampshire, then, rather than south-west from Lincolnshire, after all?

3. Earliest references to the Tetford family of Lincolnshire

References to the Tetford family or families of Lincolnshire are really very numerous from the late 12th century onwards. The earliest evidence of that family's existence we have yet uncovered comes from a deed of *c.* 1160 among the papers of the Earl of Ancaster of Grimsthorpe, Lincs. Witnesses to the deed include 'Alvredo de . . . dford, Willelmo filio Alvredi de Tedford et Radulfo fratre suo'. [*Historical Manuscripts Commission*, 13th Report, Appendix 6, (1893).]

This is interesting corroborative evidence – both of the fact that Alvred de Tedford (or Tiford) and his son William, holding land in Enderby in the late 12th century, are among the first men of that name to have had their existence recorded in a written document, but also of the connection we have suggested between the Titford and Willoughby families. Here we have the earliest 'Tedford' reference yet unearthed, appearing significantly among the papers of the Earl of Ancaster, Baron Willoughby de Eresby.

William de Tedford, almost certainly the same man who witnessed the deed referred to above, is recorded in the Pipe Roll for 1181-2 as having paid two marks for six bovates of land in Enderby, and merits a reference in the Feet of Fines for 1195 (*'Willm. fil. alur. de tiford'*).

We have to wait a further 200 years to find a direct connection between the Tetford family and East Keal, just a few miles to the south of Enderby; in 1387 Robert de Tetford of East Keal and Keal Cotes is listed as a juror. [*Sessions of the Peace, 1381-96*, Pubs. of the Lincs. Record Soc., vol. 56, p. 96.]

Other half-glimpsed characters appear from time to time:

Ralf of Tetford, tailor – release and quitclaim of all his right and claim in the land in the parish of St Margaret in Wigford, 1257-9. [*Registrum Antiquissimum*, Pubs. of the Lincs. Record Soc., vol. 62, p. 74.]
Thomas Tetford, rector of Hagworthingham, 1408. [*The register of Philip Repingdon, 1405-19*, Pubs. of the Lincs. Record Soc., vol. 57, p. 123.]

A large number of references to the Tetford family may be found in W. O. Massingberd, *History of the parish of Ormsby-cum-Ketsby, in the Hundred of Hill and County of Lincoln* (Lincoln, n.d.).

4. The Tifford family of St Ives

There is evidence of a Tifford family presence in St Ives, Hunts., 50 years earlier than we had at first thought. The will of Robert Tyfford, husbandman of St Ives, was proved in the Archdeaconry Court of Huntingdon in 1542; in it he mentions his wife Annes and his sons and daughters, who inherit between them his house and lands, his livestock, his crops and his farming equipment. Annes, the widow, made her own will in 1549; it was proved in the same year.

5. William Titford, yeoman of Cotton End, Cardington, Beds.

Like Richard Titford, yeoman of Corsley, Wilts., William Titford of Cardington is described variously as a 'husbandman' and a 'yeoman'. William's will of 1604 is that of William Titford, yeoman, but the Lay Subsidy for Eastcotts of 1592-3 had termed him a husbandman, assessing him at £3 8s. on his goods. [PRO E179/72/213.]

6. Richard Titford of Willington, Beds., son of Isaac Titford, woodward

The Titford family of Willington in Bedfordshire had been tenants of the Gostwick family since at least as early as the late 16th century. The records of the Court Baron and View of Frankpledge of William Gostwick's manor of Willington for 1599 indicate that Richard Titford was paying 1d. to the lord for his tenement within the manor, and in 1602 the same Richard was charged a 'common fine' of 1d. for the privilege of keeping five sheep and two 'beastes or bullocks' in the common fields of Willington. [Beds. CRO, R Box 212]

Somehow, clearly, the Titfords ingratiated themselves with the Gostwicks as the 17th century wore on, and proved themselves to be employees who could be trusted. Isaac Titford (bur. 1685/6), we know, was Sir Edward Gostwick's woodward, but Isaac's son Richard (1651-99) was to perform an even more invaluable service to Sir William Gostwick, 4th Baronet, in 1697: nothing less than the carefully stage-managed corruption of the electors of Bedfordshire to ensure Sir William's election to Parliament. This was a task which Richard Titford executed with consummate skill, by all accounts; as 'Mr. Tidford, Sir Wm. Gostwick's Bailiff', he features large in the Journals of the House of Commons for 1699, where his allegedly corrupt practices in securing his master's victory were considered by the Committee of Privileges.

In the event, no-one was a winner in this little drama: the cost of bribery of all sorts eventually bankrupted Sir William Gostwick, and Richard Titford, the arch-manipulator, was dead by 1699. [For more details see H. P. R. Finberg, *The Gostwicks of Willington* in Publications of the Bedfordshire Historical Record Society, vol. 36 (1955), pp. 47-115.]

Chapter 3: Thomas the Alehousekeeper

Thomas the Alehousekeeper and his wayward stepsons

Thomas Titford the Alehousekeeper of Steeple Ashton, of humble station though he was, has a habit of elbowing his way into official records more than any other of his late 16th-century and early 17th-century Titford contemporaries. Wherever one looks, it seems, there he is. Recent discoveries about his doings and those of his immediate family come from two sources: The Act Book of the Archdeacon of Sarum [WRO D2/4/1/5] and Steeple Ashton Court Book [Longleat 104611].

The Archdeacon of Sarum's Act Book throws some fascinating light upon the story of Thomas the Alehousekeeper. Featured prominently in its pages for 1592-3 is a certain 'John Davis, alias Titford'. Of all the reasons a person might have for adopting an alias, the most likely in this case is the need or the wish a son might have to perpetuate the name of his real father after his widowed mother has subsequently remarried. Working on this assumption, we have the following scenario.

Elizabeth Davis, one time wife of Richard Davis of Steeple Ashton, had two or more sons, including Edward (baptised at Steeple Ashton in 1566) and, conjecturally, John (baptised some time between 1571 and 1576, a period for which the Steeple Ashton baptismal registers are missing). Richard Davis himself died in 1577, and was buried in Steeple Ashton on 1 November that year. Elizabeth then remarried Thomas Titford fairly soon afterwards (no marriage entry having yet been found), and proceeded to have a child by her new husband, this being Mary Titford, baptised in 1579, daughter of Thomas and Elizabeth. At the time of his marriage to widow Elizabeth, then, Thomas Titford had acquired not just a wife, but also at least two stepsons, one calling himself 'John Davis alias Titford' and the other, 'Edward Davis'. Both would acquire their stepfather Thomas's taste for cocking the occasional snook at authority.

At the Archdeacon of Sarum's Court held on 29 December 1592, John Sparke, the 'apparitor', was able to declare that he had personally apprehended John Davis alias Titford, Edward Davis and Edmund Laycock of Steeple Ashton; apprehended they may have been, but present at court they were not. All were declared 'contumacious', and after a subsequent non-appearance all were duly excommunicated. This seems to have focussed young John Davis alias Titford's mind somewhat, as he graciously put in an appearance at the court in February 1593 and vehemently denied that he had had carnal knowledge of a certain Elizabeth Silvester. He was duly ordered to attend the next visitation court at Edington, to purge himself by the oaths of three neighbours. His mother, Elizabeth Titford, meanwhile, had offered a similar neighbourly oath to help out Alice Downe, wife of Peter Downe of Steeple Ashton, who was accused of unseemly conduct with a certain Timothy Wallis of Trowbridge. Titfords were regular visitors to the courts during these winter months of 1592-3. The two other Steeple Ashton bloods, Edward Davis (presumed to be John's brother, Thomas Titford's other stepson) and Edmund Laycock, followed young John through the court with similar denials of carnal knowledge committed with a couple of lasses by the names of Alice Bynney and the semi-anonymous 'Edith'. John Davis alias Titford may or may not have been guilty of the charge laid against him – and in any case the lady in question, Elizabeth Silvester, had been excommunicated for non-attendance at court herself in December 1592 – but he chose to run rather than fight. Absent from the court again in April and May 1593 as he was, he had finally tried the patience of the authorities to breaking-point, was found guilty of the charges, pronounced contumacious and excommunicated (for a second time it would seem!) on 30 June 1593. Thereafter he appears no more in the records of the court.

These few details reveal only too clearly the predicament of the ecclesiastical courts at this period; their main problem was that few people appear to have taken them seriously. They could shout and storm, declare a person contumacious and therefore excommunicated, but no-one seems to have cared very much, hoping, perhaps, that if the court and its orders were ignored, then they might go away.

Other little family gems to emerge from the Archdeacon's Court records at about this period include the discovery that William Titford, founder of the Wylye Titford line, was in Barford St Martin in February 1617/18, when he was warned for non-attendance at church. It was probably in Barford that he married his wife Rachel, with whom he was later to have several children in Wylye, the marriage registers for Barford not having survived for this period.

It was quite a surprise to discover that the archives at Longleat contained a court book for Steeple Ashton manor for the 1590s. The manor then belonged to the Crown, with John Thynne acting as seneschal to the Queen. It seems likely that when the manor passed into other hands, John Thynne, in whose possession the court book would have been, simply kept it. It remains at Longleat to this day.

We find that at the manor court held on 11 September 1593, Thomas Titford was fined the inordinately large sum of 20s. for having taken two strangers as sub-tenants. Six years later, on 5 April 1599, the jury were outraged enough to report that Thomas Titford had erected a certain 'Le flew' (an illegal chimney?) to the great danger of his neighbours.

Naturally, he was ordered to take it down forthwith, under pain of a further fine of 20s. Flues and apple trees: all part of the domestic scene in Steeple Ashton, it seems.

Chapter 9: Ralph the Pauper

Ralph Titford, pauper, and William his brother

William III, the Protestants' choice as king, had his fair share of enemies; in the wake of a Jacobite attempt against his life, the Act of Association of 1695/6 required all office-holders to take an Oath of Association, pledging themselves loyal to His Majesty and the government. The resultant lists of signatures are known as the Association Oath Rolls.

In London Ralph Titford, born in Leigh-on-Mendip, Somerset, cousin of the Frome Titfords, signed such a roll alongside his son Charles; their names appear on the roll of the Weavers' Company. Yet in many parts of the country very large numbers of people, office-holders or not, appear on the Association Oath Rolls; so the roll for Frome, for example, contains many scores of names, and acts, in effect, as a male census of the town in 1695/6. Among the 'Truely Loyall Gentlemen, Clothiers, Free-Holders and other inhabitants' of the town we find William and Ralfe Titford, flanked by their friends and eventual in-laws, the Laceys. Both William and Ralph appear to have been literate enough to sign their own names. [PRO C213/239.]

Chapter 14: Charles the Cheesemonger

Charles Titford's House and Shop in Pig Street, Frome

Thanks to the researches of Derek Gill of Frome, a number of documents relative to the Literary Institute (1 North Parade) have recently come to light. The 'Lit.' occupies the erstwhile site of Charles Titford's house and shop in what was then Pig Street.

An early owner of the house and shop in question was Joseph Mintrim, innholder, who had lived for a while in the house opposite, converted eventually into the *Black Swan* inn. Mintrim's will, proved at Wells on 14 January 1785, provided for his sister-in-law Mary Gifford to have 'all his tenement in occupation of Charles Titford'; thus it is that the said Mary Gifford was Charles's landlady in the census of 1785.

A lease and release of 1786 involving Mary Gifford, widow, and her grandson Thomas Balne, maltster, is expressed in the following terms:

> All that tenement or dwellinghouse then occupied by Charles Titford with stable coach-houses adjoining and smiths shop near thereto occupied by Benjamin Brittain, situate near the bridge and formerly occupied by William Evans cooper, and adjoining on east and south land late of Lionel Seaman clerk, fronting on west against the street leading to Welshmill, on north to garden belonging to tenement of Sir Thomas Champney late in possession of Benjamin Colston: all which then late in possession of Joseph Mintrim and devised by will to Mary Gifford . . .

Chapter 16: William Charles Titford

William Charles Titford's financial problems

William Jowett Titford was certainly fast off the mark in calling his cousin W. C. T.'s business judgment into question in a letter of 28 April 1806. Two days earlier, on 26 April, William Charles Titford had been declared bankrupt.

Financial failure in the linen-drapery business in the early years of the 19th century was a far from rare occurence: Sir Richard Phillips's *The Book of English Trades, and Library of the Useful Arts* (11th edn. 1823, p. 230) says of this branch of trade that it requires considerable capital, and that

> ... this is a business in which, we believe, more persons have failed than in any other in the United Kingdom, owing to its being liable to partake of the fluctuations, unfortunately almost inherent in the manufacturing system, and to the great versatility in fashion and dress.

There was little enough hope during the early years of the 19th century that an individual's insolvency might be kept a secret from friends, neighbours and business associates. The *London Gazette* would proclaim bankruptcies for all to see, and names and details would then be extracted with alacrity by a series of printed magazines anxious to spread the bad news far and wide. The hapless bankrupt could expect to read about himself and his misfortunes in the *Gentleman's Magazine*, the *European Magazine and London Review*, the *Monthly Magazine and British Register* and the *Universal Magazine*, all anxious to fill their pages with whatever might inform and titillate their readers. It's an ill wind ...

William Charles's bankruptcy was duly announced in the *London Gazette* for Saturday, 26 April 1806; *The Times* published the essential details two days later, together with the three dates upon which W. C. T. would have to confront his creditors at the Guildhall. The *European Magazine* was thereafter pleased to include in its appended list of bankrupts an entry for 'Titford, William Charles. Bishopgate Street Within. Linen draper. Apr. 26'. The *Monthly Magazine* tells much the same tale, adding the name of the appropriate attornies (Carpenter of Basinghall Street), as does William Smith & Co.'s publication *A list of Bankrupts* for 1806.

When the *Gentleman's Magazine* for 1778 had wanted to announce the bankruptcy of Isaac Titford, father of William Jowett Titford, 'now or late of the Strand, Middlesex, sword cutler ...' it had headed its page 'B-NK-TS'. But in 1806 such euphemisms were on the wane, and the number of people caught in the bankruptcy net was ever greater, year by year.

As W. C. T. began paying off his debts and moving towards solvency once more, the *Monthly Magazine* for 1807 includes his name under the heading of 'Dividends', announced on 16 May and again on 9 June.

So things were slowly on the mend. By the time William Jowett wrote to William Charles in person on 10 December 1806, he had mollified his tone somewhat since his April missive to Richard Titford:

> Wrote to W. C. Titford ... Sincerely sorry to hear the acct. of his misfortune but hoped by his capability of business would soon retrieve them. Remembrance to Mrs. T. the Edgar family & Frome. [From the letter book of William Jowett Titford, in the possession of Anthony R. Titford of West Horsley, Surrey.]

W. J. T. had been acting as a retailer for William Charles's shawls, as we have seen (Chapter 16); his letter book mentions a number of items despatched by his cousin for sale in Jamaica: round shawls, 'pic nics', gloves, and even the possibility of some trade in perfumery is mentioned. So William Charles must have been pleased to read in the above letter of 10 December that he was owed £7 13s. 5d. in currency – at least that might get him started on the road to financial recovery.

William Jowett Titford's letter book, then, would give us the impression that its author and his cousin Richard were financially cautious and wise compared to the bankrupt William Charles. That may well have been the case in 1806, but 10 years later W. C. T. might have had a wry smile on his face had he chosen to buy a copy of the *European Magazine and London Review* for September 1816, and scan the list of bankrupts under the heading

> An alphabetical list of bankrupts, with attornies names, from Tuesday, August 27, to Tuesday, September 24, 1816. Extracted from the *London Gazette*. N.B. All the Meetings are at GUILDHALL, unless otherwise expressed. The Country and London Attorneys Names are between Brackets.

There for all to read and comment on was the announcement of the bankruptcy of his cousins and their silk-manufacturing business:

TITFORD. W. and R. Union-st. Spital-fields, silk-manufacturers, Oct. 29. (James, Bucklersbury). Sept. 17.

The following year the same publication would include 'R. Titford' in its list of 'Certificates' for 22 March, and 'W. Titford & Co., Union St.' among 'Dividends' for 31 May. So 'Titford & Son, silk weavers, 2, Union Street, Bishopsgate' disappears as an entry in the London directories after 1816; when Richard Titford appears again in print it is as a silk manufacturer at 7 Fore Street, Spital Square, in 1827.

In the event, William Jowett himself, described as an 'accountant, agent and referee' of 1 Union Street, Bishopsgate, in the directories for 1811 and 1812, had probably been helping the family firm organise its finances. Maybe he recommended bankruptcy as a wise move in 1816? Maybe he had lost his financial touch? Here we have no letter book to help us.

William Charles Titford's descendants remember

Late in 1987 the author received a letter from Mrs. Cynthia Wilson, a great-great-granddaughter of William Charles Titford, who traces her line of descent from the marriage of W. C. T.'s daughter Sarah to William Parfitt in 1846. Mrs. Wilson has in her possession two brief but fascinating letters which reach back into history and make reference to William Charles Titford himself. These were written in 1937 and 1939 to Cynthia Wilson's aunt, and were penned by a lady by the name of Miss Lena Austen, who had lived with Georgiana Parfitt, eldest daughter of William Parfitt and his wife Sarah (*née* Titford). The letters mix fact and fiction ('Edgar Titford came to England with William the Conqueror'), but contain one or two snippets of information of the greatest value to any biographer of William Charles Titford and his family, as follows:

– W. C. T.'s eldest daughter ran away from home and married a riding master. (This is presumably represented by the marriage of Ann Titford to William Henry Perry at St Pancras Old Church on 16 January 1831. Pigot's *London Directory* for 1838 lists a William Henry Perry, engraver and printer of 47, New Compton Street, Soho, but also a Henry Perry, livery-stable keeper, of 41/2, Hart Street, Covent Garden.)

– W. C. T.'s son Charles went to sea as captain of a merchant ship, but was drowned when the ship and all its crew were lost. (This is Charles Titford, born on 17 May 1807, and baptised at St Luke's, Old Street, on 14 June in the same year. He and his cousin Robert, then, were both mariners.)

– W. C. T.'s son John became a managing clerk in a City firm and remained there until he died. His sister Emma kept house for him and they had rooms with William and Sarah Parfitt at Elm Grove, South Lambeth. (This is John, born on 18 December 1805. 'Emma' is Emely Sophia Titford, born on 26 September 1819.)

– In 1846, at the time of William Parfitt's marriage to Sarah Titford, the bridegroom was clerk of the works at Millbank Prison. (This goes some way to explaining why Sarah Titford gave her address on her marriage certificate as 'Millbank Prison'.)

– Referring to W. C. T.'s financial collapse, the writer of the letters says: 'I do not remember that he lost his money through mine shares but through falsification in the office books by one of the Co. & then failure of their bank. I think that was the end of it. Grandfather himself took it very badly.'

Letters like these, short and apparently trivial in nature, are a godsend to the genealogist; here is a person writing in the 1930s, telling us about a financial collapse which happened in 1806, to a man born in 1772. At a stroke we are back to the 18th century.

Chapter 17: Ben the Outrider

Benjamin Titford's Marriage Allegation

As well as signing his name to the requisite allegation when he applied for a marriage licence on 22 January 1808, Benjamin also had to complete and sign a marriage bond. Here he describes himself (unhelpfully) as a 'gentleman', and the other named bondsman – no doubt fictitious – is 'John Thomas'. Such fictions were commonplace at this period; William Charles Titford's fellow-bondsman in 1799 was the unlikely-sounding 'John Doe', the ubiquitous phantom signatory of many such bonds.

Chapter 21: William the Gold-Engraver

Burials at Abney Park Cemetery, Stoke Newington

Abney Park Cemetery in 1987, no longer used for burials and no longer owned by the Abney Park Cemetery Company, consists very largely of areas of wilderness in which brambles and other voracious plants have made gravestone hunting a next-to-impossible task. Some of the cemetery records are now at the Rose Lipman Library, but an almost complete series of interment books from 1840 onwards are kept in the cemetery office itself.

Full details of the family grave purchased by William Titford, the gold-engraver, appear in one of the volumes kept specifically for this purpose. There was no question here of the practice of 'digging up again' used by the sexton in the Baptist Burying Ground in Frome. Each time another body was laid to rest, the depth of the grave was re-calculated; so when Horace Charles Titford, eight months old, was buried on Wednesday 3 October 1877, the depth was 12 feet, reduced to six feet by 1946, four bodies and 69 years later. Space in the grave must have been fairly tight – normally only one foot in depth was allowed per body.

Fashions and practices in the disposal of the dead have changed considerably in the 20th century, of course; when Henry James Titford died, in 1967, his body was cremated.

Chapter 22: Charles Frederick

George Lambert, Citizen and Goldsmith – Charles Frederick Titford's master during his apprenticeship

Benjamin Titford (1814-79) certainly made commendable efforts to give his sons a good start in life. The man to whom young Charles Frederick Titford was apprenticed in Haymarket, George Lambert, was no run-of-the-mill backstreet goldsmith. The founder of the firm that became Messrs. Lambert of Coventry Street was Francis Lambert, son of an accoutrement maker in the Strand, who was born in 1778. He opened a shop for the sale of jewellery, and was also a manufacturer of silver plate at his premises at 11 and 12 Coventry Street. He died in 1841, and was succeeded by his youngest son, George Lambert, of whom we treat. George took his freedom in 1849, and

> Manufactures his choicest goods, as a rule, in fine or Britannia silver, following the most approved forms of English plate of the time of William III and Queen Anne, in flagons, tankards, and goblets, not disdaining, however, to follow occasionally the later style of the Adams period of decorative art. [William Chaffers, *Gilda Aurifabrorum: A History of English Goldsmiths and Plateworkers* (1883), pp. 95-6.]

By 1898, *Who's Who* carried an advertisement for:

> Lambert – Goldsmiths, Jewellers and Silversmiths to Her Majesty the Queen and the Royal Family. Largest collection of Presentation Plate in the world. Coventry Street, Piccadilly, London W.

The 1910 edition of the same work sported a photograph of the lavish Lambert premises at 10, 11 and 12 Coventry Street, together with the legend: 'Lambert: Goldsmiths, Silversmiths, & Jewellers to His Majesty the King'.

Chapter 23: Henry James the Goldmounter

Margaret Willox Archibald, wife of Henry James Titford

Margaret Titford used to say of herself that she had been born of Scottish parents, in England, on St. Patrick's Day: a cosmopolitan lady!

Chapter 24: Sidney Horace the Company Secretary

Sidney Horace Titford and his wife, Ethel May (née Buckler)

Ethel May Buckler can trace her own ancestry in the male line back to West Country roots; her ancestor Edward Buckler, one time chaplain to Oliver Cromwell, was eventually ejected from his living in Calbourne, Isle of Wight, in 1662, and the male pedigree extends back as far as John Buckler of Causeway in Dorset, alive during the reign of Edward IV.

The Bucklers appear in Heralds' Visitations for the County of Dorset, and one particularly prosperous branch settled at Boreham near Warminster, Wilts. Thus we have the slightly unnerving experience of seeing the name 'Buckler' regularly appearing in churchwardens' accounts for Warminster (and later in Nonconformist chapel records) alongside the Titfords of Warminster. Not only that, but a Buckler cousin, John Buckler (1770-1851), the most distinguished topographical artist of his day, painted a number of churches which have featured in the story of *Come Wind, Come Weather*, including those of Bratton, Steeple Ashton, Corsley and Frome.

The definitive work on the Buckler family was written in 1886; entitled *Bucleriana: notices of the family of Buckler*, it was written by Charles Alban Buckler, Surrey Herald Extraordinary, a grandson of John Buckler the artist. Indeed, the Buckler family seems to have had more than a passing interest in genealogy over the years; Benjamin Buckler, D.D., (1718-80), born in Warminster, was to become Keeper of the Archives of the University of Oxford, and was author of *Stemmata Chicheleana*, a genealogical work tracing all the families who could claim consanguinity with Archbishop Chichele, founder of All Souls College, Oxford.

Benjamin Buckler, John Buckler the artist and Charles Alban Buckler the Surrey Herald – all can trace their ancestry back to John Buckler of Causeway in Dorset.

Notes

Abbreviations

PRO   Public Record Office
SRO   Somerset Record Office
VCH   *Victoria County History*
WRO Wiltshire Record Office

Introduction

1. David Dymond, *Writing local history: a practical guide* (1981), p. 34. Gerald Hamilton-Edwards, *In Search of Ancestry* (1976), p. 10, writes in much the same vein, ' . . . however humble and simple the lives of your ancestors may have been, their story is in itself a contribution to our knowledge of the past'.
2. Quoted in 'The B.C.N. and Titford Valley', in *Boundary Post, the Journal of the B.C.N.*, p. 3. Commemorative edition for the Titford Canal restoration rally, 1974.
3. From Mawer and Stenton, *Place-names of Worcestershire* (1927), p. 299.
4. The unusually-named Ambrose Titford was baptised in Warminster on 23 March 1759, son of Thomas and Hester. He and his wife Charlotte (*née* Ironmonger) chose an even more intriguing name for their second son who became Pharaoh Titford at his baptism in the church of St Martin's in Birmingham in 1791. In the event, far from indicating ancient Egyptian origins, the name itself is nothing more exotic than a variation on 'Farrer' or 'Farrah'.
5. Equally intriguing is the question of the exact identity of a certain John Tetford or Tetsford of St Lawrence Pountney in the City of London, who left a P.C.C. will in 1421 – or of a family variously called Tetford or Thetford, seated at Catishall (or Catshall) in Hevingham, Norfolk. They would have been named after Thetford in Norfolk, presumably. (See Philpott's *Norfolk*, vol. 35, fol. 36.)
6. Details here from correspondence between Anthony R. Titford and J. R. B. Walker, Lancaster Herald, in 1967.
7. C. W. Bardsley, *Dictionary of English and Welsh Surnames* (1967), p. 754.
8. A map giving details of the wapentakes of Lincolnshire is included in H. C. Darby, *The Domesday Geography of Eastern England* (1971), fig. 2.
9. Details of Tetforthe and Baston are from *The Lincolnshire Domesday and the Lindsey Survey*, Lincs. Record Soc., vol. 19 (1921), p. lxix. Hearth Tax details are from 'Lincs. Hearth Tax', 17 Charles II, Lincoln, Kesteven, PRO E179/140/754.
10. From Eilert Ekwall, *The Concise Oxford Dictionary of English Place-Names* (1966).
11. Details of Titfords/Tetfords etc. from early Lincolnshire documents come from various publications of the Lincs. Record Soc.
12. Details from W. O. Massingberd (trans.), *Court Rolls of the Manor of Ingoldmells* (1902).
13. Early Chancery Proceedings, PRO bundle 123, vol. 3, p. 141 (1485-1500). A further Chancery case concerning a Tetford is that which mentions Jane, late the wife of Robert Tetford, together with land in Kerton, Laughton and Atterby – all north-west of Tetford, near Gainsborough. Early Chancery Proceedings, PRO bundle 228, vol. 3, p. 495 (1485-1500).
14. The will of Thomas Bruster, *Lincoln Wills*, vol. 2, p. 46 (L.C.C. 1520-31, f. 73d.).
15. Additionally, a certain 'S. Tifford' donated a copy of Gregory's *Moralia* to Merton College, Oxford, in the period 1325-60. One of the Lincolnshire Tiffords?
16. Chancery: Foster v. Titford, 1617 Chas. I, vol. 4, no. 231 (PRO).
17. Court of Arches: 1693. Refs.: B12/85; F9/41; F9/50.
18. Chancery: Oliver v. Litton, C24 783 L (PRO).
19. Details of Walter Titford are from *University of Cambridge Alumni* and the *Peterhouse Admission Book*, pp. 226, 230.
20. Rowland Parker, *The Common Stream* (1976), p. 122.

21. Information on Nottinghamshire from A. Peyton (1915), referred to in Peter Spufford 'Population mobility in pre-industrial England', part 1, in *Genealogists' Magazine*, vol. 17, no. 8 (1973), p. 420.

22. Details on William Paulet from Patent Rolls, 4 Edw. VI, part 2. In *Wiltshire Notes and Queries*, vol. 3, p. 155.

23. Chancery: Earl of Rutland and others v. Thomas Carr. PRO C21 R28/1. The manor of Bratton itself, of course, was only one such manor within the village and the surrounding area; several Westbury manors, for example, had lands in the parish of Bratton.

24. Robert, 4th Baron Willoughby de Eresby, grandfather of the John who married Sir Edmund Cheney's daughter Ann, took as his second wife a lady by the name of Margaret Zouch. The Zouch family were to have much influence and power in Derbyshire and Leicestershire over the years (witness the place-name Ashby-de-la-Zouch). But there is also a marriage allegation for a Mary Zouch of Littlecott, parish of Ramsbury, Wiltshire, issued in 1676. Ramsbury in the late 16th century was the home of a Henry Titford or Tickford, yeoman; could the Zouch family give us a link between Lincolnshire and Wiltshire – not Bratton but Ramsbury? (Allegation for the marriage of Mary Zouch and William Wadden, clerk, quoted in D. J. Steel's *National Index of Parish Registers*, vol. 1, p. 193).

25. Quotation from Cassandra, Duchess of Chandos, in A. C. Wood (ed.), *The continuation of the History of the Willoughby family*, p. 7.

26. Hungerford Rent Roll, 1609, WRO 442/2.

Chapter 1: Richard the Servant

1. Jean Morrison, *Bratton Church* (Westbury 1949).
2. *Wiltshire Notes and Queries*, vol. 3 (1902), p. 73.
3. *Ibid.*, p. 220. William of Edington's will, written in Latin, is reproduced in full in the reference. This particular extract reads: '*Item. Lego Johanni Moul, pagetto palefridorum mearum lx s.; Willemo garconi prime chariotter C s.; Johanni garconi secunde chariotter C s.*'
4. *Notes on the Priory Church of St. Mary, St. Katharine and All Saints, Edington, Wilts.* (1977).
5. *Wiltshire Notes and Queries*, vol. 3 (1902), p. 154.
6. The *Valor Ecclesiasticus* assessed the monastery's property in Edington alone to be worth £521 12s. 5½d. gross (£422 9s. 7¼d. net) and its manor of Bratton at £41 per annum. It also had other estates.
7. Before the Dissolution the church of St James, Bratton, was served by a visiting priest from the monastery at Edington; thereafter, until 1845, it had a curate or minister designated by the vicar of Westbury. The vicar of Westbury maintained that the church of St James was only a chapel of ease, while the villagers of Bratton insisted that their little church was entitled to all the rights peculiar to a parish church – including authority to undertake christenings, weddings, burials and a perambulation of the parish at Rogationtide. See Jean Morrison, *Bratton Church*.
8. Jean Morrison, *Bratton Church*.
9. The curate in 1558 who lost 'certaine christenings' was Sir Robert Hill.
10. Churchwardens' Presentments to the Precentor of Salisbury, 1597. WRO D25/12.
11. *Wiltshire Notes and Queries*, vol. 3 (1902), p. 243. John Rawlings's will was proved in the Prerogative Court of Canterbury, PRO PROB 11/63.
12. *Wiltshire Notes and Queries*, vol. 3 (1902), p. 160. No other Bratton document of this period mentions the name 'Tytworthe', but it would seem that spelling was not one of the scribe's strong points; every single name on this list being given an unconventional spelling.
13. Churchwardens' Presentments to the Dean of Salisbury, WRO D5/28 (undated).
14. Ralfe and Agnes Hevill had four children – two girls and two boys. Agnes died in 1608 and was buried in Bratton on 10 May, and Ralfe was buried on 6 May 1620.

Chapter 2: Thomas the Shoemaker

1. Churchwardens' Presentments to the Precentor of Salisbury, 1615. WRO D25/12
2. Survey of Part of Nunney, Somerset, 1597. PRO C110/36.
3. It was customary for members of the jury of the Hundred – like those selected to serve on the Grand Jury – to be chosen from freeholders with land worth more than £10 per annum, but neither Thomas nor most of his fellow-jurors were landowners of that quality. In fact only James Ballard and William

Deycon are listed as freeholders from Bratton on the Sheriff's list for 1607/8. See *Wiltshire Archaeological Magazine*, vol. 19, p. 265.

4. Details from *Minutes of Proceedings in Sessions, 1563 and 1574-92*, Wilts. Arch. Soc., vol. 4 (1949), Introduction.

5. Presentment of the Jury of the Hundred of Westbury, 1607, Quarter Sessions, WRO.

6. Somerset Quarter Sessions, 1608, SRO.

7. Presentment of the Jury of the Hundred of Westbury, 1613, Quarter Sessions, WRO.

8. Churchwardens' Presentments to the Precentor of Salisbury, 1614, WRO D25/12.

9. According to the dates of weddings and baptisms in the Bratton Parish Register, two other members of the Titford family were with child before they were married, and both escaped 'presentment'. Agnes Tutford, who married Sexton Bodman on 26 October 1607, had a daughter, Melior, baptised on 17 January 1607/8, while Alexander, son of John Nordine and Maud Titford, widow, who were married on 8 November 1621, was baptised on 17 February 1621/2. The latter event took place some time after the Pavvier indiscretion, and it is possible that 'Maud Titford, widow' was the relict of William Pavvier, having reverted to her maiden name after his death, as was the custom.

10. Churchwardens' Presentments to the Precentor of Salisbury, 1615. WRO D25/12.

11. Citations '*Quorum Nomina*', Precentor of Salisbury, 1615. WRO D25/8. While excommunication was the usual punishment for obstinacy in not appearing on a citation or not submitting to the orders and penalties of the ecclesiastical court, it was not generally appropriate for failure to attend church. See entry for 'Excommunication' in Canon J. S. Purvis, *Dictionary of Ecclesiastical Terms* (1962), p. 78.

12. Presentment of the Jury of the Hundred of Westbury, 1614 and 1615, Quarter Sessions, WRO. A 'hucker' was a common dealer or trader; 'quick fryth' was living underwood or hedgewood.

13. Payments made by churchwardens to those who destroyed vermin (and could produce the heads of their victims as proof) varied in different parts of the country. Typically a halfpenny would be paid for sparrows, three-farthings for jackdaws, twopence for snakes or hedgehogs, four pence for polecats, a shilling for foxes and badgers and two shillings for otters.

14. Churchwardens' Presentments to the Precentor of Salisbury, 1617. WRO D25/12. Growing dissatisfaction with church affairs is increasingly apparent in the presentments over the next decades. The presentment for Bratton in 1639 reads:

> We present the vicarage house and the parish church being in decay, the one to be mended by the Vicar, and the other by the parish. We present the minister for preaching and reading prayers without a licence. We present the minister for not catechising every Sunday and holy daie in his parish church.

In 1640 at least two of the villagers were to demonstrate their discontent more dramatically (for which demonstration they were, of course, 'presented'):

> Henry Boucher confessed that he committed fornication with Agnes Brown, and William Humphrey, having been excommunicated, came to church on Easter Day and disturbed the whole congregation and jeered the minister.

15. *Early Stuart Tradesmen*, Wilts. Arch. Soc., vol. 15 (1960), p. 35, entry 397. According to these Lenten Recognisances of 1620, Christopher White kept the only other licensed alehouse in Bratton that year, while the two alehouses in Steeple Ashton were kept by Christian Burges and Richard Brewer respectively.

Chapter 3: Thomas the Alehousekeeper

1. *Minutes of Proceedings in Sessions, 1563 and 1574-92*, Wilts. Arch. Soc., vol. 4 (1949), p. 44. These Minutes of Proceedings, of which the Wilts. Arch. Soc. has published a transcription, are the earliest-known surviving Sessions records in England. Unfortunately the complementary 'Great Rolls', which would have described the charge against Thomas Tytford, have not survived. The earliest known copy of the 'Great Rolls' for Wiltshire date only from 1603.

2. *Ibid.*, p. 113.

3. *Ibid.*, Introduction.

4. *Ibid.*, p. 129. Inns offered food, drink and accommodation; alehouses sold only ale or beer; taverns sold wine and were licensed by the Vintners and not by the Justices of the Peace, while tippling houses were low-class alehouses.

5. The only other licensed alehouse in Steeple Ashton at this time is shown in the *Minutes of Proceedings*

as having been kept by Henry Reynolds. There may, of course, have been other (illegal) alehouses: home brewing was popular and licences were expensive.

6. Queen Mary herself died in November 1558, reputedly of influenza. It has been estimated that one-fifth of the population of England died of disease or malnutrition between 1555 and 1560, and that the death-rate in the years 1596-8 from similar causes was of the same order.

7. In contrast to the sinister reputation of the Court of Star Chamber under the Stuarts, it had been highly popular among the poorer classes under the Tudor monarchs. Indeed, it was then known as 'the poor man's court', where a petitioner 'might have right without paying any money'. The court, which consisted of members of the Privy Council supported by some experienced judges, overawed the greatest of offenders, provided summary jurisdiction by Bill of Complaint and Answer and, like the Court of Chancery, sat without a Jury.

> In Star Chamber the most common ingredient in the complaint was the almost mechanical allegation of riot, forcible entry or assault – the relic of the fictitious '*vi et armis*' averments at common law merely translated into the vernacular pleadings of the English bill courts with the addition of suitable embellishments. Even in the Common Law Courts the claims that offences were committed *vi et armis* amounted often to legal fiction: the object was to catch the court's attention and to persuade the judges that the matter reported was within the orbit of royal jurisdiction. It is quite possible that such allegations merely cloaked a case of disputed title to real property which was brought to Star Chamber by an aggrieved party under the fiction of public disorder. [J.A. Guy, *The Court of Star Chamber and its Records to the reign of Elizabeth I* (1985), p. 26.]

The popularity of the Court of Star Chamber throughout Queen Elizabeth's reign is illustrated by the fact that, in the last 12 months of her reign, 732 suits were submitted. Between November 1601 and November 1602 112 cases of riot or unlawful assembly were considered, and no less than 18 per cent of complaints during that period were from South-west England, including Wiltshire. This was the largest number from any region.

8. Complaint of John Brewer of Steeple Ashton. Court of Star Chamber, 27 April 1602. PRO Sta. Ch. 5 (Eliz.) B46/3.

9. Survey of the Manor of Steeple Ashton, 1604. WRO 947 (Estate) 282.

10. *Minutes of Proceedings in Sessions, 1563 and 1574-92*, Wilts. Arch. Soc., vol. 4 (1949), p. 14

11. *Ibid.*, p. 3.

12. Survey of the Manor of Steeple Ashton, 1604. WRO 947 (Estate) 282.

13. *Early Stuart Tradesmen*, Wilts. Arch. Soc., vol. 15 (1960), p. 16.

14. According to the parish registers for Steeple Ashton, 'John, son of Walter Brewer' was baptised on 21 July 1577, 'Thomas, son of Walter Brewer' on 22 February 1583/4, 'Sibell, daughter of Walter Brewer' on 16 December 1589, and 'Agnes, daughter of Walter Brewer' on 12 November 1595, making them 22, 15, 10 and four respectively at the time of the affray. There is no record of the baptism of Edith. Reference to 'Thomas Brewer and Thomas his son' in the 'complaint' should clearly read '*Walter* Brewer and Thomas his son'.

15. Complaint of Francis Wallis of Westbury. Court of Star Chamber. PRO Sta. Ch. 8 (James I) 294/2.

16. *Wiltshire Archaeological Magazine*, vol. 12, p. 318 ff. In this article the Rev. Canon J. E. Jackson describes how he found the story among the papers of John Aubrey, the Wiltshire antiquary. A letter, written by one John Hoskins, serjeant-at-law to John Aubrey, reads as follows:

> London. Dec. 14. 1661 Mr. Aubrey – I have bin told that, in the time of Baron Tanfield [about 1620] there was indicted one John Brewer of Stiple Ashton for sheepstealing, who had a trick to keep the mutton sweet 7 weeks without salt, but would not tell his way to the judge – no, not at his trial. He was acquitted. Now, will you oblige me and some other of your servants if you can enquire how this was done?
> Your servant,
> John Hoskyns

Aubrey wrote immediately to Mr. Robert Beach of Steeple Ashton, who replied,

> The manner was this. Near Claverton, by Bath, in the stone quarries are some caves. And this Brewer kept his stolen sheep in the caves, *alive*. This was the secret.

17. Survey of the Manor of Steeple Ashton, Eliz. *c.* 1550. PRO LR2, vol. 191, fols. 145-158, and *Two Taxation Lists, 1545 and 1576*, Wilts. Arch. Soc., vol. 10 (1959), p. 34.

18. Churchwardens' Accounts for Steeple Ashton reproduced in *Wiltshire Notes and Queries*, vol. 7, pp. 374 ff.

19. Sir James Ley was born about 1552 in Teffont Evias, Wiltshire. Trained as a lawyer, he became Chief Justice of the King's Bench in 1620 and Lord High Treasurer of England in 1624. See Sir Richard Colt Hoare, *The History of Modern Wiltshire*, vol. 5 (1829), p. 35.

20. Manor Court Rolls for Steeple Ashton, Cambridge University Library, Oo.VII.8.

21. *Ibid.*

22. *Early Stuart Tradesmen*, Wilts. Arch. Soc., vol. 15 (1960). The name of John Brewer, butcher, does not appear amongst those engrossed for the Lenten Recognaissances of 1620.

23. Manor Court Rolls for Steeple Ashton. Cambridge University Library, Oo.VII.8.

24. John Brewer had married Alice Hales on 7 June 1600 – the year following the 'riot' – and they had three children. He died in 1626 and was buried in Steeple Ashton on 29 September that year at the age of forty-nine.

25. Henry Greenhill's estate in Steeple Ashton – which he inherited from his father, John Greenhill – was second only in extent to that of Prince Charles, the latter being Lord of the 'capital' Manor, whilst Greenhill owned the manor-house and farm. Henry Greenhill had married Anna, daughter of Jerome Potecary of Stockton in 1608 and, three years later, was co-defendant with George Webbe, the vicar of Steeple Ashton, and John Brewer in the complaint by Francis Wallis to the Court of Star Chamber. After selling his estate in Steeple Ashton in 1624 to John Bennett, Henry Greenhill may have returned to live in Stockton, where in the church there is a monument to his grandson, mentioning his career as Governor of the Gold Coast, a Commissioner in the Navy, and the founder of Devonport Dockyard.

26. Manor Court Rolls for Steeple Ashton. Cambridge University Library, Oo.VII.8.

27. *Ibid.* A 'lugg' is the same area as a square perch. A linear perch is $5\frac{1}{2}$ yards and, consequently, a square perch (or lugg) is $30\frac{1}{4}$ square yards. There are 160 luggs to the acre; Roger Winslowe thus occupied slightly under $\frac{1}{4}$ acre of land.

28. The Vestry of Steeple Ashton accumulated capital from the church collections taken after the sacrament on feast days, and this capital was available to the parishioners in the form of loans – the interest on these loans paying for the charitable gifts to the poor on St Stephen's Day. In 1626 the rate of interest was eight per cent.

29. WRO 947 (Estate) 892. It could be that the land described in this survey refers only to that on which the cottages stood, and that Roger Winslowe and Thomas Tytford also had allotments elsewhere. If so, no such allotments are mentioned in the survey.

30. If some mis-spelling in the Parish Register can be accepted, it would seem that Alice Foote died in 1633 and was buried in Steeple Ashton on 24 April that year. It is not clear, however, if John Foote then married again. A later entry in the parish register reads: 'John Foote and Sara Slade were married 3 December 1637', but this entry has been scratched out in the paper original of the register and appears neither in the later parchment copy nor in the Bishop's Transcript for that year. Amongst the christenings for the following year, however, is, 'Sara, daughter of John Foote, baptised 10 September 1638'.

Chapter 6: Richard the Yeoman

1. W. G. Hoskins, *Local History in England* (1960), p. 148.

2. The family is conspicuous by its absence in Bratton or any other Wiltshire parish in the years preceding 1547; admittedly the early entries in the Bratton parish registers lie hidden beneath an impenetrable brown staining, but neither the 1538 muster roll for the village nor the early 16th century lay subsidies reveal any Titfords whatever.

3. Whether by design or coincidence, the marriages of James Titford in 1585/6 and that of Richard in 1591/2 took place on the same date within the year: 24 January.

4. Details from the Hungerford Rent Roll of 1609 (WRO 442/2). Some tenants, like Richard, held their properties by indenture, others by 'copie' (copyhold). In an earlier Elizabethan rent roll of the Hungerfords (WRO 442/1), Richard Titford's name is added in different ink at the end of the list, presumably as a new tenant; possibly his move to Corsley was occasioned by the death of his father, Richard, in 1603?

Richard the Yeoman almost certainly held his cottage by virtue of a leasehold agreement, as did Thomas the Shoemaker in Nunney, with the property and land he took over from William Boudgett in 1596. We are witnessing here a stage in the gradual changeover from copyhold to leasehold tenure generally – an arrangement very much more profitable to any landowner, who could charge for lease renewals and for the addition of substitute 'lives' as required.

The names of the three freeholders in Corsley are given in the 'List of Wilts. Freeholders', *Wilts.*

Archaeol. Magazine, vol. 19, p. 265, quoted in Maud F. Davies, *Life in an English Village . . . Corsley* (1909), p. 20.

5. From the Court Book of the Manors of Sir Ed. Hungerford, 4 to 15 Car.1 (WRO 490/1541). Fulmore Common belonged to the Manor of Upton Scudamore, whereas Richard Titford was a tenant of the Manor of Corsley. As it happened, Sir Edward Hungerford was Lord of *both* Manors at this time, but that didn't entitle Richard to free grazing on the Common of Upton Scudamore even if, as was the case, it was virtually outside his front door! The common rights of the tenants of the Manor of Upton Scudamore – and of them alone – were clearly defined in the Hungerford Rent Roll for Corsley (WRO 442/1, and Upton Scudamore (WRO 442/2) with identical wording, and Richard was presented at the manor court of Upton Scudamore for having placed *'tris animalia equestria et sex animalia mulgibiles'* (i.e. three equestrian and six milking animals) on the common lands pertaining to that particular manor where, by Common Law, he had no common grazing rights. (Since the more usual Latin word for cow was *'vacca'*, it would seem that the clerk was a frustrated poet!)

   Some twenty-one years earlier a man called Richard Titford – but this time probably Richard Titford of Warminster – had been accused of a similar offence of trespass at Sir Thomas Thynne's Hundred Court held at Warminster in 1610 – Richard of Warminster then being a tenant of the Duchy of Lancaster's adjacent Manor of Furnaux, from which his 'cattell' strayed onto Sir Thomas Thynne's common.

   According to his will and the way in which he is described in the Chancery case of Rutland and others v. Carr of 1631, Richard Titford the Yeoman occupied a cottage in the hamlet of Fulmore – just north of Norridge Wood and at about an equal distance from the villages of Corsley and Upton Scudamore and from the market town of Warminster.

   Wilts. Notes and Queries, vol. 8, p. 80, has this to say about Fulmore:

   > At the Enclosures the outer parts of the parish were more populous than they are now. At Fulmoor Common, just north of Norridge Wood, stood five cottages which have all since disappeared . . . At Norridge still lay the hamlet which existed in the Middle Ages. In 1377 there were 16 poll tax payers there and 7 or 8 cottages still remained in 1807.

   One of these cottages at Fulmore could have been Richard Titford's dwelling house – though can we really think of it simply as a cottage? The inventory of his goods taken after his death would suggest a rather more substantial house altogether.

   The 1817 O.S. map, incidentally, along with some others of the period, shows Fulmore as 'Bullmoor'.

6. Map and Survey of the Manor of Upton Scudamore, 1804 (WRO 1741/33).

7. Enclosure Award for Westbury, 29 July 1808 (WRO 1A/V76). Plans ST8649 and ST8749 of the 1:2,500 scale O.S. map (1968 Series) show 'Titford Farm' at grid ref. ST864495, but sheet ST84 of the 1:25,000 scale map (1958 Series) merely has 'Titford', suggesting an area rather than a particular building. Even today, nearly 180 years after the Enclosure Award, many of the landmarks which defined the boundaries of the 1808 allotments are still visible on the site. The course of the Old Dilton road remains unchanged, while the 'private road' which bordered 'Titford Field' is now a public footpath. The whole of 'Titford Acre' now forms part of a larger field, but some twenty yards of the original boundary hedge of the 'tyning' can still be seen.

8. Even as late as 1840 the parishes of Corsley and Upton Scudamore were within the Hundred of Warminster (*VCH, Wilts.*, vol. 8, p. 3). The Hungerford Rent Roll for 1609 for both Corsley and Upton Scudamore Manors makes it clear that,

   > The tenants of this manor are within the jurisdiction of the Hundred of Warmister and the former allwayes by custome is to be Tethyngmen and is to Appeare at the iij weeke courte of the hundred and there to make his prsentmet at evy court or els doth fyne with the bayliffe of the hundred for his absence.

   Details of Richard Titford's attendance at the Hundred Court of Warminster and the presentments of the tythingmen of Little Corsley are to be found in Longleat House archives, Box 66H (ex-WRO 845/102).

9. From Chancery case, Earl of Rutland and others v. Thomas Carr (PRO C21 R28/1). Cecily, widow of Sir Edward Hungerford (he died in 1607), remarried Francis, 6th Earl of Rutland on 26 October 1608.

10. Details of the Carr affair from Maud F. Davies *Life in an English Village . . . Corsley*, pp. 20-1, and *VCH, Wilts.*, vol. 8, p. 16, and vol. 5, pp. 109 ff.

11. Richard the Yeoman died in the same year as his putative brother, Thomas the Alehousekeeper (buried

21 April 1632). There is possible evidence of one very early child of Richard and Katherine: 'Henry, the son of Richard Tutford' buried at Bratton on 2 June 1592. Little Henry would have been conceived some time before his parents' wedding – nothing unusual for a Titford! – but if he were Richard the Yeoman's son, he appears to have been the only child, and died very young.

12. In full, the 'Inventorie of the goods, chattels . . . Household stuff' of Richard Titford, taken on 14 September 1632, reads as follows (with one or two gaps occasioned by damaged sections of the manuscript now at the WRO):

	In the haule:	
Item	a table borde ij joinde stooles ij chairs . . . cubbord	vs.
Item	ij brass panns iiij brass ketles & ij chafing . . .	xxs.
Item	ij dozen of pewter vessels & v candlsticks	xs.
Item	an olde cubbord & ij chaires	vs.
Item	in the chiminie ij hanging pots ij andirons ij brandirons a fier pann a dripping pann & a girdiron	vis. 8d.
	(Som. . . . ij li. vjs. viijd.)	
	In the chamber where the testator laye:	
Item	a bedsted a bed with the furniture thereof	xxxs.
Item	a chest a sideborde ij cofears & a litle box	xs.
Item	ij paire of sheate	xs.
Item	all his aparell both linen & wolland	xxxs.
	(Som. . . . iiij li.)	
	In the chamber within the haule:	
Item	the bedsted bed & furniture to the same	xxs.
Item	a press in the same chamber	iijs. 4d.
Item	a bed & furniture in another chamber near the haule	vjs. viijd.
Item	in the buttrie iij barrels a powdring tub iij pailes iij other tubbs wth other old things	xs.
Item	dishes spoones & trenchers	vjd.
	(Som. . . . ij li. vjd.)	
	In the lought over the haule:	
Item	in mault	xs.
Item	in bacon	xs.
Item	in cheese	xs.
Item	xxx li of wooll xxxs.	
	(Som. . . . iij li.)	
	Cattell corne and haye:	
Item	fyve keine	x li.
Item	fyve horsbeasts & ij sucking coults	xj li.
Item	iiij yearlings	iiij li.
Item	iij piggs	ij li.
Item	xv sheepe	ls.
Item	in corn	x li.
Item	in haye	xxxs.
Item	a chattell grounde	iiij li.
Item	in the barton a cart wth the furniture	xs.
Item	a yoking stone	vs.
Item	in pultrie	xvjd.
	(Som. . . . xlv li. xvj s. iiijd.)	
TOTAL:		lvij li. iij s. vjd.

Once this inventory had been taken, the way was clear for Richard Titford's will to be proved in the Court of the Archdeacon of Sarum on 2 October 1632 (ref. Book 10, fol. 116).

Chapter 5: William and Mary

1. Although Frome had long been a cloth-making centre, this side of its activities saw a massive expansion in the early 17th century – William Titford was by no means the only person to find his way into the town in the 1620s. By 1623 ' . . . Frome hundred was already losing its rural character', there was a ' . . . great neglect of tillage upon many great farms' and ' . . . an increase in the number of people engaged in cloth-making'. (*VCH, Somerset*, vol. 2, p. 308.)

2. If marriage were an economic partnership for those from humbler families, it was even more so for those with property and wealth to preserve. Lord Cork talked angrily of his son's 'selfishness' in contemplating a marriage for love, a move which would ' . . . dash all my designs which concern

myself and my house', (quoted in Kirsty McLeod, *Drums and Trumpets: The House of Stuart* (1977), p. 36.)

3. William Titford may well have had a modest smallholding on the outskirts of Frome. If so, it was very probably a subsidiary enterprise to paid employment in the town itself – more like a modern allotment, perhaps.

4. Quoted in Roger Hart, *English Life in the Seventeenth Century* (1970), p. 73.

5. Magistrates were enjoined by the Statute of Artificers to modify wages ' . . . according to the plenty or scarcity of the times'.

6. Adam Smith, quoted in S. T. Miller, *Society and the State, 1750-1950* (1979), p. 120.

7. Michael McGarvie, *The Book of Frome* (1980), p. 75.

8. The same plague epidemic which had forced the Phillipses from London killed at least one Titford there in that same year of 1625: John Titford buried, dead of the plague, at St Margaret's, Westminster, 24 June 1625.

9. It would be less than fair, at this point, not to admit that there is doubt as to who precisely William's parents were. There are essentially three most likely candidates as father for our man, as follows:

a. Thomas the Shoemaker of Bratton. What we do discover in the Titford family with some degree of regularity is a naming pattern used for male children, whereby the eldest born son is named after his paternal grandfather; additionally the second son may bear the name of his maternal grandfather, leaving a third male child to take his father's name, if that has not already been used. Such a system is nothing unusual in Scotland, for example, but it was also surprisingly common amongst some English families until at least the early 19th century. What may appear to be a compliment to the paternal grandfather by naming the first son after him will often turn out to be the result of his role as the child's *godfather* rather than *grandfather per se*. If this naming pattern existed from the outset in Frome, then William Titford, married in 1625 and with an eldest son Thomas born in 1628/9, would himself be the son of a Thomas. Thomas the Shoemaker of Bratton seems a very likely candidate: his death in 1624 may have precipitated William's departure to Frome, where he married one year later. If Thomas the Shoemaker were a copyholder, then his security of tenure would have died with him. The Lord of the Manor could demand a heavy fine from the incoming heir, who might be forced to pay up or see the land handed over to someone else. Perhaps William lost out in this way? At least we can propose that it was probably not enclosure which drove him away – since ' . . . at Bratton there seems to have been but little inclosure of either pasture or arable by the middle of the 18th century'. *VCH Wilts.*, vol. 8, p. 167.)

b. Thomas the Alehousekeeper of Steeple Ashton. Another Thomas of course, but perhaps a less likely candidate as the father of William, if only because some of the other factors mentioned above would not apply.

c. Henry Titford. There is a William Titford, son of Henry Titford, christened in Sutton Veny, Wilts., on 23 April 1600. For reasons more of geographical proximity than anything else, we have assumed this to be that William who was starting a family in Wylye, Wilts., in 1622/3, a contemporary of William of Frome. But there are two significant burials in Frome in the 1630s: 'Henry Titfoord' (30 January 1633/4) and Joan Titford (7 September 1635). It is clear from the churchwardens' receipts for the Great Bell that this Joan is a widow. We might here be looking at a husband and wife, possibly Henry Titford and Joan (*née* Henton), married at Bratton on 24 April 1582 – perhaps they were William's parents?

Whatever may be the case here, one very likely explanation for the lack of any baptismal record for William Titford himself is that he was very possibly born during the period when the curate of Bratton was neglecting his duties, from June 1595 to March 1597. The lack of unequivocal proof certainly makes what we may term a provable pedigree impossible to establish; where we hope the reader will agree with us is in the belief that the general shape of the wood is clear, even if the trees within it are not.

10. The charge for ringing the 'Great Bell' at a decease or a funeral in Frome was 1s. from 1567 and for at least a century afterwards. In 1608 it was ordered that the clerk should only allow the bell to be rung if he was paid in advance – and that ' . . . the clarke doe nimbly make payment to the churchwardens'. See Samuel Cuzner, *Handbook to Froome Selwood* (1866), p. 22.

11. Roy Palmer, *A Ballad History of England* (1979), p. 16.

12. Quoted in Palmer, *ibid.*, p. 17.

13. If the Titfords were Baptists as early as the mid-17th century they may, of course, have been married before the congregation with no further religious or civil ceremony. Both the Civil Wars and the Commonwealth had a deleterious effect upon parish record-keeping: in the event a number of Titford registrations did manage to survive it all. The period from the beginning of the Civil War in 1642 up to the appointment of 'Parish Registers' on 29 September 1653, gives us three Titford baptisms, one burial and no marriages in Frome. From 1653 until the Restoration of 1660 we find two births (registered as such, of course, and not as baptisms), two burials (not deaths, but listed as '*sepult.*') and the one marriage – of Thomas Titford and Joan Newport in 1655. Interestingly, receipts for the 'Great Bell' reveal that at least one burial – that of 'Mari Titford' in 1648 – did not find its way into the registers.

Chapter 6: Thomas and Margery

1. John West, *Village Records* (1962 edn.), p. 131.
2. As a generalisation, we may say that households with one hearth were those of labouring people; those with two, those of slightly more prosperous labourers or larger plebeian families. From the Hearth Tax evidence which exists, it would seem that 75 per cent of England's 5.5 million people in the late 17th century were labouring people. For further details see R. W. Malcolmson, *Life and Labour in England, 1700-1780* (1981).

   The list of those exempt from Hearth Tax in Frome in 1670 contains no Titfords, oddly enough, though two members of the family are probably lurking hidden within some eccentric spelling which gives us 'Tho. Petford' and 'Mary Pitford'. What is also perhaps rather strange is that William Titford senior, exempt from the tax in 1674, was indeed 'rateable to church and poor', having been rated by the churchwardens for his house in the Cheap Street area since as early as 1668. If he paid rates, he should have paid Hearth Tax; the fact that he didn't serves to underline the degree of evasion which was going on – connived at or not by those charged with collecting the tax. Frome Hearth Tax details are from E. Dwelly, *Directory of Somerset*, part 4 (1932).

   Twenty years after the Hearth Tax assessment of 1674, the Marriage Duties Act (1694) involved a similar degree of legalised prying into people's homes. Passed in an attempt to raise revenue for the war against France, the Act imposed a tax on births, marriages and deaths, together with a charge levied on all bachelors over 25 and widowers without children. Lists of inhabitants were drawn up – most such lists, by now, long since lost – but the Act seems to have been widely ignored and evaded, and it would not be surprising if the Titfords escaped scot-free while it lasted (1694-1706).

Chapter 7: Henry of Southwark

1. Peter Belham, *The Making of Frome* (1973), p. 75.
2. One other male Titford appears in the registers for St Saviour's during this period: John, a waterman, whose wife Elizabeth was buried in 1662.

Chapter 8: William the Wiredrawer

1. We need not necessarily identify 'Cheep Street' exactly with the present street of that name in the town; admittedly this was the oldest trading street in Frome, but the term does appear to have been used in rate assessment lists to define a larger area, lying immediately south of the River Frome.

   William Titford the 1668 ratepayer could, in the event, be William, junior; the father would be aged approximately seventy, the son thirty-three in that year.
2. Some of the 'mahimed souldiers' were quite likely ex-Royalist troops: how some Frome worthies must have baulked at paying their rates that year!
3. Churchwardens' and overseers' accounts – the latter liberally sprinkled with what were more properly the parish constable's reckonings – were written up in separate books. Where entries exist for the same year in each series – and this was not always the case – then the information included for ratepayers (location of properties, rates paid) is nearly always identical in both sets of accounts. The overseers' accounts have much additional information on disbursements to paupers, etc.
4. From 'Wade's Narrative', quoted in W. MacDonald Wigfield, *The Monmouth Rebellion* (1980), p. 168.

The same author has a 'Roll-call of Monmouth's Army', containing roughly four thousand names, including 33 from Frome. No Titfords appear amongst them.

In 1985 the Somerset Record Society published *The Monmouth Rebels* (S.R.S., vol. 79). Over 50 names of Frome men are included, many of them 'presented' by the churchwardens of the town for 'a riot and among the Clubmen' – that is, those who opposed the Earl of Pembroke and the Wiltshire Militia when they entered Frome on 25 June 1685. In spite of the reputation of the 'Bloody Assizes', not one of the men of Frome allegedly involved in the rebellion would seem to have been executed.

There are seven wiredrawers and eight cardmakers among the Frome rebels, including a certain Joseph Bedford, cardmaker, who was very probably the ancestor, possibly the father, of the Joseph Bedford who married Ann Titford in Frome in 1715/6.

5. Arthur Mee, *The King's England: Somerset* (1945), p. 12.
6. The original eight Titford houses on Coward's Batch – later Fountain Lane (so called because of a nearby spring) – are mentioned by Michael McGarvie in *The Book of Frome*, p. 95, 'The Widow Titford had eight houses in Coward's Batch the same year' (1694). This is almost certainly 'William Titford', not 'Widow Titford', in the event.

Through the rate books (both overseers' and churchwardens'), the rentals for St Katherine's Manor (1735 and 1753) and the land tax returns from 1766 onwards, it is possible to make some attempt at tracing the owners, leaseholders and occupiers of this set of houses for the next hundred years or so. What emerges is that a series of men who married Titford girls ended up by occupying or leasing ex-Titford property at some stage or other.

7. We are working here on the assumption that the property in question is what is now no. 76 Selwood Road, a three-storey building. But the 1753 rental for St Katherine's Manor (the original now in Longleat House), laid out, as it is, street by street, would suggest nos. 77 or 78 as alternative candidates for the Lacy/Titford house.

William, son of William the Wiredrawer, was aged 17 at the time of the original lease. The close association between the Lacy and Titford families here would suggest a possible marriage relationship between the two of them: possibly William's wife, Margaret, was born a Lacy? Later, in 1732/3, William the Wiredrawer's son Thomas, was to marry Sarah Lacey. (The original indenture of 1725 on this property, referring back to 1699, is at SRO, ref. DD/X/NNT 26.)

Chapter 9: Ralph the Pauper

1. To be including an organised list of paupers in 1700 was not entirely due to the overseers' own meticulousness; an Act of 1691 (3 W & M c.11) had ruled that a register of parishioners in receipt of poor relief be kept. It had taken nine years for the act to be obeyed in Frome, it seems.
2. Details here are from W. E. Tate, *The Parish Chest* (3rd edn., 1979), p. 193.
3. R. Dunning, *Plain and Easy method of showing how the office of Overseer of the Poor may be managed* (1686), p. 13, quoted in Eleanor Trotter, *Seventeenth Century Life in the Country Parish* (1919), p. 80.

Chapter 10: William the Emigrant

1. Quoted in R. W. Malcolmson, *Life and Labour in England, 1700-1780* (1981), pp. 11, 12.
2. King's 'Scheme of the Income & Expense of the several Families of England Calculated for the Year 1688', indicates his belief that there were then 60,000 families in the category 'Artizans & handycrafts', and that each of the persons so employed had an average annual income of £10, matched by an annual expenditure of £9 10s. All that, if accurate, would give credence to the view that a typical artisan was financially, and possibly socially, closer to the employers than he was to those who were 'Labourg. People & outservts.' on an annual income of £4 10s. (R. N. Rundle, *Scenes from Stuart England, 1660-1714* (1978), p. 57.)
3. The fact that Katherine Dicks shares the same surname (albeit with a different spelling) as Margaret Dix, second wife of Henry Titford of Southwark may or may not be a coincidence.
4. Settlement certificates to cover permanent moves had been allowed by an Act of 1697 (8 & 9 W.III c.30), the Act itself being referred to on William Titford's 1711 certificate as 'an Act for the supply of some defects in the Lawes for the Relife of the poor of this Kingdome'.

The two settlement certificates issued to William Titford are now at the Kent Archives Office: that of 1710/1 to Hawkhurst (ref. P178/13) and that of 1745 to Cranbrook (ref. P100/13/1/94).

Chapter 11: Thomas the Calvinist

1. Pettus, *Words Metallic*, quoted in *VCH Somerset*, vol. 2, p. 425.
2. *Commons Journal*, 21 Jan. 1711.
3. From the original petition, House of Lords Record Office.
4. See note 15.
5. Quoted in Michael McGarvie, *The Book of Frome* (1980), pp. 94, 96.
6. Quoted in *ibid.*, p. 96
7. A measure of the difficulty encountered when relying upon the unadorned statements in parish registers to construct a pedigree may be gauged from the fact that this burial of a 'Thomas Tittford' could refer to an adult. But if so, to whom?
8. Two members of the Pollard (or Pollett or Pawlett) family from Podimore seem to have found the idea of marrying Titford girls from Frome an attractive prospect. Podimore Milton is a small and rather remote hamlet nestled around its parish church, two and a half miles north-east of Ilchester and not far from the Dorset border. The brothers William and John Pollard were both baptised there, the sons of John Pollard and Judith.

   William, baptised in Podimore in 1696/7, married Martha Titford in Frome on 16 April 1723. Martha herself had been born in 1702, the daughter of Will and Martha Titford; her father was very probably William, son of Ralph the Pauper, though no marriage entry for a William Titford and Martha has yet come to light.

   Although William Pollard and Martha married in Frome, on the bride's home territory, both of them were deemed thereafter to be officially settled in the husband's parish, a fact which accounts for a settlement certificate issued on their behalf by the churchwardens and overseers of Podimore on 10 March 1723/4. The certificate – handwritten, as most of them were at that period – allowed the pair of them to live in Frome. (Ref. SRO DD/LW/18.) William appears in the 1735 rental for St Katherine's Manor in Frome, paying 2s. 'for Titford', and is subsequently listed as a ratepayer in the town from 1736/7 until 1767 – charged from 1754 onwards for a house 'not of this parish'. (Perhaps it was within Frome but part of Marston Bigot parish?) The dearth period of 1766/7 caused enough suffering in Frome without the need to support outsiders with settlement certificates, so by 1768 poor William Pollard was back home in Podimore in receipt of parish relief of 1s. 6d. In 1772 the overseers' accounts paid 'Wm. Pollett for a pair of britches: 4s. 6d.', followed by a regular sum of 2s. a week and, in 1773: 'Paid Mr. John Dove's Bill for a new coat for William Pollett – 11s. 4d. and pair of breeches – 4s.'. William was afforded very generous treatment during this period, until 1780 when all payments cease. (Ref. SRO 13/2/1.)

   The first two of William and Martha Pollard's children were baptised in Frome, but a further five appear in the Podimore baptismal register from 1730/1 to 1741, even though the parents were apparently living in Frome at the time. Perhaps the Frome overseers were wary of such children being baptised within their parish for fear of them claiming a spurious settlement there? Two of the sons were apprenticed 'to husbandry' in Podimore: young William 'for and in respect of the parsonage' in 1741, and his brother Thomas 'for and in respect of the estate of William Ganne, Clerk' on exactly the same day. Both would serve until they were 24 years of age. Another son, Stephen Emmery Pollett, would become a thatcher, while son James, like his father, needed parish relief in 1768. After a single payment of 6s. 3d., the parish paid out a very considerable sum for his funeral and a bit of refreshment for the mourners: 'For a shroud and making for James Pollett, 6s. 4d.; for bread and chees when he was laid out 1s. 2½d.; for a cofin for same 8s.; for digging the grave and ringing the bells 2s.'. (SRO 13/2/1.) The little parish was being lavish indeed, here, with its ratepayers' money.

   Martha Pollard's own mother, Martha Titford, was to find her last resting place in Podimore; she was buried there on 12 October 1729 – possibly just visiting her daughter and son-in-law for the baptism of their daughter Judith, or else seeking refuge from the ravages of disease in Frome at this most dangerous period in the late 1720s. The long arm of pestilence, however, would seem to have reached out to touch Podimore, remotely sited as it was.

   What of William Pollard's brother John? He had been baptised in 1704, and married 'Margaret Titford' in Frome on 29 September 1731. This Margaret is almost certainly the daughter of William the Wiredrawer and Margaret, baptised in Frome in 1686. That made her old at marriage, 45, but she wasn't a bad prospect, for all that, as she had taken over a little house in Coward's Batch when her mother died in 1728. From 1734 John Pollard is paying rates on the house – 'Late Widow Titford's' – and he continued to do so until his death in 1749. They appear to have had no children – hardly surprising, in view of Margaret's age. Margaret herself had left Badcox Lane Chapel for Sheppards Barton, in 1726, just at the time of Mr. Roberts's arrival at Badcox. She is given in the Sheppards Barton Chapel Members' List for 1742, and was receiving financial support from them from the time of her husband's death in 1749 until June 1759. She and John Pollard appear to have worshipped at different chapels, as it happens; he had joined Badcox Lane from the Starve Acre meeting, being baptised into his new congregation on 15 March 1740/1.

9. We need not necessarily assume that Stephen Humphries physically ocupied the ex-Titford house for which he was paying both rent and rates. A more attractive prospect as a home for himself and Mary would have been his 'House, large Workhouse, Stable, Garden and 2 Cott. in Conigar', just round the corner. Alternatively, by 1753 he was also paying rent for 'A House late Gregory's Corner house against Bell Lane' and 'A House behind the former'. He was still being charged – this time for Land Tax – in 1766 and 1767 on 'Dellg. Ho., Connigar' as well as 'Titfords Cowards Batch Adams's'.

10. Details on this High Street property are from an original set of indentures now in the possession of Sheppards Barton Baptist Chapel, Frome.

11. There are times, even in tracing a rare surname, when all the accumulated evidence of parish register entries, rate and rent books, indentures and chapel minute books fail to throw up an unequivocal pedigree. We might invent various permutations to explain Thomas Titford's rather abrupt disappearance from the ratepayers' lists from High Street: perhaps this Thomas had died, leaving a son Thomas to appear in the chapel minutes and marry Rebekah Coles in 1763? Such a death could have occurred round about 1744, the year in which Stephen Humphries is first paying rates 'late Tittfords' on Cowards Batch and Mrs. Sheppard takes over the High Street house(s), also 'late Tittfords'. And who, we might ask, is the 'John Titford' paying the Coward's Batch rates in 1743 (a mistake for Thomas?) or 'Titford ye younger' charged at 2s. in the 1735 St Katherine's Manor rental?

Or maybe Thomas built his High Street house(s) at a time (1737) when he had a wife but no children to support. Only later, starting with son William in 1738, does he seem to have fathered a number of little Titfords; the expense of their upbringing may have left him unable to meet rent and rate demands, causing him to transfer his lease back to the Sheppards, the owners of the land. He had already let the last Cowards Batch property go to Stephen Humphries, and could leave his own male offspring no leasehold houses to inherit. It this were the case, he might well have stayed in High Street as a tenant; the 1767 Land tax returns include an entry which reads: 'Wm. Sheppard. House late Wayland. T. Titford & ... [blank] 4s. 6d.'. Thomas, it would seem, was still there as an occupier, as was a William Titford (Thomas's son?) in the rates list of 1800.

There are permutations enough, then, without pursuing in detail any further possibilities such as illness, unemployment or hard times. The wool trade in Frome had indeed been in a shaky state in the 1730s, and even in 1741 about 1,000 unemployed young men enlisted in the first two weeks of the War of the Austrian Succession, seeking marginally better times elsewhere. There was an upturn in trade, however, by the middle 1740s – can Thomas really have been impoverished or out of work at this time? Our ancestors will keep some of their secrets, delve as we may; the best the family historian can do is to approach the possibilities with honesty and a degree of objectivity, taking the most promising alternative and using it as a working hypothesis. This is what the text of this family history attempts to do.

12. Anthony R. Titford, a direct descendant of Charles Titford of Cranbrook, had for many years been in possession of a piece of paper headed 'From Charles Titford's Register', but it was only in 1984 that he unearthed the original register in Cranbrook Museum.

The register had had a chequered history; early in the 20th century a man called Ben Jameson saw it lying on the floor when some second-hand books he had bought were being carted away.

> Then it was that I saw laying upon the floor what I took at first for a piece of worn brown paper folded into the size of a small octavo sheet. I stooped to pick it up ... and then discovered it to be a simple home-made book. Across its cover, rough and of cork-like texture, was written in a laboured hand 'Charles Titford' ...

Ben Jameson, luckily for us, was fascinated by this little book, written by a man of whom he wrote,

> He probably sweated and sowed that others might reap and eat and passed away leaving nothing by which to be remembered after 200 years than the simple old diary which is in my hand as I write.

Jameson both preserved the register for posterity, and also wrote an article about it in the *Kentish*

Express of 17 August 1918, from which the above quotations are taken. He thought it appropriate to celebrate the 200th anniversary of Charles Titford's birth, and called his article 'A Cranbrook Bi-Centenary'.

Charles began his 'Regester Book' a month after his marriage, on 23 May 1747, prompted, perhaps, by his new bride, whose own father Isaac Ballard had kept a register. That register, too, has survived through the years, and includes an entry for his daughter Frances's wedding: 'My daughter Frances was married to Charls Titford in Cranbrook Church Ap:22d. 1747'. Isaac Ballard (1692-1782) and his family, like the Titfords of Cranbrook, were deeply-committed Baptist believers. Charles Titford's register, then, begins: 'According to my father and mother's account, I was born the 6th. day of Janñuary in the year 1717/8'.

His account of his journey to Frome runs as follows:

> April the 12th., 1746. Set out to Froome; stayd a week in London; got to Froom the 26th.; taken with the small pox the 3rd. of May; came out the 7th. and so on till ye 10th.; turned the 15th., from which dreadful crosid [?crisis] it was please God to rise me, and I come home the 5th. July, 1746.

We cannot be sure that Charles's journey to Frome was to collect his father's settlement certificate, but with some poetic licence have assumed this to be the case.

13. See the diary of Jeffrey Whittaker of Bratton, Wilts., quoted in Marjorie Reeves, *Sheep bell and ploughshare* (1978), p. 21, '11th. June, 1740: mobbing at Froom about Corn'.

14. Cole and Postgate (*The Common People, 1746-1946* (1976), p. 87) succeed in giving what amounts to a thumb-nail sketch of Thomas Titford almost by accident: 'The skilled craftsman knew how to read and write. He was quite commonly a Dissenter, attending the same chapel with his employer'. The Sheppards of Frome attended Sheppards Barton Baptist Chapel for the most part, rather than Badcox Lane. The Titford family might be found in either congregation.

15. The exact nature of Humphries's properties, ex-Titford, on Coward's Batch is made clear in the May 1753 rental for St Katherine's Manor: 'Stephen Humphrys. A house shop etc. late Titfords. Yearly rent: £5; Quit rent: 5s. Adjoining Coward's Batch or Barton'. (Original rental now at Longleat House, Box 29.)

16. Rowland Parker in *The Common Stream* (1976) (p. 153) speaks of,

> . . . the Archdeacon, backed by the Bishop, vigorously striving to maintain ecclesiastical control over matters which, in many cases, ought really to have been left to the individual consciences and common-sense of the parishioners. The result was a constant niggling, backbiting, prying into private affairs, which did not raise moral standards one little bit, rather the reverse.

Although we might associate detailed presentments by the churchwardens to the Archdeacon or the Bishop with 17th-century parish life, the Frome vestry was still muck-raking as late as 1708:

> Order in vestry: We . . . do consent that William Carpenter and Hester Beard, of this parish, be prosecuted henceforward for their incontinent and adulterous living . . . and we also agree to the prosecution of Joan Ray for ye disturbance she makes in ye church at ye time of Divine Service, 30th October 1708.
> 1714: Paid Mr. Brown, of Wells, for prosecuting Farmer Carpenter and Hester Beard. £2 8s. 0d. (Quoted in: Samuel Cuzner, *Cuzner's hand book to Froome Selwood* (1866), p. 49.)

The church, too, it should be remembered, demanded its tithes and its rents, its fees for baptisms, marriages and burials and its Easter offerings; it was hardly in a position in the circumstances to ingratiate itself with its poorer parishioners in any way whatever. Little wonder that so many left it behind as soon as they were able.

17. Quoted in J. H. Whiteley, *Wesley's England* (4th edn., 1954), p. 256.

18. 1689 itself gives us our first specific reference to a member of the Titford family with a clear Nonconformist allegiance; in that year a 'Mr. Titford' preached at the Old Meeting, Warminster, an Independent congregation. Whether the gentleman in question belonged to the Warminster branch of the family or was an errant son from Frome we cannot be sure. See Jerom Murch, *A history of the Presbyterian and General Baptist Churches in the West of England with some of their Pastors* (1835), p. 88.

19. From the Badcox Lane Church Memorandum Book, 1734-43. There are three such memorandum books for Badcox covering the 18th century, viz. 1734-43, 1743-61, 1762-1801. All the books are currently in the possession of Bristol Baptist College.

20. Title page of the church book, 1727.

21. Churchwardens' presentments, Dilton, Wilts. 17th century. WRO.

22. The statistics here are from Barry Coward, *The Stuart Age: a History of England, 1603-1714* (1980).

23. Robert Moss, *The Providential Division of Men into Rich and Poor* (London 1708). Quoted in R. W. Malcolmson, *op. cit.*, p. 14.

24. William Paley quoted in S. T. Miller, *Society and the State, 1750-1950* (1979), p 5.

25. 'Decent mediocrity' – a phrase from Overton and Relton, *History of the English Church*, vol. 7, p. 212. Quoted in Rev. Percy Dearmer, *Everyman's History of the English Church* (1909), p. 134.

26. Mentioned in Arthur H. Coombs, *A history of Badcox Lane Baptist Church, Frome* (1924), p. 12. 'Pilly Hill' is now effectively Willow Vale. In the early days of the Baptist movement in England, it was the Particular Baptists who had first begun the practice of believers' baptism by total immersion. Their General Baptist colleagues later followed suit.

27. Roberts's departure followed by the arrival of Thomas Hurne in 1740 changed the face of things at Badcox Lane; round the corner at Sheppards Barton, the following year was to see the death of William Hendy, 'a worthy good man' on 1 September (aged 71). He was replaced by Edward Henwood, 'a fluent and eloquent preacher', who had been assisting the older man since 1733. (Details from the Sheppards Barton Church Members' List and Accounts).

28. 'Soon after 1700 a Baptist Chapel had been provided on the Waste at Crockerton, where Five Ash Lane joins the Warminster Road. The first Minister was Mr. John Clark of Frome, who used to walk the distance of seven miles every Sunday to conduct the Service, wet or fine, sunshine or snow, and who died at the age of ninety-two'. (Frederick Myatt (ed.), *The Deverill Valley* (1982), p. 111.) John Clark of Frome had served the needs of Crockerton; now in 1740 Crockerton was able to repay the debt, by releasing Thomas Hurne.

29. Whatever James Roberts's faults may have been, he does seem here to have been the victim of a small-scale witch-hunt. For an insight into similar Puritan games where the stakes are higher, the reader is, of course, referred to Arthur Miller's *The Crucible*.

    We should not assume, either, that Sharpe was as gentle as a lamb. The Gifford affair in London reveals one side of his character, and he certainly had the knack of making enemies for himself. In 1730 he received letters threatening to murder him, 'burne his house in the Night' and pull down his meeting house unless he would give Mr. Roberts possession of it (see Arthur H. Coombs, *op. cit.*, p. 8). Eight years earlier, in 1722, Sharpe had been invited to act as a visiting minister, once a month, at the Baptist chapel at Southwick, over the Wiltshire border. Here he encountered his usual smattering of adversaries, so much so that on one occasion a certain Mr. John Greenhill seized the key of the meeting house to lock him out when he came again. See W. Doel, *Twenty Golden Candlesticks!: A history of Baptist Nonconformity in Western Wiltshire* (1890), p. 104.

30. L. G. Champion, *Farthing Rushlight: the story of Andrew Gifford 1700-1784* (1961), p. 38. Connections between Eagle Street Chapel and Badcox Lane seem to have been healthy even in the 19th century. John and Mary Lacey moved there from Frome by letters of dismission of 11 September 1809, and William Elliot, departing on 14 December 1817, is described in these terms: 'Now an itinerant preacher, 1825, to the church in Eagle Street, London'. (Details from the Badcox Lane Chapel Memorandum Book, begun in 1807.)

31. Starve Acre, later Union Street, ran south-west of Vallis Way. In the 18th and 19th centuries Frome could boast not only some substantial Baptist chapels, but also a number of subsidiary 'meetings' dotted round the town.

32. Church meeting, Thursday, 28 October 1742.

33. Church meeting, 8 July 1742.

34. From S. Tuck, *Methodism in Frome*, quoted in Coombs, *op. cit.*, p. 13.

35. The two references here to Mary Titford are from the First Church Minute Book of the Eagle Street Church, 1737-85, now at the Baptist Union Library, London.

36. An entry in the chapel minute book six years earlier, in 1751, indicates that Susannah Thatcher was received by letter from Southwark; clearly, links with the capital were fairly well forged.

37. Mary, literate where her new husband was not, does not reflect the national trend of the period. It has been estimated that in the population at large in the 1750s, about sixty-three to sixty-four per cent of women and forty per cent of men were unable (or some perhaps unwilling?) to sign their names in the marriage register. (See R. W. Malcolmson, *op. cit.*, p. 95.) Provincial towns, like Frome, boasted more literacy than country parishes at this period. Joseph Elliot himself, literate or not, would eventually become the leaseholder on ex-Titford properties in Fountain Lane/Cowards Batch.

38. We might find nothing particularly reprehensible about a man in his 70s, widowed and in need of a

bit of comfort and domestic tranquillity, taking a young wife – but such a liaison may well have attracted more than a little censure from some of their contemporaries. The people had their own way of setting moral standards independently of the established law, and an old bridegroom with a young wife – especially if he looked set to let her dominate him – ran the risk of being lampooned and cold-shouldered.

At worst, outraged neighbours might organise what was known variously as 'rough music' or the 'charivari' – and often referred to in the West Country as a 'skimmington'. An effigy of the offender against moral custom might be carried through the streets, then burnt, accompanied by a general caterwauling, ringing of cow bells, banging of warming pans and salt boxes and the like (see Thomas Hardy's *The Mayor of Casterbridge*).

One hopes that Thomas and Rebekah did not suffer any such fate; any view we might choose to hold on the subject must, in any case, be tempered by the knowledge that one in four of all 18th-century wedding ceremonies constituted a remarriage for one or other of the partners. The need to re-establish the domestic economy shattered by the death of a husband or wife was, of course, a paramount consideration.

If the hypothesis suggested later in this chapter is correct – that Thomas the Calvinist had a series of children by his marriage to Sarah Lacey – then Thomas would have been in some desperate need of a woman about the house to help look after at least three teenage children: Charles, aged 13-14; John, 12-13; Sarah, maybe no older than nine.

39. Badcox Lane Chapel was the only congregation to have its own burial ground; it was opened in about 1745.
40. Note that Rebekah is referred to, for some strange reason, as 'Eliz.', perhaps the result of a confusion of 'Becky' and 'Betty'?
41. The overseers' copy of the indenture putting John Woolly apprentice to Thomas Cray is to be found in the Settlement Papers for Frome now at SRO, ref. DD/LW/16 (Lewis papers).
42. Zion Chapel was founded by a group of Wesleyan Methodists known as 'The Calvinistic Class' in 1773. See W. J. Harvey, *The story of Zion Congregational Church, Frome* (1918).
43. A short series of court rolls for Frome Vicarage is extant for the 17th century (PRO), and Longleat House holds many court records for the Thynne family's manors in Frome East and West Woodlands. What no-one had yet been able to track down are the records for the main manor of Frome itself.
44. Rentals, leases, rate books – all refer only to a Thomas Titford; the only other significant possibility here is that at some stage or other an older Thomas gives way imperceptibly to a younger one – perhaps the son born in 1718? For the record, Thomas born in 1718, if he reached adulthood, would almost certainly have been too young to marry, say, Sarah Lacey in 1723/3, though quite definitely of an age – 44 – to be the Thomas who married Rebekah Coles in 1763. The picture would not be complete without such a secondary thesis being mentioned, albeit in passing.
45. William Charles Titford and William Jowett Titford, then, the grandson and great-grandson respectively of two brothers (Thomas and William) were thus second cousins, once removed.

Chapter 12: William the Cardmaker

1. Burn, *History of the Poor Law*, p. 121, quoted in Tate, *The Parish Chest*, p. 197.
2. 1744 was a bad year generally for those who fancied a change of scenery and a fresh parish of residence; it saw the passing of an Act (17 Geo. III c.5) whereby a justice was empowered to have vagrants conveyed, after interrogation, to the place of their last legal settlement.
3. Details from the original Removal Order. Longleat House Archives, Box 31.
4. Details from Orchardleigh Muniments, SRO, ref. DD/DU/14.
5. James Woodforde, *The Diary of a Country Parson*, ed. J. Beresford (1978), p. 70.
6. *Ibid.*, p. 73. Another excellent source for the extremes of late 18th century weather is Gilbert White, *The natural history of Selborne*. White talks of the frost of January 1768, as being 'the most severe that we had then known for many years ... the Thames was at once so frozen over both above and below bridge that crowds ran about on the ice'. (*op. cit.* (Penguin edn., 1977), pp. 253, 259) Predictably two Titford deaths followed almost immediately: William lost a child who was buried on 9 February, and Thomas Titford's second child was buried on 24 February.
7. A pyramid of society in the United Kingdom by Patrick Colquhoun, reflecting social classes at the end

of the Napoleonic Wars, places 'Shopkeepers and Hawkers' surprisingly high in the structure – above Master Craftsmen and Manufacturers, Lesser Freeholders, Farmers and Teachers, Actors, Clerks and Shopmen. Only then do we come across the category which would include cardmakers: 'Artisans and other skilled workers'. He calculates that shopkeepers and their dependants numbered 600,000 with artisans at 4,500,000. Perhaps he is thinking here of more grand shopkeepers than a humble butcher and cheesemonger like Charles Titford? For details see G. D. H. Cole and Raymond Postgate, *The Common People, 1746-1946* (1976).

8. W. E. Tate, *The Parish Chest*, p. 80.

9. *Ibid.*, p. 194.

10. Sir Frederick Norton Eden, *The State of the Poor* (1797), quoted in Michael McGarvie, *Frome through the Ages* (1982), p. 106.

11. As an indicator of just how little 2s. 6d. per fortnight might have been in real terms in the late 18th century, we might look at a table of wages for the period which appears in Cole and Postgate's *The Common People*, p. 76. It gives the daily wage of a craftsman ('chiefly skilled building operatives') in the West of England in 1790 as 2s. 4d. In other words William Titford was trying to survive on almost the same sum per *fortnight* as other craftsmen were earning per *day*.

Chapter 13: Thomas the Cardmaker

1. 1785 saw a census of the town, bearing the title *A particular Account of the number of Families & Inhabitants Within the Town and Parish of Froome Selwood*. A copy of the census, probably made by John Battle in 1789, turned up in West Woodlands in the 1980s; photocopies may be consulted at the Frome Museum or at the SRO in Taunton.

   It would seem that Thomas Titford was here occupying one of the original Titford houses on Fountain Lane, just as his brother William was apparently in an ex-Titford property on High Street. Thomas's house, indeed, is not hard to pinpoint: it was that property including a workshop which Thomas the Calvinist had leased before his move to High Street. Stephen Humphries had taken over the lease by 1744, with Mr. Adams later listed as an occupier in the Land Tax returns of 1766 and 1767. Adams himself had become the leaseholder – Thomas the Cardmaker's landlord – by the time of the 1785 census. Thereafter Mrs. Hellier took over from Adams. The Titford connection with the properties was thus continuous from the time they were built in the 1690s; members of the family or their in-laws were leaseholders and/or occupiers for over a hundred years.

2. i.e. 'grass widow'.

3. From Sheppards Barton Chapel Poor Book, in the possession of the present chapel.

4. Mary's affliction was very probably a form of epilepsy. Her chances of gainful employment may have been slim indeed; Parson Woodforde felt constrained to get rid of his servant-maid in the September of 1791 because she was 'subject to bad fits'. He was sorry to do it, ' . . . but fits are dreadful, they are so very alarming and come on so suddenly'. See Woodforde, *The Diary of a Country Parson*, p. 404.
   How odd, incidentally, that the Frome overseers should be referring in 1793 to 'Thomas Titford's child'; she was, after all, a 20-year old woman in that year.

5. The wheat price of 119s. 6d. was the yearly average for 1801. Grain prices in that year made even the crisis of 1795 appear to be minor by comparison; in effect the 1795 situation was in danger of becoming a permanent state of affairs, as a worsening climate and consequent high prices set in. See Geoffrey W. Oxley, *Poor Relief in England and Wales, 1601-1834* (1974), p. 113.

   It is interesting to note that the overseers were helping Thomas Titford in 1801 because he had no work; interesting, because he was 60 years old at the time.

Chapter 14: Charles the Cheesemonger

1. Dr. John Ross, minister at St John's from 1760 to 1792, never officiated at a marriage in his church, for reasons best known to himself. In the event, Charles and Elizabeth's marriage was solemnised by Peter Mayson, the curate and master of Frome Grammar School.

2. Cheesemongers had to be careful about prices, of course; in the crisis year of 1766 there had been riots in Nottingham during which cheeses were rolled downhill in protest at their high cost. It has been estimated that in 1795 an average labourer's family spent roughly 3d. per week on cheese and 1s. per

week on meat; as Charles could offer both commodities, he was perhaps not doing so badly, providing
he had enough customers.

3. For further details on naming patterns, see D. J. Steel, *National Index of Parish Registers* (1976), vol. 1,
p. 112.

4. The fact that William Charles was almost certainly called simply 'Charles' most of the time might
help explain why Charles the Cheesemonger's burial in the chapel records is described as being that
of 'Charles, senr.'

5. Benjamin Titford, along with most of his brothers and sisters and a few million other people over the
years, was to be baptised twice over; once in the Anglican Church, and then – almost 150 years later –
by the Church of Jesus Christ of Latterday Saints (the Mormons). The Mormons baptise deceased
individuals into their church retrospectively in extremely large numbers; their records show that
Benjamin was thus baptised on 13 January 1938, based upon information supplied by a descendant-
in-law, a certain James Miller Jones (details from Mormon archive records).

6. 'Stocks' could conceivably refer to the charge made to traders for the use of stalls and selling space
on market days. A more likely explanation is one given by J. O. Lewis in his own thoughts on Frome
stocks: 'Probably the taxable goods of Frome merchants as apart from their property or houses'. (From
a handwritten note in SRO, ref. DD/LW/36, extracts from churchwardens' and overseers' books for
Frome, 1679-1734.)

7. What was once called Pig Street is now more demurely known as Bridge Street. .

8. The original 1783 Turnpike Trustees indenture is now lost, but a copy exists at SRO, ref. DD/LW/37.
Daniel Rossiter died only four years after the indenture was drawn up, in 1787. See Musgrave's
Obituary, *Gentleman's Magazine*, 1787.

9. For details of the 1794/5 crisis, see Geoffrey W. Oxley, *Poor Relief in England and Wales, 1601-1834* (1974),
pp. 111 ff.

10. Details from the original Act of Parliament, House of Lords Record Office.

11. Woodforde, *The Diary of a Country Parson*, p. 444.

12. The tennis court mentioned here is presumably the one attached to the *Champneys Arms*, built in 1739:
'also shall and will Build Erect and finish a Tennis or Ball Court . . . the same to containe in Length
One Hundred ffoot and in Breadth fforty foot'. (From the original lease of 1739, quoted in Michael
McGarvie, *Frome through the Ages*, pp. 79, 80.) This would have been an enclosed court for the playing
of Real Tennis, of course.

13. The late 1720s saw the deaths of six Titfords in Frome; across the border in Wiltshire, six more members
of the Warminster branch of the family were to die between December 1727 and December 1730.

14. For a series of tables showing British wheat prices from the late 17th century onwards, see Cole and
Postgate, *The Common People*, pp. 76-7 and 119 ff.

15. G. M. Trevelyan, *English Social History* (1946), p. 466.

16. Even William Pitt himself was to say in 1795 that he believed that 'trade, industry and barter would
always find their own level'. (Pitt, speaking against Whitbread's bill for reviving wage regulation,
quoted in S. T. Miller, *Society and the State*, p. 33.)

17. From Prothero, *English Farming*, p. 211, quoted in Charlotte Waters, *A Short Economic History of England*
(1928), p. 324.

18. The information on the Frome Military Association here comes from three principal sources: **a.** Michael
McGarvie, *The Book of Frome*, p. 111. **b.** The Diary of Edmund Crocker, *A Journal of Remarkable Occurrences
in Frome, 1798-1801*, SRO ref. DD/SAS c/27 10. (Also printed, with a few omissions, as *Frome at end of
18th century: diary kept by Blue School master's son*, in *Frome & District Directory* (1936), pp. iii-xv.) **c.** Anon.
(Captain Francis Haviland), *The North Somerset Regiment of Yeomanry Cavalry* (1850), pp. 5, 6, 13, 14.

The French had actually made a small landing on English shores, near Fishguard, on the Pembroke-
shire coast, in February 1797. See E. H. S. Jones, *The Last Invasion of Britain* (Cardiff 1950), cited in
E. P. Thompson, *The Making of the English Working Class* (1979), note to p. 180.

Thompson points out that many a volunteer corps was formed as much against internal conspiracy
as against the French. Several farmers at this period had become 'upstart gentleman' and were 'ready
to ride over all they met . . . on the way; but this was nothing compared to the pride and folly which
took possession of their empty or fume-charged heads, when they got dressed in scarlet . . . and were
called "yeomanry cavalry". (T. Bewick, *A Memoir*, ed. M. Weekley (1961), pp. 146-8, 153, quoted in
Thompson, *op. cit.*, note to p. 198.)

19. John's name appears in the list of infantry for 1798 – mis-spelt as 'John Tizford', a forgiveable error. The list itself is included in Haviland, *op. cit.*, pp. 5 and 6.

20. Nonconformist zeal, then, we might say with a degree of cynicism, was not always an inherited characteristic. Many sociologists studying patterns of religious belief would claim that Dissent would often last no longer than three generations. See David Martin, *A Sociology of English Religion*, pp. 16 ff. This thesis would certainly be borne out by the history of the Titfords in Frome: Thomas the Calvinist was an ardent chapel-goer; his son Charles, disillusioned, perhaps, by what he had seen of the goings-on at Badcox Lane, or feeling some revulsion at the treatment meted out to his step-mother Rebekah, was to baptise his children at the parish church, though he buried them at the chapel burying-ground. He was, in any case, never a full member of that chapel. Finally his son, William Charles, seems to have found the Anglican Church quite cosy enough for his liking – and if you're in trade in the City of London, even working alongside Baptist cousins, why risk offending any customers by admitting to being a Dissenter? William Charles's spiritual energy, such as it was, seems to have been channelled into trade. The Titfords might even serve as a model for E. P. Thompson's contention that, 'When the democratic revival came in the last years of the [18th] century, Old Dissent had lost much of its popular following, and those artisans who still adhered to it were permeated by the values of enlightened self-interest', *op. cit.*, p. 58.

    Nonconformists, incidentally, did not have the right to enlist with the forces voluntarily until well towards the close of the 18th century. See J. H. Whiteley, *Wesley's England*, p. 138.

21. By 1801, 800 Frome men had joined the forces, and payments to Militiamen's families were straining the overseers' resources. The Militia, of course, unlike the Regular Army, was a conscripted, not a volunteer force. Anyone keen enough to join it at times of national crisis could have achieved that ambition by making it known that he was prepared to act as a substitute for those chosen by ballot who were unwilling to serve.

22. Even in 1845, the *Second Report of the Commissioners for Inquiring into the State of Large Towns and Populous Districts* was saying that, 'The percentage of population who die annually at Frome is above the average, and the class of persons who attain the least average age, and who suffer most from consumption and epidemics are the tradespeople', quoted in McGarvie, *Frome through the Ages*, p. 141. This seems to have been the case well before 1845, if we consider Charles the Cheesemonger's family; he himself died at 52, and two of his three sons were struck down in their twenties.

23. Woodforde, *The Diary of a Country Parson*, p. 576.

24. Crocker's Diary, *op. cit.* John Titford was not the only volunteer to be buried with military honours in Frome; Crocker also mentions 'Mr. Gregory at the Bell. He being a private in the Infantry, was buried with military honours'. (11 September 1798.) The *Bath Chronicle*, meanwhile, reveals that a similar honour was accorded to Mr. Smart, a member of the Salisbury Armed Association, who died within a week of John Titford. One gets the impression that, had Napoleon waited long enough, the weather might have killed off more of his enemies than his cannon could ever have done . . . Even the appalling weather, we should note, did not prevent Mrs. Sarah Siddons from performing in 'The Mourning Bride' at the Theatre Royal, Bath, that very week.

25. Woodforde, *op. cit.*, pp. 579-80.

26. Details from Crocker's Diary, *op. cit.*

27. Perhaps it behoves us to be a little more charitable to the Shatford family. After all, they did put on a performance of the 'Wheel of Fortune' for 'the benefit of the poor', and staged 'Cure for the Heart Ache' because it was 'desir'd by Frome Infantry'.

28. Crocker's Diary, 19 June 1801.

29. Prices noted by Edmund Crocker in his diary. Cheese was, of course, a good commodity to be selling at the time; together with bread, it constituted an important element in the diet of most working families.

30. From a contemporary newspaper account included in Crocker's Diary. We may make what judgments we choose, in retrospect, about the 'let them eat cake' inequity of the rich downing pheasant while the poor starved, but the late 18th century in England is marked, as we have seen, by an apparently deep-seated political apathy on the part of the poorer classes. Starvation is as likely to cause revolution as resignation, but for many Englishmen in the late 1700s there seems to have been a stoical and fatalistic acceptance of God's overriding wisdom in these matters. It was Mrs. Alexander in the following century who would speak in a hymn of,

> The rich man in his castle,
> The poor man at his gate,
> God made them, high or lowly,
> And order'd their estate.
> (from *All Things Bright and Beautiful*, 1848.)

Thus it was that when King George III and his Queen visited Longleat, near Frome, in September 1789 (the year of the French Revolution), 30,000 locals crowded into the park to wave their hats and shout at the Royal retinue of 125 people who had just consumed between them three oxen, six fat bucks, 17 fat sheep, game, poultry, fish, fruit and 'all other good things that could be thought of'. (Samuel Cuzner, *op. cit.*, p. 114.) Jubilation, we note with interest, not revolution.

31. An 18th-century German traveller through England, C. P. Moritz, wrote in a similar vein, 'Nothing in London makes a more detestable sight than the butchers' stalls . . . the grits and other refuse are all thrown out on the street and set up an unbearable stink'. (Carl Moritz, *Journeys of a German in England*, quoted in Roger Hart, *English Life in the Eighteenth Century* (1970), p. 13.

32. Correspondence of William Jowett Titford, now in the possession of Mr. A. Titford of West Horsley, Surrey.

Chapter 15: John the Cardmaker

1. Details from John Kingdon's church book, Badcox Lane Baptist Chapel, 1762-1801.

2. 'Oldbury' or 'Oldberry' is a distinctive and unusual name for Frome; one with a bit of a West Midlands ring about it?

3. We have included William and Joseph here as the sons of John, though positive evidence of baptism is lacking. Who more likely than John, after all, not to baptise his children!

   One boy, 'John Titford's son', was buried at Badcox Lane in 1783. William, born in 1774-5, would seem to be a further son, given the later connection between his widow Sarah, and John's daughters. There is a Whittox Lane connection, too, with those daughters: William lived there, as they were to do, working as a mason. He had married Sarah Moon in 1817, having two children soon afterwards: William, baptised in 1818, of whom nothing further is known, followed by Mary Ann. She worked as a burler, but was to die a pauper in the fetid and overcrowded workhouse in 1857, aged only 36; the parish paid for her burial. William the mason, meanwhile, was interred at Christ Church in 1822, aged 47, his widow Sarah living on until 1841. She died at Brandy Lane, aged 56, carried off – like her ill-fated daughter – by apoplexy.

   Joseph, too, is probably the son of John Titford, though his year of birth 1776-7 (or 1778-9?) could make him a child of Thomas and Elizabeth. This is unlikely, perhaps, given Elizabeth's poor state of health at the time. And the 1785 census for Fountain Lane only lists one male in Thomas Titford's family: that is, Thomas himself.

   Poor Joseph appear to have ended up sick and in the workhouse: the overseers are including payments of 4s. and 6s. in their list of 'Workhouse expences – extras' for 'Titford' just before his death in May 1800. The sexton of the burial ground and the person who kept the register at Badcox Lane Chapel seemed unable to agree either on his age, or even on the date of his burial! So we know that he was *either* 21 or 23, and that he was buried *either* on 11 May or 12 May.

4. Badcox Lane Chapel deed of 1 November 1805. Close Rolls, no. 6, part 1, 46 George III. Transcript in SRO, DD/LW/30.

5. Details from the original document for Badcox Lane Chapel, now in the possession of Bristol Baptist College.

6. From Badcox Lane Church Book, 1806-70, Bristol Baptist College.

7. The commercial directories for Frome for this period would indicate that Mary was quite possibly a dressmaker as well as a milliner; such ladies, while they might keep a shop as a central base, would be quite likely to do a great deal of their work in customers' own homes.

8. For William Cobbett's idiosyncratic comments on Frome in 1826, see Michael McGarvie, *Frome through the ages*, pp. 121, 122. For extracts from Thomas Clark's journal, see *ibid.*, pp. 124, 125.

9. Rates lists for Behind the Hill, naming paupers as well as ratepayers, refer to 'Jane Titford'. This is clearly Sarah, in fact; perhaps she was known as 'Sarah Jane'?

10. A mortgage of 1846 refers to John Ellitt of Croydon, Surrey, who has a house on the east side of Whittox Lane, then occupied by 'Miss Titford'. (Details from Derek Gill of Frome.)

Chapter 16: W. C. T.

Not every source for material in this and subsequent chapters is noted specifically. Sometimes details are given in the text itself, but the following records – nearly all very familiar to family historians undertaking 19th-century research – have been referred to extensively: parish registers, non-parochial registers, records of the Registrar General, census returns, wills, commercial directories. Also family notes and correspondence in the possession of Anthony R. Titford and John S. Titford.

1. The sewer rate was levied annually for the year ending on Lady Day. The rate was two pence in the pound on 'real yearly rack Rents'. William Charles Titford, entered simply as 'Titford', first appears in the rate list for Bishopsgate Ward Within, St Ethelburga's Precinct, in 1799, replacing Joseph Ready. . Guildhall Library MS 2137/49, fol. 22.
2. Groseley and Archenholz, quoted in J. H. Whiteley, *Wesley's England*, p. 146.
3. Roger Hart, *English Life in the Eighteenth Century*, p. 47.
4. Defoe, visiting Yeovil in the early 18th century, found its dialect harder to understand than that used in any other part of the country, '. . . 'tis certain that tho' the tongue be all meer natural English, yet those that are but a little acquainted with them, cannot understand one half of what they say'. Quoted in J. H. Bettey, *Rural Life in Wessex, 1500-1900* (1977), p. 105. Defoe's more detailed analysis runs as follows, 'The difference [i.e. between the speech in the Dorset/Somerset region and that of London] is not so much in the orthography of words, as in the tone and diction; their abridging the speech, *cham* for *I am*, *chil* for *I will*, *don* for *put on* and *doff* for *put off*, and the like'. (Daniel Defoe, *A tour through the whole Island of Great Britain*, 2 vols., (Everyman ed., 1962), vol. 1, pp. 218-19.)

   Dialect variation, of course, was more widespread in an age of much illiteracy: Defoe's comment on Yeovil in the early 18th century could be held to apply, albeit in a slightly modified form, to Frome at the end of that century.
5. James Woodforde, *The Diary of a Country Parson*, p. 283.
6. This impressive list of drapers' fineries comes from Roger Hart, *op. cit.*, p. 47.
7. From the original Weavers' Company Court Minutes. Guildhall Library MS 4655/18.
8. The Order of the Court of Aldermen to admit William Charles Titford to the City Freedom is dated 15 January 1799. He duly swore the Freeman's oath before the City Chamberlain and was formally admitted during March of the same year. Details are in the City Freedom admission bundle CF1/1226 (Corporation of London Records Office). W. C. T. must have been well aware that to call his father a 'cheesemonger' during these proceedings would have sounded softer on City ears than 'butcher'.
9. Weavers' Company Court Minutes, 1798-1826. Guildhall Library.
10. From the ballad, *A short sketch of the times* (1794). Quoted in Roy Palmer, *A Ballad History of England*, pp. 80, 81. When the fortunes of the silk industry finally plummeted for good some years later, the City Titfords were not caught napping: they made a hasty move into the scale-making business.
11. The original Faculty Office Marriage Allegation is in Lambeth Palace Library.
12. See Anthony R. Titford, 'A biographical study of William Jowett Titford (1784-1823/7) and *Sketches towards a Hortus Botanicus Americanus*', in *J. Soc. Bibliog. Nat. Hist.* (1977), no. 8 (2), pp. 120-142.
13. When W. C. T.'s son Charles was baptised at St Luke's, Old Street, in 1807, it was to be the surname that gave the clerk problems: 'son of William Charles and Ann TILFORD'. He was neither the first not the last scribe to make that simple error.
14. Joseph Titford and Elizabeth are known to have had at least three sons: Frederick James (b. 1837); Joseph Henry (b. 1853); William (b. 1855). Frederick James died in 1857 and was buried in Abney Park Cemetery on 19 January of that year; Joseph Henry died in Islington on 12 January 1924, aged 70; William died in Islington in 1875.
15. From David Iredale's introduction to Charles Trice Martin, *The Record Interpreter* (2nd. edn., 1982), p. 6.

Chapter 17: Ben the Outrider

For a general statement on 19th-century records used, see notes to Chapter 16. Details on the Stepney and Whitechapel area are in part taken from contemporary maps now at the Greater London Record Office.

1. In some ways both W. C. T. and Ben were going against the tide by leaving Frome as they did. Admittedly the population of London was growing, but this was true of Frome, too; its 9,000 inhabitants in 1801 had risen to 12,500 by 1821 – an increase of over forty per cent in 20 years.

2. An 'outrider' sounds as if he ought to be riding shotgun on a coach, or going ahead to clear the road of highwaymen. The word could have this meaning, but Joseph Wright's *Dialect Dictionary* (1898-1905) gives the definition 'a commercial traveller' as used in the dialect of Cheshire, Leicestershire, Warwickshire, Shropshire, Berkshire and Somerset itself. This, reinforced by *O.E.D.*'s dialectical 'a tradesman's travelling agent', seems to be the correct meaning in this case. Wright also gives the verb, 'to outride'; 'a commercial traveller/to travel as a commercial traveller', together with a number of Somerset examples, including 'He's doin' well 'nough – he've a-got in out-ride vor Mr. Jones up in Bristol, zillin' o' hats and that', and, 'He d'outride vor Mr. Hannibal, zillin' crockery and shop goods', both from West Somerset.

3. No expert on Somerset dialect would forgive us if we suggested that speakers in the county simply replaced all 'f's with 'v's and 's's with 'z's – technically, a substitution of a voiced consonant for an unvoiced one in each case. In theory, it is only words of an Anglo-Saxon origin or earlier which are accorded the 'v' or 'z' substitution, and an 's' is always sounded as such when followed by a consonant. See G. W. and J. H. Wade, *The Little Guides: Somerset* (1949), pp. 1, 2.

4. Princes Square was later renamed 'Swedenborg Square'. In the 1790s, incidentally, the *Cock and Neptune* in Well Close Square had been the meeting place of a division of the London Corresponding Society – just the kind of group which seemed to be sailing close to the edge of revolution, and which the authorities feared so much. See E. P. Thompson, *The Making of the English Working Class*, p. 186.

5. From the original Faculty Office Marriage Allegation, Lambeth Palace Library. The Faculty Office of the Archbishop of Canterbury could authorise a marriage at any parish in England and Wales, though it had been a stipulation of Hardwicke's Marriage Act of 1753 that a licence could only be granted when one of the parties had resided in the parish for four weeks previous to the grant being made. See D. J. Steel, *National Index of Parish Registers*, vol. 1, pp. 225, 228.

6. Details from Sewerage Rate Lists, St Mary Whitechapel, Midsummer 1809-Midsummer 1810. Ref. P 93/MRY 1/202. Greater London Record Office. For further general details of such records, see Ida Darlington, *The London Commissioners of Sewers and their Records*.

7. Charles Benjamin, the eldest son of Benjamin and Elizabeth, appears to vanish without trace. Nowhere is his name recorded in the Registrar General's Office, and an informed guess would say that he died young – or emigrated? His burial may well be recorded in the voluminous records of St Leonard's, Shoreditch, where his mother went to live very soon after Ben the Outrider's death.

8. It had long been the custom to bury suicides at a crossroads with a stake through the heart. This man was a sailor named Williams, who had hanged himself in prison on the night he was arrested. He had so terrified the local populace that those who could afford to bought blunderbusses or watchmen's warning rattles.

9. C. P. Hill, *British Economic and Social History, 1700-1939* (1966), p. 114.

10. Tuberculosis was almost exclusively an urban disease. See S. T. Miller, *Society and the State, 1750-1950*, p. 157.

11. From the register of Zion Chapel, Frome.

12. Details from Shoreditch Workhouse registers, 1823-27 and 1837-45. Greater London Record Office.

13. In the mid-1840s the plight of sempstresses – many working for starvation wages in slop-shops – was a matter for great public concern. There was even a class of women (maybe Elizabeth Titford was once among them?) referred to as 'distressed needlewomen'.

    Rev. William Quekett, deeply concerned about the plight of the poor in the capital, collected statistical returns over a number of years to establish just how many people had resorted to the workhouse in time of need. On 27 November 1848, the year before Elizabeth Titford died in Shoreditch, returns for 35 unions and workhouses covering 200 parishes in London and its suburbs revealed the following numbers of people spending the night in such an establishment: 7,381 men, 11,775 women, 5,425 children. Total: 24,581. Women, clearly, were much more vulnerable in this way than men were. Rev. William Quekett, *My Sayings and Doings* (1888), p. 102.

Chapter 18: Robert the Mariner

For a general statement on 19th-century records used, see notes to Chapter 16.

1. Details about the *Orynthia* are from the following sources: Lloyd's Register of Shipping, 1840, 1842, 1846; Merchant shipping records (PRO): BT 107/36; BT 107/61; BT 107/300; BT 111/31. Details on Robert Titford are from (PRO): Register of Seamen, 1835-44 (BT 120/5) – 'Robert Tilford' [sic] – and BT 112/69.

2. Details on voyages and crew for the *Orynthia* are from (PRO) Crew Lists and Agreements, ref. BT 98 376 (Part I), 1835-44.

3. The master's wage in the schedule in question is given at £250 per year – massively in excess of that of anyone else on board, even bearing in mind the extra responsibility carried. Whether Captain William Cox was here being generous with himself as half-owner of the vessel is not made clear.

4. Inaccurately-recorded ages seem to have been a feature of this voyage. To begin with, Robert Titford lists his own age as 25, when in fact it was 30; and George Groves, previously given as a 15-year old in 1838, appears to have achieved the age of 19 when he joined the *Orynthia* in Honduras just over a year later.

5. Details of crew agreements from a printed Schedule 'A' form for the *Orynthia*, 1843-4. Ref. BT 98 376.

6. Given the Hasted/Titford connection with Mile End Old Town Zion Chapel, it would seem likely that Selina Elizabeth Titford was named after Selina, Countess of Huntingdon, a one-time friend of John Wesley, who had founded the breakaway Lady Huntingdon's Connexion.

7. Both Alexander Cowley and Selina Elizabeth Titford were, as it happens, children of mariners.

Within the limits of the present family history we will not be able to follow the descendants of Robert Titford in any detailed way. In barest outline the story runs as follows: Robert Edward, the only son of Robert the Mariner, married Sarah Ann Farrow, daughter of Henry Farrow, an engineer, at St Mary's Bermondsey in 1857. Their sons were: Robert Henry (born 1860); Herbert Edward (born 1866); Charles Ernest (born 1868); Frederick Arthur (born 1871).

Robert Edward had been a warehouse clerk and a traveller. Robert Henry was an entrepreneur with erratic success: a tobacconist, publican, owner of cinemas and bookmaker. Of his sons (Robert John, John Henry and Charles Edward) only the eldest, Robert John, had sons in his turn: Hedley Robert, an electrical engineer; Clifford Dennis, a shopfitter, and Russell John, a stockbroker (and family historian *par excellence*).

Herbert Edward, the next of Robert Edward's sons, died in Harlesden in 1962, but of his family nothing is presently known. Charles Ernest, the next brother, married twice and fathered one daughter; he died in Hackney in 1948.

Frederick Arthur, the youngest son, was a haberdasher and drapery buyer in North London; he married Sarah Annie Usher, daughter of William Usher, gentleman and cheesemonger of Pimlico, in Leytonstone on 16 August 1902. Of their two sons, one is still alive and a great fan of family history: Arthur Osmond, a retired Lloyds underwriter of Winchmore Hill. He has a wife and two married daughters, Margaret and Shelagh. Arthur's brother Leonard Frederick died in 1977: a wholesale button manufacturer, member of the Worshipful Company of Horners and a Freeman of the City of London, he left a widow, Joyce, and two sons, Derek and Richard. Derek is married with two daughters, and Richard, now an Anglican clergyman, married· in 1980.

Through the kindness and interest of Robert the Mariner's descendants, new links have been forged between that side of the family and their cousins, descendants of Benjamin the Silversmith, of whom the present author is one. The author and his parents now count Arthur Titford, his wife Muriel and their daughters and sons-in-law, together with Joyce Titford and her sons and daughters-in-law, and Russell Titford, son of Robert John, and his wife Jan and daughter Lucinda amongst their closest friends. Proof, after all, that blood is thicker than water.

Chapter 19: Benjamin the Silversmith

For a general statement of 19th-century records used, see notes to Chapter 16.

1. The borders between the skilled artisan, the petty trader and the manual worker had long been blurred. In modern parlance we might use terms like 'plebeian' and 'petty bourgeois' to try and identify the relevant socio-economic classes. Not that those terms help a great deal, when there was so much fluidity between those classes.

'2. The family crest appears in James Fairbairn's *Crests of the families of Great Britain*: 'Titford: a demi-lion, rampant'. Several branches of the Titford family seem to have been aware of the existence of such a crest, though there is no evidence for its provenance. The Titfords of Wylye and St Pancras very probably chose their up-market mottoes, '*Cui debeo fidus*' (Loyal to whom loyalty is due) and '*Suscipere et finire*' (to undertake and to accomplish – a deliberate pun on their activites as funeral directors, perhaps?) from some handbook of mottoes or other, both being well-established and in use by several families. There was no shortage of entrepreneurial stationers and others who would provide any family with a set of armorial bearings, however spurious, in exchange for a modest fee.

3. We need not necessarily assume that Benjamin was being callous by allowing his mother to be looked after in the workhouse: she was paralysed, after all, and could probably receive the kind of nursing in an institution which her son and daughter-in-law would be in no position to provide.

4. The wording of a 19th-century indenture was, of course, anachronistic; the form of words had remained very much the same since at least the 17th century, seeming to suggest a feudal relationship between master and apprentice. One could expect an indentured apprentice to be treated with more civility than a parish apprentice, though there may well have been some who slept under the counter.

5. Quoted in W. J. Reader, *Victorian England* (1974), p. 136.

6. From Charles Dickens, 'What a London curate can do if he tries'. Originally published in *Household Words*, 16 November 1850, but printed in full in Rev. W. Quekett, *My Sayings and Doings*, pp. 75-86. This quotation is from pp. 76 and 79. Quekett, for all his later dedication to his job, had thought that the living in London he was being offered was St George's Hanover Square, not the lowly St George's in the East. His first reaction was one of mild horror: 'so we drove on through the crowded, low streets, and my heart sank within me as I saw the squalor and wretchedness of the neighbourhood' (*ibid.*, pp. 74, 75). This was in about 1830.

7. In 1847 Quekett was living at 51 Well Close Square, while John Frederick Hasted, cooper, (the son of John Frederick Hasted, brother to Elizabeth Titford *née* Hasted) was at no. 27. Well Close Square had been highly fashionable in its time – the home of the Danish Ambassador and other such luminaries.

8. From *The Times*, 13 September 1849. Cholera had spread to Russia from India and Afghanistan in the spring of 1830, thence to England by the autumn of 1831. Its successive outbreaks caused widespread deaths, especially in towns. Pump water would very quickly become lethal once contaminated by sewage; it was thus very much to the Victorians' credit that they improved sanitation to the point where the disease could be eradicated.

9. Native Hoxtonians would have their own very distinctive London accents at this time, of course:

> *The Sarcastic Bystander*: Do you know where *I* come from?
> *The Note-taker (Henry Higgins)*: Hoxton. (*Titterings . . .*)
> *The Sarcastic One (amazed)*: Well, who said I didn't? Bly me! You know everything, you do.
> (George Bernard Shaw, *Pygmalion*, first published 1916.)

10. We may be looking at a connection here with the Parkes family, who were by no means short of money, and one of whose ancestors is rumoured to have invented the wooden blocks once used to pave so many of the roads in Britain's cities. Benjamin Titford's mother-in-law, Harriott Parkes (*née* Brook) had died in 1854, the very year during which he made his move into Wilmington Square; she was interred in Highgate cemetery. Ebenezer Parkes, left a widower, remarried with almost indecent haste. Already in his middle fifties, he set off hot-foot down to the Isle of Wight, obtained a marriage licence, and celebrated his wedding to a spinster by the name of Charlotte Wallis, daughter of a Bembridge pilot – and all this on 28 June, three months after his first wife's death. He described himself, with a certain lack of modesty, perhaps, as a 'gentleman', and it may well have been he who made it possible, even in his absence, for the Titfords to start up as boarding-house keepers in Wilmington Square. Or maybe Harriott had left Benjamin and Elizabeth a legacy?

Nearly 20 years later the Titfords were to return to Wilmington Square once more: first to no. 2, then to no. 24, where William's son, Henry James, was born.

11. Here is Dickens, writing in 1879 on the subject of Common Lodging Houses:

> The Common Lodging House Act has worked a marvellous revolution in the housing of the London poor. Every establishment of the kind throughout the metropolis is now under direct and continual police supervision . . . Every bed, moreover, has to be furnished weekly with a complete supply of fresh linen.
> (*Dickens's Dictionary of London 1879: an Unconventional Handbook* (ed. H. Baker, 1972), p. 77.)

12. This family bible was given by Henry James Titford to the minister at Bowes Park Methodist Church

in the 1960s and has never been seen since. Robert Edward Titford, son of Robert the Mariner, was given a similar bible at his marriage in 1857, which he and his wife duly filled in with family details; it is currently in the possession of his Titford descendants.

13. It is just possible that the compiler of the 1860 family details was Benjamin's cousin Joseph, a younger son of William Charles. Joseph, a house painter, and his wife Elizabeth were living at 46 Milner Square, Islington in 1853, just round the corner from Benjamin and Elizabeth at James Street. Not only that, but at his death Joseph is described as being 'late of 15 James Street, Islington' – of interest to us when we consider that Benjamin was at 14 James Street in 1849. Clearly the cousins were very much in touch with each other, so perhaps Joseph had written those details on the mysterious blue sheet?

14. W. J. Reader, *op. cit.*, p. 24.

15. 'Comfortable working class' is a term used by Reader, *ibid.*, pp. 120-44.

16. Roger Hart, *English Life in the Nineteenth Century* (1971), p. 103.

17. Working from home as he did for periods of his life, Benjamin must have known both his wife and children rather better than, say, a modern city commuter.

18. Notice that three Elizabeth Titfords had outlived their husbands in the 19th century in London: Elizabeth, wife of Ben the Outrider; Elizabeth, wife of Robert the Mariner; and now Elizabeth, wife of Benjamin the Silversmith.

Chapter 20: Benjamin James

For a general statement on 19th-century records used, see notes for Chapter 16. The 20th-century sources for births, marriages and deaths, etc., are essentially the same as for the preceding century.

1. Just one example of an outstandingly successful self-made man in the later years of the 18th century would be Sir Richard Arkwright; from a very humble background, he rose in the social scale to the point where he was made High Sheriff of Derbyshire. Not all social movement was upwards, however: the Lancashire proverb 'There's nobbut three generations between clog and clog' reminds us that a ne'er-do-well son could soon spend his father's legacy and reduce the family to penury once more. See Gerald Hamilton-Edwards, *In Search of Ancestry* (1974), p. 69.

2. The information here on schoolmaster apprenticeships is from Roger Hart, *English Life in the Nineteenth Century*, p. 95. Details from the archives of St Paul's College, Cheltenham, were very kindly supplied by Mr. Peter Brooks.

3. The family of 'Titeford/Tightford', farmers and landowners, were in the hamlet of Stathe, near Stoke St Gregory, from at least as early as 1576, in which year William Titeford married Agnes Garlant at Stoke St Gregory parish church. The last evidence of their presence in the area comes in a marriage of 1683, after which time they appear to have died out without trace. One of the Titefords, Richard, even had his will proved in the Prerogative Court of Canterbury, in 1596. Despite the rather unusual spelling of the surname – it even appears as 'Titefoot' on occasions – it looks very much as if William and Richard Titeford had moved to Stathe from the original family home of Bratton in Wiltshire in the late 1570s. Names and dates seem to support such a supposition. One distinguishing feature of the family in the 17th century is their entanglement in paternity suits – either as the wronged woman, or as the wronging man.

4. Maps of London in the 1860s and 1870s show Canonbury and Islington, the outer northern suburbs, on the edge of open countryside; Stoke Newington and Finsbury Park were then very rural settlements. Caroline Titford, writing of Islington in the 1860s, says that it 'still retained somewhat of its rural character; tall elms flanked the Upper Street'. (Caroline Titford, *History of Unity Church, Islington* (1912), p. 40). Caroline Titford, *née* Spiller, had married Sydney Titford, one of the decendants of William the Emigrant, in Hackney in 1867. Dickens, in his *Dickens's Dictionary of London 1879*, p. 124, tells a slightly different story: 'High-street and Upper-street have grown to be amongst the noisiest and least agreeable thoroughfares in London'.

5. Much material on Benjamin James's time in Curry Rivel has been provided by the great kindness of Mr. Donald Mounter, who still lives in the village. His own father was born in 1867 – a year before Benjamin's arrival – and died there in 1957; he could remember having once owned a cricket bat with a silver shield which read, 'Presented to Benjamin Titford'. 'Not much of a bat' was his laconic comment on this treasure!

The commercial directories appear to give Benjamin James's later place of residence as 'Church Hay', but Donald Mounter says no such place exists in the village, and he had understood that the Titfords lived at 'Coombstock House'. When Mr. Mounter was at school in Curry Rivel there were only 176 pupils; in the 1980s the total at Curry Rivel Junior School had risen to 235. Keen-eyed as he is, Mr. Mounter spotted an entry in the Curry Rivel church visitors' book for 24 November 1972, which read: 'E. M. Rudkin, granddaughter of B. Titford'. Whoever this elusive person may have been, she certainly chose to define herself in an interesting enough way!

6. The man so much moved by the funeral was Donald Mounter's elder brother.

7. Details from Benjamin Foote, son of Frank Foote and Alice Maud (*née* Titford) now living at Stroud (1983).

8. Marwood's nephew, Benjamin Foote, can even remember hearing his uncle referred to as 'Harry'. From Marwood James *Henry*, presumably.

Chapter 21: William the Gold-Engraver

1. On 30 June 1783, Parson Woodforde noted in his diary that, 'I privately named a Child this morning of Dinah Bushell's by name Keziah One of Job's Daughters Names'. (Woodforde, *op. cit.*, p. 206). The original reference is from Job 42, 12-15: 'Job . . . has also seven sons and three daughters. And he called the name of the first, Jemima; and the name of the second, Kezia; and the name of the third, Kerenhappuch. And in all the land were no women found so fair as the daughters of Job'. Mercifully, Mary Ann was named after the second of these daughters, rather than the third: 'Mary Ann Kerenhappuch Titford' would hardly trip off the tongue!

2. Abney Park Cemetery had been opened on a site of approximately 30 acres in 1840. For details of this and other such cemeteries, see Patricia S. Wolfston (ed. Michael J. Gandy), *Greater London Cemeteries and Crematoria and their Registers* (1982).

3. Although the grandchildren can remember their Titford grandmother very clearly, they have only dim recollections of grandfather William. 'A gruff old boy' is the nearest they can get by way of a description of him in his later years.

Chapter 22: Charles Frederick

Much of the detail included in this chapter comes from the album and accumulated papers of Charles Frederick, now in the possession of the present author. Information concerning individual ships comes largely from various crew lists now held by the Memorial University of Newfoundland, Canada.

1. From *London in the Sixties*, quoted in Roger Hart, *English Life in the Nineteenth Century*, p. 90.

2. A series of letters concerning the *Chimborazo* graced the correspondence columns of *Sea Breezes* in the late 1940s and 1950s. The one quoted is by Captain T. W. Pickard (May 1947). The four Orient Line sister ships were built originally for the Pacific Steam Navigation Company in the 1870s: the *Lusitania*, the *Cuzco*, the *Garonne*, on which Charles Titford became steerage steward in 1883 but which was also run aground, like the *Chimborazo*, before being pensioned off to run Norwegian cruises, and finally the *Chimborazo* itself. She was eventually renamed the *Cleopatra*, and bought by the Ocean Cruising and Highland Yachting Co., Ltd., for Mediterranean cruises and other such humble little jobs. (By a strange coincidence, just as the *Chimborazo* was heading south with Charles Titford on board, on 4 February 1878, another ship called the *Cleopatra* was making its way up the Thames with Cleopatra's Needle. No-one was quite sure what to do with the obelisk when it arrived: use it in St James's Park, or set it right in the middle of the Serpentine?)

The four sister ships were all slightly different in their own way, but each had been based upon the design of the *John Elder*, built in 1868. For an account of a journey from New Zealand to England aboard the *John Elder* ('a fine steamship of the Pacific Steam Navigation Company') see J. H. Hillary, *Westland: Journal of John Hillary, emigrant to New Zealand, 1879* (1979). The *John Elder*, built, appropriately enough, by J. Elder & Co. of Glasgow, finally ran ashore off the coast of Chile in 1892 and became a total loss. A graphic story of sailing to New Zealand aboard a full-rigged ship at this period is provided by *Plum duff and cake: the journal of James Nichols, 1874-5; an account of his voyage to Picton, New Zealand, on the Ship* Carnatic *& some of his new experiences in the colony* (ed. J. Neill, 1975).

3. Brief details of the *Chimborazo* striking the rocks are given in Jack Loney, *Sea Adventures and Wrecks on the*

N.S.W. South Coast, p. 75. A fuller account of the incident appears in the *Australian Town and Country Journal* for 23 March 1878, p. 552, while the subsequent enquiry is reported at length in the *Sydney Morning Herald*, 25 April 1878. A very fine engraving of the *Chimborazo* in the Fitzroy Dock, Sydney, appears on the front page of the *Illustrated Sydney News*, 20 April 1878.

By a strange coincidence, the author of 'My name is Blacket', a fellow competitor with 'Come Wind, Come Weather' in the Institute of Heraldic and Genealogical Studies' '700' Competition (1984) was Mr. Nick Vine Hall of Sydney, Australia, a great-grandson of Captain John Vine Hall of the *Chimborazo*. *My name is Blacket*, published by the author in 1983, recounts how Alice Blacket (1846-1934), the second daughter of Edmund and Sarah Blacket, married her cousin Captain John Vine Hall (1845-1932) at Christ Church, Paddington, in 1872. In 1883 – after the *Chimborazo* incident – Captain Hall settled in Sydney, becoming a successful marine surveyor and assuming the surname 'Vine Hall' in 1910. He and his wife had nine children, and the book carries a photograph of him.

4. Details of George Lambert's signed declaration are from the Chamberlain's Court, London, who also hold the one half of Charles's apprenticeship indenture to match the other now in the possession of the author. A certain Francis Lambert was firmly established as a goldsmith and jeweller at 12 Coventry Street, on the corner of Panton Square, by the first half of the 19th century. See Ambrose Heal, *The London Goldsmiths, 1200-1800* (1972), p. 190.

Even greater fame and success would come to the Lamberts; *Who's Who* of 1910 carries a rather grand advertisement, complete with a photograph of the Coventry Street shop, for 'LAMBERT, Goldsmiths, Silversmiths, & Jewellers TO HIS MAJESTY THE KING. 10, 11, 12 Coventry Street, Piccadilly, London, W.'

5. Benjamin the Silversmith was already terminally ill in June 1879, when Charles received his Freedom of the City (presumably he did so in person). Charles may in fact have been in London when his father died, still giving him time to be in South Africa by December; if that were the case, the black-bordered envelope of 1 January 1880, may have brought news of another death, but whose?

6. Charles's album contains a small sepia photograph of another ship from the Union Steamship fleet: the S.S. *Anglian*, a small brig of just over 2,000 tons, seen in full sail as well as steam.

7. Quotation from J. H. Hillary, *Westland*, *op. cit.*, p. 84. Passengers aboard the *John Elder* in 1880 would, says the author, never forget the terrific heat of the Red Sea – and what of the stokers below deck? Hillary mentions *Ishmaelia* in passing: 'A drove of about 200 camels and 2 ponies in charge of a few Arabs on the right and camels bearing burdens with an Arab trudging by their sides on the left hand' (p. 84).

Chapter 23: Henry James the Goldmounter

1. Quoted in Roger Hart, *op. cit.*, pp. 121, 122.
2. The family were first at 48 Freegrove Road, then at no. 17.
3. In 1943 Grace had to produce a number of family documents to prove her birth and parentage for the purposes of National Health Insurance; a birth certificate was issued to her in July of that year, 'Supplied at the special fee of 6d. applicable in certain statutory cases'.
4. One person only just missed Harry's wedding: his grandmother, the widow of Benjamin the Silversmith, who had died in March 1902.
5. There is some difference of opinion as to why Harry was not involved in the First World War. Doris maintains it was because he had suffered from a weak heart (from that wretched parrot bite, so it is said) and was classified as Grade 3; Sidney believes he was called up, but only on Armistice Day. Perhaps both of these were true?
6. From a letter to the author from Mr. Harold Cropp of Cropp & Farr, 15 May 1979.

Bibliography

1. History: General

Ashley, Maurice, *The English Civil War* (Thames 1974)

Aspin, Chris., *The Woollen Industry* (Shire Publications 1982)

Asquith, Stuart, *New Model Army* (Osprey 1981)

Bentley, Nicholas, *The Victorian Scene (A picture book of the period 1837-1901)* (Weidenfeld and Nicolson 1968)

Berkman, Evelyn, *Creators and Destroyers of the English Navy*, (Hamish Hamilton 1974)

Buchan, John, *Oliver Cromwell* (Hodder and Stoughton 1934)

Cheney, C. R. (ed.), *Handbook of Dates for Students of English History* (Royal Historical Society 1978)

Clapham, Sir John, *A Concise Economic History of Britain. From the Earliest Times to A.D. 1750* (Cambridge 1949)

Cole, G. D. H., and Postgate, Raymond, *The Common People 1746-1946* (Methuen 1976)

Coleman, D. C., *Industry in Tudor and Stuart England* (MacMillan 1975)

Court, W. H. B., *A Concise Economic History of Britain. From 1750 to Recent Times* (Cambridge 1967)

Coward, Barry, *The Stuart Age: a History of England 1603-1714* (Longmans 1980)

Creighton, Charles, *A History of Epidemics in Britain* (Cass 1965)

Dearmar, Rev. Percy, *Everyman's History of the English Church* (Mowbray 1909)

Emmison, F. G., *Introduction to Archives* (Phillimore 1977)

Emmison, F. G. and Gray, Irvine, *County Records* (Historical Assoc. 1973)

Flinn, Michael W., *An Economic and Social History of Britain since 1700* (MacMillan 1966)

Galbraith, V. H., *The Historian at Work* (BBC 1962)

Gordon, A., *Freedom after Ejection* (1917)

Gregg, Pauline, *A Social and Economic History of Britain, 1760-1965* (Harrap 1969)

Harrison, Molly, and Wells, A. A. M., *Picture Source Book for Social History: Eighteenth Century* (George Allen and Unwin, n.d.)

Hart, Roger, *English Life in Tudor Times* (Wayland 1972)

Hart, Roger, *English Life in the Seventeenth Century* (Wayland 1970)

Hart, Roger, *English Life in the Eighteenth Century* (Wayland 1970)

Hart, Roger, *English Life in the Nineteenth Century* (Wayland 1971)

Hill, Christopher, *The World Turned Upside Down: Radical Ideas during the English Revolution* (London 1972)

Hill, C. P., *British Economic and Social History, 1700-1939*, 2nd edn. (Arnold 1966)

Holland, A. J., *British Economic and Social History since 1700: The Age of Industrial Expansion* (Nelson, n.d.)

Jones, J. R., *Country and Court, 1658-1714* (Edward Arnold 1978)

Laslett, Peter, *The World we have Lost* (Methuen 1975)

Lyon Turner, G., *Original Records of early Non-conformists ... under Persecution and Indulgence* (London 1911-14)

MacDonald Wigfield, W., *The Monmouth Rebellion* (Moonraker Press 1980)

McLeod, Kirsty, *Drums and Trumpets: the House of Stuart* (Andre Deutsch 1977)

Malcolmson, R. W., *Life and Labour in England 1700-1780* (Hutchinson 1981)

Manning, Brian, *The English People and the English Revolution* (Peregrine 1978)

Martin, Geoffrey, *A Visual History of Modern Britain: the Town* (Vista 1961)

Miller, S. T., *Society and the State, 1750-1950* (Macdonald and Evans 1979)

Oxley, Geoffrey W., *Poor Relief in England and Wales, 1601-1834* (David and Charles 1974)

Palmer, Roy, *A Ballad History of England from 1588 to the Present Day* (Batsford 1979)

Quennell, Marjorie and C. H. B., *A History of Everyday Things in England*, 4 vols. (Batsford)

Reader, W. J., *Victorian England* (Batsford 1974)

Rundle, R. N., *Scenes from Stuart England* (Hodder and Stoughton 1978)

Shrewsbury, J. F. D., *A History of Bubonic Plague in the British Isles* (Cambridge 1970)

Steinberg, S. H., *Historical Tables, 58 B.C.-A.D.1961*, 6th edn. (MacMillan 1961)

Thompson, E. P., *The Making of the English Working Class*, (Penguin 1979)
Trevelyan, G. M., *English Social History*, 3rd edn. (Longmans 1946)
Waters, Charlotte, *A Short Economic History of England* (Oxford 1928)
Wedgwood, C. V., *The King's War* (Collins 1958)
Whiteley, J. H., *Wesley's England*, 4th edn. (Epworth Press 1954)
Wrightson, Keith, *English Society, 1580-1680* (Hutchinson 1982)

2. Local History: London

Barker, Rev. Thomas B., *Abney Park Cemetery: a Complete Descriptive Guide to Every Part of this Beautiful Depository of the Dead* (Houlston & Wright, London 1869)
Berresford Ellis, Peter, *The Great Fire of London* (N.E.L. 1976)
Blatch, Mervyn, *A Guide to London's Churches* (Constable 1978)
Cobb, Gerald, *The Old Churches of London* (Batsford 1941-2)
Darlington, Ida, *The London Commissioners of Sewers and their Records* (Phillimore 1970)
Dickens, Charles, *Dickens's Dictionary of London – an Unconventional Handbook*, first pub. 1879 (Howard Baker edn., 1972)
Esdaile, Katharine A., *St. Martin in the Fields, New and Old*, (S.P.C.K. 1944)
Hayes, John, *London: a Pictorial History* (Batsford n.d.)
Hibbert, Christopher, *London: the Biography of a City* (Penguin 1980)
Kent, William, *An Encyclopaedia of London* (Dent 1970)
Lillywhite, Bryant, *London Signs* (George Allen and Unwin, n.d.)
Rudé, George, *Hanoverian London, 1714-1808* (Secker and Warburg 1971)
Walford, Edward, *Old and New London*, 6 vols. (Cassell, Petter and Galpin 1880)

3. Local History: Somerset

Belham, Peter, *The Making of Frome* (Frome Society for Local Study 1973)
Collinson, John, *The History and Antiquities of the County of Somerset* (Bath 1791)
Coombs, Arthur H., *A History of Badcox Lane Baptist Church, Frome* (Harvey and Woodland, Frome 1924)
Cuzner, Samuel, *Cuzner's Handbook to Froome Selwood* (Frome 1866)
Daniel, Rev. W. E., 'The street names of Frome', Text of an original lecture of 1897, reprinted in the *Somerset Standard.*
Dunning, Robert (ed.), *Christianity in Somerset* (Somerset County Council 1976)
Dunning, Robert, *A History of Somerset* (Somerset County Library 1978)
Dwelly, E., *Dwelly's National Records, vol. 2, XVII century: Directory of Somerset, Part 4, Lay Subsidy Rolls/Hearth Tax* (privately printed, Fleet, Hants. 1932)
Gill, Derek J., *The Sheppards and Eighteenth-century Frome* (Frome Society for Local Study 1982)
Harvey, W. J., *The Story of Zion Congregational Church, Frome* (Harvey and Woodland, Frome 1918)
Haviland, Francis, *The North Somerset Regiment of Yeomanry Cavalry* (Bath 1850)
Howard, A. J., and Stoate, T. L., *Somerset Protestation Returns and Subsidy Rolls* (1975)
Hunt, T. J., and Sellman, R. R., *Aspects of Somerset History* (Somerset County Council 1973)
King, J. E. (ed.), *Inventory of Parochial Documents in the Diocese of Bath and Wells and the County of Somerset* (Somerset County Council 1938)
Leech, Roger, *Early Industrial Housing: the Trinity Area of Frome* (H.M.S.O. 1981)
Little, Bryan, *Portrait of Somerset*, 4th edn. (Robert Hale 1976)
McGarvie, Michael (ed.), *Eighty years of Frome, 1894-1974* (Frome U.D.C. 1974)
McGarvie, Michael, *Light in Selwood: a short history of St. John's Church, Frome* (Frome Society for Local Study 1976)
McGarvie, Michael, *The Bounds of Selwood* (Frome Society for Local Study 1978)
McGarvie, Michael, *The Book of Frome* (Barracuda 1980)
McGarvie, Michael (ed.), *Frome Through the Ages – Frome Anthology* (Frome Society for Local Study 1982)
McGarvie, Michael, *Frome Place-names: their Origin and Meaning* (Frome Society for Local Study 1983)
Mee, Arthur, *The King's England: Somerset* (Hodder and Stoughton 1945)
Tuck, S., *Methodism in Frome* (1837)

Wade, G. W. and J. H. (revised by Maxwell Fraser), *The Little Guides: Somerset*, 10th edn. (Methuen and Batsford 1949)

Woodforde, Rev. James (ed. by John Beresford), *The Diary of a Country Parson* (O.U.P. 1978)

4. Local History: Wiltshire

Baker, Mark, *From Wiltshire to Australia in 1851* (WRO monograph 1974)

Colt Hoare, Sir Richard, *The History of Modern Wiltshire* (John Bowyer Nichols and Son 1829)

Daniell, J. J., *History of Warminster* (Simpkin, Marshall & Co. 1879)

Daniell, William, *Warminster Common* (1850)

Davies, Maud F., *Life in an English Village: an Economic and Historical Survey of the Parish of Corsley in Wiltshire*, (T. Fisher Unwin 1909)

Doel, W., *Twenty Golden Candlesticks: a History of Baptist Nonconformity in Western Wiltshire* (Trowbridge and London 1890)

Gough, P. H., *The Story of Corsley and its Church* (1966)

Gunn, Rev. H. M., *History of Non-Conformity in Warminster* (Jackson and Walford 1853)

Hudson, W. H., *A Shepherd's Life* (Compton Press 1910)

Kirby, J. L., *The Estates of Edington Priory* (Friends of Edington Priory Church 1966)

Morrison, Jean, *Bratton Church* (Westbury 1949)

Myatt, Frederick (ed.), *The Deverill Valley* (Deverill Valley History Group 1982)

Ponting, K. G., *The Weavers and Fullers of Edington* (Friends of Edington Priory Church 1974)

Reeves, Marjorie, *Sheep Bell and Ploughshare* (Moonraker Press 1978)

Wall, Alison D., *Riot, Bastardy and other Social Problems – the Role of Constables and J.P.s, 1580-1625* (Wiltshire Monographs No.1, Wilts. County Council 1980)

Whitelock, Dorothy, *The Importance of the Battle of Edington, A.D. 878* (Friends of Edington Priory Church 1977)

5. Local History: General

Bettey, J. H., *Rural Life in Wessex, 1500-1900* (Moonraker Press 1977)

Darby, H. C., *The Domesday Geography of Eastern England* (Cambridge 1971)

Dymond, David, *Writing Local History: A Practical Guide* (Bedford Square/N.C.V.O. 1981)

Godber, Joyce, *History of Bedfordshire* (Beds. County Council 1969)

Hoskins, W. G., *Local History in England*, 3rd edn. (Longmans 1984)

Hughes, Anne, *The Diary of a Farmer's Wife (1796-1797)* (Penguin 1981)

Massingberd, W. O. (trans.), *Court Rolls of the Manor of Ingoldmells* (Spottiswoode 1902)

Murch, Jerom, *A History of the Presbyterian and General Baptist Churches in the West of England with some of their Pastors* (London 1835)

Parker, Rowland, *The Common Stream* (Paladin 1976)

Richardson, John, *The Local Historian's Encyclopedia* (Historical Publications 1974)

Rodgers, Alan, *This Was Their World: Approaches to Local History* (BBC 1972)

Tate, W. E., *The Parish Chest* (Phillimore 1983)

Trotter, Eleanor, *Seventeenth Century Life in the Country Parish* (Cambridge 1919)

Turner, Thomas, *The Diary of a Georgian Shopkeeper* (O.U.P. 1979)

Victoria County History, Volumes covering Bedfordshire, Somerset and Wiltshire (O.U.P. various dates)

West, John, *Village Records* (Phillimore 1982)

White, Gilbert (ed. by Richard Mabey), *The Natural History of Selborne* (Penguin 1977)

6. Genealogy

Burns, Nancie, *Family Tree* (Faber and Faber 1962)

Camp, Anthony, *Tracing your Ancestors* (John Gifford 1964)

Colwell, Stella, *The Family History Book* (Phaidon 1980)

Cox, Jane, and Padfield, Timothy, *Tracing your Ancestors in the Public Record Office* (H.M.S.O. 1981)

Currer-Briggs, Noel, and Gambier, Royston, *Debrett's Family Historian* (Debrett/Webb and Bower 1981)

Graham, Norman H., *The Genealogists Consolidated Guide to Parish Register Copies and Indexes in the Inner London Area, 1538-1837* (1981)
Hamilton-Edwards, Gerald, *In Search of Ancestry* (Phillimore 1974)
Iredale, David, *Discovering your Family Tree* (Shire 1979)
Linder, Bill R., *How to Trace your Family History* (Fawcett, New York 1979)
Mander, Meda, *How to Trace your Ancestors* (Granada 1977)
Smith, Frank, and Gardner, David E., *Genealogical Research in England and Wales* (Salt Lake City 1956-64)
Steel, D. J., *Discovering your Family History* (BBC 1980)
Steel, D. J., *National Index of Parish Registers* (Society of Genealogists vols. 1, 1976, and 2, 1980)
Westin, Jean Eddy, *Finding your Roots* (Ballantine, New York 1978)
Willis, A. J., *Genealogy for Beginners* (Phillimore 1970)
Wolfston, Patricia (ed. Michael Gandy), *Greater London Cemeteries and Crematoria and their Records* (Society of Genealogists 1982)

7. Miscellaneous

Bardsley, C. W., *Dictionary of English and Welsh Surnames*, (Genealogical Publishing Co., Baltimore, U.S.A. 1967)
Champion, L. G., *Farthing Rushlight: the Story of Andrew Gifford, 1700-1784* (Carey Kingsgate Press 1961)
Chandos, Cassandra, Duchess of (ed. by A. C. Wood), *The Continuation of the History of the Willoughby Family* (Shakespeare Head Press, n.d.)
Defoe, Daniel, *Journal of the Plague Year* (Dent 1961)
Dunkling, Leslie, *The Guinness Book of Names* (Guinness 1974)
Ekwall, Eilert, *The Concise Oxford Dictionary of English Place Names* (O.U.P. 1966)
Freeman, J. W., *Discovering Surnames* (Shire 1968)
Garrett, R. E. F., *Chancery and other Legal Proceedings* (Pinhorns, Isle of Wight 1968)
Guy, J. A., *The Court of Star Chamber and its Records to the Reign of Elizabeth I* (H.M.S.O. 1985)
Heal, Ambrose, *The London Goldsmiths 1200-1800* (David and Charles 1972)
Hillary, J. H., *Westland: Journal of John Hillary, Emigrant to New Zealand, 1879* (Acorn 1979)
Latham, R. C., and Matthews, W., *The Diary of Samuel Pepys* (G. Bell and Sons 1976)
Loney, Jack, *Sea Adventures and Wrecks on the N.S.W. South Coast*
Martin, Charles Trice, *The Record Interpreter*, 2nd edn. facs. (Phillimore 1982)
Martin, David, *A Sociology of English Religion* (Heinemann n.d.)
Milward, Rosemary, *A Glossary of Household, Farming and Trade Terms from Probate Inventories* (Derbys. Record Society 1982)
Neill, Joyce (ed.), *Plum Duff and Cake: the Journal of James Nichols, 1874-5: an Account of his Voyage to Picton, New Zealand, on the Ship* Carnatic *& Some of his New Experiences in the Colony* (Pegasus, N.Z. 1975)
Quekett, Rev. William, *My Sayings and Doings (with Reminiscences of my Life – an Autobiography . . .)* (Kegan, Paul, Trench 1888)
Reaney, P. H., *A Dictionary of British Surnames* (Routledge and Kegan Paul 1958)
Stamp, Dudley, and Beaver, S. H., *The British Isles: a Geographic and Economic Survey* (Longmans 1971)
Titford, Anthony R., 'A biographical study of William Jowett Titford (1784-1823/7) and *Sketches towards a Hortus Botanicus Americanus*', in *Journal of The Society for Bibliography of Natural History*, vol. 8 (1977), pp. 120-42
Titford, Caroline, *History of Unity Church, Islington*, (Essex Hall, Strand 1912)
Titford, William Jowett, *Sketches towards a 'Hortus Botanicus Americanus'* (Privately published 1811)

Index

Introductory Note

Women are indexed under their maiden name where known. Except in the Introduction and Addenda, all Titfords are indexed as Titford, rather than under variations of the name. In the Notes, with a few exceptions, only the Titfords are indexed.

List of Subscribers

Mrs. E. K. Julie Ambrose
Mary Appleton
Dr. Simon Bailey
John A. Baker, Sara and Alan
Helen Letitia Jane Bavister
J. N. Beardsley Jnr.
D. F. Bench
Jo Birkbeck
Mr. and Mrs. Paul Blackburn
Paul A. Blake
Mrs. B. E. Blight
B.M.S.G.H. Stourbridge Branch
Mrs. Valerie A. Boddy (*née* Dare)
Margaret Bonney (*née* Titford)
Miss D. H. Bridge
Mrs. Diane L. Brook
Bernard H. Buckler
John D. Burton
Mr. and Mrs. Butler
Peter D. Campkin
Philip C. Candy, Armidale, Australia
Irene Chisnall
The Clayburn Society
Amethy Coles
J. F. Collinson
Angela Carolyn Cooke
Danny and Barbara Corns
Miss P. R. Cotton
Ian and Ruth Cowley
John and Gloria Cuerden
David J. W. Cutten
Gil Damsell
Mrs. Gillian P. Davies
Heather Duckett
R. D. Dunn
Shirley Janet Edgar (Miss)
Mr. and Mrs. Leslie Edwards
T. V. H. Fitzhugh
Virginia Franklin
Michael J. Garrett
Vanessa Ann Gist (*née* Titford)
Commander and Mrs. A. S. Goldup
Dr. Harvey M. Good
Natalie Francisca Good
Mrs. Joan Evaline Gouldson
Gerald J. Gracèy-Cox
Geoff Gration

Alick Griffin
Joan Hagens
Miss R. G. Halford
Enid Doreen Hallam
Marjorie Hammond
Ronald V. Handley
Dorothy Hartley
William Hewlett Dew Harvey
Dr. Peter Shayle Hawkins
Peter Henry
John C. Higgs
Ernest H. Holland
Mr. R. N. Hollinghurst
Sue and Maxwell Hollyhock
Emma Littlejohns Hooper
Vice-Admiral Sir Ted and Lady Horlick
Roy Horridge
A. G. Hurle
Ian W. Jardine
Miss Gwen Jones
John M. Kelly
John A. Köhler
John Lally
M. A. Lincoln
Paul Linford
Mrs. Annie Lloyd
Mrs. Clare Longworth (*née* Titford)
Mrs. Rachel Lovelace
D. G. Lynall
Mrs. H. G. Marson
George and Hilda Massey
Carole Ann Mattingly
Michael McGarvie
Miss Grace McLaren
Margaret McNerney (*née* Titford)
Jaroslaw Melnyk
Mrs. J. M. Metcalfe
Mrs. Doris G. Mills
Lorna Mills
Roger B. Mitchell
W. J. Mitchell
A. L. Morris
Anne G. Morris
Jean Morrison
Donald Mounter
Stan Nelson
Lionel Offord

Rosemary M. Oliver
John and Eileen Perkins
Jo Pierce
Alison and Peter Place
T. Pool
Mrs. H. Presbury
G. W. Quartley
Brenda Remington
Jean I. Ruskin
Betty Ryde (*née* Titford)
Muriel C. Sainsbury
Richard Scollins
Mrs. Margaret A. Scott
Mr. F. P. Smedley-Stevenson
Somerset Record Office
David Sommerlad
J. W. Spendlove
Sidney E. Targett
Keith R. Taylor
Alan J. Tew
Mrs. Mary Thornley
Kathleen Timms
Alan Frank Titford
Anthony R. Titford
Adele Julie Titford
Austen Jeffery Titford
B. G. Titford
Brian R. Titford, Macclesfield
Charles Henry Victor Titford
Charles William Titford
   Basil Titford (son)
   Cedd Titford &
   Benjamin Titford (grandsons)
Christine Margaret Titford
Colin Richard Titford
Derek S. Titford, F.C.A.
Rear-Admiral Donald Titford
Douglas M. Titford
Freda Titford
Mr. and Mrs. G. J. Titford

Henry John Titford
J. A. Titford and J. L. A. Titford
J. C. Titford
J. J. Titford
Jack Titford
James H. Titford
Jeanne Titford
Jeffrey William Titford
John Edmund Howard Titford 1913 – 1987
Keith Laurence Titford
Leslie Phillip Titford
Marc Laurence Titford
Michael Titford
Michael and Rebecca Titford
Miriam C. Titford
Reginald Frederick Titford
Reginald M. Titford
Richard Titford
Richard G. Titford, London
The Revd. Richard K. Titford, B.A.
Robert Titford
Russell John Titford
Mr. and Mrs. S. H. Titford
Stephen Michael Titford
Charles Trevail
Mr. B. Trevette
P. Tritton
Mr. and Mrs. Paul Trueman
Anne Walker
Muriel Walker (*née* Titford)
Mrs. Jean M. Whiting
Matthew W. Wilkinson
B. A. Williams
Dr. Williams's Library
Mrs. Cynthia M. Wilson
Wiltshire Archaeological and Natural
   History Society
Leonie Wright
John Edward Frowd Young